Studia Fennica
Linguistica 21

The Finnish Literature Society (SKS) was founded in 1831 and has, from the very beginning, engaged in publishing operations. It nowadays publishes literature in the fields of ethnology and folkloristics, linguistics, literary research and cultural history.

The first volume of the Studia Fennica series appeared in 1933. Since 1992, the series has been divided into three thematic subseries: Ethnologica, Folkloristica and Linguistica. Two additional subseries were formed in 2002, Historica and Litteraria. The subseries Anthropologica was formed in 2007.

In addition to its publishing activities, the Finnish Literature Society maintains research activities and infrastructures, an archive containing folklore and literary collections, a research library and promotes Finnish literature abroad.

Studia Fennica Editorial Board
Editors-in-chief
Pasi Ihalainen, Professor, University of Jyväskylä, Finland
Timo Kallinen, University Lecturer, University of Helsinki, Finland
Taru Nordlund, Professor, University of Helsinki, Finland
Riikka Rossi, Title of Docent, University Researcher, University of Helsinki, Finland
Katriina Siivonen, Title of Docent, University Teacher, University of Turku, Finland
Lotte Tarkka, Professor, University of Helsinki, Finland

Deputy editors-in-chief
Anne Heimo, Title of Docent, University of Turku, Finland
Saija Isomaa, Professor, University of Tampere, Finland
Sari Katajala-Peltomaa, Title of Docent, Researcher, University of Tampere, Finland
Eerika Koskinen-Koivisto, Postdoctoral Researcher, Dr. Phil., University of Helsinki, Finland
Laura Visapää, Title of Docent, University Lecturer, University of Helsinki, Finland

Tuomas M. S. Lehtonen, Secretary General, Dr. Phil., Finnish Literature Society, Finland
Tero Norkola, Publishing Director, Finnish Literature Society, Finland
Virve Mertanen, Secretary of the Board, Finnish Literature Society, Finland

oa.finlit.fi

Editorial Office
SKS
P.O. Box 259
FI-00171 Helsinki
www.finlit.fi

On the Border of Language and Dialect

Edited by
Marjatta Palander, Helka Riionheimo and Vesa Koivisto

Finnish Literature Society · SKS · Helsinki · 2018

STUDIA FENNICA LINGUISTICA 21

The publication has undergone a peer review.

© 2018 Marjatta Palander, Helka Riionheimo and Vesa Koivisto
License CC-BY-NC-ND 4.0 International

A digital edition of a printed book first published in 2018 by the Finnish Literature Society.
Cover Design: Timo Numminen
EPUB: Tero Salmén

ISBN 978-952-222-916-8 (Print)
ISBN 978-951-959-003-7 (PDF)
ISBN 978-951-858-004-4 (EPUB)

ISSN 0085-6835 (Studia Fennica)
ISSN 1235-1938 (Studia Fennica Linguistica)

DOI: http://dx.doi.org/10.21435/sflin.21

This work is licensed under a Creative Commons CC-BY-NC-ND 4.0 International License.
To view a copy of the license, please visit http://creativecommons.org/licenses/by-nc-nd/4.0/

 A free open access version of the book is available at http://dx.doi.org/10.21435/sflin.21 or by scanning this QR code with your mobile device.

BoD – Books on Demand, Norderstedt, Germany 2018

Contents

MARJATTA PALANDER, HELKA RIIONHEIMO, AND VESA KOIVISTO
Introduction: Creating and Crossing Linguistic Borders 7

DENNIS R. PRESTON
What's Old and What's New in Perceptual Dialectology? 16

JOHANNA LAAKSO
Language Borders and Cultural Encounters
A Linguistic View on Interdisciplinarity in the Research of
Intercultural Contacts 38

VESA KOIVISTO
Border Karelian Dialects – a Diffuse Variety of Karelian 56

MARJATTA PALANDER AND HELKA RIIONHEIMO
Imitating Karelian
How Is Karelian Recalled and Imitated by Finns with Border Karelian
Roots? 85

NIINA KUNNAS
Viena Karelians as Observers of Dialect Differences in Their Heritage
Language 123

TAMÁS PÉTER SZABÓ
Reflections on the Schoolscape
Teachers on Linguistic Diversity in Hungary and Finland 156

ANNA-RIITTA LINDGREN AND LEENA NIIRANEN
The Morphological Integration of Scandinavian and Saami Verbal
Borrowings in Kven and Their Impact on Contact-Induced Language
Change 191

Vesa Jarva and Jenni Mikkonen
Lexical Mixing in a Conversation between Old Helsinki Slang
Speakers 222

Contributors 253

Abstract 256

Index 257

Marjatta Palander
 http://orcid.org/0000-0002-4370-8493

Helka Riionheimo
 http://orcid.org/0000-0002-9294-6201

Vesa Koivisto
 http://orcid.org/0000-0003-1256-6477

Introduction: Creating and Crossing Linguistic Borders

The present volume aims to shed light on the various complex dimensions and manifestations of borders between languages and dialects: how language varieties have emerged because of geographical or administrative borders; how linguistic borders are created by contrasting varieties with each other; how borders are mentally maintained by individual language speakers, how they are ideologically co-constructed through interaction; and how different borders are crossed so that language contacts begin to shape language varieties. Multidisciplinary border studies have a long history at the University of Eastern Finland where the border theme has been approached within various academic disciplines, including social sciences, history studies, cultural studies, and linguistics, among others. In 2014, an international symposium took place titled "On the Border of Language and Dialect", which in turn spawned the current volume. The symposium was organized by the FINKA research project: "On the Borderline of Finnish and Karelian: Perspectives on Cognate Languages and Dialects", and the articles in this volume bring together different fields of linguistics, as well as related disciplines, thus, presenting a fascinating multifaceted picture of the complex notion of linguistic border.

In their most concrete form, borders are administrative, sometimes (especially in the case of state borders) visibly demarcated in the terrain. Contrary to nation state ideology (still commonly held by laymen), these borders are not natural language borders but rather often cut across areas that have been linguistically and culturally uniform. However, once established, administrative borders begin to affect the language varieties spoken both within the borderline area and on the other side of it. Since borders steer the social networks of language speakers, contacts inside a border increase and contacts across a border are hindered. In this way, state borders are dual in nature as they cause both convergence and divergence: varieties spoken inside the border area begin to influence each other and develop towards convergence, whereas the varieties spoken on the other side of border begin to diverge and may even ultimately evolve into a new language. One such instance is the case of the Eastern Finnish dialects and the Karelian language, which are very closely related as they share the same ancestor language origin (Proto-Karelian) and form a dialect continuum. However, the presence of the border between Finland and Russia has caused changes: the Eastern Finnish dialects have begun to converge with the other varieties of Finnish (and have also been influenced by Standard Finnish), whereas the Karelian varieties spoken in Russia have maintained many of their old features while still being strongly influenced by the Russian language. (For details, see Vesa Koivisto's article in this volume.) The turmoil of the events of World War II, and indeed more recent events, have left their mark on the linguistic map of Europe, and these offer further illustrations of the effects of shifting borders. The dialect divergence between Polish and Belarusian illustrates diverging development (see Woolhiser 2005), and reunified Germany, by contrast, presents a case of convergence (see Auer, Barden, and Grosskopf 1998; Auer, Barden, Grosskopf, and Mattheier 2000). A further well-known recent example of divergence is the division of Serbo-Croatian into several languages (Serbian, Croatian, and Bosnian) after the collapse of Yugoslavia in the 1990s. Once new political states were established, their inhabitants sought to distinguish their languages from the varieties spoken in neighbouring states (see, e.g., Hawkesworth 2006, van der Wouden 2012).

An extreme case of the impact of political borders (together with many other political, social, and cultural factors) is the endangerment and extinction of the small minority languages that are spoken within the same given administrative area, along with a much more dominant language, and that do not have official status in that country (see, e.g., Thomason 2015). The situation of the Karelian language exemplifies language endangerment, and several articles in this volume examine this issue. Varieties of Karelian have been spoken in two countries, Russia and Finland, and wherever Karelian has been spoken, it has been a suppressed minority language, which has led to the present situation where the language is now rapidly losing speakers despite efforts and activities to revitalize it (see, e.g., Laakso et al. 2016, Sarhimaa 2016). In Russia, the dominance of Russian has led to a large-scale language shift and the same phenomenon has occurred in Finland, aided by the close resemblance of Finnish and Karelian. Indeed, the fate of the Karelian language is the focus of the articles written by Vesa Koivisto, Niina Kunnas, and Marjatta Palander and Helka Riionheimo.

Unlike administrative borders, actual linguistic boundaries are not sharp, rather they are expansive and vague areas where the distinctions between varieties are gradual and can be subtle, and where the isoglosses of linguistic features do not necessarily coincide with state borders. Consequently, the boundary of a language and a dialect is nebulous and is, in practice, often based on political and administrative borders rather than on linguistic differences or mutual unintelligibility. For instance, Swedish and Norwegian are quite easily mutually intelligible, but, since they are languages spoken in separate states, they are generally considered distinct languages. A corresponding situation exists in Western Europe where national boundaries divide some dialects of the West Germanic dialect continuum, resulting in some classified as Dutch and others as German. Still another example is provided by Meänkieli and Kven, both originally dialects of Finnish, but which are now often referred to as languages in their own right because they are spoken outside the state of Finland, and because both have official minority language status in the country where they are spoken (Sweden and Norway, respectively) (see, e.g., Sulkala 2010, 10–13 and Lindgren & Niiranen in this volume).

It should be noted, however, that inside administrative boundaries, linguistic reality is not uniform but consists of many kinds of mental and subjective borders. Human beings are sensitive to more overt and subtle differences in the ways other people speak, and they tend to contrast languages and groups of speakers on the basis of linguistic features (also known as the social indexicality of linguistic phenomena). Numerous minority languages confront this very situation because their speakers form a small minority amongst speakers of a dominant language. To illustrate this, the fate of the Border Karelian speakers in Finland after World War II will be highlighted. Border Karelia is a border zone that has, over the past centuries, belonged at times to Russia (and the Soviet Union) and at other times to Sweden, and later to an independent Finland (see Sarhimaa 2000). After World War II, the area was ceded by Finland to the Soviet Union, and its Karelian-speaking inhabitants (who were citizens of Finland) had to evacuate their homes and resettle in other parts of Finland. In their new Finnish-speaking environment, these evacuees were faced with many kinds of prejudice due to their different religion (Eastern Orthodox Church), different customs, and different language. Throughout the first post-war decades, the Karelian spoken by these people was officially considered a dialect of Finnish, but the linguistic differences between the Finnish dialects and the Border Karelian dialects drew the attention of Finnish members of society, and Karelian speakers often came up against negative attitudes. In this way, Finnish speakers created a language barrier between themselves and the evacuees, even though the languages in question are very closely related. (For details, see, e.g., Raninen-Siiskonen 1999.) In this volume, the articles by Kunnas and Palander and Riionheimo focus on situations in which language barriers seem to exist between closely related language varieties.

One additional salient point when dealing with borders is recognizing the fact that political or linguistic borders are not absolute barriers, but may act as bridges that may be crossed. Throughout history, trade has been an activity that has united people, and many cultural as well as linguistic influences have travelled across the world via trade routes. Migration and travel are another ancient phenomenon that leads to crossing all manners of borders (political, cultural, linguistic, etc.) by individuals or larger groups of people. In the modern world, many additional forms of international collaboration bring together people from different countries and with different linguistic backgrounds. Language contacts, i.e., the encounters between people who speak different dialects or languages, thus make it possible for words and grammatical features to be borrowed by one language from another. Cross-linguistic influence may thus be seen as a manifestation of crossing linguistic borders. The linguistic effects of language contact – especially lexical borrowing – are discussed in the articles by Anna-Riitta Lindgren and Leena Niiranen, and Vesa Jarva and Jenni Mikkonen.

Furthermore, large-scale migration waves cause linguistic changes in both the migrating group's language and the language of the host population.

This is demonstrated dramatically by the languages of colonization in the Americas, Australia, and Asia, which have both shaped the local languages and been shaped by them. This development may be exemplified by the emergence of various Colonial Englishes (see, e.g., Trudgill 2004; Kerswill and Trudgill 2005) and the development of Afrikaans from a Dutch dialect (van der Wouden 2012). In the Finnic language area, one of the notable migration situations was the movement of Karelian speakers from Kexholm County (including the areas of present-day North Karelia in Finland and Border Karelia in Russia) after the county was incorporated from Russia into Sweden in the 17th century. The Karelians slowly travelled towards Inner Russia and finally settled in Tver Oblast. This migration resulted in the emergence of Karelian language islands scattered throughout Russian-speaking areas, in isolation from other varieties of Karelian. Within these exclaves, the Karelian language was maintained for centuries and evolved into a new variety. The development of Tver Karelian is described by Vesa Koivisto in this volume.

The linguistic borders between a language and a dialect as well as the administrative, cultural, and mental borders that affect the linguistic ones are considered from multiple perspectives in this volume. The articles approach mental borders between dialects, dialect continua, and areas of mixed dialect, language ideologies, language mixing, and contact-induced language change. In addition to the theme of borders or bordering, the articles have one thing in common: they all describe multilingualism, whether past or present, societal or individual. Karelian receives particular attention, as the research subject of the FINKA project, and Karelian is examined from multiple perspectives with attention to variation, maintenance, and the dialect perceptions of its speakers. Together, these articles paint a picture of multidimensional, multilingual, variable, and ever-changing linguistic reality where diverse borders, boundaries, and barriers meet, are intertwined, and cross each other. The combination of the articles also aims to cross disciplinary and methodological borders and present new perspectives on earlier studies and their interpretations.

The volume opens with Dennis R. Preston's article "What's Old and What's New in Perceptual Dialectology?", which is a review of the development of this branch of research from its early days until the present. Perceptual dialectology belongs to a larger field of folk linguistics, where research focuses on the layman's (i.e., the non-linguist's) perceptions and views on language. Language users observe their language continuously, and their beliefs always influence their language attitude and their actual language use. Early studies were aimed at determining whether the informants regarded neighbouring dialects as similar to or different from their own dialect, and, on the basis of these conceptualizations, it was possible to discern perceptual or mental dialect borders. Since the 1980s, the methodology of perceptual dialectology has developed rapidly, especially due to the work of Dennis R. Preston, and has included, for instance, ranking tasks and drawing mental dialect maps. At present, complex computer-aided techniques are utilized for the same purposes. At the same time, the scope of research has expanded, and it now involves the investigation of linguistic attitudes (e.g., the perception of how 'correct' or 'pleasant' the dialects are according to non-linguists). Recently, the studies of linguistic attitudes have applied discourse analysis and experimental methods (such as reaction time studies and eye tracking studies). What comes to the question of demarcating a language and a dialect, the article shows that perceptual dialectology provides significant insights not only on what laymen believe about dialect boundaries but also on the relevance of these perceptions and attitudes when explaining regional and social variation.

In the article "Language Borders and Cultural Encounters: A Linguistic View on Interdisciplinarity in the Research of Intercultural Contacts", Johanna Laakso problematizes the common notion that languages are closed systems with clear boundaries. The writer stresses the artificialness and conventionality of borders, especially in a linguistic sense. In the spirit of national idealism, strict borders have been drawn between languages (and concurrently nation-states), although the reality behind this kind of national monolingualism might be more complicated. As the author notes, "What is traditionally called 'the same language' is in practice realized as 'a bundle of varieties' ". Deep down there may also be a common human striving towards making a distinction between oneself and others, 'us' vs 'them'. In linguistics, however, it should be kept in mind the universally common coexistence and use of various languages, i.e., multilingualism. The author stresses the central role of multilingualism in societies throughout the centuries and points out its gradual re-emergence in the Europe of today.

A noteworthy example of language and dialect mixing are the Border Karelian dialects that are introduced in Vesa Koivisto's article "Border Karelian Dialects – a Diffuse Variety of Karelian". These dialects of the Karelian language were spoken in the former Eastern Finnish territories in the vicinity of the Russian border. Contact between Karelian and Finnish in Border Karelia have taken place ever since the 17th century, since many Karelians moved to Russia and the area was settled by a Finnish-speaking population. The border line between the Karelian and Finnish languages has traversed Border Karelia, but in practice this border was realized as a continuum along which Karelian dialects showed characteristics of mixed or transitional dialects. The language border was indefinite both geographically and in terms of the use of the two languages, Karelian and Finnish, in villages. In addition to two distinct languages, there were also two dialects of Karelian that met in Border Karelia and that influenced each other: Karelian Proper (more precisely, its subdialect South Karelian) and Olonets Karelian. The border between these two also formed a continuum. Thus, a mixed dialect may consist not only of constituents of one and the same language but also – as Border Karelian does – of elements of two related languages (Karelian and Finnish). For such close linguistic relatives, grammatical integration is also possible to a certain extent. Border Karelian dialects reveal a situation in which defining a language may be elusive, as the language idiolectally represents varying proportions of two neighbouring languages or dialects. Border Karelian dialects, thus, call into question the traditional concept of a linguistic border in several respects.

The remaining two Karelian-related articles in this volume represent perceptual dialectology. In Marjatta Palander's and Helka Riionheimo's study "Imitating Karelian: How Is Karelian Recalled and Imitated by Finns with Border Karelian Roots?" an imitation task is applied to a research setting involving language contact and language memory. The informants have their roots in Border Karelia (the area described above): the oldest ones were born in Border Karelia before World War II while the younger ones are children or grandchildren of the Border Karelian evacuees who were resettled in Finland after the war. In Finland, the Border Karelians have largely experienced a language shift, and, thus, the younger generations speak mostly the local Finnish dialect and remember only sporadic Karelian elements. The purpose of the research task was to discover the kinds of recollections the informants have of the Karelian language spoken by themselves as children or which they had heard spoken by their older relatives. In other words, they were asked to cross many boundaries: the boundary between generations and the boundary between Finnish and Karelian. The task revealed that Karelian is mostly remembered lexically as single words or short fixed phrases. However, there were also informants who were able to produce spontaneous dialogue in Karelian or even use Karelian throughout the entire interview. On the basis of the results, the researchers suggest that the childhood memories of Karelian could help in reviving the language, should the informants wish to do so.

Niina Kunnas's article "Viena Karelians as Observers of Dialect Differences in Their Heritage Language" focuses on the White Sea Karelian variety and how its speakers conceptualize their own language. The research material includes interview data and a listening task. White Sea Karelian is the northern dialect of Karelian Proper and is clearly distinct from the other main Karelian dialect, Olonets Karelian. The Viena Karelians themselves seem to consider the dialect boundary between their dialect and Olonets Karelian wider than the boundary between their dialect and Finnish, even though the speakers of White Sea Karelian and Olonets Karelian live in the same geopolitical state (the Karelian Republic in the Russian Federation), and the geographical distance between these two varieties is only about 500 km. The study also confirms the earlier finding that laymen are not aware of the definitions or the names of the varieties employed by linguists. Furthermore, Niina Kunnas discovered that for the Viena Karelians, vocabulary and some phonological or phonetic features are salient when determining dialect boundaries. The comments about different sibilants used in White Sea Karelian and Olonets Karelian demonstrate that laymen are able to perceive even relatively small phonetic differences between the varieties.

Working within the framework of language ideology studies, Tamás Péter Szabó approaches the ways in which linguistic borders are interactionally constructed in two countries, Hungary and Finland, in the article "Reflections on the Schoolscape: Teachers on Linguistic Diversity in Hungary and Finland". This research material comes from metadiscourses in which a local teacher and the researcher co-explore the school building and discuss its schoolscape (i.e., the material environs of education, presented by pictures on the walls and the like). Microanalyses of the recordings focus on the multilingual practices of these schools through the narratives, evaluations, and explanations that touch upon current educational practices, which also reflect elements of nation-wide discourses of linguistic diversity. The analyses consider accounts that draw connections between English and multilingualism. In a Hungarian example, a view emerges in which the standard language is accorded preference, and the students are portrayed as deficient speakers of English. The Finnish examples present a more pluralistic approach since they are not focused on the standard language or linguistic norms, but represent the students in a positive light as active users of all their linguistic resources. By examining the labelling of language varieties and boundary-making practices, the study illustrates how notions such as 'mother tongue' and 'foreign language' are reconstructed in interaction and how the participants construct language borders, revealing some of the language ideologies that belie the use of these borders.

In their article "The Morphological Integration of Scandinavian and Saami Verbal Borrowings in Kven and Their Impact on Contact-Induced Language Change", Anna-Riitta Lindgren and Leena Niiranen present a contact-linguistic study that investigates the Kven language, a language variety that, in itself, lies on the fuzzy border between a language and a dialect. The Kven are a small minority in northern Norway, and their language derives from the dialect of Finnish spoken by their ancestors who moved to Norway in the 18th and 19th centuries. As the dialect has been spoken in a different country, and with little or no connections to Finland, the variety has diverged from the Finnish of Finland. In 2005, Kven was recognized as a national minority language in Norway, and, thus, it was accorded the status of an autonomous language, distinct from Finnish. The emergence of Kven, thus, reflects the influence of nation-state borders during the era of modernization in the 20th century. The article focuses on different kinds of language borders while examining linguistic borrowing from two sources: from two Scandinavian languages, Norwegian and Swedish, and from the Saami languages that are the closest cognates of the Finnic language family. The Saami languages and the Finnic languages share many structural similarities, such as rich inflectional and derivational morphology. This study addresses different forms of borrowing (the matter and pattern replication) and show that there are clear differences brought about by the borrowing source. The borrowings from typologically different Scandinavian languages are integrated into one inflectional type, and this language contact does not exhibit any kind of pattern replication (i.e., borrowing of morphological patterns instead of borrowing the sound-meaning pairs). By contrast, the impact of the Saami languages is more multifaceted and consists of integrating the Saami borrowings into many inflectional and derivational types, as well as various types of pattern replication. In this way, this article demonstrates that the linguistic border between two related languages is not as wide as that between languages that are typologically distant.

In addition to language borders dividing geographical areas, there are also more "tacit" linguistic borders, e.g., within a more restricted area, as within a single city. This kind of linguistic border can be described as demographic rather than geographic. An example of this is the Old Helsinki Slang (OHS), a variety of urban Finnish spoken by the "lower classes" that is discussed by Vesa Jarva and Jenni Mikkonen in their article "Lexical Mixing in a Conversation between Old Helsinki Slang Speakers". In the article, OHS is represented by a unique audio recording from the 1960s. OHS is a nonstandard (spoken) variety that shows considerable linguistic variation (both diachronically and synchronically). It is a mixture of dialectal and borrowed lexical material that combine features of Swedish (both lexical and structural) with a Finnish (multi-dialectal) basis originating in the dialects of the rural population that moved to Helsinki in the late 1800s and early 1900s. The quantity of (mostly Swedish) loan words in OHS is well over the universal average, thus, allowing it to be classified in the high borrowers category. The lexical material of OHS has been adapted to Finnish phonology, but it also displays phonological features foreign to the rest of Finnish. Due to its multifaceted origin, OHS has a medial status between a mixed speech form and a variant of Finnish.

Now that this article compilation nears completion, we wish to express our gratitude to all of the persons or institutions that have contributed or lent support to the book. First and foremost, the participants of the symposium "On the Border of Language and Dialect" are thanked for their fascinating perspectives on our central theme of demarcating languages and dialects. Most of the present articles are based on the papers presented during this symposium. Also, the writers of the articles are thanked for their patience and cooperation during the several phases of editing this volume. Furthermore, the reference group of the research project FINKA are gratefully acknowledged: Professors Riho Grünthal, Dennis R. Preston, and Anneli Sarhimaa, and Docent Maria Vilkuna, who have supported the project from its initial stage. The project was funded by the Academy of Finland during 2011–2014 (Project 137479), and the symposium received additional funding from the Federation of Finnish Learned Societies, the Joensuu University Foundation, the University of Eastern Finland, and the City of Joensuu. Thanks are in order, as well, to the publisher, the Finnish Literature Society, that has included this book in their esteemed series *Studia Fennica Linguistica*. Two anonymous referees provided valuable advice for finalizing the articles. The editors of this series, as well as the publishing editor of the Finnish Literature Society, have managed the editing process with competence and expertise. All in all, we are grateful to have had the opportunity to work with such a variety of scholars and experts.

References

Auer, Peter, Birgit Barden, and Beate Grosskopf. 1998. "Subjective and Objective Parameters Determining 'Salience' in Long-Term Dialect Accommodation." *Journal of Sociolinguistics* 2:2:163–187.

Auer, Peter, Birgit Barden, Beate Grosskopf, and Klaus Mattheier. 2000. "Long-Term Linguistic Accommodation and Its Sociolinguistic Interpretation: Evidence from the Inner-German Migration after the Wende." In *Dialect and Migration in a Changing Europe*, edited by Klaus Mattheier, 79–98. VarioLingua: Nonstandard-Standard-Substandard. Frankfurt: Peter Lang.

Hawkesworth, E. C. 2006. "Serbian-Croatian-Bosnian Linguistic Complex." In *Encyclopedia of Language & Linguistics* (2nd ed.), editor-in-chief Keith Brown, 258–260. Boston: Elsevier.

Kerswill, Paul, and Peter Trudgill. 2005. "The Birth of New Dialects." In *Dialect Change. Convergence and Divergence in European Languages*, edited by Peter Auer, Frans Hinskens, and Paul Kerswill, 196–220. Cambridge: Cambridge University Press.

Laakso, Johanna, Anneli Sarhimaa, Sia Spiliopoulou Åkermark, and Reetta Toivanen. 2015. *Towards Openly Multilingual Policies and Practices. Assessing Minority Language Maintenance Across Europe*. Linguistic Diversity and Language Rights 11. Bristol: Multilingual Matters.

Raninen-Siiskonen, Tarja. 1999. *Vieraana omalla maalla. Tutkimus karjalaisen siirtoväen muistelukerronnasta*. [As a stranger on one's own ground. Research of the Karelian occupants' oral history.] SKST 766. Helsinki: Finnish Literature Society.

Sarhimaa, Anneli. 2000. "The Divisive Frontier: the Impact of the Russian–Finnish Border on Karelian." In *Dialect Convergence and Divergence across European Borders*, edited by Jeffrey Kallen, Frans Hinskens, and Johan Taeldeman. *International Journal of the Sociology of Language* 145:153–180.

Sarhimaa, Anneli. 2016. *Karelian in Finland. ELDIA Case-Specific Report*. Studies in European Language Diversity 27. Accessed December 12, 2016. https://fedora.phaidra.univie.ac.at/fedora/get/o:471733/bdef:Content/get.

Sulkala, Helena. 2010. "Introduction. Revitalisation of the Finnic Minority Languages." In *Planning a New Standard Language. Finnic Minority Languages Meet the New Millennium*, edited by Helena Sulkala, and Harri Mantila, 8–26. Studia Fennica Linguistica 15. Helsinki: Finnish Literature Society.

Thomason, Sarah G. 2015. *Endangered Languages. An Introduction*. Cambridge Textbooks in Linguistics. Cambridge: Cambridge University Press.

Trudgill, Peter. 2004. *New-Dialect Formation: The Inevitability of Colonial Englishes*. New York: Oxford University Press.

Woolhiser, Curt. 2005. "Political Borders and Dialect Divergence/Convergence in Europe." In *Dialect Change. Convergence and Divergence in European Languages*, edited by Peter Auer, Frans Hinskens, and Paul Kerswill, 236–262. Cambridge: Cambridge University Press.

van der Wouden, Ton. 2012. *Roots of Afrikaans: Selected Writings of Hans den Besten*. Amsterdam: John Benjamins.

Dennis R. Preston

What's Old and What's New in Perceptual Dialectology?

Abstract

The systematic study of perceptual (or folk) dialectology dates back to at least the 19th century but was seriously developed in the mid 20th century, especially in The Netherlands and Japan. A late 20th century revival has now established this mode of enquiry as one commonly attached to general studies of varieties or carried out independently. In this article, the various goals, methods, and findings are summarized and evaluated with special regard to the following questions:

1) Where do people believe speech differs?
2) To what extent and where do the folk boundaries determined in 1) differ from those discovered by professionals?
3) In what way do people believe speech differs – linguistically (i.e., with reference to details) and/or incrementally (e.g., by degree).
4) Which linguistic signals do (and can) people use to identify varieties?
5) Which variant linguistic facts influence comprehension?
6) What sorts of factors (e.g., social stereotypes, caricatures) accompany and influence any of the answers sought in 1) through 5) above.

The methodological approaches taken to answer each question are examined, ranging from the map-oriented work of the early approaches to more recent experimentally grounded procedures, using resynthesized material and increasingly sophisticated experimental protocols (e.g., implicit evaluation tasks). The sorts of results obtained with each method are outlined and comparisons provided among them, as well as evaluations of their contributions to dialectology, contact (between languages and dialects), and, in some cases, sociolinguistics, and even general linguistics. This article concludes with an encouraging call for developing and future research that includes a variety of approaches.

1 Introduction

In a discussion of old and new trends in perceptual dialectology (PD), it is helpful to understand its place within the broader framework of folk linguistics (or "language regard"[1]), as shown in Figure 1.

Folk Linguistics			
Perceptual Dialectology		Social Psychology of Language	Speech Perception
Regional	Social	Language Attitudes	Variety

Figure 1. The place of perceptual dialectology within folk linguistics.

These nonexhaustive subcategories of folk linguistics are so intertwined with PD, however, that research that begins in one inevitably leads to one or more of the others. This article begins by focusing on regional dialectology, the birthplace of PD, but expands to show both newer trends in its analysis and interpretation as well as its interconnectedness with all the areas represented in Figure 1.

2 Regional PD

PD was first suggested by scholars whose reputations were firmly established in traditional dialect study. Although the early days of the subfield are represented in articles collected in Preston (1999b), some of the highlights of that work are reviewed here. The first use of the "little-arrow" ("Pfeilchen") method was apparently Willems (1886), but the earliest extensive studies were carried out in The Netherlands and gave rise to such representations as those shown in Figure 2.

---

[1] I have come to use "language regard" as a broad cover term for folk linguistics (Preston 2010, 2011). I do so due to the unfortunate interpretation of "folk" as "false," as in the long-standing use of "folk etymology" within historical linguistics, an interpretation that has infected understandings in even the Wikipedia entry for "Folk Linguistics", in spite of vigorous denials in Niedzielski and Preston 2000. I also do not use "language attitudes" as a general cover term so as to avoid the connection between "attitudes" and "evaluation" (e.g., Kruglanski and Stroebe, 2005) since many instances of folk linguistics or language regard are not evaluative at all: they are simply "beliefs," although I do not want to exclude language and variety evaluation. Finally, I also want a term that will include the more anthropologically and ethnographically oriented approach to "language ideology" (e.g., Schieffelin et al. 1998).

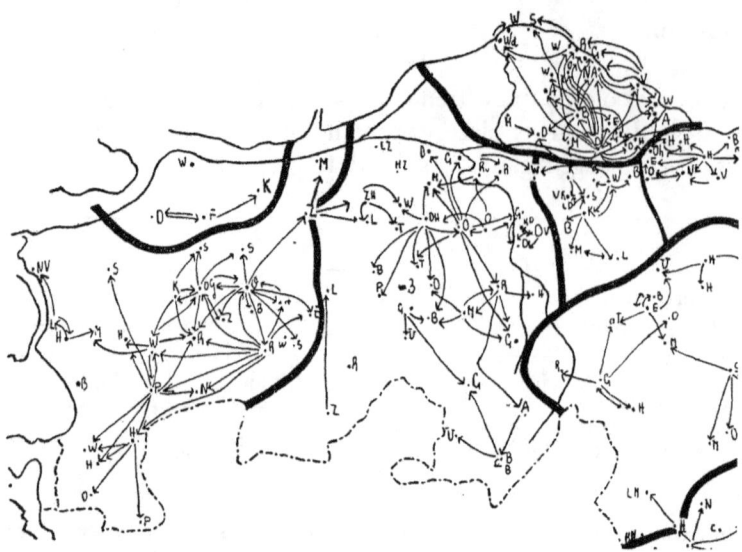

Figure 2. "Little arrows" perception in the North Brabant (Weijnen 1946).

In this research, arrows are drawn between a respondent's home site and others around them where they indicate speakers that sound the same. As Figure 2 shows, bundles of these interconnected sites arise so that tentative perceptual dialect areas (the darker lines in Figure 2) can be determined.

This Flemish-Netherlands approach to regional perception was soon added to with Japanese contributions. Figure 3 shows the results of early research carried out there.

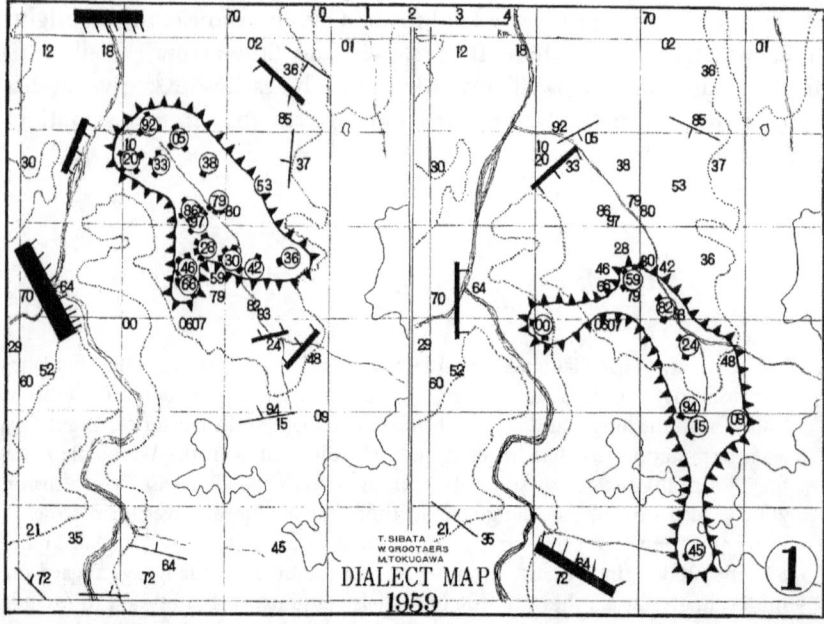

Figure 3. The determination of two perceptual areas in Itoigawa, left and right panels of the same area (Sibata 1959 [1999, 42]).

In this work in the Itoigawa River valley in the west of Japan, respondents indicated which villages speak differently, and a node pointing in the direction of each named site was attached to the outside of the circle of the respondent's identifying number. The sites indicated were then identified with lines (heavier for those mentioned by more respondents) and with small lines extending from those lines that point back in the direction of the respondents who identified the site as different. The respondents grouped together in the left panel with the toothed line are considered a perceptual area on the basis of their agreement about sites that are different, in this case those predominately to the upper left of the left panel in Figure 3; in contrast, in the panel on the right, very few respondents indicated differences in the upper left-hand portion of the same area; instead they focused their identifications of difference on the bottom center left, an area hardly identified at all by the respondents grouped together in the left panel.

Interestingly, although both research teams asked respondents where areas were similar and different, the Dutch argued that perceptual areas were not distinct from and, in fact, usually followed professionally determined dialect areas (e.g., Weijnen 1968), but the Japanese said that their results reflected only prefectural boundaries, school district limits, and the like rather than traditional dialect boundaries (e.g., Grootaers 1964). The Dutch said that was because the Japanese based their maps primarily on where varieties were said to differ while the Dutch maps were based on where respondents identified areas that were the same or similar, an argument well-covered in the various articles in Preston (1999b). The Japanese scholar Mase (1964a, 1964b) was the first to provide maps of both similarity and difference judgments and to develop a numeric protocol to determine their strength.

The little-arrow method was used subsequently in ways that illustrate the potential for a historical focus in PD. Figure 4 shows a detail of a little-arrow map of the German-Netherlands border in Landkreis Grafschaft Bentheim in Lower Saxony (Kremer 1984) in which respondents indicated only a few national border crossings.[2] This PD map surely reflects the trend for many fewer actual cross-border similarities at the time of Kremer's study. This can be illustrated in one lexical feature ("wren"); the right-hand panel of Figure 5, a map dated 1975, close to the time of Kremer's study, shows very few items shared across the national border compared to the numerous shared items in 1940, shown in the left-hand panel.

---

2   Only one German site (Wi1 at 6.5 – q) and three Dutch sites (Os at 8 – p, Ns at 8.5 – p, and Tb at 7.5 – s) show crossings at the international border.

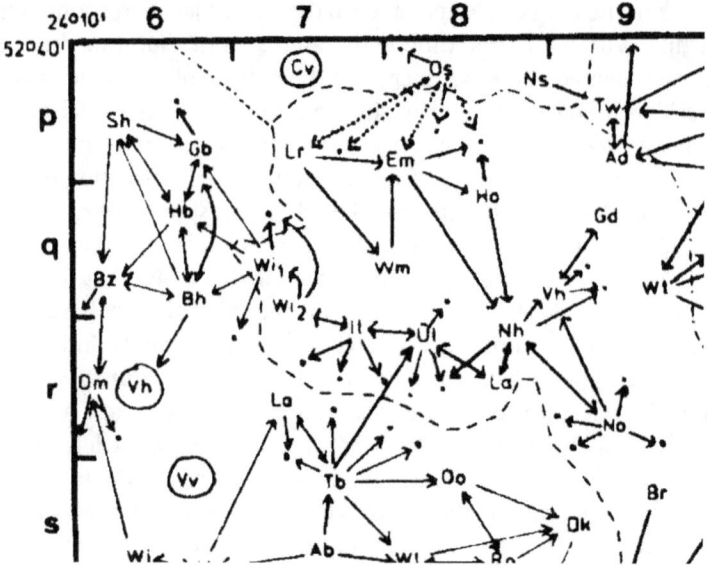

Figure 4. Kremer (1984 [1999]) the Dutch-German national border (dashed line) as a folk dialect boundary (detail).

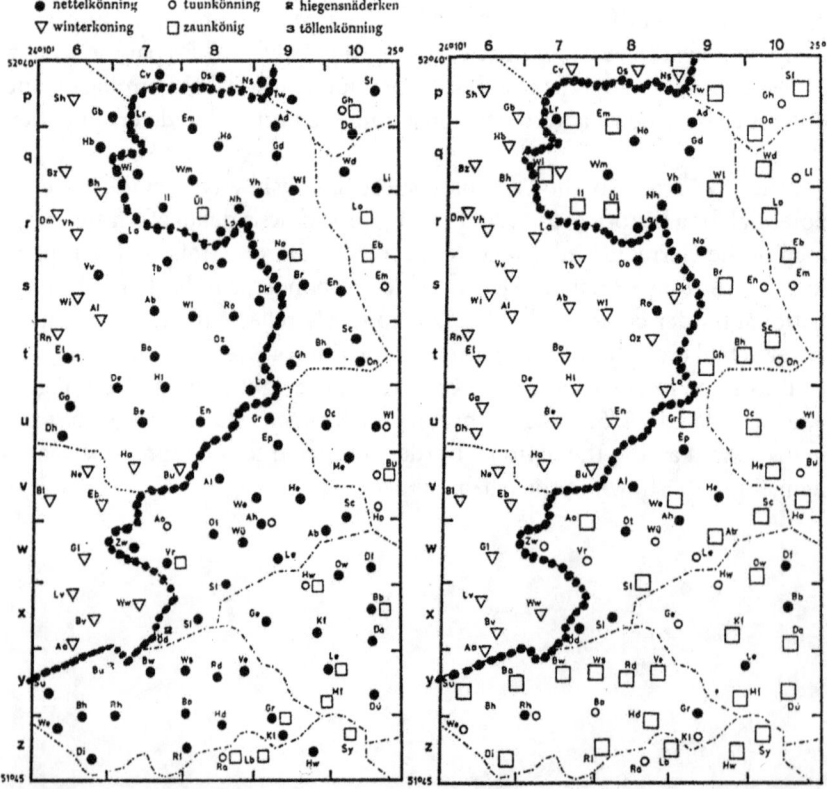

Figure 5. Map for "wren" at the Germany-Netherlands border; left–1940, right–1975 (Auer 2005, 19).

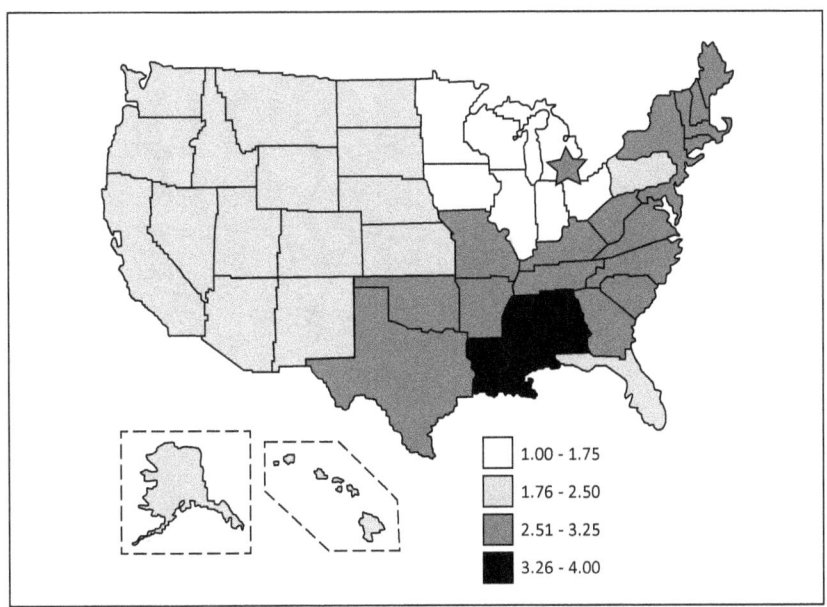

Figure 6. Southeastern Michigan (indicated with the star) respondents' rating of degree-of-difference for the 50 US states (Preston 1996a, 318).

There are no perceptual maps for this territory before the 1970s nor more recent ones, but it is interesting to speculate that earlier perceptual maps, from around the time of the 1940s investigations, might have shown many more border crossing perceptions of similarity and that later ones, with even more vigorous entrenchment of the standard languages, even fewer such crossings.

The Japanese and Dutch ratings of similarity and difference were later used in a modified task ("degree-of-difference"), in which respondents ranked areas as 1 = same, 2 = a little different, 3 = different, and 4 = unintelligibly different (Preston 1993a, 1996a). Figure 6 shows the results for such a task for respondents from southeastern Michigan (the area starred in the figure), in which the mean scores were divided into even groups. Although this alternative technique was first applied to larger areas, some work has focused on smaller regions, as in the Dutch and Japanese models (e.g., Benson 2005 for the US state of Ohio). An alternative similarity-difference technique known as "pile sort" and borrowed from anthropology was introduced into PD by Tamasi (2003). In this alternative technique, predetermined areas (e.g., states, prefectures) are printed on cards and respondents sort them into piles of similar items, in this case on the basis of linguistic similarity.

A more recent technique in PD that continues the similarity-difference approach is one that has come to be known as "draw-a-map." Borrowed from cultural geographers (e.g., Gould and White 1974), this technique, introduced in Preston 1981, asks respondents to draw regional speech boundaries and assign labels to them. Figure 7 shows a typical hand-drawn map for the entire United States. Although the labels and respondent interview comments after the task are valuable for ethnographic and attitudinal research (Why

Figure 7. Hand-drawn map of US dialects by a 20-year old (in 1983) female European American from Western New York (Preston, personal collection).

do speakers in Michigan and Wisconsin use "Wishy Washy ling"?), the ability to make general maps from many respondent drawings attracted early attention. Preston and Howe (1987) and Long (1999) were the first to use this method, and their innovations allowed the boundaries of many hand-drawn maps to be traced in a computer-processed system from which generalizations about the outlines of perceived areas could be made.

Newer GIS-based computer mapping systems have replaced these early models and allow not only such elegant maps as shown in Figure 8 but also demographically sensitive ones as shown in Figure 9. Figure 8, for example, shows not only areas in England and Scotland identified as dialectally distinct by north of England respondents but also the degree of agreement about the areas in a "heat map." Figure 9 shows not only the heat map of a perceived dialect area in the Southwest of Germany but also the correspondence of the perception to Catholic and Protestant areas. An introduction to the use of GIS systems in perceptual mapping is available in Montgomery and Stoeckle (2013).

In the techniques examined so far, respondents were not given voice samples; Preston (1996a) presented a scrambled north-south continuum of voices of nine middle-aged, college-educated males to respondents from southeastern Michigan (the area starred in Figure 6), who identified each with a city (shown in Figure 10). A cluster analysis of the results (Figure 11) shows a much closer linkage (i.e., ones further to the left) of the northern voices than the linkage of the association of the southern voices at the bottom of the figure. There is a steady progression from the northernmost (Saginaw, the one closest to the respondents' home area) through Coldwater, to South Bend, to Muncie, and finally, New Albany, before there is a sharp division in the attachment of the southern cluster to the northern. In fact, the southern cluster of Nashville, Florence, and Bowling Green is attached

What's Old and What's New in Perceptual Dialectology?

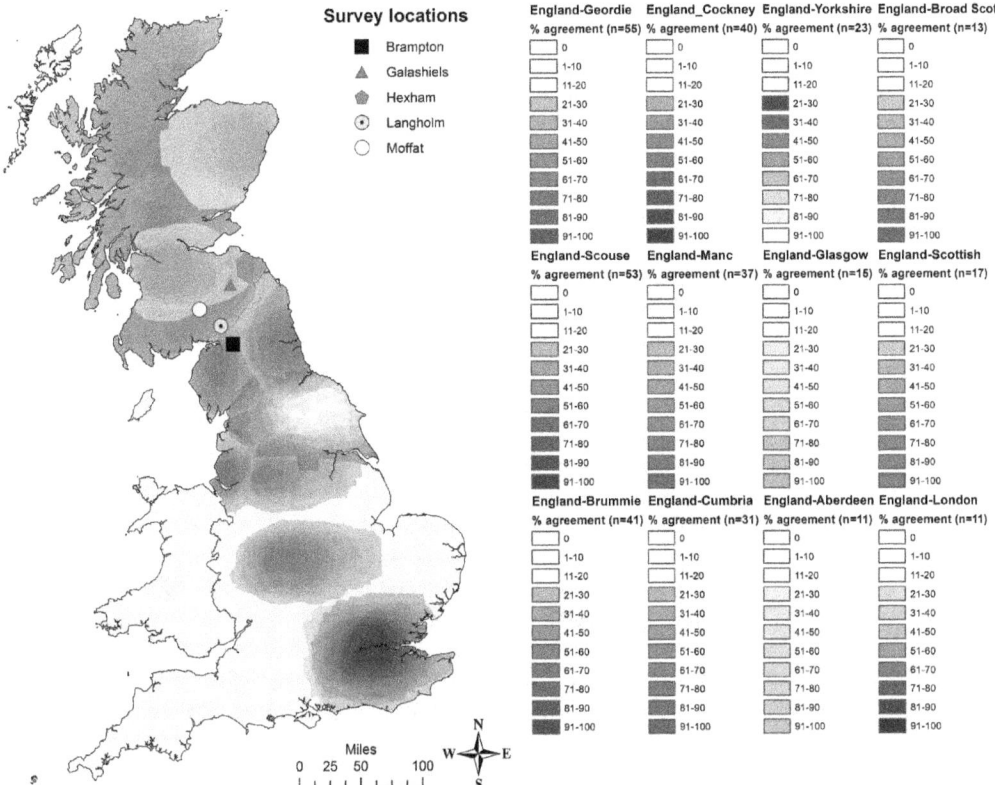

Figure 8. Perceptual map of UK dialects from the point of view of three north of England sites – Brampton, Hexham, and Langholm (Montgomery and Stoeckle 2013, Map 25).

to the entire northern cluster before the southernmost voice (Dothan) is attached to the entire array.

While one might admire the north-south sensitivity of these identifications, the groupings would not make US dialectologists very happy. Saginaw and Coldwater both belong to the Inland North, but South Bend does not, evidencing such features of the North Midland as the [ɔ] pronunciation of "on" (speakers to the north say [ɑ]). South Bend should be much more closely related to Muncie, with which it shares regional affiliation, but the entire group of northern sites would then be closely related to New Albany, a city in the "Hoosier Apex" area of Indiana (Carver 1987) that shares many more features with the southern group and should have been closely tied to Bowling Green. That Dothan is attached to all other voices before being aligned with its southern neighbors, with which it shares many features, would also confuse professionals.

23

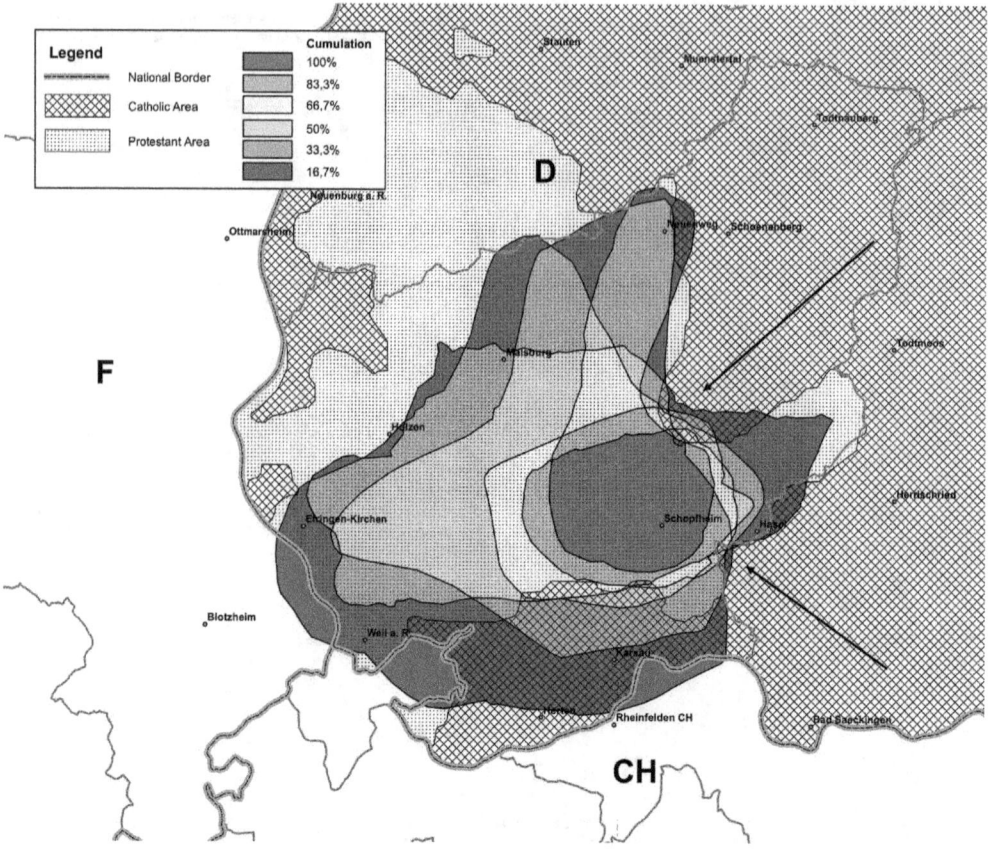

Figure 9. Perceptual map of Schopfheim identification of the local dialect compared to Catholic and Protestant areas (Montgomery and Stoeckle 2013, Map 16).

3 Social PD

The next subcategory in Figure 1 suggests that social factors should be added to PD, as they no doubt should be to dialectology in general: "[d]ialectology without sociolinguistics at its core is a relic" (Chambers and Trudgill 1998, 188). In PD, the social distinctions studied may concern both respondent status as well as the perceived demographic identity of the speakers in the areas delimited. The respondent who drew the dialect outlines shown on the map in Figure 7 believes that Southern US speakers are not just dialectally distinct but are also "tough acting dudes." The Southwestern German respondents whose local dialect identification shown in Figure 9 may use religion to guide dialect identification, or religion (perhaps due to network alliances) may have guided dialect formation.

In other PD work, statistical procedures, such as factor analyses and multidimensional scaling, have allowed the introduction of social factors. Figure 12 shows the degree-of-difference results for Madrid respondents (with the same 1–4 values used in the earlier PD studies) in their evaluation of 17 regions of Spain.

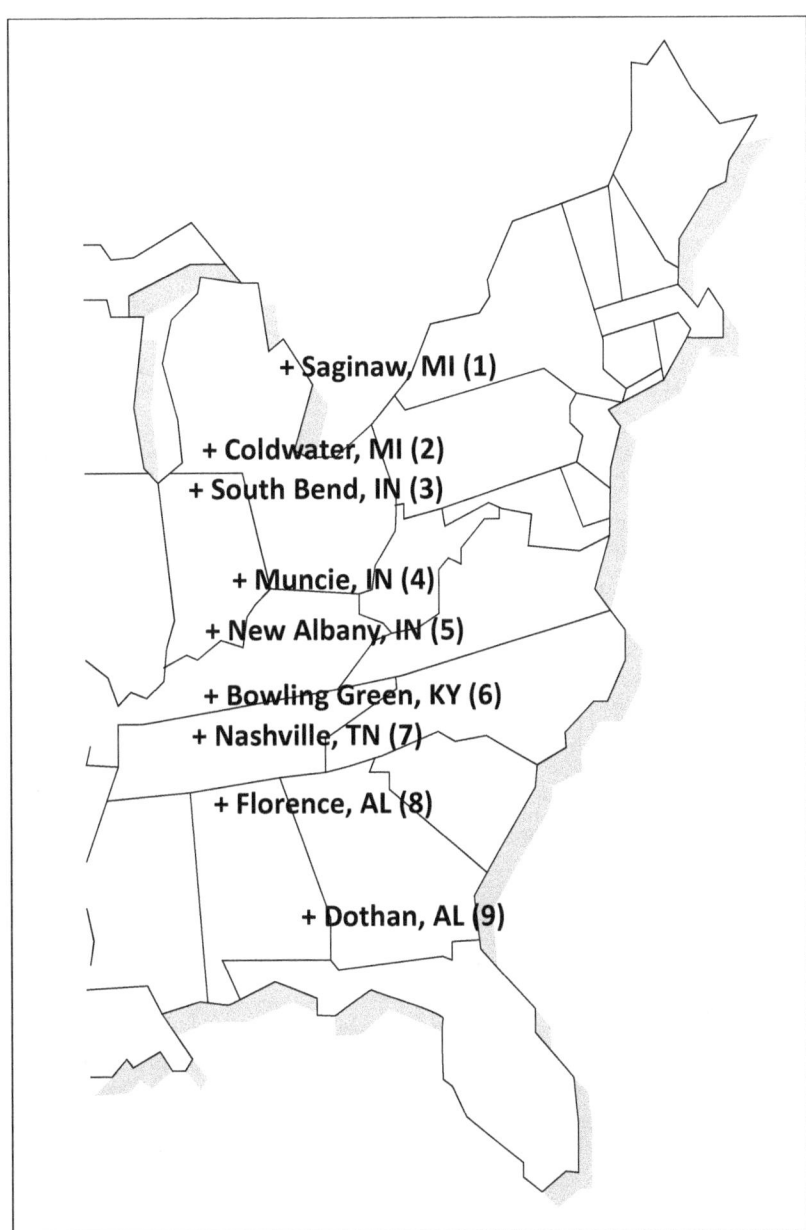

Figure 10. The home sites of the nine male voices presented for regional identification (Preston 1996a, 322).

The horizontal dimension (#1) is perhaps a multilingual one: "non-Spanish" areas – 1 (Galicia), 4 (Basque Country), 7 (Catalonia), 13 (Valencia), and 14 (Balearic Islands) – cluster to the right. The vertical dimension (#2) reflects dialect differences; one group at the top – 5 [Navarra], 10 [Extramadura], 16 [Murcia], 17 [Canary Islands]), and a second at the bottom – 9 [Rioja], and 15 [Andalusia], although the wide separation of the second group on Dimension #1, suggests that Rioja is more native-like. The local area (11 [Madrid]) is closely linked to 12 (Castille-La Mancha), and

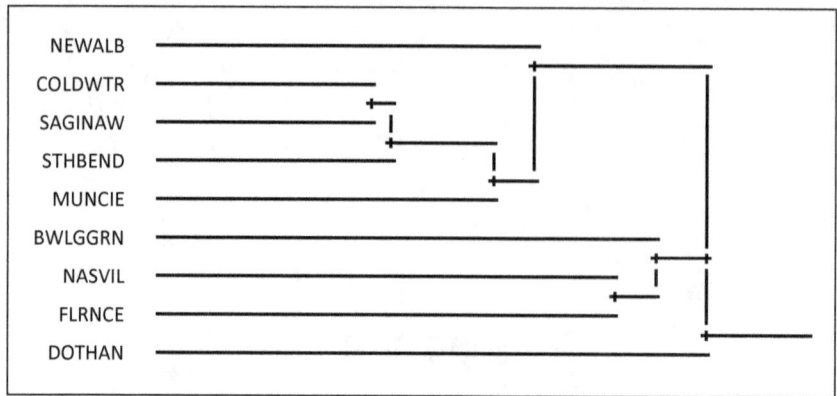

Figure 11. Cluster analysis of southeastern Michigan placement of nine voices on the map in Figure 10.

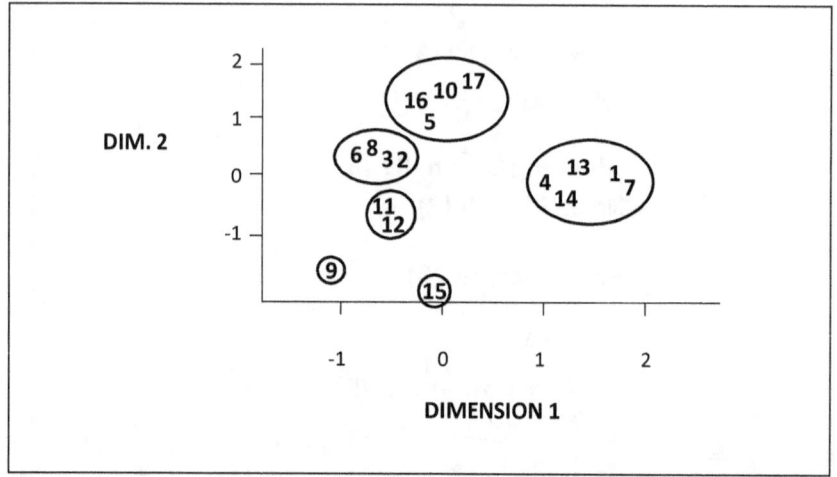

Figure 12. A multidimensional scale of Madrid respondents' evaluations of degree-of-difference for 17 areas of Spain (1 = Galicia, 2 = Asturias, 3 = Cantabria, 4 = Basque Country, 5 = Navarra, 6 = Aragon, 7 = Catalonia, 8 = Castile-Leon, 9 = Rioja, 10 = Extramadura, 11 = Madrid, 12 = Castile-La Mancha, 13 = Valencia, 14 = Balearic Islands, 15 = Andalusia, 16 = Murcia, 17 = Canary Islands) (Moreno and Moreno 2002, 304).

both are not far from the group of 2 (Asturias), 3 (Cantabria), 6 (Aragon), and 8 (Castile-Leon), which, since it is above 11 and 12 on Dimension 2, is slightly more marked dialectally, perhaps, in the direction of the topmost group (Moreno and Moreno 2002, 303).

The study includes social dimensions, which compare men and women, three age groups, and three educational levels. Dimension #1 (language) is more important for male, middle-aged, and university-educated respondents, and Dimension #2 (dialect) is more significant for women and youth. Although some similar social factors were considered in earlier degree-of-difference studies, these more sophisticated quantitative approaches have improved the discussion of social dimensions in PD.

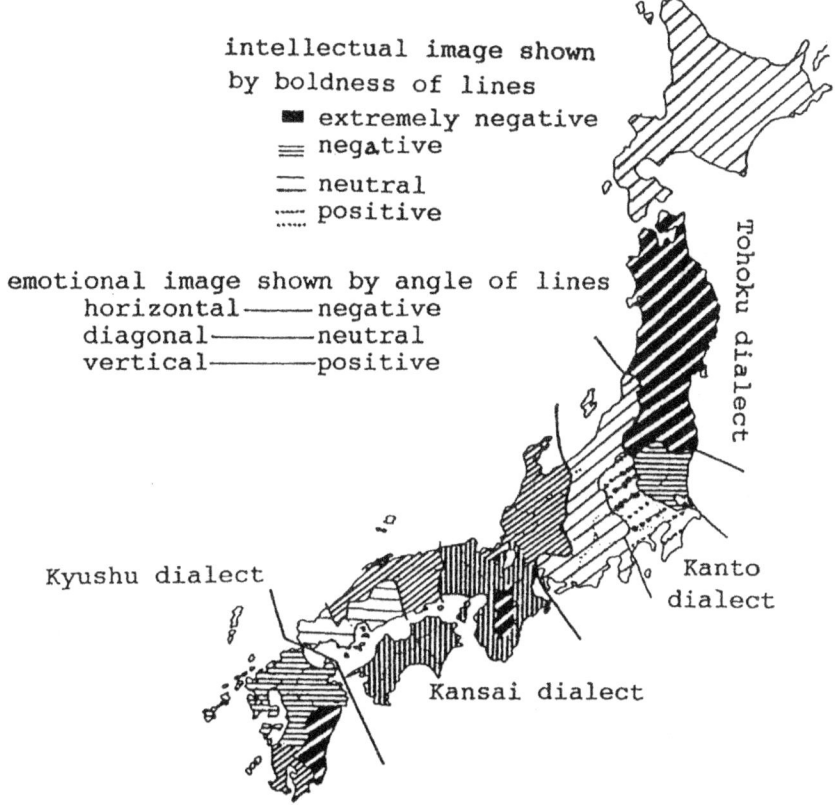

Figure 13. Dialect classification of status ("intellectual") and solidarity ("emotional") characteristics by region in Japan (Inoue 1999, 149).

4 Attitudes in PD

Both the social and regional dimensions of PD, however, require evaluation as a necessary component, and many would point to early work on the evaluation of regional and ethnic varieties (e.g., Giles 1970, Tucker and Lambert 1969), although respondent identification of region or ethnicity was not a part of their work nor of subsequent work in the social psychological tradition. An early PD study that approached attitude directly was Inoue 1988 and 1989, summarized in Inoue 1999. Using semantic differential and factor analytic techniques, Inoue found that the usual components of language attitudes – one that refers to status ("intellectual" in Figure 13) and the other to solidarity ("emotional" in Figure 13) – are associated with regions in Japan. Preston (1985), again using the geographical techniques outlined in Gould and White (1974), directly appealed to these two components by simply asking respondents where the "most correct" and "most pleasant" varieties were spoken. Figure 14 shows the results of the "correct" evaluations for US respondents from southernmost Indiana (area "5" in Figure 10).

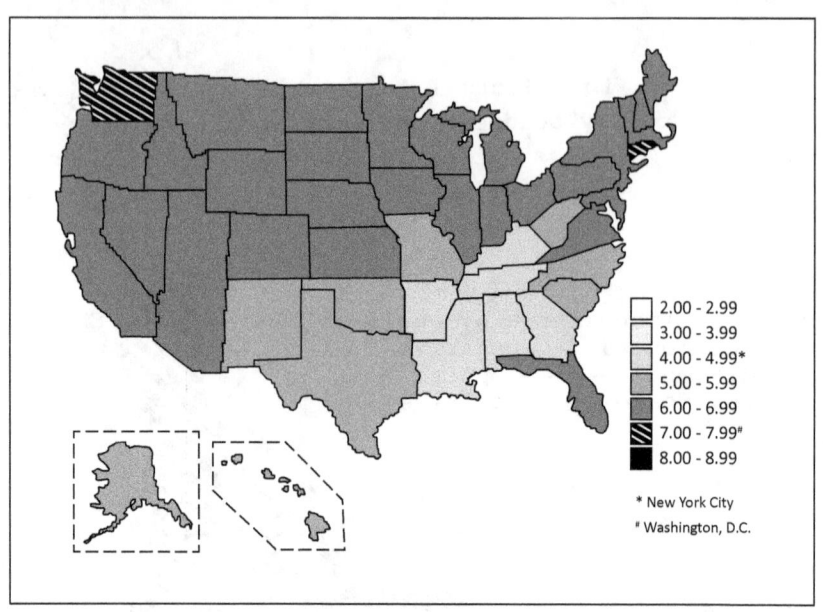

Figure 14. Southern Indiana respondent classifications of the US states, Washington D.C., and New York City for "correct English" (1 = least correct and 10 = most correct) (Preston 1996a, 312).

People from Southern Indiana don't think very much of New York City; it scored the lowest for correctness (in the 4.00 – 4.99 range) and also the lowest for pleasantness, but there is something even more intriguing in these correctness evaluations. Indiana itself is assigned to a fairly Northeastern, Northern, and Western band of 6.00 – 6.99 ratings, but right across the Ohio River, the State of Kentucky is rated lower (in the 4.00 – 4.99 band, as low even as New York City). As pointed out above in the discussion of the voice placement task (Figures 10 and 11), Southern Indiana is dialectally indistinguishable from at least the part of Kentucky that it borders. Since the river causes no dialect difference, it appears that even the southernmost Indiana residents cling to the idea that good English is spoken in the North and bad English in the South, and they couple this belief with the geographical perception that even the part of Indiana where they live is northern and Kentucky is southern.

Correctness and pleasantness, however, do not always coincide. The core of the US South (assigned a "4" in Figure 14) is considered rather more pleasant, friendly, down-to-earth, and casual than the home area by respondents from southeastern Michigan (Preston 1999a), who, like the Indiana respondents, found the South in general to be the most incorrect. This study, like Inoue's cited above, uses a "silent" matched-guise approach with semantic differential Likert scale evaluations subjected to factor analytic analysis. The regions submitted to the respondents were the ones discovered earlier in the draw-a-map task done by respondents from the same southeastern Michigan area (Preston and Howe 1987), combining attitudinal research directly with the results of regional PD.

Attitude research in PD has moved forward more recently along two fronts: discoursal and experimental, the latter discussed in the following section. The treatment of discourse and interaction is so broad that only a small sampling of some of the techniques used to examine "talk about talk" (i.e., folk metalanguage, e.g., Preston 2004) can be illustrated in this article. Excluded from consideration in this study are methods in social psychology (e.g., Potter and Wetherell 1987), ethnomethodological investigations of interaction (e.g., Sacks 1972), critical discourse analysis (e.g., Fairclough 1992), content analysis (e.g., Bauer 2000), and anthropological approaches (e.g., Goddard 2009) that all lie outside the scope of more linguistically oriented techniques.

Preston (1993b) illustrates a number of linguistically-oriented techniques that focus on respondent talk about language variety and reveal both overt and covert expressions of their attitudes and beliefs. One illustration will suffice here. In an informal group conversation about language varieties, two airplane pilots (S and D) have the following interaction (Rodgers and Preston 2015):

92S: Is there a – is there a – an a – an a – an opinion or correlation or – about – – intelligence – related to – how somebody speaks?

93D: No. – If **A** was who I fly with, – he sounds like the hickest of hicks – but that dude can do some crazy things with an airplane,=

In this exchange, the 92S question[3] about the relationship between intelligence and manner of speaking is immediately denied in 93D, but the remainder of 93D requires an analysis of nonasserted material. Characterizing parts of this exchange as a "nonoppositional argument" (e.g., Schiffrin 1985) makes it clear that it should be classified as support for the 93D denial of the ability to detect a relationship between speaking and intelligence, but it is understood to be so only if S does some pragmatic work. The support for D's denial is a counterexample; one cannot tell the intelligence of a speaker from their manner of speaking because A is one who "sounds like the hickest of hicks" but can do "crazy things with an airplane." However, if the hearers do not know that "hicks" are widely assumed in the culture to be rural, uneducated, unsophisticated, and unintelligent, how will they know that "sounds like the hickest of hicks" is D's example of one who sounds as if they were unintelligent? He never asserts this overtly. Equally mysterious without implicational work is that his ability to do "crazy things with an airplane" is an example of A's intelligence. Recall, however, that S and D are

---

3 Questions themselves may not be pragmatically simple. Here it is ignored that, in a given context (defined narrowly or broadly), there might be a preferred or dispreferred answer, both from the point of view of the asker and the answerer. Also ignored here is the fact that a question might serve such conversational work as topic initiation (which it probably does in this example).

pilots, and this expression is an acknowledgement of A's considerable skill.[4] Such pragmatic analyses are highly recommended for discoursal PD data in order to uncover the tacit beliefs held by the respondents.

Talk about language variety, however, is interesting from any perspective, and discussion with respondents after such PD tasks as outlined above and in the next section is highly recommended. Mielikäinen and Palander (2014) is a recent book-length compilation of respondent comments from all over Finland about Finnish varieties and is an excellent example of the value of recording and studying respondent comment in PD.

5 Speech perception

It is by no means a new idea that linguistic detail plays an important role in PD (e.g., Preston 1996b); Graff et al. (1986) have called the use of such detail in experimental procedures "a new method for sociolinguistic research." Increasing sophistication in experimental models and sophisticated but inexpensive programs for acoustic analysis and resynthesis have expanded this style of investigation. In Graff et al., for example, the /aʊ/ diphthong of Philadelphia US English was modified to have a backer (e.g., /ɑ/) or fronter (e.g., /a/) onset in the word "house". It was placed in a sentence spoken by an African-American Philadelphia speaker in which the rest of the phonology was typically African-American. Philadelphia judges, both Black and White, then listened to the samples with the fronter and backer onsets, and, in spite of the African-American character of the rest of the sentence, overwhelmingly agreed that the sentence with the fronter onset in "house" was spoken by a White speaker and the backer one by a Black speaker.

In this case, the folk perception was correct in assigning a fronted onset to Philadelphia European-American speakers, but experimental work in PD has revealed more subtle factors at work. Niedzielski (1999) asked Southeastern Michigan speakers to tell her which of three vowels matched one previously presented. She first played the word "last" with the speaker's typical southeastern Michigan vowel – one considerably raised and fronted[5] (F1 = 700Hz, F2 = 1900Hz). She then played three resynthesized versions of the word "last": 1) the same vowel, 2) one more typical of American English (F1 = 775Hz, F2 = 1700Hz), 3) and a third exaggeratedly low and back (F1 = 900Hz, F2 = 1530Hz). She identified the speaker of the first sample word as "from Michigan." Not one of her forty-two respondents succeeded in correctly matching the vowel, although the wrong answers were phonetically quite distinct. Thirty-eight thought the first word matched #2

---

4   In fact, the fieldworker, not a pilot, had to confirm the admiration embedded in "do some crazy things with an airplane" from the respondents. Ordinary airline passengers would no doubt not be reassured by the phrase.
5   This is the position of this vowel in the "Northern Cities Shift" system, a vowel configuration typical of the large cities around the Great Lakes of the US (e.g., Labov et al. 2006).

above, the more common vowel of American English, and four chose even the exaggeratedly lower and backer vowel (#3).

Why did Michiganders fail at this simple task? Niedzielski notes previous PD work (especially of the "correct" and "pleasant" sort) that shows that Michiganders believe their own area to be dialect-free – the best example of "correct English" in the US (e.g., Preston 1996a). One of the Michigan respondents in Niedzielski and Preston (2000), when asked where "Standard English" was spoken, told the fieldworker that it was the "Midwestern" English that the respondent himself spoke. Such evidence led Niedzielski to believe that Michigan respondents rejected any phonetic evidence that would deny the correct or standard status of Michigander English (although they were users of the fronted variety themselves). These Michiganders appear to have two systems available to them; the one, their own native dialect that produces raised and fronted tokens of the vowel of "last," and another from media, historical, and other sources that puts a much lower and backer version of that vowel in what might be called their "mind's ear" (Preston 2011). It is that vowel they refer to as correct and standard, and, since they believe themselves to be speakers of the most correct English in the US, it is that vowel they select when presented with a choice that should identify a "Michigan speaker."

Perception experiments expose folk knowledge of regional and ethnically-based linguistic characteristics that both correspond and do not correspond with what linguists know about those characteristics. Plichta and Preston (2005), for example, have shown that speakers from southeastern Michigan are fairly good at placing increasingly monophthongal versions of the /aɪ/ diphthong along a north-south line in the middle of the US, corresponding to the linguistic reality that Northern varieties are diphthongal and Southern ones monophthongal. In this web-based experiment that elicited responses from all over the US, another interesting result was revealed. Male and female versions of the word "guide" were resynthesized, using exactly the same formant frequencies in increasingly monophthongal tokens, but respondents always heard the male voice as at least one step farther south or the female one as one step farther north. As all sociolinguists know (e.g., Labov 1990), male speakers are more vernacularly oriented and female speakers more oriented to standard varieties; as all folk US speakers assert, people speak bad English in the South and better English in the north (with exceptions such as New York City) (e.g., Preston 1996a). Therefore, the folk know that even a minimal clue of southernness, such as monophthongization or even a degree of monophthongization of the /aɪ/, will more obviously identify a speaker as male.

Other studies of specific features have focused on local sensitivity to regional norms and age. Labov (2011) studied high school (HS) and college (Col) students who were local Inland Northern speakers from Chicago, Illinois (Chi) and non-locals of the same age groups from Philadelphia, Pennsylvania (Phi) and Birmingham, Alabama (Bir). They listened to the word *socks*, the phrase *wear socks*, and the sentence *You had to wear socks, no sandals.*

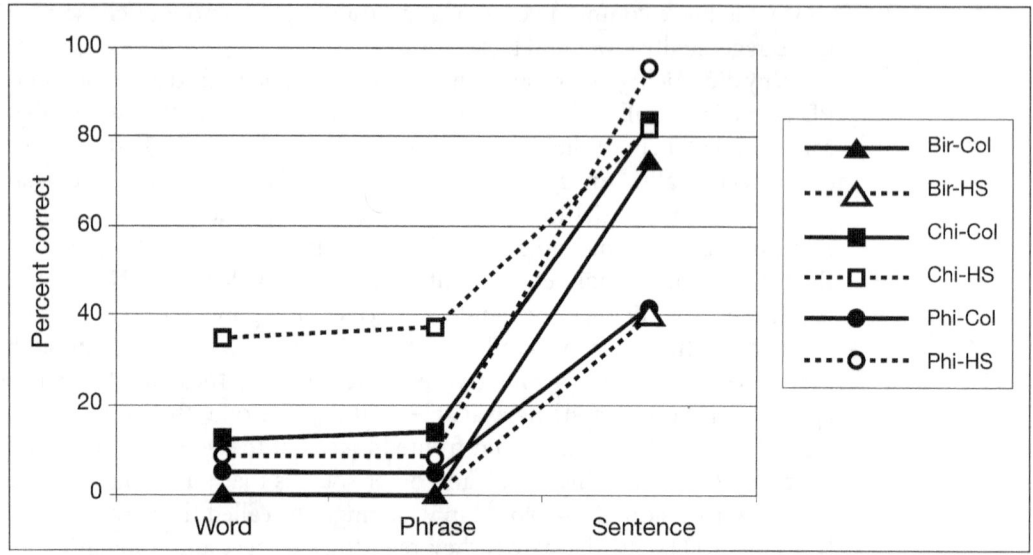

Figure 15. Local and non-local respondent groups' correct understandings of the item socks as an isolated word, in a phrase, and in a sentence (Labov 2011, Figure 4.7).

The Chicagoans are involved in the "Northern Cities Shift" (see above) in which the vowel of *socks* is pronounced farther forward, in the direction of the vowel in "trap." Figure 15 shows that the younger (HS) locals outstripped all other groups (even only slightly older locals) in understanding this word in isolation and in the short phrase, but even they fell below forty percent correct on the isolated word test, an important fact for a dialectology that involves perception as well as production, which PD does.

Such experimental work in perception and its clear relationship to the attitudes and beliefs associated with PD has led to even newer techniques to elicit unconscious responses to varieties: reaction-timed techniques (including so-called implicit tests), eye-tracking measures, and even neurological responses. Koops, Gentry, and Pantos (2008) have revealed implicit knowledge of the correlation between variation and age using photographic priming and eye-tracking. In Houston, Texas, older Anglo speakers merge high front lax vowels before nasals, but these vowels are not merged in younger Anglos. Direct measures of language attitudes do not reveal knowledge of this variation, but Koops et al. have shown results that suggest that respondents are in fact implicitly aware of the merger and even related social facts. When primed with a photo of an older speaker, respondents fixated longer on words that were homophonous (e.g., *rinse* versus *rents*) in the merged (but not the unmerged) dialect.

This conscious-unconscious split in PD studies is an important one since in a recent study Kristiansen (2009) finds that Danes from all over Denmark say that they like their home variety best, but, when a matched-guise test is given, they prefer the emerging "New Copenhagen" standard, the one that is currently influencing the entire country. If matched guise is an actually nonconscious (or implicit) method of collection (see Preston 2009), and, if the generalization reached about this dichotomy for Denmark is found in other areas, then these different methods of investigation will prove essential not only to PD but also to dialectology and variation and change in general, perhaps particularly in those places where standardized or more widespread forms are replacing local ones.

Even more recently, some perception studies of specific features of regional and social linguistic diversity have attempted to elicit nonconscious ("implicit") responses, either with the design of the experimental input or by measuring neural responses in the brain. Campbell-Kibler (2012), for example, used a version of the Implicit Association Test (IAT), in which reaction times to expected and unexpected pairings were studied to test associations beyond the control of the respondent (Greenwald et al. 1998). In her experiment, the use of the alveolar rather than the prescriptively preferred velar consonant in the -*ing* morpheme was shown to be implicitly associated with Southern speech rather than Northern (confirming the negative stereotype of Southern US speech cited in several places above) as well as with Southern [ɑɪ] monophthongization.

In an even more complex design, Loudermilk (2015) compared respondents with high stereotypical responses ("High D") to variation to those with low responses ("Low D"), as determined with an IAT measure. He then measured their EEG brain signals, focusing on the component known as N400, which shows a more dramatic inflection for the presentation of less-expected linguistic stimuli, presumably an indication of a requirement for greater processing effort (e.g., Brown and Hagoort 1993). In his presentation he considered the velar representation of -*ing* (ING) to be consistent with California speakers and the alveolar variant (IN) to be consistent with Southern speakers. The results were as follows:

1) High D listeners showed a more dramatic effect when hearing IN in Southern speech and ING in California speech (the incongruent pairs)
2) Low D listeners showed a more dramatic effect when hearing IN in California speech and ING in Southern speech (the incongruent pairs)

For the High D listeners, the presentation of the congruent pair caused a dramatic N400 effect, but, for Low D listeners, it was the incongruent pair that caused the most processing difficulty. Loudermilk concluded that High D listeners repress the processing effect that an incongruence might have, but it is clear that we need to know more about the brain and PD.

6 Conclusion

It has been shown in this article that PD is necessarily more than the study of folk perceptions about regional dialect boundaries. It is one part of the wider interest in folk linguistics or language regard. In fact, however, it is doubtful that any effective study of language variety perception can be done without consideration of the other categories identified in Figure 1. First, any modern definition of dialect includes social categories, and the PD investigations surveyed in this article show that that is just as true of perceptual matters as it is of production ones. Second, attitudinal influences on PD are also highlighted in much of the research discussed in this article and are essential to the explanation of regional and social identifications as well as to the more finely-tuned study of perception. Third, the more recent study of perception and the focus on conscious versus nonconscious responses open interesting new avenues for research.

The necessary interconnectedness of PD with other areas should not come as a surprise to any who value the study of language in social life. PD, especially when coupled with these other areas of concern, is not just a study conducted for the sake of understanding folk perceptions, although its ethnographic value should be obvious. Those who are interested in the evaluation problem (Weinreich et al. 1968) in the study of language variation and change, however, may find in PD even more directly explanatory evidence than of the more traditionally sociolinguistically oriented study of the facts of production.

References

Auer, Peter. 2005. "The Construction of Linguistic Borders and the Linguistic Construction of Borders." In *Dialects Across Borders*, edited by Markku Filppula, Juhani Klemola, Marjatta Palander, and Esa Penttilä, 3–30. Current Issues in Linguistic Theory 273. Amsterdam: John Benjamins.

Bauer, Martin W. 2000. "Classic Content Analysis: A Review." In *Qualitative Researching with Text, Image and Sound: A Practical Handbook*, edited by M. W. Bauer and G. Gaskell, 131–151. London: Sage.

Benson, Erica J. 2005. "Folk Perspectives of Dialects in Ohio." In *Language Diversity in Michigan and Ohio*, edited by Brian Joseph, Dennis R. Preston, and Carol Preston, 35–60. Ann Arbor: Caravan Books.

Brown, C., and P. Hagoort. 1993. "The Processing Nature of the N400: Evidence from Masked Priming." *Journal of Cognitive Neuroscience* 5:34–44.

Campbell-Kibler, Kathryn. 2012. "The Implicit Association Test and Sociolinguistic Meaning." *Lingua* 122,7:753–763.

Carver, Craig M. 1987. *American Regional Dialects: A Word Geography*. Ann Arbor: The University of Michigan Press.

Chambers, J. K., and Peter Trudgill. 1998. *Dialectology*. (2nd ed.) Cambridge: Cambridge University Press.

Fairclough, Norman. 1992. *Discourse and Social Change*. Cambridge: Polity Press.

Giles, Howard. 1970. "Evaluative Reactions to Accents." *Educational Review* 22:211–227.

Goddard, Cliff. 2009. "Cultural Scripts." In *Culture and Language Use* (Handbook of Pragmatics Highlights 2), edited by Gunter Senft, Jan-Ola Östman, and Jef Verschueren, 68–80. Amsterdam: John Benjamins.

Gould, P., and R. White. 1974. *Mental Maps*. Harmondsworth, Middlesex: Penguin.

Graff, David, William Labov, and Wendell Harris. 1986. "Testing Listeners' Reactions to Phonological Markers of Ethnic Identity: A New Method for Sociolinguistic Research." In *Diversity and Diachrony*, edited by David Sankoff, 45–58. Amsterdam: John Benjamins.

Greenwald, A. G., D. E. McGhee, and J. L. K. Schwartz. 1998. "Measuring Individual Differences in Implicit Cognition: The Implicit Association Test." *Journal of Personality and Social Psychology* 74:1464–1480.

Grootaers, Willem A. 1964 (1999). "La discussion autor des frontières dialectales subjectives." *Orbis* 13:380–398 (translated as "The Discussion surrounding the subjective boundaries of dialects", in Preston 1999b, 115–129).

Inoue, Fumio. 1988. "Dialect Image and New Dialect Forms." *Area and Cultural Studies* 38:13–23.

Inoue, Fumio. 1989. "*Kotoba-zukai Shin-fukei*" [New landscape of spoken Japanese]. Tokyo: Akiyama Shoten.

Inoue, Fumio. 1999. "Classification of Dialects by Image: English and Japanese." In Preston (ed.), 1999b, 147–159.

Koops, Christopher, E. Gentry, and Andrew Pantos. 2008. "The Effect of Perceived Speaker Age on the Perception of PIN and PEN Vowels in Houston, Texas." *University of Pennsylvania Working Papers in Linguistics* 14:2. http://repository.upenn.edu/pwpl/vol14/iss2/

Kremer, Ludger. 1984 (1999). "Die niederländisch-deutsche Staatgrenze als subjektive Dialektgrenze." In *Grenzen en grensproblemen. Een bundel studies uitgegeven door het Nedersaksisch Instituut van de R. U. Groningen ter gelegenheid van zijn 30-jarig bestaan.* (= Nedersaksische Studies 7; zugleich: Driemaandelikse Bladen 36), 76–83. (Translated as "The Netherlands-German Border as a Subjective Dialect Boundary," in Preston (ed.), 1999b, 31–36.)

Kristiansen, Tore. 2009. "The Macro-Level Social Meanings of Late-Modern Danish Accents." *Acta Linguistica Hafniensia* 41:167–192.

Kruglanski, Arie W., and Wolfgang Stroebe. 2005. "The Influence of Beliefs and Goals on Attitudes." In *The Handbook of Attitudes*, edited by Dolores Albarracín, Blair T. Johnson, and Mark P. Zanna, 323–368. Lawrence Erlbaum Associates, Mahwah, NJ & London. Albarracín et al.

Labov, William. 1990. "The Intersection of Sex and Social Class in the Course of Linguistic Change". *Language Variation and Change* 2:205–254.

Labov, William. 2011. *Principles of Linguistic Change, Vol 3*. Cambridge: Cambridge University Press.

Labov, William, Sharon Ash, and Charles Boberg. 2006. *The Atlas of North American English*. Berlin: Mouton de Gruyter.

Long, Daniel. 1999. "Geographical Perceptions of Japanese Dialect Regions." In Preston (ed.), 1999b, 177–198.

Loudermilk, Brandon C. 2015. "Implicit Attitudes and the Perception of Sociolinguistic Variation." In *Responses to Language Varieties: Variability, Processes and Outcomes*, edited by Alexei Prikhodkine, and Dennis R. Preston, 137–156. Amsterdam: John Benjamins.

Mase, Yoshio. 1964a (1999). "Hôgen ishiki to hôgen kukaku." In *Nihon hôgen kenkyûkai*, edited by Misao Tôjô, 270–302. Tokyo: Tokyodo (translated as "Dialect consciousness and dialect divisions", in Preston (ed.), 1999b, 71–99).

Mase, Yoshio. 1964b (1999). "Hôgen ishiki ni tsuite: Washa no genkyûshita hôgenteki tokuchô." *Nagano-ken Tanki Daigaku Kiyô* [Collected Papers of the Nagano Junior College] 18:1–12 (translated as "On dialect consciousness: dialect characteristics given by speakers", in Preston (ed.), 1999b, 101–113).

Mielikäinen, Aila, and Marjatta Palander. 2014. *Miten suomalaiset puhuvat murteista? Kansanlingvistinen tutkimus metakielestä.* [How do Finns talk about dialects? Folk linguistic research on metalanguage.] Helsinki: Finnish Literature Society.

Montgomery, Christopher, and Phillip Stoeckle. 2013. "Geographic Information Systems and Perceptual Dialectology: A Method for Processing Draw-A-Map Data." *Journal of Linguistic Geography* 1,1:52–85.

Moreno Fernández, Juliana, and Francisco Moreno Fernández. 2002. "Madrid Perceptions of Regional Varieties in Spain." In *Handbook of Perceptual Dialectology: Volume 2*, edited by Daniel Long and Dennis R. Preston, 295–320. Amsterdam: John Benjamins.

Niedzielski, Nancy. 1999. "The Effect of Social Information on the Perception of Sociolinguistic Variables." *Journal of Language and Social Psychology* 18.1:62–85.

Niedzielski, Nancy, and Dennis R. Preston. 2000. *Folk Linguistics* (rev. paperback edition, 2003). Berlin: Mouton de Gruyter.

Plichta, Bartłomiej, and Dennis R. Preston. 2005. "The /ay/s Have It: The Perception of /ay/ as a North-South Stereotype in United States English." *Acta Linguistica Hafniensia* 37:107–130 (special issue, *Subjective Processes in Language Variation and Change*, edited by Tore Kristiansen, Peter Garrett, and Nikolas Coupland).

Potter, Jonathan, and Margaret Wetherell. 1987. *Discourse and Social Psychology: Beyond Attitudes and Behaviour*. London: Sage.

Preston, Dennis R. 1981. "Perceptual Dialectology: Mental Maps of United States Dialects from a Hawaiian Perspective (summary)." In *Methods IV/Méthodes IV* (Papers from the Fourth International Conference on Methods in Dialectology), edited by Henry Warkentyne, 192–198. University of Victoria, British Columbia.

Preston, Dennis R. 1985. "Southern Indiana Perceptions of 'Correct' and 'Pleasant' Speech." In *Methods/Méthodes V* (Papers from the Fifth International Conference on Methods in Dialectology), edited by Henry Warkentyne, 387–411. Department of Linguistics, University of Victoria, British Columbia.

Preston, Dennis R. 1993a. Folk Dialectology. In *American Dialect Research*, edited by Dennis R. Preston, 333–377. Amsterdam: John Benjamins.

Preston, Dennis R. 1993b. "The Uses of Folk Linguistics." *International Journal of Applied Linguistics* 3,2:181–259.

Preston, Dennis R. 1996a. "Where the Worst English Is Spoken." In *Focus on the USA*, edited by Edgar Schneider, 297–360. Amsterdam: John Benjamins.

Preston, Dennis R. 1996b. "Whaddayaknow?: The Modes of Folk Linguistic Awareness." *Language Awareness* 5.1:40–74.

Preston, Dennis R. 1999a. "A Language Attitude Approach to the Perception of Regional Variety." In Preston (ed.), 1999b, 359–373.

Preston, Dennis R., ed. 1999b. *Handbook of Perceptual Dialectology: Volume 1*, Amsterdam: John Benjamins.

Preston, Dennis R. 2004. "Folk Metalanguage." In *Metalanguage: Social and Ideological Perspectives*, edited by Adam Jaworski, Nikolas Coupland, and Dariusz Galasiński, 75–101. Berlin: Mouton de Gruyter.

Preston, Dennis R. 2009. "Are You Really Smart (or Stupid or Cute, or Ugly, or Cool)? Or do You Just Talk That Way?" In *Language Attitudes, Standardization & Language Change – Perspectives on Themes Raised by Tore Kristiansen on the Occasion of His 60th Birthday*, edited by Marie Maegaard, Frans Gregerson, Pia Quist, and J. Normann Jørgensen, 105–129. Oslo: Novus Forlag.

Preston, Dennis R. 2010. "Variation in Language Regard." In *Variatio Delectat: Empirische Evidenzen und theoretische Passungen sprachlicher Variation* (für Klaus J. Mattheier zum 65. Geburtstag), edited by Peter Gilles, Joachim Scharloth, and Evelyn Zeigler, 7–27. Frankfurt am Main: Peter Lang.

Preston, Dennis R. 2011. "The Power of Language Regard – Discrimination, Classification, Comprehension, and Production." *Dialectologia* (Special Issue II, edited by Dirk Speelman, Stefan Grondelaers, and John Nerbonne; Proceedings of the Conference on Production, Perception, Attitude. Leuven, April 2–3, 2009), 9–33. http://www.publicacions.ub.es/revistes/dialectologiaSP2011/.

Preston, Dennis R., and George M. Howe. 1987. "Computerized Studies of Mental Dialect Maps." In *Variation in language: NWAV-XV at Stanford* (Proceedings of the Fifteenth Annual Conference on New Ways of Analyzing Variation), edited by Keith Denning, Sharon Inkelas, F. C. McNair-Knox, and John R. Rickford, 361–378. Stanford CA: Department of Linguistics, Stanford University.

Rodgers, Elena, and Dennis R. Preston. 2015. "Language Diversity: Arguments and Analysis." Paper presented at the annual Georgetown University Round Table on Languages and Linguistics, Washington, DC, March 13.

Sacks, Harvey. 1972. "An Initial Investigation of the Usability of Conversational Data for Doing Sociology." In *Studies in Social Interaction*, edited by D. N. Sudnow, 31–74. New York: Free Press.

Schieffelin, Bambi, Kathryn A. Woolard, and Paul Kroskrity, eds. 1998. *Language Ideologies: Practice and Theory*. New York: New York University Press.

Schiffrin, Deborah. 1985. "Everyday Argument." In *Handbook of Discourse Analysis: Volume 3*, edited by Tean A. van Dijk, 35–46. London: Academic Press.

Sibata, Takesi. 1959. "Hôgen Kyôkai no Ishiki." *Gengo Kenkyû* 36:1–30. (Translated as "Consciousness of dialect boundaries" in Preston (ed.), 1999b, 39–62).

Tamasi, Susan L. 2003 "Cognitive Patterns of Linguistic Perceptions." PhD diss., University of Georgia.

Tucker, G. Richard, and Wallace E. Lambert. 1969. "White and Negro Listeners' Reactions to Various American-English Dialects." *Social Forces* 47:463–468.

Weijnen, Antonius A. 1946. De grenzen tussen de Oost-Noordbrabantse dialecten onderling [The borders between the dialects of eastern North Brabant]. In *Oost-Noordbrabantse dialectproblemen* [Eastern North Brabant Dialect Problems], edited by Antonius A. Weijnen, J. M. Renders, and Jac. van Ginneken, 1–15. Amsterdam: Bijdragen en Mededelingen der Dialectencommissie van de Koninklijke Nederlandse Akademie van Wettenschappen.

Weijnen, Antonius A. 1968 (1999). "Zum Wert subjektiver Dialektgrenzen," *Lingua* 21:594–596. (Translated as "On the value of subjective dialect boundaries" in Preston (ed.), 1999b, 131–133.)

Weinreich, Uriel, William Labov, and Marvin I. Herzog. 1968. "Empirical Foundations for a Theory of Linguistic Change." In *Directions for Historical Linguistics*, edited by Winfred F. Lehmann, and Yakov Malkiel, 95–188. Austin: University of Texas Press.

Wikipedia. Accessed April 17, 2015. http://en.wikipedia.org/wiki/Folk_linguistics.

Willems, P. 1886. *De enquête werd gehouden in 1886 de antwoorden zijnhet eigendom ca de Koninklijke Vlaamsche Academie voor Taal- en Letterkunde, en worden daar bewaard* [The enquiry was done in 1886; the responses are the property of the Royal Flemish Academy of Languages and Literatures in Ghent where they are preserved]. Microcopies are at the institutes of Dialectology and Phonetics in Leuven, the Catholic University, Nijmegen, and the P. J. Meertens Institute, Amsterdam.

Johanna Laakso
http://orcid.org/0000-0002-4892-9885

Language Borders and Cultural Encounters
A Linguistic View on Interdisciplinarity in the Research of Intercultural Contacts

Abstract

This article reflects on the role of *borders* from the point of view of languages and linguistics. Languages are commonly perceived as markers of community borders and ethnic identities, often corresponding to essentialized "racial" or cultural communities. This is connected with the idea of languages as closed systems or entities with clear boundaries. For a number of conspiring ideological, political, and theoretical reasons, this view has long dominated in Western research and language policies. In recent decades, however, it has been increasingly challenged by the so-called cultural turn in the humanities, connected with the political developments of the late 20th century.

Sociolinguistics and variation linguistics show that the borders of languages are not always clear, nor can humankind be uncontroversially divided into communities characterized each by one sole or dominant mother tongue. The assumption of monolingualism as the primary and natural state of human beings and communities is also challenged by theoretical, cognitive, and historical linguistics. At the same time, however, cultural studies are increasingly interested in multilingualism and multiculturalism, sometimes in a way that seems to imply an essentializing view on languages and identities, confirming borders while contesting them.

The problems in interdisciplinary approaches involving linguistics and cultural studies often actualize not only on the border of languages, but also on the border between nature and culture. Crossing borders is fashionable and attractive, but it should not tempt us to naturalize culture or culturalize nature at the cost of empirical adequacy.

1 The Border: How language separates Us from Them?

On the LanguageLog website, Mark Liberman (2003) has written about typical lay ideas about language, ethnicity, and multilingualism, using the title "This Is Not Middle-Earth." In the imaginary world of *The Lord of the Rings*, as well as in many latter-day works of fiction and fantasy, peoples, nations, or ethnic groups are distinct entities, each of them characterized by a certain language, culture, worldview, and physical appearance (hair, skin color, etc.). Moreover, all these characteristics are organically interconnected and inherited as an organic whole: people 'have it in their blood.' As a rule, ethnic groups do not mix and their borders cannot be crossed (you cannot become something other than what you were born to be), everybody or almost everybody unequivocally belongs to one group only, and only some exceptional individuals know other groups' languages – problems with mutual understanding are normally solved with international lingue franche or, as often in science fiction, with the help of technical devices.

This is the view within which very many Europeans are socialized, at least since the times of Romantic Nationalism. We just love the idea that different peoples look, dress, smell, and talk differently, that there are always clear borders between US and THEM. In our days, these ideas, as *gesunkenes Kulturgut,* appear in the world of popular fiction, but, until the early 20th century, they were taught at schools and even at universities. School textbooks that reproduced stereotypical ideas about the appearances, national costumes, characters, and mentalities of different ethnic groups belong to this tradition along with the darker sides of European race ideologies (see, e.g., Hagerman 2006), from the history of slavery up to the well-known crimes against humanity in the 20th century. And even in our days, the essentialization of 'culture' into a clearly demarcated something that dictates a person's actions keeps surfacing in political discourse, about immigration in particular, in both openly racist and more well-intentioned forms. For instance, the European debate about the integration of immigrants always threatens to become mired in the essentialization of 'culture' and 'cultural differences' or even 'intercultural communication' – these people "come from a different culture," so they are essentially different – instead of focusing on the real and practical everyday problems that immigrants face (see, e.g., Bachinger and Schenk 2012).

The need to draw borders between US and THEM is deeply rooted in our culture, and some researchers have even claimed that it might have arisen in the course of the evolution of humankind. As our ancestors needed to distinguish edible plants from poisonous ones and harmless animals from dangerous ones, they perhaps extended this cognitive schema to other human beings as well, as Francisco Gil-White (2001) claims:

> ... humans process ethnic groups (and a few other related social categories) as if they were 'species' because their surface similarities to species make them inputs to the 'living-kinds' mental module that initially evolved to process species-level categories.

In other words: we love essentializing differences in culture and culturally conditioned behavior, such as language. Of course, there are many other important ethno-differentiating factors as well, such as clothing or ethnic cooking, but language is one of the most powerful, or perhaps even the most powerful of these factors, as it directly affects mutual communication and understanding. From the perspective of a Finnish linguist, I will start in my own comfort zone and first reflect on how linguistics has been used and misused in building and strengthening borders between US and THEM, which very much involves essentializing culture, naturalizing nurture.

2 Languages as separate entities in historical-comparative Finno-Ugric studies

Modern nations are, as Benedict Anderson famously said, 'imagined communities,' or even imaginary or metaphorical families, 'a family writ large' (Fox 1993), in which the members are metaphoric blood relations and men and women are assigned roles corresponding to the usual gendered roles of family members (cf., e.g., Lempiäinen 2003; Laakso 2005, 95). In classical nation-state projects, language played a crucial role. This is not just because language was both the means and the product of what could be called the national culture, but especially because linguistics in the 19th century offered the best views into what could be understood as the history of the nation. This is something that Finns know all too well: the discovery of the Finno-Ugric language relatedness puts the Finnish people in a place on the ethnolinguistic map of Eurasia, and this, in fact, was the explicit goal of the pioneers of Finno-Ugric studies, such as M. A. Castrén.

> There is only one thing that has affected me deeply and powerfully, I can live only for that, everything else is subsidiary. I have decided to show the Finnish people that we have not been torn apart from the world and world history, but that we are related to at least one sixth of mankind. Grammars are not my principal aim, but without grammars this aim cannot be achieved.
> (M. A. Castrén in a letter to J. V. Snellman in 1844; translation quoted from Korhonen 1986, 66).

And why is this so? Because historical linguistics was the first discipline that could offer something like hard (or semi-hard) facts about the otherwise undocumented past of a group of people. Languages that had been spoken thousands of years ago could be reconstructed and, at least, approximations made as to how they had really sounded. What's more, the family-tree model of linguistic relatedness was not just a scientific-sounding way of describing the national past. Due to its misleading analogy to elite genealogies – in which not the branching and spreading roots but the strategically important noble lineage played a central role – the family trees of languages could be understood as reflections of pure lineages, and not just of languages but of peoples.

The following classical illustration (Figure 1), from a school textbook by the distinguished linguist Lauri Kettunen from the 1930s (Kettunen and Vaula 1938), shows how the concepts of language and nation are conflated and confused. The caption says "The kindred peoples of the Finns," the sections into which the tree trunk is divided represent periods of time (for instance, "Finno-Ugric period" until 2500 BC), while the branches represent individual languages such as Hungarian *(unkari)*, or subgroups of languages, for instance, the Ob-Ugric languages *(obin-ugrilaiset kielet)*.

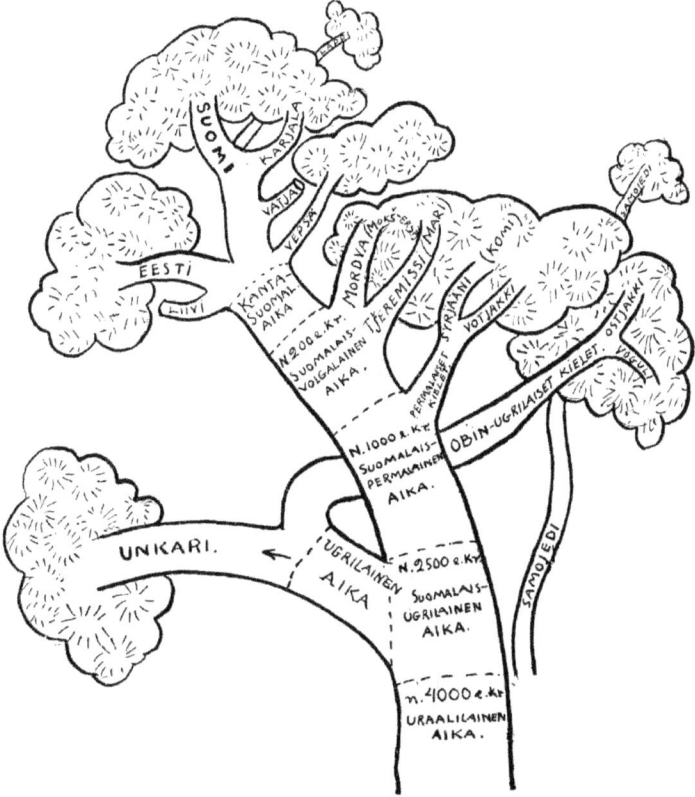

Suomensukuiset kansat.

Figure 1. The family tree of the Uralic languages, presented in Kettunen and Vaula (1938) as the family tree of the "kindred peoples of the Finns".

Interestingly, the branches representing racially 'different' peoples, the Samoyed (on the right-hand side) and the Saami (the uppermost branch entitled *Lappi* behind the top of the tree) do not really, organically, belong to the tree, they begin from nowhere. The reason is obvious: for the Finnish nationalists of those times, it was inconceivable that the tall blonde Nordic Finns and these exotic peoples with dark colors and slanting eyes could descend from the same ancestors. The Saami and Samoyed branches that belong to the tree, but are not visibly connected to it, illustrate this controversy between linguistic relatedness and (perceived) lack of genetic relatedness.[1]

1 Concerning the origins of the Saami, the so-called Proto-Lapp hypothesis was very popular in the early 20th century. It was believed that the ancestors of the Saami were a non-Uralic people who had given up their original language, adopting the language of their culturally superior Finnic neighbors. This was in accordance with the racist thinking of those days; for the history of the ideas about the racial 'otherness' of the Saami, see Isaksson 2001. Actually, recent research has, in a certain sense, rehabilitated this idea, showing that an unknown, non-Uralic ethnolinguistic group must have participated in the ethnogenesis of the Saami; see especially Aikio 2004; 2012.

One important detail about which misunderstandings and misleading statements abound must be emphasized. Historical linguistics does *not* ignore language contacts; in the field of historical Uralic studies, language contacts have been of central importance practically since the very beginning. The point is just that the comparative method – and the family tree model, its visual representation – treats inherited and borrowed elements as phenomena of different levels and can only represent contact-induced change in an indirect way. For this reason, it is easy for a naïve outsider to interpret family trees as 'pure' lineages, parthenogenetic generations of virgin mothers and their daughters. This, in turn, is the wet dream of a romantic nationalist: basically, it can be interpreted as supporting the idea of nations as eternal, closed, and discrete entities. Our nation, with its singularly 'pure' heritage and with its singularly pure language, which testify to its glorious past, has always existed, as if moving in an ethnolinguistic vacuum, and the main question for our prehistory simply concerns the localisation of our *Urheimat:* where did we come from? (Again, please note that this simplifying view was not typical of historical linguistics inside the discipline but, rather, interpretations and uses of historical linguistics in the research into the national prehistory and its representations in popular literature, school textbooks, etc. This is one of the risks of so-called interdisciplinarity.)

Linguists working within the political framework of nation-state projects have had further reason to focus on pure, monolingual identities and ignore the existing multilingualism and fuzziness of language and identity borders. Namely: many of them worked with linguistic minorities in a language shift situation. The Finnish Finno-Ugrists in the first golden age of fieldwork before World War I saw what was happening with the Finno-Ugric minorities in Russia; marginalisation and a massive loss of identity, culture, and language, the physical and spiritual destruction of whole nations. Their field reports and memoirs often contain heart-rending accounts of the effects of apathy, alcoholism, and marginalization, foreboding the extinction of languages and cultures (see, e.g., Korhonen et al. 1983; Salminen 2008; Laakso 2011, 19–20).

Note that the Finno-Ugric field linguists at the turn of the 20th century typically came from a background of Finnish nationalism and the – by then already successful – emancipation project of the Finnish language. Within their romantic nationalist framework, it was easy to simplify the situation: once upon a time there had been a pure monolingual precolonial world of indigenous languages, then came the colonization and language contact that could only lead to a language shift and loss of the original languages. Certainly, language shift and language death as observed by these researchers were and are real phenomena. However, all language contacts and cultural encounters do not necessarily follow this colonization scenario, nor does multilingualism necessarily mean just a phase in the inevitable process of language shift.

3 Nature vs. Culture: The distinctness of language in folk views, in national language policies and in linguistics

During the 19th and the 20th centuries, up to current times, linguists working with national philologies and state language planning have often been employed to draw and define clear borders between languages. Purism in language planning (see, e.g., Thomas 1991), the idea that native, inherited words and elements are inherently better and that foreign influences should be avoided, has a long tradition in the language policy of many European countries. Currently, puristic language policies may be motivated by the dangers of globalization. The global lingua franca English, in particular, is identified as a danger in quite a few national language policy papers or language laws, as in the current language development plan of the Estonian government:

> According to the strategy [i.e., the strategy *Sustainable Estonia 21*], the most significant danger is rapid internationalization of cultural space, including the emergence of English as the most important language of communication in several spheres of life. (*Development Plan of the Estonian Language 2011–2017*, 11).

In the interim report on this development plan[2], the expression *inglise keele pealetung* 'the attack/invasion of the English language' is used.

Perhaps the most blatant examples of the unholy alliance between linguistics and nationalism can now be seen in Hungary, where the political situation favors the ideas of imagined authenticity. In that country, a new Language Strategy Institute was founded recently as a result of purely political decision-making: the new institute is separate from existing academic institutions and reports directly to the Prime Minister, and the already existing Research Institute for the Hungarian Language of the Hungarian Academy of Sciences (which already has a research group for language policy) was not consulted nor even informed.[3] Interestingly, the director of the institute has profiled himself not as a practician of language policy but as a vehement supporter of the – now politically very convenient – ideas of linguistic relativism. Vulgar relativism, the idea of a language being inherently connected to a national worldview and culture and, thus, inherently distinct from everything else, fits in perfectly with today's Hungarian politics of 'our way,' the nationalist populism of the present government. To quote a somewhat baffling article recently published by the director of the new institute:

---

2 Online at http://ekn.hm.ee/system/files/Vahearuanne+%2819.12.2013+VV+ot-susega%29.pdf, accessed April 24, 2015.
3 A translation of the government decree and some other relevant texts in English at http://www.nytud.hu/archives/lsi.html. More information in Hungarian at http://www.nytud.hu/archiv/nyelvstrategiai_intezet.html. See also my guest post in the "Hungarian Spectrum" blog: https://hungarianspectrum.wordpress.com/2014/07/07/johanna-laakso-brave-new-linguistics/.

> "Omnes leones leonizare" [sic] – all lions lionize [a grammatically maltreated reference to Nicolaus Cusanus, *Quando enim omnes leones qui fuerunt et nunc sunt leonizare videmus...*], this is their habit. As the linguist, too, is a human being, all linguists primarily see the world, including language and their own linguistics, from the perspective of their mother tongue [...] The endeavour to describe non-Indo-European languages, including Hungarian, with the grammatical categories of the Indo-European languages has up to our days led to major misunderstandings [...] (Bencze 2013, 37–38, my translation.)[4]

Note the ultimate essentialism, the analogy between different animal species and humans speaking different languages: one is reminded of the famous dialogue between Huck and Jim in *Adventures of Huckleberry Finn* (Twain 1884), where Huck tries to educate Jim about the French language, the point of course being that poor ignorant Jim has never heard of any language other than English:

> "Looky here, Jim, does a cat talk like we do?"
> "No, a cat don't."
> "Well, does a cow?"
> "No, a cow don't, nuther."
> "Does a cat talk like a cow, or a cow talk like a cat?"
> "No, dey don't."
> "It's natural and right for 'em to talk different from each other, ain't it?"
> " 'Course."
> "And ain't it natural and right for a cat and a cow to talk different from us?"
> "Why, mos' sholy it is."
> "Well, then, why ain't it natural and right for a Frenchman to talk different from us? — you answer me that."
> "Is a cat a man, Huck?"
> "No."
> "Well, den, dey ain't no sense in a cat talkin' like a man. Is a cow a man? — er is a cow a cat?"
> "No, she ain't either of them."
> "Well, den, she ain't got no business to talk like either one er the yuther of 'em. Is a Frenchman a man?"
> "Yes."
> "*Well*, den! Dad blame it, why doan' he *talk* like a man? – you answer me *dat*!"

But the pressure to describe languages as distinct entities with clear and unquestionable borders and to focus on one such unit at a time comes not only from society and our cultural need to classify human beings and ethnic groups, but also from the tradition of linguistics itself. Within linguistics, as well, there is methodological pressure to see monolingualism as a natural

---

4 The original text:
„Omnes leones leonizare" – minden oroszlán oroszlánol, ez a szokása. Lévén a nyelvész is ember, minden nyelvész elsősorban anyanyelve szerint látja a világot, benne a nyelvet és a saját nyelvtudományát is, [...] Az a törekvés, hogy indoeurópai nyelvtani kategóriákkal akartuk leírni a nem indoeurópai nyelveket, köztük a magyart is, nagy félreértésekhez vezetett mindmáig [...].

state, starting from Noam Chomsky's "idealized monolingual speaker in a homogeneous speaker community" – or actually not starting from Chomsky, as the idea of languages as autonomous systems goes a long way back in the history of Western linguistics and language philosophy. But as Chomsky put it, in a famous interview with the multilingualism researcher François Grosjean:

> Why do chemists study H_2O and not the stuff that you get out of the Charles River? ... You assume that anything as complicated as what is in the Charles River will only be understandable, if at all, on the basis of discovery of the fundamental principles that determine the nature of all matter, and those you have to learn about by studying pure cases. (Cook and Newson 2007, 222).

In other words: if language is an autonomous system and the human language faculty is, in essence, monolingual, then all meaningful research must begin with the 'pure case,' an idealized monolingual system. It is no coincidence that the analogy is taken from science, not the humanities or social sciences: the border is drawn between nature and culture, and 20th century mainstream linguistics, as Noam Chomsky understood it, positions itself on the side of 'nature.' Linguists, accordingly, work with 'pure cases,' like the chemical composition of water, moreover, with cases that are beyond our conscious control and outside such fuzzy and messy issues as the free will of human beings.

The Chomskyan view of language as an autonomous, distinct system comes with a few important corollaries or underlying assumptions. First, the borders between languages are, in principle, always clear and distinct: you speak either English or German, or you speak either the German language of Germany or Austrian Standard German, etc. Second, language is hard-wired into our brain and based on a genetically conditioned language facility or 'Universal Grammar' (or 'the language instinct,' as it is called in the famous bestseller book by Steven Pinker [1994]), which means that all the languages of the world are basically just different realizations of the same underlying human language (in his debate with Huckleberry Finn, poor ignorant Jim was right after all). This hypothesis is used to explain why young children acquire any language of their environment so easily, as it seems, and why language learning later in life is so much more difficult: we are born with a language acquisition device that switches itself off after a critical age.

This, in turn, means that there is a fundamental difference between (first) language acquisition and (second) language learning and, correspondingly, between true bi- or multilingualism (having two or more first languages) and acquired multilingualism. Furthermore, real language change can only take place in the course of native language acquisition: the parameters (the switches in the virtual switchboard that we all are born with) are set in a certain way, and after that, no substantial or real change is possible. This view, still endorsed even in recent literature on language change ("it seems increasingly clear that most language changes arise as errors in native language learning;" Ringe and Eska 2013, xii), means heavy constraints on contact-induced change: whatever you learn later in life, whatever you do consciously, will actually not affect your mother tongue in a permanent or significant way.

This hypothesis comes with numerous empirical and technical problems, but it also has many aspects that quite obviously have promoted its popularity. The idea of languages as distinct systems and the mother tongue as a system with a special position is not only in line with classical Western ideals of objectivity in science and the whole tradition of theoretical and speculative language philosophy, of describing complex phenomena as systems based on rules, the more economically and elegantly, the better. It is also coherent with the romantic nationalist idea of the one and only true mother tongue, and it corresponds to the way of thinking that many citizens of Western nation-states have learned in the course of their language education: there is the mother tongue, which is the only language you can really master because it comes 'naturally' to you, and there are 'foreign languages,' which are rule-based systems you can only learn with a major effort, if at all. The only exception to this are those few people who grow up with many languages, but they are exceptions or anomalies, the normal thing is (would be) that you and everybody around you just speak your language.

To sum up: both diachronic and synchronic linguistics are largely based on the idea of languages as discrete entities with clear borders. This is in line with the 'living kinds mental module,' that is, essentializing and naturalizing the borders of ethnic groups and speaker communities, and also with various political aspirations. In the last couple of centuries, both cultural, political, and theoretical or methodological factors have conspired to support this view. As shown by a long tradition of linguistic research, seeing language as a closed system with clear boundaries is a working hypothesis that does work. In the same way as the famous hypothesis of sound changes being 'laws of nature' without exceptions, it is a very good scientific hypothesis, proven in the practice of historical linguistics (cf., Ringe and Eska 2013, xxiii).

4 Linguistic challenges to the monolingual assumption

The idea of languages as autonomous systems, the 'philosophical-logical' view (as M. A. K. Halliday [1977] calls it, as opposed to the 'descriptive-ethnographic' view), has often been contested also within linguistics. Not all linguistic studies support the idea of languages as distinct systems in human cognition and human behavior. This can be seen already in the subdiscipline of linguistics that first made linguistics a science in our sense of the word, and that has largely been inspired by scientific approaches to the nature of humankind: historical linguistics. In this field, evolutionary approaches sometimes bring in quantitative and computational methods taken over from genetics, calculating, for instance, absolute chronologies for the splits in a family tree: the proto-forms of these two sister languages were separated from each other so and so many thousand years ago (for examples from a recent project in Uralic studies, see Honkola et al. 2013, Syrjänen et al. 2013). This means, in essence, relativizing the borders between languages and showing language change and divergence realistically, as a gradual process.

Evolutionary approaches have their own problems, especially as concerns the quantifiability of language change and reconstruction and if the amount of data available is very restricted (as it happens to be in Uralic studies). However, there is another aspect that is even more relevant in this context: instead of the language system as a whole, evolutionary approaches focus on the replication process that takes place in a population and refrain from essentializing language as such.

In the evolutionary view of Croft (2000), languages are like populations of grammars of individual speakers: individual languages, such as English, Estonian, or Mansi, are abstractions that do not exist in space and time; what exists is only the population of individual speakers' ideas of what English, Estonian, or Mansi is like. This view makes language borders fluid and difficult to define in the same way as boundaries between species. According to the usual definition, two organisms belong to the same species if interbreeding is possible and two people speak the same language if they can understand each other. However, in reality, a clear demarcation is not always possible in either of these cases. Interbreeding may be possible between some, neighboring subspecies but not between geographically more distant ones, and in the same way Eastern Finnish and White Sea Karelian are very close to each other and mutually fairly intelligible while Western Finns and Olonets Karelians will have much more difficulty understanding each other (cf., Koivisto's article in this volume).

Even more challenges to the essentialist view about languages as distinct systems come from what Halliday has called the descriptive-ethnographic view on linguistics, an umbrella concept for various approaches that stress culture, variation, functionalism, and interaction. The crucial point is acknowledging the reality of multilingualism, not just as a transitory phenomenon, an in-between stage preceding the loss of a language and the full acquisition of another, but as a stable characteristic of a multilingual community. In this connection, it is frequently pointed out that multilingual situations used to be different before Romantic Nationalism and nation-state projects introduced the idea of regimes ideally based on monolingual language management. According to Braunmüller (2007, 30), for instance, in the Late Middle Ages, many Europeans lived in pragmatic multilingual regimes. Latin was the supranational language of higher education and the church, while common people practised various forms of receptive multilingualism, ad hoc multilingual communication or semicommunication (for example: I speak Low German, you speak Swedish, we understand each other). R. M. W. Dixon (1997) speaks of equilibrium, the hypothetical situation in precolonial Australia, for instance, in which there were no major hierarchical or cultural differences between languages. Ansaldo (2010) calls these situations 'Ecology A' (his argumentation, however, is somewhat flawed, as his examples all come from language situations that involve colonization, social stratification, and hierarchies). In contrast to historical multilingualism situations created by historical migration and colonization processes connected with nationalism, it is often thought that pre-colonial indigenous peoples lived in a fairly stable multilingualism, in which ethnic groups did not strive to assimilate each other.

Motivated by this insight, historical linguistics is gradually understanding that reconstructions of prehistoric language geography must take multilingualism into account. Uralic studies offer interesting examples of changing views (see also Laakso 2014): After WWII and especially from the 1970s on, a 'continuity' view was widely accepted, reconstructing large and ethnically homogeneous primeval homes, for instance, extending the area of Proto-Finno-Ugric from the Volga region to the eastern Circum-Baltic area and more or less ignoring the possibility of other languages (beyond the well-known Indo-European and 'Altaic' neighbors) being present in the same area. Now, with modern substratum studies (see, e.g., Saarikivi 2006; Aikio 2004; Aikio 2012; Häkkinen 2014), it seems more and more realistic to assume that Northeastern Europe was originally home to many languages of unknown ancestry and affiliation and that this diversity only gradually gave way to the spread of Uralic and Indo-European language varieties. It seems probable that this language situation has resembled the situation in pre-agrarian societies in the diversity zones of Amazonia or New Guinea.

Monolingual bias is also being challenged in the study of language acquisition and language learning. There seems to be accumulating evidence that bilingual first language acquisition is not an anomaly or an aberration; it is perfectly normal; in some communities it is the rule rather than the exception. In the words of Cook (1991),

> Chomsky's idealisation rules out most of the human race and does not cope with the perfectly normal condition of the human mind.

This means that the idea of Universal Grammar as a built-in monolingual switchboard in which the switches (the parameters) are set in a certain way when the one and only Mother Tongue is acquired simply does not hold true; instead, many researchers now call for dynamic models of 'multicompetence' (Cook 1991; Herdina and Jessner 2002).

Multilingual individuals are no exceptions or anomalies, instead, there are many communities all over the world in which it is considered normal to know many languages. This is reality for many linguistic minorities; the Saami, for instance, have often been multilingual, knowing and using one or more state languages (for instance, Finnish and Norwegian) in addition to Saami. Knowing this, it is actually somewhat strange that multilingualism in itself is still not legally or institutionally endorsed anywhere. A nice example was provided recently by the research project ELDIA, which involves both traditional and migrant minorities in Europe. Although in all the eight countries included in the study, language laws or minority laws have been passed or amended in the last few years, the ELDIA law research group could state that what these laws protect is, in the best case, the right of a certain group of people to use a certain language in a certain area, not everybody's right to learn and speak two or more languages, for instance (see, e.g., Laakso et al. 2016, 173–182, 190–192). However, the issue of multilingualism as part of everybody's identity, not just limited to a few privileged elite multilinguals or a handful of minority members still awaiting assimilation, will be central in the years to come in connection with globalization and diversity.

A recent survey on the status of the English language in Finland (Leppänen et al. 2011) has shown that only some 6% of today's Finns, the 'have-nots,' have nothing to do with English, while 16%, the 'have-it-alls,' use English so much that it forms an essential part of their everyday life. However, this does not mean that these people are giving up Finnish completely; rather, the authors see this development as emerging new multilingualism, in which the knowledge of English essentially belongs to the linguistic identity of (at least younger and more educated) citizens of the Nordic countries. In other words, globalization forces us to realize that not just minorities but even speakers of nation-state languages in their home countries must come to grips with everyday multilingualism and the coexistence of more than one language in daily life. The idyllic monolingual worlds of Romantic Nationalism are not real and cannot be.

There is one final aspect in which the fundamental and essential character of multilingualism has been highlighted in linguistics in the last few decades: variation linguistics means a serious challenge to the idea of languages as homogeneous systems. This does not merely refer to speaking traditional dialects or sociolects that belong to certain areas or certain groups of people but to the fact that one and the same person knows and uses many varieties of what is traditionally called 'the same language,' and that it is not at all easy to regulate the use of 'a language' that, in reality, is a bundle of varieties. Globalization has brought the phenomenon of Lingua Franca English and World Englishes into focus, but also in the German-speaking area there is strong sensitivity towards the fact that German is spoken in very different varieties; de Cillia (2010) speaks of 'language-internal multilingualism' *(sprachinterne Mehrsprachigkeit)*, in the sense that even so-called monolingual speakers are normally expected to be able to use many varieties, dialects, registers, or styles of their mother tongue.

Pluricentricity is slowly gaining recognition even in linguistic cultures that have been characterized by national monism and prescriptivism. Since 1920, when the peace agreement of Trianon turned large groups of ethnic Hungarians into ethnic minorities in the new neighbor states of the new Hungary, the Hungarian language has developed in different directions. Recently, this insight has given rise to new initiatives that highlight the pluricentricity of the Hungarian language. Above all, the *határtalanítás* (de-bordering, de-Trianonizing) project collects vocabulary from the Hungarian-speaking minority areas and tries to include it into dictionaries of Standard Hungarian.[5]

To sum up: In linguistics, there have been both approaches that analyze and focus on distinct, discrete units, autonomous systems, that present the borders between these systems as something natural, and diametrally opposite approaches that question and contest the borders between languages and language varieties, that highlight their fluidity and fuzziness or regard them as socially constructed rather than natural. Both approaches

---

5 More information (in Hungarian) at http://ht.nytud.hu/. See also Maráz 2004.

are theoretically and empirically justified to some extent, but both are also connected with empirical problems and open questions. As mentioned above, this is also an issue of interdisciplinarity. Is it better to concentrate on systems of language as closed systems, to strive for scientific objectivity and methodological purism, which detach language from the emotions, intentions, bodies, culture, society, and social interactions of its speakers? Or is it better to connect language with society and behavior and develop a mix of methods from different disciplines to research what is often called cultural encounters or intercultural contacts?

5 Attractive borders: Language, culture, and the challenge of interdisciplinary approaches

The last few decades have witnessed what could be called a cultural turn in the humanities (Best 2007) – at least this is what it looks like from a linguist's point of view. Instead of static, autonomous, hierarchically organized structures that are often embedded in patriarchal power constellations (such as the nation-state projects and the idea of *Nationalwissenschaften,* the academic disciplines that are perceived as central to the nation-state, such as the national philologies, history, or ethnography of the nation), linguistic and cultural studies have, in the last few decades, often positioned their theories in another, dynamic framework. This has entailed highlighting mutual interactions rather than unilateral power relations, diversity rather than unity, constructs rather than nature, and focusing on the individual's choices (free will) and agency rather than showing the individual as a carrier of folklore, religion, or language understood as suprahuman, autonomous systems. There seems to be a connection between this turn and the political processes in the Western world in the late 20th century, such as the rise of the movements for greater equality, women's and minorities' rights, the criticism of objectivity and positivism – and the political criticism of the values of Western nation-state projects.

In the course of this cultural turn, the interest in language has partly shifted from the structure of language-as-a-system to the culture and actions that carry and surround language: to linguistic ethnography, discourse, and conversation analysis and other ways of investigating spoken language in action, to cognitive linguistics or to sociolinguistics and language sociology. Instead of *languageness* (cf., Garner 2004), the idea of language as a system – whether a genetically conditioned, innate language faculty or a socially constructed accumulation of behavioral patterns, based on institutional power structures – there is a lot of talk about *languaging*: 'language' as a verb. The deconstruction of languageness culminates in some approaches that contest the idea of language as a system altogether: Makoni and Pennycook (2007) claim that languages, in essence, do not exist, they are socially constructed epistemic violence against the real, existing diversity. Once again, diversity and multilingualism are key issues.

Paradoxically, while linguistics is partly moving away from language to the cultural and social mechanisms of language use (or, rather, claiming that these cannot be detached from language in itself), in cultural studies there seems to be a growing interest in language. These two interests meet in the research of multilingualism and intercultural contacts. For cultural studies, language is not only the medium of culture and communication but also the symbol and emblem of ethnic identities. Language is the medium by which cultural communities or narrative communities *(Erzählgemeinschaft;* Müller-Funk 2008, 14) are constructed, language is the object of cultural activities (literature, media) and policies (language-related identity policy) – and, above all, language is the supreme border marker. The last few decades have witnessed an upsurge of interest in almost anything inter-, supra-, and transcultural in the area of cultural studies, from 'intercultural communication' to 'transcultural spaces,' 'hybridization,' *mestizaje* or even 'transdifference' (Breinig and Lösch 2002). Borders are attractive in that they can be approached from many directions and used for both splitting and lumping; as conceptual tools, they are indispensable.

And this is where the risks of interdisciplinarity arise. The first is the challenge of terminology transfer (cf., Tileagă and Byford 2014). In order to describe how people perceive and conceptualize diverse aspects of reality and how these are reflected in culture, cultural studies must adopt concepts and terms from other disciplines, and, in the worst case, these will be redefined ad absurdum, become meaningless from the point of view of their source discipline. In the relationship between cultural studies and linguistics, this risk is particularly relevant, as cultural studies approach their object through and with the help of language. Objects of study are defined, 'cultural spaces' are carved out with linguistic criteria, sometimes without looking closely at what these criteria contain. For example, there is a growing interest in Austria in the multilingual and multicultural areas of the old Habsburg Monarchy, such as 'Galizien,' areas in today's Poland and Ukraine with their ethnolinguistic mix of Eastern and Western Slavic, German, Jewish, and other populations; in this connection, multilingualism is often mentioned but seldom analyzed in linguistic detail.

> Der „Galizische Text" wurde im Laufe von etwas mehr als zwei Jahrhunderten narrativ und dementsprechend kulturell produziert; dabei zählt zu seinen „grundlegenden" Perioden die fast anderthalbhundert Jahre dauernde Zugehörigkeit Galiziens zur Habsburger Monarchie. Eines der wichtigsten Merkmale des „Galizischen Textes" war immer seine Polyphonie, da der Kulturraum Galizien von Anfang an vielsprachig war. (Cybenko 2014).

Even 'language' itself can be understood in a variety of ways. I could refer to Lacan and his ideas of 'language' as a symbol of phallogocentric power structures, but I will merely quote Deleuze and Guattari (2004, 109), who have written about *littérature minoire* (such as that written by Kafka as a representative of German-language literature in Prague):

> To be a foreigner, but in one's own tongue, not only when speaking a language other than one's own. To be bilingual, multilingual, but in one and the same language, without even a dialect or patois.

From the point of view of an empirical linguist, this simply does not make sense. If you can be bilingual or multilingual within one language, even excluding variation (dialect or patois), then *language* is used to denote something so completely different from what linguists understand by language that an interdisciplinary dialogue is no longer possible. Of course, cultural studies can define language or other concepts of linguistics in their own way, but, in doing so, they will make real interdisciplinarity impossible.

6 Conclusion

The issue of border(s) and language was approached from three viewpoints in this article: the border between US and THEM as a fundamental conceptual tool with which human beings construct their society and culture (including language, 'ours' and 'theirs,' as a central emblem of nations as imagined communities), the border between nature and culture as a central issue in the history and practice of linguistics, and the border between linguistics and cultural studies as an issue of research practices, terminology, and theory.

The problems in interdisciplinary approaches involving linguistics and cultural studies, which often actualize cultural, ethnic, and linguistic borders, are obviously often connected with how borders between disciplines and conceptual frameworks are drawn. From the point of view of linguistics, problems arise around the border between nature and culture. On the one hand, there is the temptation to naturalize what is really (also) connected with culture, as in the overuse of the universal grammar model, which explains all aspects of language as genetically conditioned and innate even where it would be more realistic to describe language as a construction of social conventions. This can be understood or marketed as interdisciplinarity; crossing the border to language philosophy, computing, or science. On the other hand, there is the risk of interpreting nature as culture and drawing unjustified conclusions based on speculative analyses of issues that are really of an empirical character – the most blatant example of this is the Sokal affair (the parodic article about gravitation as a social construction which a renowned journal published without recognizing the parody; Sokal 1998), but there are many less spectacular examples of literature scholars jumping to conclusions about language.

Perhaps we could say that nature and culture constrain each other: culture dictates which possible scenarios of language change are realized in language contact, but language also influences culture. Internal explanations in either direction are inherently flawed; knowledge of substance on both sides of the border is needed. Borders are attractive, 'crossing borders' seems to carry an inherent positive value in our academic contexts (almost as positive as 'innovation' or 'pathbreaking'), and everything with the prefix 'inter-' or 'trans-' sounds sexy and exciting. The trick is knowing where the border runs in border crossing as well.

References

Aikio, Ante. 2004. "An Essay on Substrate Studies and the Origin of Saami." In *Etymologie, Entlehnungen und Entwicklungen: Festschrift für Jorma Koivulehto zum 70. Geburtstag* [Etymology, borrowings, and developments: a Festschrift for Jorma Koivulehto on his 70th birthday], edited by Irma Hyvärinen, Petri Kallio, and Jarmo Korhonen, 5–34. Mémoires de la Société Néophilologique de Helsinki 63. Helsinki: Société Néophilologique de Helsinki.

Aikio, Ante (= Luobbal Sámmol Sámmol Ánte). 2012. "An Essay on Saami Ethnolinguistic Prehistory." In *A Linguistic Map of Prehistoric Northern Europe*, edited by Riho Grünthal and Petri Kallio, 63–118. Mémoires de la Société Finno-Ougrienne 266. Helsinki: Finno-Ugrian Society.

Ansaldo, Umberto. 2010. "Identity Alignment and Language Creation in Multilingual Communities." *Language Sciences* 32:615–623.

Bachinger, Eva, and Martin Schenk. 2012. *Die Integrationslüge: Antworten in einer hysterisch geführten Auseinandersetzung* [The integration lie. Answers in a hysterically conducted conflict]. Wien: Deuticke.

Bencze, Lóránt. 2013. "Omnes leones leonizare." In *II. Czuczor-Fogarasi-konferencia: "Ha szabad a magyart a magyarból magyarázni"* [2nd Czuczor-Fogarasi Conference: "If it is allowed to explain Hungarian on the basis of Hungarian"], edited by Katalin Horváth, 23–46. A Magyar Művészeti Akadémia Konferenciafüzetei 2. Budapest: Magyar Művészeti Akadémia.

Best, Steven. 2007. "Culture Turn." In *Blackwell Encyclopedia of Sociology*, edited by George Ritzer. [S.l.:] Blackwell. Accessed December 1, 2014. http://www.sociologyencyclopedia.com/public/book.html?id=g9781405124331_yr2013_9781405124331.

Braunmüller, Kurt. 2008. "Receptive Multilingualism in Northern Europe in the Middle Ages: A Description of a Scenario." In *Receptive Multilingualism: Linguistic Analyses, Language Policies, and Didactic Concepts*, edited by Jan D. ten Thije and Ludger Zeevaert, 25–48. Hamburg Studies on Multilingualism 6. Amsterdam: John Benjamins.

Breinig, Helmbrecht, and Klaus Lösch. 2002. "Introduction: Difference and Transdifference." In *Multiculturalism in Contemporary Societies: Perspectives on Difference and Transdifference*, edited by Helmbrecht Breinig, Jürgen Gebhardt, and Klaus Lösch, 11–36. Erlanger Forschungen: Reihe A, Geisteswissenschaften, Bd. 101. Erlangen: Universitätsbund.

Cook, Vivian. 1991. "The Poverty-of-the-Stimulus Argument and Multi-Competence." *Second Language Research* 7:03–117.

Cook, V. J., and Mark Newson. 2007. *Chomsky's Universal Grammar: An Introduction*. Third edition. Malden: Blackwell.

Croft, William. 2000. *Explaining Language Change. An Evolutionary Approach*. London: Pearson Education.

Cybenko, Larissa. 2014. *"Galizischer Text." Mehrsprachigkeit in der vielsprachigen gemeinsamen Erzählung eines Raumes*. [Galizian Text. Multilingualism in the multilingual common narrative of a space.] Habilitationsschrift zur Erlangung der *venia docendi* für das Fach "Vergleichende Literaturwissenschaft" an der Philologisch-Kulturwissenschaftlichen Fakultät der Universität Wien.

de Cillia, Rudolf. 2010. "Mehrsprachigkeit statt Zweisprachigkeit – Argumente und Konzepte für eine Neuorientierung der Sprachenpolitik an den Schulen" [Multilingualism instead of bilingualism: Arguments and concepts for a new orientation of language policies in schools]. In *Discourse – Politics – Identity. Diskurs – Politik – Identität. Festschrift für Ruth Wodak*, edited by Rudolf de Cillia,

Mathias Gruber, Michał Krzyżanowski, and Florian Menz, 245–255. Tübingen, Stauffenburg.

Deleuze, Gilles, and Félix Guattari. 2004. *A Thousand Plateaus. Capitalism and Schizophrenia.* Translated by Brian Massumi. London: Continuum.

Development Plan of the Estonian Language 2011–2017. Translated by Enn Veldi. Tallinn: Estonian Language Foundation, 2011. Accessed August 28, 2015. http://ekn.hm.ee/node/53.

Dixon, R. M. W. 1997. *The Rise and Fall of Languages.* Cambridge: Cambridge University Press.

Fox, Jennifer. 1993. "The Creator Gods: Romantic Nationalism and the En-genderment of Women in Folklore." In *Feminist Theory and the Study of Folklore,* edited by Susan Tower Hollis, Linda Pershing, and M. Jane Young, 29–40. Urbana: University of Illinois Press.

Garner, Mark. 2004. *Language: An Ecological View.* Bern: Peter Lang.

Gil-White, Francisco J. 2001. "Are Ethnic Groups Biological 'Species' to the Human Brain? Essentialism in Our Cognition of Some Social Categories." *Current Anthropology* 42:4:515–554.

Hagerman, Maja. 2006. *Det rena landet: om konsten att uppfinna sina förfäder* [The pure country: On the art of inventing one's ancestors]. Stockholm: Prisma.

Häkkinen, Jaakko. 2014. Kielet Suomessa kautta aikain [The languages in Finland throughout times] Accessed December 1, 2014, http://www.elisanet.fi/alkupera/Kielet_Suomessa_kautta_aikain.pdf.

Halliday, M. A. K. 1977. "Ideas About Language." In *Ideas and Perspectives in Linguistics,* edited by M. A. K. Halliday, 32–49. Occasional Papers 1. Applied Linguistics Association of Australia.

Herdina, Thomas, and Ulrike Jessner. 2002. *A Dynamic Model of Multilingualism: Perspectives of Change in Psycholinguistics.* Clevedon: Multilingual Matters.

Honkola, Terhi, Outi Vesakoski, Kalle Korhonen, Jyri Lehtinen, Kaj Syrjänen, and Niklas Wahlberg. 2013. "Cultural and Climatic Changes Shape the Evolutionary History of the Uralic Languages." *Journal of Evolutionary Biology* 26:1244–1253. http://onlinelibrary.wiley.com/doi/10.1111/jeb.12107/pdf.

Isaksson, Pekka. 2001. *Kumma kuvajainen. Rasismi rotututkimuksessa, rotuteorioiden saamelaiset ja suomalainen fyysinen antropologia.* [A strange mirror image. Racism in racial studies, the Saami in race theories, and the Finnish physical anthropology.] Inari: Kustannus Puntsi.

Kettunen, Lauri, and Martti Vaula. 1938. *Suomen kielioppi sekä tyyli- ja runo-opin alkeet oppikouluille ja seminaareille* [Finnish grammar and the basics of stylistics and poetics, for grammar schools and teacher seminars]. Porvoo: WSOY.

Korhonen, Mikko. 1986. *Finno-Ugrian Language Studies in Finland 1828–1918.* Helsinki: Societas Scientiarum Fennica.

Korhonen, Mikko, Seppo Suhonen, and Pertti Virtaranta. 1983. *Sata vuotta Suomen sukua tutkimassa: satavuotias Suomalais-Ugrilainen Seura* [A hundred years of research into the kinship of the Finns: the centenary of the Finno-Ugrian Society]. Espoo: Weilin+Göös.

Laakso, Johanna. 2005. *Our Otherness: Finno-Ugrian Approaches to Women's Studies, or vice versa.* Wien: LIT Verlag.

Laakso, Johanna. 2011. "Being Finno-Ugrian, Being in the Minority. Reflections on Linguistic and Other Criteria." In *Ethnic and Linguistic Context of Identity: Finno-Ugric Minorities,* edited by Riho Grünthal and Magdolna Kovács, 13–36. Uralica Helsingiensia 5. Helsinki: Finno-Ugrian Society.

Laakso, Johanna. 2014. "The Prehistoric Multilingual Speaker: What Can We Know About the Multilingualism of Proto-Uralic Speakers?" *Finnisch-Ugrische Mitteilungen* 38:98–114.

Laakso, Johanna, Anneli Sarhimaa, Reetta Toivanen, and Sia Spiliopoulou Åkermark. 2016. *Towards Openly Multilingual Policies and Practices: Assessing Minority Language Maintenance Across Europe.* Bristol: Multilingual Matters.

Lempiäinen, Kirsti. 2002. "Kansallisuuden tekeminen ja toisto" [Creating and reproducing nationality]. In *Suomineitonen hei! Kansallisuuden sukupuoli* [Hi there, Finnish Maid! The gender of nationality], edited by Tuula Gordon, Katri Komulainen, and Kirsti Lempiäinen, 19–36. Tampere: Vastapaino.

Leppänen, Sirpa, Anne Pitkänen-Huhta, Tarja Nikula, Samu Kytölä, Timo Törmäkangas, Kari Nissinen, Leila Käänta, Tiina Räisänen, Mikko Laitinen, Päivi Pahta, Heidi Koskela, Salla Lähdesmäki, and Henna Jousmäki. 2011. *National Survey on the English Language in Finland: Uses, Meanings and Attitudes* (VARIENG 5). Accessed December 12, 2016. http://www.helsinki.fi/varieng/series/volumes/05/index.html.

Liberman, Mark. 2003. "This Is Not Middle-Earth." Accessed December 1, 2014. http://itre.cis.upenn.edu/~myl/languagelog/archives/000214.html.

Makoni, Sinfree, and Alastair Pennycook. 2007. "Disinventing and Reconstituting Languages." In *Disinventing and Reconstituting Languages*, edited by Sinfree Makoni and Alastair Pennycook, 1–41. Bilingual Education and Bilingualism 62. Clevedon: Multilingual Matters.

Maráz, Gabriella. 2004. "Sprachrettung oder Sprachverrat: Zur Diskussion über die Norm des Ungarischen" [Language rescue or language treason: On the discussion about the norms of the Hungarian language]. *Trans: Internet-Zeitschrift für Kulturwissenschaften.* Accessed May 27, 2013. http://www.inst.at/trans/15Nr/06_1/maraz15.htm.

Müller-Funk, Wolfgang. 2008. *Die Kultur und ihre Narrative. Eine Einführung.* [Culture and its narrative. An introduction.] Wien: Springer.

Pinker, Steven. 1994. *The Language Instinct.* New York: William Morrow.

Ringe, Don, and Joseph F. Eska. 2013. *Historical Linguistics: Toward a Twenty-First Century Reintegration.* Cambridge: Cambridge University Press.

Saarikivi, Janne. 2006. "Substrata Uralica". PhD diss., University of Helsinki. Accessed December 12, 2016. http://ethesis.helsinki.fi/julkaisut/hum/suoma/vk/saarikivi/.

Salminen, Timo. 2008. *Aatteen tiede. Suomalais-Ugrilainen Seura 1883–2008.* [Science with a sublime purpose. The Finno-Ugrian Society 1883–2008.] Helsinki: Finnish Literature Society.

Sokal, Alan. 1998. "What the *Social Text* affair does and does not prove." *Critical Quarterly* 40:2:3–18.

Syrjänen, Kaj, Terhi Honkola, Kalle Korhonen, Jyri Lehtinen, Outi Vesakoski, and Niklas Wahlberg. 2013. "Shedding More Light on Language Classification Using Basic Vocabularies and Phylogenetic Methods. A case study of Uralic." *Diachronica* 30:3:323–392.

Thomas, George. 1991. *Linguistic Purism.* London: Longman.

Tileagă, Cristian, and Jovan Byford. 2014. "Introduction: psychology and history – themes, debates, overlaps and borrowings." In *Psychology and History: Interdisciplinary Explorations,* ed. by Cristian Tileagă and Jovan Byford, 1–11. Cambridge: Cambridge University Press.

Twain, Mark. 1884. *Adventures of Huckleberry Finn.* Electronic edition by Victor Fischer and Lin Salamo. Berkeley/Los Angeles/London: University of California Press 2003, 2009. http://www.marktwainproject.org/xtf/view?docId=works/MTDP10000.xml;style=work;brand=mtp.

Vesa Koivisto
http://orcid.org/0000-0003-1256-6477

Border Karelian Dialects – a Diffuse Variety of Karelian

Abstract

The article gives an overview of Border Karelian dialects: a variety of the Karelian language that was spoken in Eastern Finland before World War II. Border Karelia (Fi. *Raja-Karjala*) belonged to Sweden after 1621. The area where the Border Karelian dialects were spoken was located along the border of two states, Sweden (later Finland) and Novgorod (later Russia), and Border Karelia was an area of diverse language contacts. The division of religion (Orthodox and Lutheran) simultaneously marked a division of language (Karelian and Finnish) in Border Karelia.

Russian has been a contact language for Karelian for centuries. Since the 17th century, there have been contacts between the Karelian and Finnish languages in Border Karelia as many Karelians moved to Russia, and a Finnish-speaking population partly replaced them. In addition to these languages, there were two dialects of Karelian that met in Border Karelia and affected each other: South and Olonets Karelian. In practice, they formed a dialect continuum. Border Karelian dialects have a historical connection and close genetic ties to the so-called enclave dialects of Tver Karelian, which developed due to the migration of Karelians from Border and North Karelia.

1 Introduction

This article introduces Border Karelian dialects, a variety of Karelian that is no longer spoken in its original territory, Border Karelia, which was the easternmost part of Finland before World War II. Border Karelian dialects formed the part of the Karelian language that was spoken in Finland, and they have been a rather unknown vernacular both in the field of linguistic studies and in Finland in general. After WWII, Border Karelians were evacuated and the position of their language in Finland deteriorated. This article will bind together the linguistic history and the known demographic history of Border Karelia.

The structure of this article is as follows: Section 2 introduces the Karelian language and Section 3 the dialectal area, Border Karelia. Section 4 presents the language contacts that have taken place in Border Karelia. Section 5 illuminates the situation of Border Karelian dialects and their speakers in the years after WWII. Section 6 presents characteristics of Border Karelian dialects. Section 7 lists Border Karelian materials for linguistic study, and Section 8 gives an overview of previous research on Border Karelian dialects. In Section 8 and the concluding Section 9, the position of Border Karelian dialects in Finnic linguistics is also analyzed.

2 On the Karelian language

Karelian is a Finnic[1] language that is currently spoken mainly in Russia. Karelian belongs to the eastern branch of the Finnic languages and is very closely related to Finnish, especially to its eastern dialects. There are estimated to be 20,000–30,000 speakers of Karelian in Russia today. This estimate is fairly unprecise, though, and it is somewhat lower than the estimates presented in recent decades.

Karelian is an indigenous language not only in Russia but also in Finland, where it was spoken in the easternmost parts of the country, in Border Karelia, until WWII. At that time, there were approximately 40,000 speakers of Karelian in Finland. After WWII, its speakers were scattered in various parts of Finland, and, presently, the number of speakers of Karelian in Finland has been estimated to be from less than 2,000 up to more than 10,000 (Jeskanen 2005, 278; Hämynen 2012, 266; 2013, 205; Munne 2013, 389–390; Laakso et al. 2013, 46–47). As can be seen, the estimate is quite inaccurate.

Karelian is divided into two (or three) main dialects, which are sometimes referred to as separate languages: Karelian Proper, consisting of North (White Sea) and South Karelian dialects, and Olonets Karelian (Olonec Karelian, Olonetsian, Livvian) (see Map 1). All these dialects are spoken in the Republic of Karelia in Russia. South Karelian is also spoken in the Tver district that is situated in Central Russia, in territories between St. Petersburg and Moscow. The dialects spoken in former Finnish Border Karelia were South and Olonets Karelian.

Karelian is a minority language, and it is nowadays also classified as an endangered one. It is currently undergoing a rapid decrease in the number of native speakers. At present, all speakers of Karelian are bilingual both in Russia and Finland (the Russian and Finnish languages being strongly pervasive). Although Karelian has no official status in Russia, it is recognized as "a national language" (along with Veps and Finnish) in the Republic of Karelia. There, Karelian is an everyday language for some 4.5–5% of the population (see Karjalainen et al. 2013, 22 Table 2), but there are also areas in the Republic where the proportion of Karelian speakers is considerably higher, e.g., in the areas surrounding the town of Olonets. In Finland,

---

1 The Finnic (or Baltic-Finnic) languages are Finnish, Karelian, Ludian, Veps, Ingrian, Votic, Estonian, and Livonian.

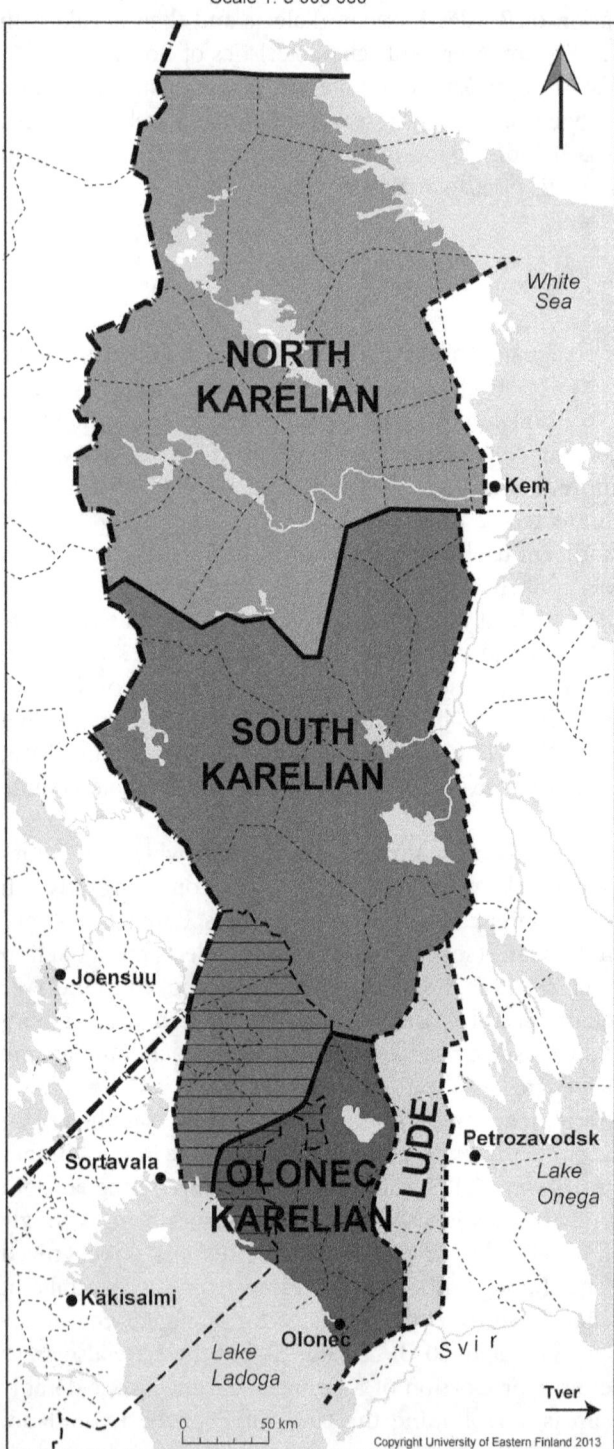

Map 1. The main dialects of Karelian and the area of Border Karelia.

Karelian has had the status of an autochthonous non-territorial minority language since 2009.

The development of Karelian can generally be described as a process of deterioration under the pressure of a dominant language: Russian in Russia, and Finnish in Finland. On UNESCO's scale for assessing language vitality and endangerment, Karelian is classified as "definitely endangered" (Karjalainen et al. 2013, 9). In this situation there are hardly any children who speak Karelian any longer.

3 Border Karelia and Border Karelian dialects

The so-called Border Karelian dialects of the Karelian language were spoken in former Finnish Karelia north of Lake Ladoga. This area, Border Karelia, was ceded to the Soviet Union after WWII in 1944 (along with the Karelian Isthmus south of Lake Ladoga), and its entire population was evacuated to the remaining territories of Finland, mostly to the northern parts of the counties of Savo and North Karelia in Eastern Finland. Due to the displacement of population, Border Karelian dialects became a vernacular that no longer exists in its original area. In present-day Finland, these dialects are still spoken to some extent by elderly people who were born and lived in Border Karelia before WWII or who acquired the language after the war in their Karelian-speaking families.

Border Karelian dialects represent two main dialects of Karelian: the majority of these are the southern dialects of Karelian Proper, i.e., South Karelian. These dialects were spoken in Border Karelia in the municipalities of Suistamo, Korpiselkä, and Suojärvi; in the eastern parts of Ilomantsi; and in some villages of Impilahti as well. Forming a smaller dialect area in Border Karelia, Olonets Karelian dialects were spoken in the municipality of Salmi and parts of Impilahti.[2] (Turunen 1982, 66.)

The border line between Karelian Proper and Olonets Karelian crossed Border Karelia, but in practice the border was realized as a continuum along which Border Karelian dialects show characteristics of mixed or transitional dialects (e.g., Nirvi 1961, 129). The dialect continuum in Suojärvi has been documented by Genetz (1870, 206; see also Turunen 1982, 72; Jeskanen 2011, 353–354). All in all, the dialects in Border Karelia were not uniform within a single municipality (see, e.g., Nirvi 1932 on Suistamo).

The population density was quite low in most of Border Karelia. Only the southern parts of Salmi and the western parts of Suistamo had a somewhat denser population (Forsström 1894, 41) along with the southern parts of Impilahti, whereas the municipalities of Ilomantsi, Korpiselkä, and large parts of Suojärvi and Suistamo were sparsely populated. Settlement was concentrated to villages separated by wide forest and swamp areas. The

---

2   In addition to Salmi and Impilahti, there were Olonets Karelian speakers in the southeastern parts of Suistamo (Nirvi 1932, 11–16) and Suojärvi (Hämynen 2012, 248) as well.

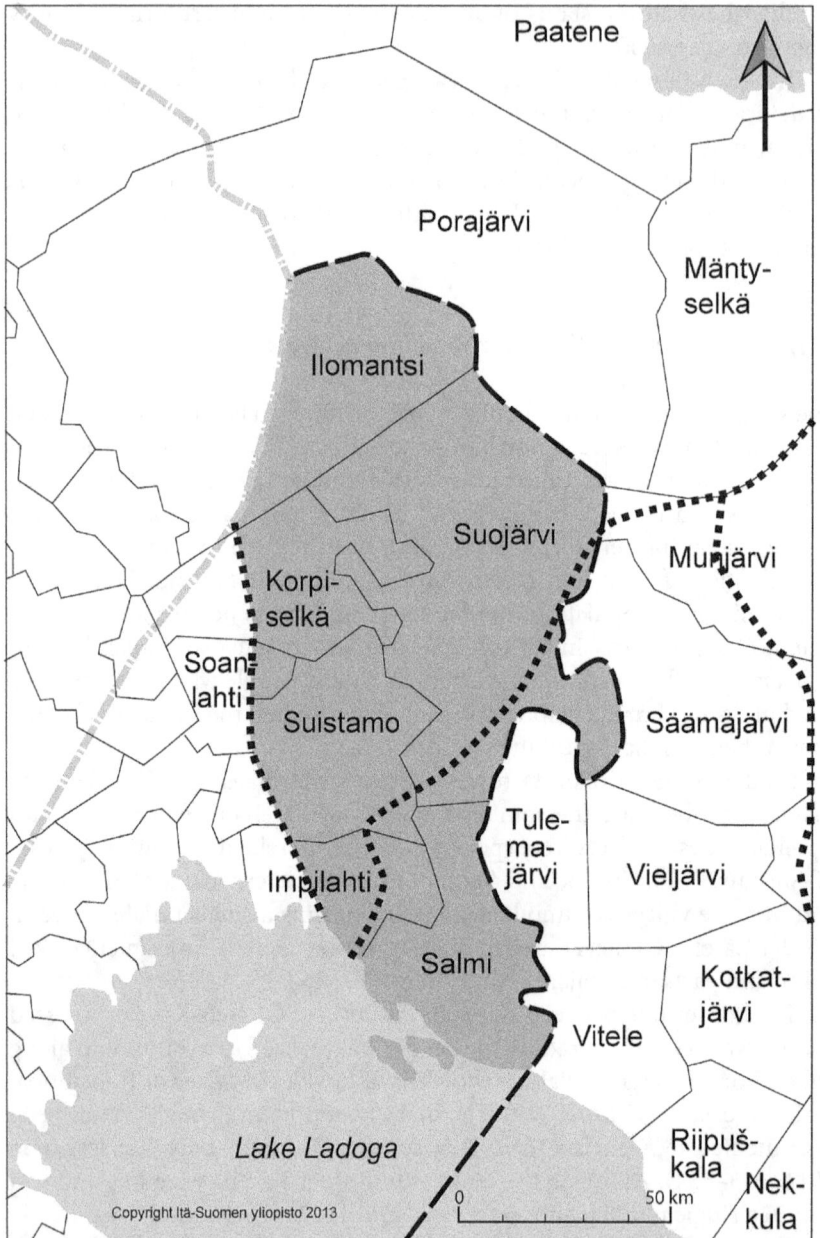

Map 2. Border Karelia and its municipalities.

uneven spread of inhabitancy and the small size of local speech communities undoubtedly had an effect on the development of local dialects.

One of the central characteristics of Border Karelian dialects is the influence of Finnish (for more on the characteristics of these dialects see Section 6). Beginning in the 17th century, both Karelians (Orthodox) and Finns (Lutheran) lived in Border Karelia (Kuujo 1963; Björn 2013, 409–414), and they remained in close contact for more than three centuries. Eventually

Karelian and the eastern dialects of Finnish overlapped with the western part of Border Karelian dialects.[3] (For contacts, see Section 4.)

In Border Karelia, there was a clear division between the Orthodox and Lutheran religions in respect to the language people spoke as their native tongue: the Orthodox (or the great majority of the people) spoke Karelian, and the Lutherans spoke Finnish. The Karelian language remained the vernacular of the Orthodox population over the centuries, and Karelians had, along with religion, a linguistic and cultural identity that differed from the speakers of Finnish. In the constant contact situation with Finns, the Orthodox religion has been a uniting factor and the maintaining force for the linguistic identity of the Karelian-speakers in Border Karelia.

The Border Karelian contact languages, Karelian and Finnish, are genetically very close to each other. They are mutually intelligible to a certain extent and share a long common history as they have evolved from a joint ancestor language, Proto-Karelian. At the beginning of the first millenium (A.D.), there was a Proto-Karelian population living in the northern and northwestern coastal areas of Lake Ladoga. During the following centuries, this population spread gradually westwards and northwards, eventually also covering the areas of North Karelia of present-day Finland. Simultaneously the eastern branch of the language, the future Karelian, and the future Finnish gradually grew apart. More and more differences emerged, and the separation of Eastern Finnish dialects from Karelian was mostly complete by the 14th century. On the state level, the boundary between Sweden and Novgorod defined in the Peace Treaty of Nöteborg (Fi. *Pähkinäsaari*) in 1323 consolidated the division of these two languages.

Until the 17th century, the Karelian dialects spoken in Border Karelia shared their history with the rest of Karelian. Border Karelia was originally part of Novgorod (later Russia), but, after wars between Sweden and Novgorod, it was ceded to Sweden in 1621 along with the entire county of Käkisalmi (which included the area of Finnish North Karelia and the whole of Ingria). Consequently, in Border Karelia there were administrative measures taken by the new Swedish regime that were directed towards the original non-Lutheran, Karelian-speaking population. These measures included heavy taxes and religious oppression. As a reaction to these, a considerable part of the Orthodox inhabitants of Border Karelia moved to Russia (see, e.g., Saloheimo 1973; 2010; H. Leskinen 1998, 358–359, 362). The migration was massive (estimated from 25,000 up to 50,000 persons; Virtaranta 1970, 461, 463; Björn 2013, 409), and even entire villages in Border and North Karelia were left empty (especially in the western parts of the area). The result of this was a reduction in population in Border Karelia to a minimum in the latter half of 17th century. Respectively, the proportion of speakers of Finnish increased from the 17th century onwards as the diminishing Karelian population was immediately replaced with an invasion of Finnish-speaking Lutherans. The Savo dialects expanded rapidly at that time. There was a constant flow of Finns from the west to Border Karelia (Kuujo 1963,

---

3   The subdialects of Finnish spoken west of Border Karelia were the Savo dialects and the southeastern dialects.

59–68), and eventually only less than 10% of the inhabitants of the county of Käkisalmi were Orthodox (Leskinen 1998, 359). The ongoing presence of the Finnish language has had a considerable effect on Border Karelian dialects ever since.

At the beginning of the 17th century, the area where Karelian was spoken extended further west- and southwards than in later times. The Karelian language covered the areas of the northwestern shores of Lake Ladoga that belonged to Finland up to WWII and parts of present-day Finland in North Karelia. This area was under Novgorod's rule up to 1621, and its population consisted mostly of Orthodox speakers of Karelian. The Karelian language has left a substratum layer in the North Karelian dialects of Finnish, which developed through the spread of Savo Finns over the originally Karelian-speaking area from the 17th century onwards.

A consequence of the migration from Border and North Karelia eastwards was new Karelian-speaking territories further off in Central Russia (e.g., in Tver).[4] In these new domiciles of the Karelians, their language gradually developed into a dialectal variety of its own, the so-called enclave dialects of Karelian (also called "Daughter Karelian"), which form part of the South Karelian dialects. By the end of the 17th century, the Tver Karelian population had grown to approximately 20,000–30,000, and it was in the 1930s that the Karelian-speaking population of Tver was at its largest, about 155,000 speakers. The Karelian enclave dialects developed from the 17th century onwards on the basis of the South Karelian dialect spoken in Border Karelia (about which there are no documents; Ruoppila 1956, 12). At that time, the South Karelian of Border Karelia was not yet separated from the rest of South Karelian, and, thus, it was not very similar to the Border Karelian dialects of the 20th century. Thereafter linguistic innovations have emerged both in the new enclave dialects and in the remaining Border Karelian dialects (see Section 6). Thus the political changes of the 17th century meant a start for the development of two new Karelian dialectal varieties: Border and "Daughter" Karelian.

As part of Sweden (and later Finland), Border Karelia was a lateral area in the vicinity of the Novgorod border. Due to its geographical position, Border Karelia formed simultaneously a meeting place and a collision zone for two languages (Karelian and Finnish), two religions (Orthodox and Lutheran), and two cultures (Slavic and Western European). Religion was the most central of these divisive factors in people's lives.

Language does not seem to have been a crucial factor in people's ethnic orientation in Border Karelia. The basis of ethnicity was formed by religion as well as material and mental culture. Language, for its part, created no sense of solidarity and was actually a rather irrelevant factor for people in those times; in real life, it was just important that everyone understood each other. It was only after the national awakening in the 19th century that language attained more importance in the formation of selfhood and whole nations. (Katajala 2005, 49, 51, 54, 241, 243; Björn 2013, 411–412.)

---

4 In addition to Tver, there were two other enclave dialects: the dialects of the Tihvin and Valdai areas.

4 Language contacts in Border Karelia

From the 17th century onwards, the Karelian dialects in Border Karelia were in close contact with the eastern dialects of Finnish. The contacts resulted in mixed idiolects, the basis of which was Karelian but which acquired numerous linguistic features from Finnish. This led to the finnicization of Karelian in Border Karelia.

4.1 General remarks

For a long time, the study of the Finnic languages was mainly diachronic. Due to extensive studies in the context of Neogrammarians in the 19th and 20th century, the common origin of the Karelian language and the Eastern Finnish dialects is a well-known fact and has been described quite adequately. These languages are descendants of Proto-Karelian, and they have many phonological, morphological, and lexical similarities in which they differ from the western dialects of Finnish (Nirvi 1961, 112–121; Itkonen 1983, 209–212; H. Leskinen 1998, 354–355). The division of Proto-Karelian has been explained with the spread and movements of settlement, language, and dialect contacts, and their mixing.

Language contacts cause, drive, and enhance language change. Contacts between languages and dialects have been and are a constant formative force and an impulse for change in the history and development of languages. This applies to the Finnic languages as well: both Karelian and Finnish and their predecessor languages have had plenty of contacts with both cognate and non-cognate languages over the centuries and even millenia of their existence. These contacts have undoubtedly, in some respects, made the directions and paths of change different from an alternative imaginative situation in which these contacts did not exist. The study of the contacts of Karelian (and other Finnic languages) has become more diversified since the 1990s (Palander et al. 2013, 362–363). A new focus of interest in contact linguistics is the sociolinguistic conditions of the contact situation and the linguistic processes that contacts have led to; Anneli Sarhimaa has described the extralinguistic situation in the overall history of Karelia in the following way: "The history of Karelia is marked by repeated waves of migration that have led to a continuous loss of population, especially on the margins of the inhabited region" (Sarhimaa 1999, 43).

In order to produce credible explanations, adequate information on the historical, social, and mental circumstances in which a cross-linguistic contact has taken place is necessary (Riionheimo 2013, 222). In the context of Border Karelian dialects, the difficulties in this kind of diachronic research lie, e.g., in distinguishing and timing historical facts, phases, and temporal layers of contact-induced changes (such as the influence of Eastern Finnish dialects over Border Karelian dialects during different periods of time), or linguistic features received through them. As Sarhimaa (1999, 18) has put it: understanding the situation of Karelian "requires insight into the complex socio-historical setting within which the contacts have been occurring for more than a thousand years." All in all, it may be difficult to "get in" to the historical contact situation (see Riionheimo 2013, 243). In the case of Border

Karelia, there is enough information to sketch the linguistic history of the area, but it is not easy to provide explanations with a more detailed picture.

Contacts may occur not only between two (or more) languages, but also between dialects of one and the same language. A contact between two separate but genetically close languages (as Karelian and Finnish) or dialects (as South and Olonets Karelian) may create contact phenomena or linguistic consequences that differ from those generated by a contact situation in which the languages are not genetically related to each other. In the contact of two closely related vernaculars, their elements can easily become mixed or intertwined, so that, e.g., a single word form may contain morphological or phonological elements of both languages, or there may be variations among variants of each contact language or dialect. The genetic closeness of contact languages may also strengthen the intensity and pace of change. However, there has been little research on the contacts between two Finnic languages (an exception is Riionheimo 2007). The study of mixed varieties (dialects or languages) has also been quite scant so far in the context of the Finnic languages, although the concept of a mixed language or dialect has been utilized since the very beginning of linguistic studies of the Finnic languages, especially in diachronic explanations.

4.2 Contacts among Border Karelian dialects

Karelian and Finnish were in close contact in Border Karelia, especially in its western parts, for centuries. Although the contacts are an adequately documented historical fact, very little attention has been paid to the mutual linguistic influences of Finnish and Karelian. Contacts with and the influence of Finnish are related to language change and development here: features of Finnish in Border Karelian dialects can be treated as contact-induced changes.

Speakers of the eastern dialects of Finnish entered Border Karelia from the 17th century onwards. The remaining speakers of Karelian gradually started to adopt features of Finnish. Their language eventually developed into mixed idiolects and dialects (Ruoppila 1956, 12), that, however, maintained the linguistic status of representing Karelian (and not Finnish), which was supported for its part by the Orthodox religion.[5] As a result, in the 20th century, there were idiolects in which the degree of "finnicization" or "Finnish-ness" was considerable; however, these varied idiolectally and areally. All in all, Border Karelian dialects can be said to have exhibited a linguistic continuum from Finnish to Karelian dialects (Ojansuu 1910, 10–11).

As Finns and Karelians lived side by side in the same villages – although not usually in the same families – it is evident that some kind of bilingualism also existed in Border Karelia. In Impilahti, for example, the language border was indefinite both geographically and in terms of the use of the two languages: many could speak and almost everyone could understand both

---

5   The contacts have also led to some degree of "karelianization" of the local Finnish dialects in Border Karelia; e.g., Olonets Karelian had some influence on the dialect of Finnish spoken in Impilahti, mainly on the vocabulary (Koponen 1982, 11).

languages (Punttila 1992, 6).⁶ In addition to fully bilingual Karelian–Finnish speakers (whose native Karelian was a mixed, finnicized Border Karelian dialect), there were most probably also Karelian-speakers who modified their native Karelian in the direction of Finnish when communicating with Finns (if they did not switch entirely to Finnish), and, conversely, there must have been speakers of Finnish who modified their speech towards Karelian.⁷

In Border Karelia, there were also contacts between distinct dialects of the same language, namely between South and Olonets Karelian. This situation is attested in the South–Olonets Karelian dialect continuum, which extended over the municipality of Suojärvi (see Jeskanen 2011, 353–354). Olonets Karelian has also had some influence on the South Karelian dialect in westernmost Border Karelia (see Section 6.1).

The Olonets Karelian speaking area was spread across two states, but, despite the divisive frontier, the speakers of Olonets Karelian in Border Karelia had close ties to and contacts with the speakers of the same dialect on the Russian side of the border. The mutual bonds within the entire speaking area of Olonets Karelian were strong. Traditionally Olonets Karelia, including areas on both sides of the border, formed a joint cultural and ethnic region. People had various kinds of "inter-border" activities and they, e.g., participated in the same feasts. Marriages over the border were also common up to the 1920s, so there were bonds of kinship between the Olonets Karelians of Finland and Russia as well. These diverse contacts over the border also enhanced the preservation of the local Karelian dialect in the area and its unification, despite the state border. (See Sauhke 1971, 13; Hämynen 1995, 28–29; 2012, 249; 2013, 186; Kokkonen 2012, 32–33; Pyöli 2013, 163; 2015, 510.)⁸

For most of its existence beginning in 1323, the Swedish-Russian border has not been a thoroughly guarded zone. In the 19th century, during the Grand Duchy period of Finland, the border was primarily a customs boundary, which created, in practice, no physical obstacle for the inhabitants of the border zone. During this time, the border could be described as more like a bridge than a barrier between the Karelians living unnaturally split in two countries (Katajala 2005, 36; Kokkonen 2012, 25).

---

6   It has been reported that as late as in the 1920s and 1930s in Salmi and Suojärvi, speakers of Finnish also used Karelian in everyday communication (Hämynen 2013, 189).
7   There may have been a distinction between some kind of "functional modes" of the same language (i.e., here, Karelian): in the 1800s, Lönnrot observed that it was as if there were actually "two languages" in Impilahti; one spoken by people (especially Orthodox) among themselves, and another spoken with authorities ("vallasihmisten kanssa") and Finns (Lönnrot 1980, 308). According to this obervation, a division existed between distinct varieties or modes of one language or dialect (in a similar way as reported from the Hindi-speaking area of northern India by Gumperz 1971, 27, 107), which display varying proportions of narrow local features (Gumperz's "village dialect") vs. areally wider-known features ("regional dialect").
8   There is not much information on contacts between speakers of South Karelian across the state border, but it is known that there were, e.g., marital ties.

Russian has been an important contact language for the development of Karelian over time. The influence of Russian was essential in the division of Karelian and the eastern dialects of Finnish, Karelian having considerably more Russian influence of the two. But the Russian language has also played a role in Border Karelia after the administrative separation of the area from the control of Novgorod and Russia. Under Swedish rule, there were still lively contacts with Russia and the Russian language, as Border Karelia (like all of Southeastern Finland) had close economic and demographic ties with Russia. The eastern contacts were strengthened anew when Finland became an autonomous Grand Duchy of Russia in 1809.

The Orthodox religion was also a uniting factor in the direction of Russia. In the late 1800s, during a period of Russification in Finland, approximately half of the children in Border Karelia attended Finnish schools, whereas the other half went to schools maintained by the Russian Orthodox church in which the instruction language was Russian (Hämynen 1995, 75–82; Pyöli 2013, 163–164). The Karelian language used to be strongly connected to the Greek Orthodox church, but, despite this, the language officially used in the Orthodox church in Finland was and is Finnish (see Hämynen 1995, 110–111; 2012, 252; Jeskanen 2005, 223–224; Pyöli 2013, 166).

After the revolution in Russia and Finland's independence in 1917, the relations to and influence of the Russian language diminished to practically none in Finland (concerning both the Finnish and Karelian languages spoken in the Finnish territories). In the 20th century, Border Karelia became closer to and started to assimilate to the rest of Finland as part of the independent Republic of Finland. Children in Border Karelia attended Finnish schools in which the language of instruction was Finnish, so they learned the standard written and spoken forms of Finnish in school. Karelian was not (at least officially) used in Border Karelian schools.[9] (Hämynen 2012, 251–252.) Karelian remained the language of communication at home and in the rural communities of Border Karelia.

The Karelian-speaking community in Border Karelia remained unified up to the end of the Grand Duchy period of Finland and WWI. The unity was maintained by strong religious and cultural bonds among the Karelians and also by their internal marriages within the Orthodox religion. However, in the 1920s and 1930s, changes were to come. In practice, in 20th century Finland, Karelian turned more and more into a secondary (or simply a domiciliary) language for children of Karelian-speaking parents.

5 Border Karelians and their dialect in post-war Finland

In the 20th century, and especially during the time of Finland's independence, the position of the Finnish language became more central in Border Karelia. By the 1930s, the influence of Finnish – also written Finnish – on Border Karelian dialects grew considerably along with the governmental and

---

9 Locally, however, there may have been teachers who used their native Karelian inofficially and colloquially to some extent in the context of school instruction.

educational unification in the independent state of Finland and the social development connected to it. The mixing and merging of the two languages, Karelian and Finnish, was typical of Border Karelian dialects to a certain extent already long before the post-war years and WWII in Finland. Development in the 20th century led to further finnicization of Border Karelian dialects, a process that was to accelerate further after WWII when the Border Karelian population was evacuated to Finland. (Turunen 1965, 27; 1982, 84–85; H. Leskinen 1998, 376; Hämynen 2012, 251–252; Pyöli 2013, 166; 2015, 511, 517.)

After WWII, the evacuees of Border Karelia were resettled in Finnish-speaking parts of Finland, and the community of speakers of Karelian became scattered. This led to linguistic assimilation with the dominant language, Finnish, even by the older generation, resulting in mixed idiolects that contained an increasing number of Finnish elements and displayed individual mixtures of Karelian and Finnish. This linguistic phase of Border Karelian dialects is represented in audio recordings made in the 1960s (The Corpus of Border Karelia prepared by the FINKA[10] project, see Section 7; on audio recordings of the dialect of Salmi see Pyöli 2015, 520–523).

As Finnish and Karelian were not fully mutually comprehensible, a need for linguistic adaptation was inevitable for the speakers of Karelian in their new situation in Finland. The stories of Border Karelians in the audio recorded material of the 1960s reveal evidence of communication problems between Karelians and Finns, so there were also practical reasons for adapting one's individual language to the language of the environment – even if it led to a decrease in or loss of the original characteristics of Karelian and, in this way, weakened the linguistic identity of Karelians (see Pyöli 2013, 172). According to Hämynen, there were few linguistic features in common between Border Karelian and the local Finnish dialects (2012, 265; 2013, 204). The Karelian features to disappear first were probably those that were unknown to both the standard Finnish language and the local Finnish dialects and, thus, were incomprehensible to Finnish speakers.

In their new domiciles in Finland, due to language differences and cultural incomprehension, Border Karelians were exposed to disparagement and discrimination, e.g., by being called Russian. Some even felt that it was shameful to speak Karelian at that time in Finland. Areal splitting, mingling with the dominant Finnish-speaking majority, and the lack of recognition of the Karelian language in Finnish society led to a process where the already narrowed spectrum of use of Karelian narrowed still more, and there was soon a process of language shift at hand. Karelian was rapidly left "under" Finnish and its position grew weaker. In the new demanding situation, Karelians simply did not have the strength to maintain their language. (Pyöli 2013, 170–172; Lemmetyinen 2015, 34, 36.) Thus, the number of speakers of Karelian began to decline. The younger generation acquired Finnish (both the local Eastern Finnish dialect and the written standard language) but not

---

10 *FINKA – On the Border of Finnish and Karelian* – was a research project at the University of Eastern Finland in 2011–2014, funded by the Academy of Finland (Project 137479).

necessarily Karelian any longer, or at least its acquisition remained much thinner and more defective than was the case for the previous generation (for different types of Karelian speakers, see Palander and Riionheimo in this volume).

A language shift to Finnish took place after the war. In addition to areal displacement and negative attitudes towards the Karelian language, an important factor in the process of the fading of Karelian was the increasing number of mixed marriages (between Orthodox and Lutherans) in which the Lutheran religion – and simultaneously the Finnish language – was usually accorded a dominant position. In Border Karelia, mixed marriages were rare up to the 20th century, and, even as late as in the 1920s and 1930s, mixed marriages comprised only a little less than 40% of all recorded marriages in Border Karelia. This situation helped the preservation of the Karelian language, but after WWII, in the new domiciles, mixed marriages became more common (e.g., in the period 1944–1947, the proportion of mixed marriages was 88% of all marriages of the people of Suojärvi). The children of these families usually adopted the Lutheran religion (and the Finnish language). This development along with the low societal status of the Karelian language had an immediate weakening effect on the use of Karelian in homes. (Hämynen 2012, 252–253, 262.)

Thus, for various reasons, the development of Karelian in Finland after WWII can be characterized as a rapid finnicization that severely disturbed the transmission of Karelian and, in practice, cut the natural continuum of passing the language on to the next generation. The final blow to the Karelian language in Finland was post-war urbanization. In rural communities, Karelian was still used as a spoken language in the homes of Karelian evacuees, but the hefty migration of the younger generation to towns all around Finland dispersed the potential young speakers of Border Karelian dialects and simultaneously the Karelian language. (Hämynen 2012, 259–260; 2013, 197–198, 203–205.)

Estimating the number of speakers of Karelian and their proportion of the whole population of Border Karelia has been difficult because there has been no precise data on the native language of the inhabitants. The Karelian language is not usually mentioned in historical sources, and there are no direct documents or statistics of the language of the population of Border Karelia, either from the 17th or from the following centuries. The only historical documents available are linguistically secondhand, mostly judicial material. (Björn 2013, 410, 412–413.)

In practice, the number of speakers of Karelian can be estimated on the basis of the number of those inhabitants of Border Karelia who belonged to the Orthodox Church and, for this reason, can be expected to have spoken Karelian as their first language. Drawing on this, in 1870, according to Hämynen (2012, 248–249), there were some 20,000 speakers of Karelian in Finland, and by WWII the number had doubled. In 1944, the number of Border Karelian evacuees who spoke Karelian is estimated to have been from approximately 35,000 (Harakka 2001) to 40,000 (Hämynen 2012, 251, 257; 2013, 187, 196) or even a little more (see Turunen 1976, 123).

In 2009, there were, according to Hämynen (2012, 266), still 8,400 persons in Finland who were born in Border Karelia and were Orthodox by religion, and who, thus, presumably had Karelian as their first language at home. However, these persons have more or less experienced a process of linguistic finnicization during the post-war years, and it is evident that only some of them have preserved their native language, even to a certain extent. Using the situation of the Saami languages and the decline of their speakers in Finland as a comparison, Hämynen estimates (2012, 266; 2013, 205) that some 1,700 of the total of 8,400 of Border Karelian born people would possibly still be able to speak Karelian. Thus, the decline in the number of Karelian speakers in Finland during the latter half of the 20th century has been dramatic. A population of some tens of thousands of native speakers has faded to a fraction of a few thousand "part-time speakers" (Munne 2013, 391; for the various types of speakers of Karelian, see Palander and Riionheimo in this volume).

6 Characteristics of Border Karelian dialects

The common characteristics of the Karelian language (as described in, e.g., Ojansuu 1918; Turunen 1982, 78–80; H. Leskinen 1998, 376–381) form the basic linguistic features of Border Karelian dialects. Although these dialects have experienced considerable influence from Finnish, they are classified as representing the Karelian language (and not Finnish). Below are some examples of the characteristic features of Border Karelian dialects, especially such features in which this vernacular differs from the rest of Karelian. The Corpus of Border Karelia (see Section 7) will be used as the material.

How do the Border Karelian dialects differ from their "mother" dialects, South and Olonets Karelian? One of the main characteristics of Border Karelian dialects is their rich, even lavish linguistic variation mainly concerning phonological and morphological features.[11] The cause of variation is long-term contacts with speakers of Finnish, and the variation often exhibits varying linguistic elements of Karelian and Finnish. In this variation and the strong influence of Finnish, Border Karelian dialects differ from other dialects of Karelian (on the contacts with Finns, see Section 4.2). The variation of Border Karelian dialects has not been studied or described before, but now it is possible to make observations about it on the basis of the extensive textual material of The Corpus of Border Karelia. Section 6.1 presents some examples of the variation of Border Karelian dialects.

Veikko Ruoppila (1956, 12) has pointed out that in the mixed dialects of Border Karelia there may also be innovations that have emerged after these dialects were separated from the rest of the Karelian language: there are both Karelian and Finnish features in these dialects, but, according to Ruoppila, "probably also some that evolved during a later local special development." Ruoppila does not, however, name or describe any of these innovations. Section 6.2 deals with such special Border Karelian features.

11 There was also lexical variation (e.g., Punttila 1992, 9; Pyöli 2015, 520).

The age of Finnish influence (and variation) in Border Karelian dialects may vary, according to feature, from the age of more than a hundred years to more recent development that has taken place in the new domiciles after WWII. The influence of Finnish can basically be attested through comparison with the Karelian language spoken in Russia, which does not contain such Finnish features (as these have been adopted after the separation of Border Karelian dialects). Another point of comparison is the Tver Karelian dialects, which are clearly similar to the Border Karelian dialects (the Tver dialects are not dealt with in this article, however). The Tver dialects derive from a 17th century variety of South Karelian and have preserved well most of the original South Karelian dialectal features of that time. Thus, they offer a peephole into the history of Border Karelian dialects. Linguistic features of the Border Karelian dialects of the 20th century can be compared to the same features in the Tver dialects, and the comparison may reveal facts about original features or later developments of these dialects.

6.1 Variation

Examples of features of Border Karelian dialects in which there is variation between a Karelian and a Finnish variant (the latter one representing the Eastern Finnish dialects) include: (1) voiced and voiceless stops, (2) palatalization, and (3) 3rd person plural verb forms. A similar kind of Karelian–Finnish variation can be detected in numerous other linguistic features in Border Karelian dialects. The material of the examples is mainly from the South Karelian dialects of Border Karelia. The variation described here is idiolectal, i.e., it occurs in the speech of one and the same person. The occurrences of variants may vary featurewise from equal variants to only rarely or sporadically occurring ones. There can be great diversity in the proportions of the same varying elements among different speakers of the same municipality or even the same village. Instead of a varying pair of forms, there may also be several alternative variants within the same instance of variation, as in (3). In general, there is more variation, and the Finnish variants are more common in the western parts of Border Karelia.

(1) In South and Olonets Karelian, original voiceless short stops *k*, *t*, *p*, and sibilants *s*, *š* have become voiced in a voiced environment, e.g., *hangi* 'snowdrift,' *šilda* 'bridge,' *ambuo* 'to shoot' (Ojansuu 1918, 5–6), *izä* 'father,' *kyžyjä* 'asker' (id. p. 37). In these cases in Border Karelian dialects, there is variation between a voiced and the original voiceless variant (Turunen 1982, 85). Occurrences of this variation in The Corpus of Border Karelia are, e.g., *niidä ~ niitä* 'them' (Partitive) (Suojärvi, SKNA 275:1a), *tuhmembii ~ tuhmempii* 'more stupid' (Pl. Partitive) (Korpiselkä, SKNA 303:1a), *konza ~ konsa* 'when' (Korpiselkä, SKNA 437:1b). The voiceless variants are more common especially in the western parts of Border Karelia (where the influence of Finnish is stronger).

(2) The consonantal palatalization typical of Karelian (see Ojansuu 1918, 84–88), e.g., *naińe* 'woman,' *tüönd'i* '([s]he) sent,' *pert't'ih* 'to the house' (id. p. 85), has been reported to be labile in Impilahti (Punttila 1992, 8) and in Salmi (Kujola 1910, 41; see also Pyöli 2015, 509, 521). Additionally, in other Border Karelian dialects there is free variation between the palatalized and

non-palatalized variant, as can be seen in The Corpus of Border Karelia, e.g., *ol'i ~ oli* 'was' (Suojärvi, SKNA 101:2a), *luatinnu ~ luat'innuh* '(has) made' (Suistamo, SKNA 065:1b). (In the Eastern Finnish dialects, there is less palatalization than in Karelian, and in Standard Finnish none; see also Palander and Riionheimo in this volume.)

(3) In Karelian the original passive verb form is used also as a 3rd person plural form (see Zaikov 2013, 157–158; Pyöli 2011, 79–80), e.g., *tytöt tullah ~ tuldih* 'the girls come ~ came' (cf., Finnish passive forms *tullaan, tultiin* 'some ~ we come, came'), whereas in Finnish dialects the singular 3rd person form is widely used in the plural 3rd person, e.g., *tytöt tuli* 'the girls came' (cf., *tyttö tuli* 'the girl came'). In Russian Karelian, the passive form is used invariantly in 3rd person plural, but, in Border Karelian dialects, the Finnish 3rd person singular form varies with the Karelian passive form (*hyö tuli ~ hyö tuldih* 'they came'); e.g., *ne ol' ~ ne oldih* 'they were' (Korpiselkä, SKNA 437:1a; also the 3rd person plural pronoun *ne* has been borrowed from the Finnish dialects); *herrat **piettii** lystii – – semmosiihan ne **piti*** 'the masters had ("held") fun – – (it was) such [feasts] they held;' *niiŋ ku nytki verkot **ollah** – – harvat verkot **ol'** ni – –* 'as now the (fish)nets are – – the nets were sparse' (Korpiselkä, SKNA 303:2a).[12] (See also Palander and Riionheimo in this volume.)

Examples (1–3) represent variation between Karelian and Finnish variants. There is also another kind of variation in Border Karelia. As there were two dialects of Karelian spoken in Border Karelia, i.e., South Karelian (of Karelian Proper) and Olonets Karelian, it is not surprising that there has been internal influence between these main dialects. In the South Karelian dialect spoken in Border Karelia, there may occur occasional Olonets Karelian features that vary with the expected South Karelian variant.

(4) As an example of Olonets Karelian features in such Border Karelian dialects that clearly represent South Karelian (e.g., in Korpiselkä), occasional occurrences of the lacking consonant gradation of *ht*, a feature typical of Olonets Karelian (Ojansuu 1918, 26), can be noticed, e.g., *lähtimmä* 'we left' (Korpiselkä, SKNA 437:1b), *kah**t**estoista* 'twelfth' (Suistamo, SKNA 065:1a), *unoh**t**uttu* '(they) have been forgotten' (Impilahti, SKNA 127:1a) (cf., South Karelian and Eastern Finnish dialects: *lähimmä, kahestoista, unohuttu*).

(5) Another Olonets Karelian feature is nominative word forms in which the original final vowel *-a, -ä* is represented by *-u, -y* (this is a regular representation in Olonetsian; Ojansuu 1918, 131–132). This feature may occur – speakerwise – in the South Karelian idiolects of Border Karelia, but only sporadically, never as a common or expected variant, e.g., *äij**y*** 'much' (Suistamo, SKNA 065:1a), *luterilaist**u*** 'Lutheran' (Sg. Partitive) (Suojärvi, SKNA 166:1b), *niid**y*** '(of) them' (Partitive) (Impilahti, SKNA 681:1b) (cf., South Karelian: *äijä, luterilaista, niidä*).

Features (4) and (5) are undeniably of Olonetsian origin and clearly detectable as their representations differ from both South Karelian and Finnish. Both example features may occur in several idiolects of the same

---

12 Cf., 3rd person plural in written Standard Finnish: *pojat menevät, tulivat* 'the boys go, came,' a form that is not used in Border Karelian dialects.

municipality in The Corpus of Border Karelia. Compared to the influence of Finnish (1-3), Olonets Karelian features perceived in the South Karelian dialects of Border Karelia (4-5) are fewer and less frequent, mostly sporadic, and "hidden below the surface." However, it is important to notice that there are Olonetsian features all over the South Karelian area of Border Karelia, including the dialects of the westernmost municipalities of Korpiselkä and Ilomantsi. The South Karelian dialects of Border Karelia are, thus, more "Olonetsian" than the rest of South Karelian (spoken in Russia). There is no previous research on this kind of Olonetsian influence and not even any observations of such occurrences.

There is no data on internal movements of population in Border Karelia after the 17th century, which could explain the Olonetsian features in the South Karelian dialect of Border Karelia. The Tver dialects also have some (sporadic) features of Olonets Karelian (Sarhimaa 1999, 32-33).

6.2 Border Karelian features

There are also Border Karelian features that are areally restricted to Border Karelian dialects only and that are clearly of Border Karelian origin (and not common South Karelian features). Here are some examples (6-9) of these types of feature.

(6) In consonant gradation, the weak grade representatives of geminate stops *kk, tt, pp* are expectedly and commonly *k, t, p* in Karelian (Ojansuu 1918, 13) as well as in Finnish.[13] In Border Karelian dialects, however, there is generalization of voicing in these cases: in the weak grade there may unexpectedly occur the voiced stops *g, d, b* instead of the original and expected voiceless ones *k, t, p*, e.g., *hybätää* 'it is jumped,' *hybähettih* 'it was jumped' (Suistamo, SKNA 065:1b), *keidettih* 'it was boiled,' *käydettih* 'it was used,' *obedettih* 'it was taught' (Korpiselkä, SKNA 303:1a). So, in the weak grade of *kk, tt, pp* there is variation *k, t, p ~ g, d, b* in Border Karelian dialects (cf., in the rest of Karelian invariantly *hypätäh, hypähettih, keitettih, käytettih, opetettih*; cf., Finnish: *hypätään, hypähdettiin, keitettiin, käytettiin, opetettiin*). This voicing phenomenon can be described as hypercorrect. The model for the wrong generalization (voicing) in Border Karelia is the development of short originally voiceless stops that become voiced in voiced environments in South and Olonets Karelian (e.g., *siga < sika* 'pig,' *randa < ranta* 'shore') (see feature (1) in Section 6.1). Usually (i.e., in the rest of Karelian), the weak grade variants *k, t, p* of *kk, tt, pp* do not comply with the voicing development as they go back to former geminates ($k < {}^*\check{k}k$, $t < {}^*\check{t}t$, $p < {}^*\check{p}p$).

(7) In Karelian, the indicative 3rd person present suffix is usually *u, y* (Zaikov 2013, 151-152, 157-158; Pyöli 2011, 79, 82), e.g., *tulou, mänöy* ('comes, goes'). However, in part of Olonets Karelian (and in Finnish), the singular 3rd person present tense ending is *-V* (i.e., lengthening of the final vowel of the verbal stem). The suffix *-V* is also typical of Border Karelian dialects, e.g., *tuloo, mänöö, pidää, työndää* ('comes, goes, holds, pushes')

---

13 The consonant gradation of geminate stops: e.g., (Sg. Nominative : Sg. Genitive) *takki : takin* 'coat,' *hattu : hatun* 'hat,' *pappi : papin* 'priest.'

(Jeskanen 2011, 354, 356–357).[14] In some parts of Border Karelia (Suistamo, Korpiselkä), the suffix -*V* may also have been extended with the original 3rd person present tense suffix *bi* ~ *pi* (in which case, the sg. 3rd person suffixal element is *Vbi*), e.g., *luatiibi* 'makes', *maksaabi* 'pays' (Suistamo, SKNA 065:1a), *painaltaabi* 'presses' (Suistamo, SKNA 065:1b), *ruppiepi* 'begins' (Korpiselkä, SKNA 303:2a); with one-syllable stems, the ending is plain *bi* ~ *pi*: *käybi* 'goes' (Suistamo, SKNA 065:1b), *suapi* 'gets' (Suistamo, SKNA 065:1a) (*pi*-final 3rd person forms like these are used in some Finnish dialects, too). The final vowel *i* may also be omitted and the ending is then *(V)b* ~ *(V)p*: *huomuab* '(he) notices' (Suistamo, SKNA 065:1b), *siunauduub* 'there will be' (Suistamo, SKNA 065:1b), *syöb* 'eats', *jiäp* 'stays' (Korpiselkä, SKNA 303:2a), *tuloop* 'comes' (Korpiselkä, SKNA 303:1a). In the Salmi dialect, the 3rd person ending *bi* may occasionally have the form *bin*, e.g., *jiäbin* '(he) stays' (SKNA 166:3a) (*p* also in Finnish North Karelian dialects; Turunen 1956, 20, 86). – This Border Karelian mixture of 3rd person endings and their variation is different from the rest of Karelian; in other Karelian dialects (spoken in Russia), the indicative 3rd person present suffix is mainly *u*, *y*.

(8) In the material of the municipality of Korpiselkä, there are some morphological variants of the preterite participle that do not exist in any other Karelian dialect (see Moshnikov 2014, 70). These Border Karelian participle suffixes that occur simultaneously with Karelian suffixes *nun*, *nyn*, *n*, *nuh*, *nyh* (corresponding to the Standard Finnish *nut*,-*nyt*) are (a) *h*, (b) *V*, (c) *nuu*,-*nyy*, and (d) *Ø*, e.g., (a) *myö emmä lähteh* 'we did not leave' (SKNA 437:1a), *engä muistah* 'and I did not remember' (SKNA 437:1b), *ei t'iedäh* 'did not know' (SKNA 304:1a); (b) *ois ottaa* 'would have taken' (SKNA 304:1a), *ol' ampuu* 'had shot' (SKNA 749:1a), *olet porskahuttaa* 'you have splashed' (SKNA 437:1a); (c) *emmä syönyy* 'we did not eat' (SKNA 304:1a), *ei osannuu* 'could not;' (d) *olem piästä* 'I have left (sthg)' (SKNA 303:1a), *en ruve* 'I did not start' (SKNA 304:1a), *emmä ois lähte* 'we would not have left' (SKNA 437:1b) (all examples are from Korpiselkä). These participle types (a–d) are Border Karelian innovations. It can further be added to the Olonets Karelian features (5–6) in Section 6.1 that the Olonetsian preterite participle variant that has a final *h* in the suffix *nuh*, *nyh* also appears in the South Karelian dialect of Korpiselkä (but not in the speech of all informants), e.g., *uskonuh* 'believed' (SKNA 437:1a), *nähnyh* 'seen' (SKNA 438:1a), *kuulluh* 'heard' (SKNA 438:1a).

(9) In the use of the local cases, Border Karelian dialects combine the case systems of Olonets Karelian and Karelian Proper (and Finnish). In both of these main dialects of Karelian, there are special syncretic cases in which a single inflected case form corresponds to two (or more) *case* functions. In Karelian Proper, i.e., South and White Sea Karelian, there is a syncretic Adessive-Allative case marked with the suffix *l* ~ *(l)lA*, which represents the original Adessive suffix *lla* ~ *llä* and has both locative (Adessive) and lative

---

14 In Suojärvi, there are also infinitive-like 3rd person form variants, e.g., *pideä* 'holds' (also: 'to hold'), *load'ie* 'makes' (also: 'to make'), *ottoa* 'takes' (also: 'to take'), varying with 3rd person *pidäy* ~ *pidää* ('holds'), etc. (see Jeskanen 2011, 354, 356–357).

(Allative) use in these Karelian dialects (Zaikov 2013, 96–98). In Olonets Karelian, there is a syncretic Inessive-Elative case the suffix of which is the original Inessive suffix *s ~ ssA* (Pyöli 2011, 41–43), combining locative (Inessive) and separative (Elative) use. These are called interior local cases, and in Olonets Karelian there is a similar syncretism between the exterior local cases Adessive and Ablative: the locative case suffix *l(lA)* (Adessive) can also be used in separative meaning (Pyöli 2011, 44–46).[15] Border Karelian dialects exhibit all three types of syncretism listed above: e.g., Adessive (locative) form in Allative (lative) use: *yhellä mummozel annoin* 'I gave (it) to an old woman' (Korpiselkä, SKNA 304:1a); Adessive (locative) form in Ablative (separative) use: *kulgukauppihiel osti ńiillä vuokkilazilla* 'from the peddlers (he) bought from the peddlers of Vuokkiniemi' (Korpiselkä, SKNA 304:1a); *puusta lua̦ittih ašt´ivo da, kuuzen_oksissa* 'the container was made of wood and branches of spruce' (Korpiselkä, SKNA 303:1a). In the last example, one finds the morphological Elative (separative) form *puusta* 'of ~ from wood,' which represents the case systems of Karelian Proper and Finnish, whereas the form *oksissa* has the suffix of an originally locative case (Inessive) but the meaning of a separative case (Elative; 'of ~ from branches') in this clause; this is an Olonets Karelian feature. This kind of mixed use of the case systems of both South and Olonets Karelian (and Finnish) is a Border Karelian specialty. In practice, it has not been studied at all. (See also Palander and Riionheimo examples 11–13 in this volume.)

7 Border Karelian materials for study

In Finland, there is a long tradition of collecting linguistic data that has resulted in extensive dialect archives of Finnish and other Finnic and Finno-Ugrian languages. Linguistic research on the Finnic languages has been essentially connected to the establishment, maintenance, and accumulation of these collections. The relevant archives for Karelian are the Lexical Archive of Karelian and the Audio Recordings Archive, both of which are hosted by the Institute for the Languages of Finland (*Kotimaisten kielten keskus*) in Helsinki.

The Audio Recordings Archive contains originally tape-recorded samples (dating from 1959 onwards) of all dialects of Finnish as well as a wealth of audio recordings of minor Finnic languages (Karelian, among others). The material of Border Karelian dialects in the archive consists of some 550 hours of speech, recorded mostly in the 1960s in Finland when it was still possible to reach Karelian-speaking informants who had lived most of their lives in Border Karelia. The conversational form of the material is in an interview format that concentrates on themes of traditional life and its phenomena and is conducted by a linguist.

---

15 In separative (Elative, Ablative) use, the case can also be expressed in a more explicit way with an extending element *päi* attached to the case suffix (*päi* originally: 'from some direction'), e.g., Elative *moa-s-päi* 'from the ground' (cf., *moa-s* 'on ~ from the ground'), Ablative *ranna-l-päi* 'from the shore' (cf., *ranna-l* 'on ~ from the shore').

In 2010–2014, the FINKA project of the University of Eastern Finland prepared a corpus through transcribing approximately 120 hours of audio recorded speech of Border Karelian dialects into written form. This text corpus is called *The Corpus of Border Karelia*. Its material has not been previously used in linguistic research, and, thus, it makes a substantial contribution to the research material available on Border Karelian dialects. The corpus exhibits a wide range of Border Karelian mixed idiolects, and it provides researchers with unique access to the process of language mixing and dialect levelling in a Karelian–Finnish context. As Border Karelian dialects are a defectively documented and sparsely studied variety of Karelian, all available material is relevant. In addition to the 120 hours of material of The Corpus of Border Karelia, more than 400 hours of still "unexploited" audio recorded material of Border Karelian dialects is located in the Audio Recordings Archive. The fact that Border Karelian dialects can no longer be reached and recorded in their original "pre-war" form reinforces the importance of the existing speech material of these dialects in The Corpus of Border Karelia and the Audio Recordings Archive.

The Lexical Archive of Karelian contains more than 550,000 archive cards of Karelian dialect entries, dating from the end of the 19th century to the 1970s. Most of the Karelian lexical material was collected before WWII. The contents of the Archive form the basic material of an extensive dictionary of Karelian dialects, *Karjalan kielen sanakirja* (KKS), which was published in six volumes in 1968–2005 and republished via the Internet with identical contents in 2009 (http://kaino.kotus.fi/cgi-bin/kks/kks_etusivu.cgi). This dictionary has approximately 83,000 lexical entries, and its target language is Finnish. (Dictionaries of dialects of single Border Karelian municipalities are Pohjanvalo (1947) on the Salmi dialect and Punttila (1998) on the Impilahti dialect.)

The dialectal area of Border Karelia is represented in the lexical material of both the dictionary of Karelian (KKS) and the Lexical Archive of Karelian. In the study of Border Karelian dialects, the lexical material of the dictionary and the archive form an important supplement to the audio recorded corpus and other material. Much of the lexical archive material is not included in the lexical entries ("word articles") of the dictionary; this unutilized "hidden" material may also be useful when sketching an overview of Border Karelian dialects or for more specific studies.

In addition to dictionaries and archives, there are some other sources of Border Karelian dialects that are available as research material: text collections and dialect atlases. There are quite a few published text collections of Karelian in which there is, however, very little material on Border Karelian dialects. The largest samples of Border Karelian dialects are included in a three-volume collection from the 1930s (E. Leskinen 1934, 83–145). Sample texts of Border Karelian dialects have also been published by Kujola (1910, 77–88; Salmi dialect), Virtaranta (1960, 121–187; Salmi dialect written down by Kujola), Nirvi (1932, 86–96; Suistamo dialect), and Punttila (1992; Impilahti dialect). With its 120 hours of transcribed texts The Corpus of Border Karelia forms the most extensive textual material of Border Karelian dialects for linguistic studies.

The large dialect atlas of Karelian by Bubrih et al. (1997) was compiled in the Soviet Union from 1937 onwards and eventually published in Finland sixty years later. It contains 209 lexical maps with 186 villages as observation points. This atlas does not, however, include Border Karelian dialects in its material as Soviet citizens were not able to visit Finland in the 1930s, and right afterwards, in the following decade, Border Karelian dialects were no longer spoken in their original Finnish territories. It is for this reason that Border Karelian dialects are not represented in Kalevi Wiik's (1998) study on the "dialectometrics" of Karelian, as this study is directly based on the material of the atlas of Bubrih et al. Another, even smaller dialect atlas of Karelian was published by Heikki Leskinen in 1992; it contains 25 maps of eastern–western word pairs, and the maps cover both Karelian (including Border Karelian dialects) and Finnish dialects. These maps illustrate the lexical parallelism of Karelian and Eastern Finnish dialects, the latter of which usually share the eastern lexical variant with Karelian. Finally, the dialect atlas of Finnish (Kettunen 1940) with its 213 maps also contains some information on the Karelian dialects of Border Karelia.

8 On the research on Border Karelian dialects

Linguistic research on the Karelian language has focused on the main dialects of Karelian – the northern and southern dialects of Karelian Proper and Olonets Karelian, which are all spoken in Russian Karelia – whereas the dialects of Border Karelia have been almost totally neglected in linguistic studies (see Jeskanen 2005, 273). (However, Border Karelian dialects are well represented in the lexical material of the dictionary of Karelian, KKS.) This section will give an overview of the study of Border Karelian dialects.

The study of Karelian has traditionally been phonetic, phonological, and morphological description, dialectological surveys, and study of lexicon, and all of this mostly from a diachronic perspective, like the study of the Finnish language and its dialects, respectively. One synchronic research task has been the compilation of dictionaries (on dictionaries of Karelian see Section 7).

Border Karelian dialects are included in the material of the very first Karelian language studies by Arvid Genetz (1870; 1880; 1884). There are also a few monographs on the phonology and phonetics of Border Karelian dialects from the first half of the 20th century (Kujola 1910; Donner 1912; Nirvi 1932). Subsequently, in the latter half of the 20th century, Aimo Turunen published several articles that offer a general description of Border Karelian dialects (Turunen 1965; 1973; 1976; 1982).

The municipalities of Border Karelia have been studied to varying degrees. The dialect that has been described most thoroughly is the dialect of Suojärvi, which was situated in the border zone of Olonets and South Karelian, next to the state border with Russia. This dialect was first studied in detail by Genetz who published a description of it in 1870 (Genetz 1870; see also Korhonen 1986, 111–125). Another linguist to be mentioned in the context of Karelian studies, and Suojärvi in particular, is E. V. Ahtia who collected the vocabulary of Suojärvi in 1908–1919. This material consists of 54,000 lexical cards, and the Suojärvi collection is one of the largest in the Lexical Archive of Karelian. (Turunen 1965, 21.)

The Border Karelian dialects of Suistamo have been studied by R. E. Nirvi. In addition to his sound historical study on the vowels of the central dialect of Suistamo (1932), Nirvi also collected lexical material (approximately 11,000 lexical cards in the Lexical Archive of Karelian). The dialect of Impilahti is represented in a publication of two hours of transcribed texts (Punttila 1992; the introduction contains a short description of the dialect) and a small dictionary (Punttila 1998). Juho Kujola studied his native dialect of Salmi, and he also collected and published some texts in it (Kujola 1910; Virtaranta 1960). The least studied Border Karelian dialects are the dialects of the northwestern municipalities of Korpiselkä and Ilomantsi.

The collection of lexical material also forms part of the study of Border Karelian dialects. The collection of Karelian vocabulary was started in the 1890s as part of a larger project on the study and recording of Finnish and other Finno-Ugric languages. From early on, the main interest was directed at Russian Karelian, and in the 20th century, and especially in the 1930s, attention was paid to the Karelian refugees who represented dialects spoken on the Russian side of the border (Palander et al. 2013, 361). However, in the 1930s, Border Karelian vocabulary was also collected to some extent.

Border Karelian vernaculars were mixed dialects with multifaceted roots, strong influence from Finnish, and ample idiolectal variation. Mixed dialects have, however, not been of interest to researchers or collectors who have preferred "pure" original and invariant dialects (Punttila 1992, 6–7; 1998, 5–6; Uusitupa 2017, 72). Traditional folk poetry and ethnological material has been collected in Border Karelia, but there has been no linguistic interest in the dialects of the area.[16] Thus little research has been conducted on Border Karelian dialects, and they are until now a relatively unexplored language variety. Only quite recently, the FINKA project and its corpus (The Corpus of Border Karelia) have brought Border Karelian dialects to light in the context of mixed dialects and language contacts.

During WWII, the recording of dialects (and toponyms) also concentrated on Russian Karelia (which was called "East Karelia" in Finland at that time), parts of which were occupied by Finland from 1941 to 1944. As some Russian Karelian population remained in their home villages through the war, it was possible for Finnish linguists (as well as ethnologists and other scholars) to come into contact with them (see, e.g., Järvinen 2004; Kaukonen 2004; Närhi 2004; Pimiä 2007). During the so-called Continuation War (1941–1944), the scientific study of East Karelia became officially organized (Katajala 2013, 41–42).

After the war, the study of and interest in the Karelian language was scant (Palander et al. 2013, 361–362) although Karelian, as a member of the Finnic language family and an essential part in the chain of explanation of its historical development, remained part of Finnish language studies at the

---

16 It was in these parts of Karelia that the traditional Finnic folk poetry was preserved the latest in its original form (Härkönen 1932, 490–491; Salminen 1932, 484, 487).

universities in Finland. However, linguists showed no interest in Finnish Karelians although there would have been a pool of some 40,000 Karelian-speaking evacuees resettled in Finland to study. Their fate and that of their descendants was to finnicize rapidly in Finnish society during the subsequent decades (see Section 5). Some research has been conducted on the linguistic adaptation of Finnish-speaking evacuees (H. Leskinen 1974), and there are a couple of MA theses on the finnicization of the Border Karelian dialect of Ilomantsi (Hirvonen 1972; Karvinen 1983), but the process of finnicization of Border Karelian evacuees has not been studied (except: Lehikoinen 2008; see Jeskanen 2005, 273).[17]

This ignorance of "domestic" Karelian dialects is peculiar as Border Karelian dialects were a vernacular spoken in the territories of Finland, and, thus, they would have been easily accessible for study both before and after the war. Yet at the same time, it was primarily other "purer" dialects of Karelian that attracted the interest of linguists in Finland. This discrepancy may be related to the general attitude in folkloristics and other national sciences in Finland in the 19th and the first half of the 20th century: genuine Karelia is situated on the Russian side of the border. It is possible that an image of another national Finnic language beside Finnish was also not considered appropriate although this attitude has probably not been explicitly articulated anywhere.

9 Conclusion

Today the study of Border Karelian dialects is historical in the sense that the dialects are no longer spoken in their original territories. In this sense, the formation of Border Karelian dialects is a fascinating linguistic puzzle. Contacts with neighbouring languages and dialects have been crucial in different phases of the development of Border Karelian dialects. These dialects have stood at the intersection of two languages, nations, and cultures. Thus they represent dialect continua across borders (as meant by Auer 2005). The development of Border Karelian dialects has been influenced by linguistic, historical, and demographic factors. The population of Border Karelia has always been quite small, and locally, during some historical periods, extremely small, so it is possible to talk about real bottlenecks in the history of Border Karelia as well as in the formation of its dialects.

The linguistic analysis of the original Border Karelian dialects as represented in The Corpus of Border Karelia is based on material that is at least 50 years old. It can, however, be treated using normal methods of synchronic linguistics. The input of present-day linguistic research into the study of Karelian will apply current theories and methodologies to Karelian data. In recent years, interest in mixed dialects has arisen, and new methods of analysis have already been tried on the Border Karelian material, e.g., in

---

17 A study of the finnicization of the White Sea Karelian dialect spoken in some villages in northern Finland is Virtaranta 1968.

MA theses and doctoral dissertations at the University of Eastern Finland (Massinen 2012; Moshnikov 2014; Tavi 2015; Uusitupa 2017).

The future research of Border Karelian dialects will aim to present new information of a little known and unique language variety and of contacts between the Karelian and Finnish languages. The study of Border Karelian dialects can contribute to the international discussion on, e.g., language contacts, variation analysis, dialect geography, grammaticalization, language typology, or perceptual linguistics. Only now is it possible (both theoretically and technically) to handle a large and multifaceted collection of material like that of the Border Karelian dialects in The Corpus of Border Karelia. The data offers non-Indo-European language material for the comparison of linguistic hypotheses that have primarily been formulated on the basis of Indo-European languages.

Language decay – and, finally, language death – is a commonplace and even natural phenomenon. The number of languages in the world is currently rapidly diminishing. Karelian belongs to the fading languages. It has never held an official position in either of the countries in which it has been spoken. In Finland, after being practically ignored for decades, the Karelian language finally obtained the status of an autochthonous non-territorial minority language in 2009.

In 19th and 20th century Finland, Border Karelia was regarded – in comparison with the rest of Finland – as an exotic original region marked by the Greek Orthodox religion and as exhibiting the last remnants of traditional Eastern Finnic culture and folklore. Conceived of as an impressive and enthralling embodiment of the home country, Border Karelia served as a source of inspiration (along with Russian Karelia) for Finnish culture, which was in the process of awakening and strengthening. In this context, the original Karelian language was, however, not treated on equal terms, and its fate was to remain a less esteemed language variety in Finnish society.

It may be challenging to motivate the study of an endangered language in the modern world, but, without a doubt, it can be said that investigating Karelian is relevant at this moment. It is important to document small languages as thoroughly and widely as possible, but studying them is also important in terms of revitalization. The study of Karelian can enhance efforts to revive the presently fading Border Karelian language variety and the Karelian language in general. Studying these "forgotten" dialects is simultaneously a gesture of reconciliation with their former and present speakers who have been denied the linguistic rights that would have naturally belonged to them in the 20th century.

Today Border Karelia lives mostly through vague and fading images of a formerly lively linguistic community (see Katajala 2013, 60–61; also Palander and Riionheimo in this volume). In their present status, Border Karelian dialects can be compared to Vrouw Maria, the well-preserved shipwreck at the bottom of the Baltic Sea with goods and articles of value that sank with it, or the Saimaa ringed seal, an endemic relic, which, although a species on the edge of extinction, still has potential to continue to live in the diversity formed by its environment.

References

Auer, Peter. 2005. "The Construction of Linguistic Borders and the Linguistic Construction of Borders." In *Dialects Across Borders. Selected Papers from the 11th International Conference on Methods in Dialectology (Methods XI), Joensuu, August 2002*, edited by Markku Filppula, Juhani Klemola, Marjatta Palander, and Esa Penttilä, 5–30. Amsterdam: John Benjamins.

Björn, Ismo. 2013. "Kuka puhuu karjalasta, puhuiko kukaan karjalaa?" [Who speaks of Karelian, did anyone speak Karelian?]. In *Karjala-kuvaa rakentamassa* [Constructing the image of Karelia], edited by Pekka Suutari, 404–438. SKST 1389. Helsinki: Finnish Literature Society.

Donner, Kai. 1912. "Salmin murteen kvantiteettisuhteista" [On the quantity relations of the dialect of Salmi]. In *Suomi* IV: 9. Helsinki: Finnish Literature Society.

Forsström, O. A. 1894. *Kuwia Raja-Karjalasta* [Pictures of Border Karelia]. Helsinki: Finnish Literature Society.

Genetz, Arvid. 1870. "Kertomus Suojärven pitäjäästä ja matkustuksistani siellä v. 1867" [A report on the parish of Suojärvi and my travellings there in 1867]. In *Suomi* II: 8. Helsinki: Finnish Literature Society.

Gumperz, John J. 1971. *Language in Social Groups*. Stanford, California: Stanford University Press.

Harakka, Paavo. 2001. "Karjalan kieli Suomessa" [Karelian language in Finland]. Talk at National home region days, August 2001. Valtimo, Finland. [http://www.karjalankielenseura.fi/tekstit/kirjoituksia/valtimo082001.html]

Hirvonen, Tauno. 1972. "Ilomantsin Mutalahden tienoon karjalaismurteen savolaistuminen sandhi-ilmiöiden valossa" [The finnicization of the Karelian dialect of Mutalahti (Ilomantsi) in the light of sandhi phenomena]. MA thesis. University of Jyväskylä.

Hämynen, Tapio. 1993. *Liikkeella leivän tähden. Raja-Karjalan väestö ja sen toimeentulo 1880–1940*. [On the move for bread. The population of Border Karelia and its subsistence in 1880–1940.] Historiallisia Tutkimuksia 170. Helsinki: Suomen Historiallinen Seura.

Hämynen, Tapio. 1995. *Suomalaistajat, venäläistäjät ja rajakarjalaiset. Kirkko- ja koulukysymys Raja-Karjalassa 1900–1923*. [Finnicizers, Russifiers, and Border Karelians. The church and school question in Border Karelia in 1900–1923.] Ortodoksisen teologian laitoksen julkaisuja 17. Joensuu: University of Joensuu.

Hämynen, Tapio. 2012. "Changes in the Linguistic Identity of the Borderland Karelians in Finland up to the Year 2009". In *Nation Split by the Border. Changes in the Ethnic Identity, Religion and Language of the Karelians from 1809 to 2009*, edited by Tapio Hämynen and Aleksander Paskov, 246–271. Joensuu: University Press of Eastern Finland.

Hämynen, Tapio. 2013. "Rajakarjalaisen kieliyhteisön rapautuminen ja karjalankielisten määrä Suomessa" [The attrition of the Border Karelian language community and the number of Karelian speakers in Finland]. In *Karjala-kuvaa rakentamassa* [Constructing the picture of Karelia], edited by Pekka Suutari, 182–213. SKST 1389. Helsinki: Finnish Literature Society.

Härkönen, Iivo. 1932. "Erinäisiä kansanrunouden lajeja Raja-Karjalassa ja muilla karjalaisalueilla" [Diverse types of folk poetry in Border Karelia and other Karelian regions]. In *Karjalan kirja* [The book of Karelia], 2nd edition, edited by Iivo Härkönen, 490–496. Porvoo: WSOY.

Itkonen, Terho. 1983. "Välikatsaus suomen kielen juuriin" [On the origin of Finnish – an intersurvey]. *Virittäjä* 87:190–229, 349–386.

Jeskanen, Matti. 2005. "Karjalan kieli ja karjalankieliset Suomessa" [Karelian language and Karelian speakers in Finland]. In *Monenlaiset karjalaiset. Suomen karjalaisten kielellinen identiteetti* [Karelians' many faces: The linguistic identity of Karelians in Finland], edited by Marjatta Palander and Anne-Maria Nupponen, 215–285. Studia Carelica Humanistica 20. Joensuu: University of Joensuu..

Jeskanen, Matti. 2011. "Karjalan kieli Suojärvellä" [Karelian language in Suojärvi]. In *Omal mual vierahal mual. Suojärven historia III.* [On one's own land, on strange land. The history of Suojärvi III.], edited by Tapio Hämynen, 352–357. Saarijärvi: Suojärven Pitäjäseura ry.

Järvinen, Irma-Riitta. 2004. "Kylä ja erämaa. Helmi Helmisen perinteentallennusmatkat Itä-Karjalaan 1941–1944." [Village and desert. The journeys of Helmi Helminen for collecting folklore in East Karelia in 1941–1944.] In *Kenttäkysymyksiä* [Field questions], edited by Pekka Laaksonen, Seppo Knuuttila, and Ulla Piela, 43–60. Kalevalaseuran vuosikirja 83. Helsinki: Finnish Literature Society.

Karjalainen, Heini, Ulriikka Puura, Riho Grünthal, and Svetlana Kovaleva. 2013. *Karelian in Russia. ELDIA Case-Specific Report.* Studies in European Language Diversity 26. Mainz.

Karvinen, Erja. 1983. "Havaintoja Melaselän murteen savolaistumisesta" [Observations on the finnicization of the dialect of Melaselkä]. MA thesis. University of Joensuu.

Katajala, Kimmo. 2005. *Suurvallan rajalla. Ihmisiä Ruotsin ajan Karjalassa.* [On the border of a great power. People in the Karelia of the Swedish era.] Historiallinen Arkisto 118. Helsinki: Finnish Literature Society.

Katajala, Kimmo. 2013. "Konstruoitu Karjala. Suomalaisen historiantutkimuksen Karjala-paradigmat 1900-luvulla." [The construed Karelia. The paradigms of Karelia in Finnish historical sciences in the 20th century.] In *Karjala-kuvaa rakentamassa* [Constructing the picture of Karelia], edited by Pekka Suutari, 29–82. SKST 1389. Helsinki: Finnish Literature Society.

Kaukonen, Väinö. 2004. "Tutkimusmatka Vienan Karjalaan 1942" [A research journey to White Sea Karelia in 1942]. In *Kenttäkysymyksiä* [Field questions], edited by Pekka Laaksonen, Seppo Knuuttila, and Ulla Piela, 61–72. Kalevalaseuran vuosikirja 83. Helsinki: Finnish Literature Society.

Kettunen, Lauri. 1940. *Suomen murteet III A. Murrekartasto.* [The Finnish Dialects III A. Dialect Atlas.] SKST 118. Helsinki: Finnish Literature Society.

KKS = *Karjalan kielen sanakirja 1–6* [Dictionary of Karelian 1–6]. Lexica Societatis Fenno-Ugricae XVI,1–6. Helsinki: Finno-Ugrian Society. 1968–2005.

Kokkonen, Jukka. 2012. "Origins of the Modern Finnish-Russian Border: the Border and Crossing it from the Grand Duchy Period until the Winter War". In *Nation Split by the Border. Changes in the Ethnic Identity, Religion and Language of the Karelians from 1809 to 2009*, edited by Tapio Hämynen and Aleksander Paskov, 24–45. Joensuu: University Press of Eastern Finland.

Koponen, Paavo. 1982. *Esi-isiemme Impilahti* [The Impilahti of our forefathers]. Lappeenranta: Impiranta-Säätiö.

Korhonen, Mikko. 1986. *Finno-Ugrian Language Studies in Finland 1828–1918.* The History of Learning and Science in Finland 1828–1918 11. Helsinki: Societas Scientiarum Fennica.

Kujola, Joh. 1910. "Äänneopillinen tutkimus Salmin murteesta" [A phonological study on the dialect of Salmi]. *Suomi* IV: 10.

Kuujo, Erkki. 1963. *Raja-Karjala Ruotsin vallan aikana* [Border Karelia during Swedish rule]. Joensuu: Karjalaisen Kulttuurin Edistämissäätiö.

Laakso, Johanna, Anneli Sarhimaa, Sia Spiliopoulou Åkermark, and Reetta Toivanen. 2013. *Summary of the Research Project ELDIA (European Language Diversity for All). Abridged English-language Version of the ELDIA Comparative Report.* Vienna: University of Vienna. Accessed April 3, 2015. https://phaidra.univie.ac.at/detail_object/o:304813.

Larjavaara, Matti. 1986. "Itämerensuomen koillisryhmän synkretistiset paikallissijat" [The syncretic local cases in the north-eastern group of Finnic]. *Virittäjä* 90:413–427.

Lehikoinen, Sanna. 2008. "Karjalaa vai suomea? Karjalan kielen säilymisestä suojärveläissyntyisillä siirtokarjalaisilla" [Karelian or Finnish? On the preservation of the Karelian language of Karelian evacuees born in Suojärvi]. MA thesis. University of Joensuu.

Lemmetyinen, Anne-Mari. 2015. "Karjalan kielen taival ei-alueelliseksi vähemmistökieleksi Suomessa" [The journey of the Karelian language to a non-territorial minority language in Finland]. MA thesis. University of Eastern Finland.

Leskinen, Eino. 1934. *Karjalan kielen näytteitä II. Aunuksen ja Raja-Karjalan murteita.* [Samples of the Karelian Language II. Dialects of Olonets and Border Karelia.] Helsinki: Finnish Literature Society.

Leskinen, Heikki. 1974. "Karjalaisen siirtoväen murteen sulautumisesta ja sen tutkimisesta" [On the merging of the dialect of Karelian evacuees and its research]. *Virittäjä* 78:361–378.

Leskinen, Heikki. 1992. *Karjalan kielikartasto. Idän ja lännen sanastoeroja.* [Language atlas of Karelian. Differences in the vocabulary of east and west.] Jyväskylän yliopiston suomen kielen laitoksen julkaisuja 35. Jyväskylä: University of Jyväskylä.

Leskinen, Heikki. 1998. "Karjala ja karjalaiset kielentutkimuksen näkökulmasta" [Karelian and the Karelians from the viewpoint of linguistics]. In *Karjala: Historia, kansa, kulttuuri* [Karelia: History, people, culture], edited by Pekka Nevalainen and Hannes Sihvo, 352–382. Helsinki: Finnish Literature Society.

Lönnrot, Elias. 1980. *Matkat 1828–1844* [Journeys 1828–1844]. Espoo: Weilin+Göös.

Massinen, Henna. 2012. "Yleis- ja erikoisgeminaatio Ilomantsin karjalankielisten siirtolaisten idiolekteissa" [Primary and secondary gemination in the idiolects of the Karelian evacuees of Ilomantsi]. MA thesis. University of Eastern Finland.

Moshnikov, Ilia. 2014. "NUT-partisiipin variaatio Ilomantsin rajakarjalaismurteessa" [The variation of active preterite participle in the Border Karelian dialect of Ilomantsi]. MA thesis. University of Eastern Finland.

Munne, Timoi. 2013. "Karjalan kielen voimavarat Suomessa" [The resources of the Karelian language in Finland]. In *Karjala-kuvaa rakentamassa* [Constructing the picture of Karelia], edited by Pekka Suutari, 386–403. SKST 1389. Helsinki: Finnish Literature Society.

Nirvi, R. E. 1932. *Suistamon keskusmurteen vokalismi* [Vocalism of the central dialect of Suistamo]. Helsinki: Finnish Literature Society.

Nirvi, R. E. 1961. "Inkeroismurteiden asema" [The status of Ingrian]. *Kalevalaseuran vuosikirja* 41:99–132.

Närhi, Eeva Maria. 2004. "Mannerheim ja Itä-Karjalan paikannimet" [Mannerheim and the toponyms of East Karelia]. In *Kenttäkysymyksiä* [Field questions], edited by Pekka Laaksonen, Seppo Knuuttila, and Ulla Piela, 73–90. Kalevalaseuran vuosikirja 83. Helsinki: Finnish Literature Society.

Ojansuu, Heikki. 1910. "Karjalan (ja Aunuksen) kielestä" [On the language of Karelia (and Olonets)]. In *Karjalan kirja* [The book of Karelia], edited by Iivo Härkönen, 10–16. Porvoo: WSOY.

Ojansuu, Heikki. 1918. *Karjala-aunuksen äännehistoria* [Sound history of Karelian-Olonetsian]. Helsinki: Finnish Literature Society.

Palander, Marjatta, Pekka Zaikov, and Milla Uusitupa. 2013. "Karjalan kielen tutkimusta ja opetusta kahden puolen rajaa" [Research and education of Karelian on both sides of the border]. In *Karjala-kuvaa rakentamassa* [Constructing the picture of Karelia], edited by Pekka Suutari, 358–385. SKST 1389. Helsinki: Finnish Literature Society.

Pimiä, Tenho. 2007. *Sotasaalista Itä-Karjalasta* [Spoils of war from East Karelia]. Jyväskylä: Gummerus.

Pohjanvalo, Pekka. 1947. *Salmin murteen sanakirja* [Dictionary of the dialect of Salmi].

Punttila, Matti. 1992. *Impilahden karjalaa* [Karelian of Impilahti]. Castrenianumin toimitteita 41. Helsinki: Yliopistopaino.

Punttila, Matti. 1998. *Impilahden karjalan sanakirja* [Dictionary of the Karelian dialect of Impilahti]. Lexica Societatis Fenno-Ugricae XXVII. Helsinki: Finno-Ugrian Society.

Pyöli, Raija. 2011. *Livvinkarjalan kielioppi* [Grammar of Olonets Karelian]. Helsinki: Karjalan Kielen Seura.

Pyöli, Raija. 2013. "Rajakarjalaiset ja muuttuva identiteetti" [Border Karelians and changing identity]. In *Karjala-kuvaa rakentamassa* [Constructing the picture of Karelia], edited by Pekka Suutari, 159–181. SKST 1389. Helsinki: Finnish Literature Society.

Pyöli, Raija. 2015. "Salmilaisten kieli" [The language of the people of Salmi]. In *Rajoil da randamil: Salmilaiset 1617–1948* [Rajoil da randamil: the people of Salmi 1617–1948], edited by Jukka Kokkonen, 499–525. Saarijärvi: Salmi-Säätiö.

Riionheimo, Helka. 2007. *Muutoksen monet juuret. Oman ja vieraan risteytyminen Viron inkerinsuomalaisten imperfektinmuodostuksessa.* [The multiple roots of change. Mixing native and borrowed influence in the past tense formation of Ingrian Finns living in Estonia.] SKST 1107. Helsinki: Finnish Literature Society.

Riionheimo, Helka. 2013. "Kieltenvälinen vertailu kielikontaktitutkimuksessa" [Cross-linguistic comparison in language contact research]. In *Kielten vertailun metodiikkaa* [Methodology of language comparison], edited by Leena Kolehmainen, Matti Miestamo, and Taru Nordlund, 219–250. Helsinki: Finnish Literature Society.

Ruoppila, Veikko. 1956. *Etelä-Karjalan murreopas* [A handbook of the dialects of Finnish South Karelia]. Helsinki: Otava.

Salminen, Väinö. 1932. "Karjalan runoalueet ja muinaisrunot" [The poem regions and ancient runes in Karelia]. In *Karjalan kirja* [The book of Karelia], 2nd edition, edited by Iivo Härkönen, 483–488. Porvoo: WSOY.

Saloheimo, Veijo. 1973. "Kyläkunnittainen muutto Tverin Karjalaan ennen vuotta 1651" [The villagewise migration to Tver Karelia before 1651]. *Kalevalaseuran vuosikirja* 53:43–54.

Saloheimo, Veijo. 2010. *Entisen esivallan alle, uusille elosijoille. Ortodoksikarjalaisten ja inkeroisten poismuutto 1500- ja 1600-luvuilla* [To the former authorities, to new domiciles. The migration of Orthodox Karelians and Ingrians in the 16th and 17th century]. Joensuu: Pohjois-Karjalan historiallinen yhdistys.

Sarhimaa, Anneli. 1999. *Syntactic transfer, contact-induced change, ande the evolution of bilingual mixed codes. Focus on Karelian-Russian language alternation.* Studia Fennica Linguistica 9. Helsinki: Finnish Literature Society.

Sauhke, Niilo. 1971. *Karjalan praašniekat.* [The feasts of Karelia.] Jyväskylä: Gummerus.

SKNA = Suomen kielen nauhoitearkisto [The Audio Recordings Archive]. The Institute for the Languages of Finland, Helsinki.

SKST = Suomalaisen Kirjallisuuden Seuran toimituksia [Editions of The Finnish Literature Society].

Tavi, Susanna. 2015. "Rajakarjalaismurteiden venäläiset lainasanat" [Russian loan words in Border Karelian dialects]. MA thesis. University of Eastern Finland. http://epublications.uef.fi/pub/urn_nbn_fi_uef-20160039/urn_nbn_fi_uef-20160039.pdf.

Turunen, Aimo. 1956. *Pohjois-Karjalan murreopas* [A handbook of the dialects of Finnish North Karelia]. Helsinki: Otava.

Turunen, Aimo. 1965. "Suojärven murre" [The dialect of Suojärvi]. In *Suojärvi I,* edited by Lauri Pelkonen, 21–38. Pieksämäki: Suosäätiö.

Turunen, Aimo. 1973. "Raja-Karjalan murteet ja vepsän kieli" [Border Karelian dialects and Veps]. In *Karjala. Idän ja lännen silta* [Karelia. A bridge between east and west], edited by Hannes Sihvo, 83–94. Porvoo: WSOY.

Turunen, Aimo. 1976. "Suomen entisen Raja-Karjalan murteet ja niiden suhde rajantakaisiin ja Suomen-puoleisiin naapurimurteisiin" [The dialects of the former Finnish Border Karelia and their relation to the neighboring dialects behind the border and in Finland]. In *Suomalainen tiedeakatemia: Esitelmät ja pöytäkirjat 1975* [Finnish Academy of Sciences: Papers and minutes 1975], 123–133. Helsinki.

Turunen, Aimo. 1982. "Raja-Karjalan murteet" [The dialects of Border Karelia]. In *Karjala 2. Karjalan maisema ja luonto* [Karelia 2. The landscape and nature of Karelia], edited by Yrjö-Pekka Mäkinen and Ilmari Lehmusvaara, 65–89. Hämeenlinna: Arvi A. Karisto.

Uusitupa, Milla. 2017. *Rajakarjalaismurteiden avoimet persoonaviittaukset* [Open person constructions in Border Karelian dialects]. Publications of the University of Eastern Finland. Dissertations in Education, Humanities, and Theology 117. Joensuu: University of Eastern Finland.

Wiik, Kalevi. 1998. *Karjalan dialektometriikkaa* [On the dialectometrics of Karelian]. A manuscript.

Virtaranta, Pertti. 1960. *Juho Kujola, karjalan ja lyydin tutkija* [Juho Kujola, researcher of Karelian and Lude]. SKST 266. Helsinki: Finnish Literature Society.

Virtaranta, Pertti. 1968. "Suomussalmen karjalaiskylien kielioloista" [On the language of the Karelian villages in Suomussalmi]. In *Fenno-Ugrica. Juhlakirja Lauri Postin kuusikymmenvuotispäiväksi 17. 3. 1968* [Fenno-Ugrica. A jubilary book on the 60th birthday of Lauri Posti 17. 3. 1968], 254–275. Suomalais-Ugrilaisen Seuran toimituksia [Editions of The Finno-Ugrian Society] 145. Helsinki: Finno-Ugrian Society.

Virtaranta, Pertti. 1970. "Karjalan kielen tutkimuksesta Neuvostoliitossa toisen maailmansodan jälkeen" [On the research of Karelian in the Soviet Union after WWII]. *Virittäjä* 74:458–469.

Zaikov, Pekka. 2013. *Vienankarjalan kielioppi. Lisänä harjotukšie ta lukemisto*. [Grammar of White Sea Karelian. With exercises and readings.] Helsinki: Karjalan Sivistysseura ry.

Marjatta Palander
ⓘ http://orcid.org/0000-0002-4370-8493

Helka Riionheimo
ⓘ http://orcid.org/0000-0002-9294-6201

Imitating Karelian

How is Karelian Recalled and Imitated by Finns with Border Karelian Roots?

Abstract

This folk linguistic study focuses on the Karelian language as remembered by the Border Karelian evacuees who moved to Eastern Finland after World War II, or their descendants. Karelian is the closest cognate of Finnish and is currently severely endangered both in Finland and in Russia. As the research method, the study applies an imitation task, performed during a half-structured interview, in which the informants (altogether 32 Finnish-Karelians) were asked to replicate the way their parents, grandparents, or other older relatives had spoken. The aim was to investigate how long imitated sequences the informants could produce in a language they do not actively use themselves and how authentic their imitations are. The methological goal was to apply folk linguistic imitation task to research on an endangered language.

The study reveals considerable individual differences. Four informants were not able to imitate Karelian at all in the interview situations. Most commonly, short phrases or sentences in Karelian were produced, and some informants named isolated Karelian words. A few of the informants were capable of switching from Finnish to Karelian, and one informant spoke Karelian throughout the whole interview. In most cases, the imitated Karelian sequences contained much influence from Finnish, but many Karelian phonetic, morphological, or syntactic features were reproduced as well. Sometimes the informants produced hypercorrect words when trying to speak Karelian, showing that they have knowledge of the characteristic features of Karelian but not necessarily of the exact distribution of these features. The most often occurring phonological phenomena were features that differ from the Eastern Finnish dialects, such as voiced stops and the diphthongisation of *aa/ää* in non-initial syllables. Karelian morpho-syntax was best mastered by those informants who were able to produce longer sequences in Karelian. All in all, many informants can be considered latent speakers of Karelian who have good recollections of the language and who probably could learn or relearn Karelian in the right circumstances.

1 Introduction

This article focuses on the traces of Karelian preserved in the minds of those Finnish Karelians who have roots in the Border Karelia region and whose parents or grandparents have been Karelian speakers. Border Karelia is a region situated on the border of Finland and Russia, and it belonged to Finland until the end of World War II, at which time it was incorporated into the Soviet Union. The inhabitants of Border Karelia were citizens of Finland, and they were resettled in various locations in Finland among the Finnish-speaking majority. After the war, the Border Karelian speakers largely shifted to using Finnish in their daily life, and the use of their native language was mainly restricted to the domestic domain. The present-day speakers of Karelian mostly belong to the oldest generation, and even they have, in practice, shifted to Finnish in their daily life. Karelian has seldom been transferred to younger generations, and the number of Karelian speakers has been rapidly decreasing. In this context, our research subject is of topical interest since Karelian speakers have lately been actively revitalising their language. This study provides information about how Karelian is produced by those Karelians who have neither fully acquired nor ever actively used this language – but who are potentially able to revive and improve their language skills.

The study represents the field of folk linguistics, a relatively new branch of sociolinguistics that examines the conceptions that non-linguists have about language. Folk linguistics is interested in lay people's conscious or subconscious observations about language and their linguistic attitudes. In the present study, these questions are approached by applying the imitation method: the informants were asked to reproduce or mimic the Karelian language that resides in their recollections of older relatives. Imitation tasks have earlier been used within a folk linguistic framework to study dialect or accent differences and the salience of linguistic features (see Section 3). The present attempt to apply this form of eliciting data in the research of an endangered language and language contacts is methodologically and theoretically innovative.

The article is structured as follows: First, Section 2 introduces the linguistic and historical background of Border Karelia and the Border Karelian dialects. Section 3 gives an overview of imitation as a research method, presents data, and states the research questions to which answers were sought by using an imitation task. In Section 4 the results are presented by arranging the informants into several different categories according to their abilities to produce Karelian language in the imitation task. Section 5 examines the imitated utterances with respect to phonetic and phonological features, and Section 6 presents analyses of morphological and morpho-syntactic features. Finally, the findings are discussed, and the applicability of imitation tasks to a contact-linguistic study of an endangered language is assessed.

2 The Border Karelian dialects

Karelian belongs to the Finnic language family (also known as the Baltic Finnic languages) that consists of several very closely related languages spoken around the Gulf of Finland. It is the closest cognate of Finnish, and the Eastern Finnish dialects, in particular, resemble Karelian to a great extent due to their development from a common protolanguage (Proto-Karelian). Karelian differs from the Finnish dialects especially because of Russian influence (loanwords, borrowed phonetic features, borrowed grammatical patterns), due to long coexistense with Russian speakers. Karelian is traditionally divided into two main dialects, namely Karelian Proper and Olonets Karelian (see Map 1), and these varieties are nowadays considered as separate languages by some linguists (Grünthal 2007; Salminen 2009; Moseley 2010; Lewis et al. 2015). Karelian Proper is further divided into White Sea Karelian and the South Karelian dialects. Karelian has also been spoken in small areas in Inner Russia where the language was brought by South-Karelian migrants during the 17th century. The eastern dialects are spoken on the Finnish side of the border: in the province of North Karelia, the eastern *Savo* dialects are spoken and in the province of South Karelia the southeastern dialects are spoken. (It should be noted that even though the Finnish provinces are named North and South Karelia, the language spoken in these areas is Finnish.)

During the 20th century, the number of Karelian speakers began to decrease rapidly, and, currently, Karelian is a severely endangered language. Karelian is spoken in Finland and in Russia as a small minority language: in Finland the estimated number of Karelian speakers is approx. 5,000–11,000 and in Russia 25,000 (Sarhimaa 2016, 3; Laakso et al. 2013, 46; Laakso et al. 2015, 97, 108). The estimates vary considerably, e.g., according to whether the knowledge of Karelian is based on using Karelian daily or regularly or being able to understand Karelian. In Finland, there may be as many as 20,000 people who can understand Karelian (Laakso et al. 2015, 108), but according to a more cautious estimate, the number of Karelian speakers is now fewer than 2,000 (Hämynen 2013, 205). In neither of the countries does Karelian have the status of an official language, and it has, in practice, little institutional support, even though in Russia (in the Karelian Republic), Karelian is nominally protected by the law. In 2009, Finland recognised Karelian as a non-regional minority language (Laakso et al. 2013, 46, 47). Attempts to revitalise the Karelian language have been carried out since the end of the 1980s in both countries, including developing a written standard, publishing literature and newspapers in Karelian, and organising language nests (Pasanen 2010; Knuuttila 2011; Palander et al. 2013).

This article focuses on Border Karelia, which is an area that lies on the border of Finland and Russia and currently belongs to the latter (see Map 2) and has a complex history as the borderland between Sweden and Russia. Originally, it was a part of the Novgorod Republic and then of the Russian Empire, but, in 1617, it was incorporated into Sweden. In 1721, the area again came under Russian rule, and, in 1809, Finland became part of the same empire as an autonomous Grand Duchy. In 1917, Finland gained

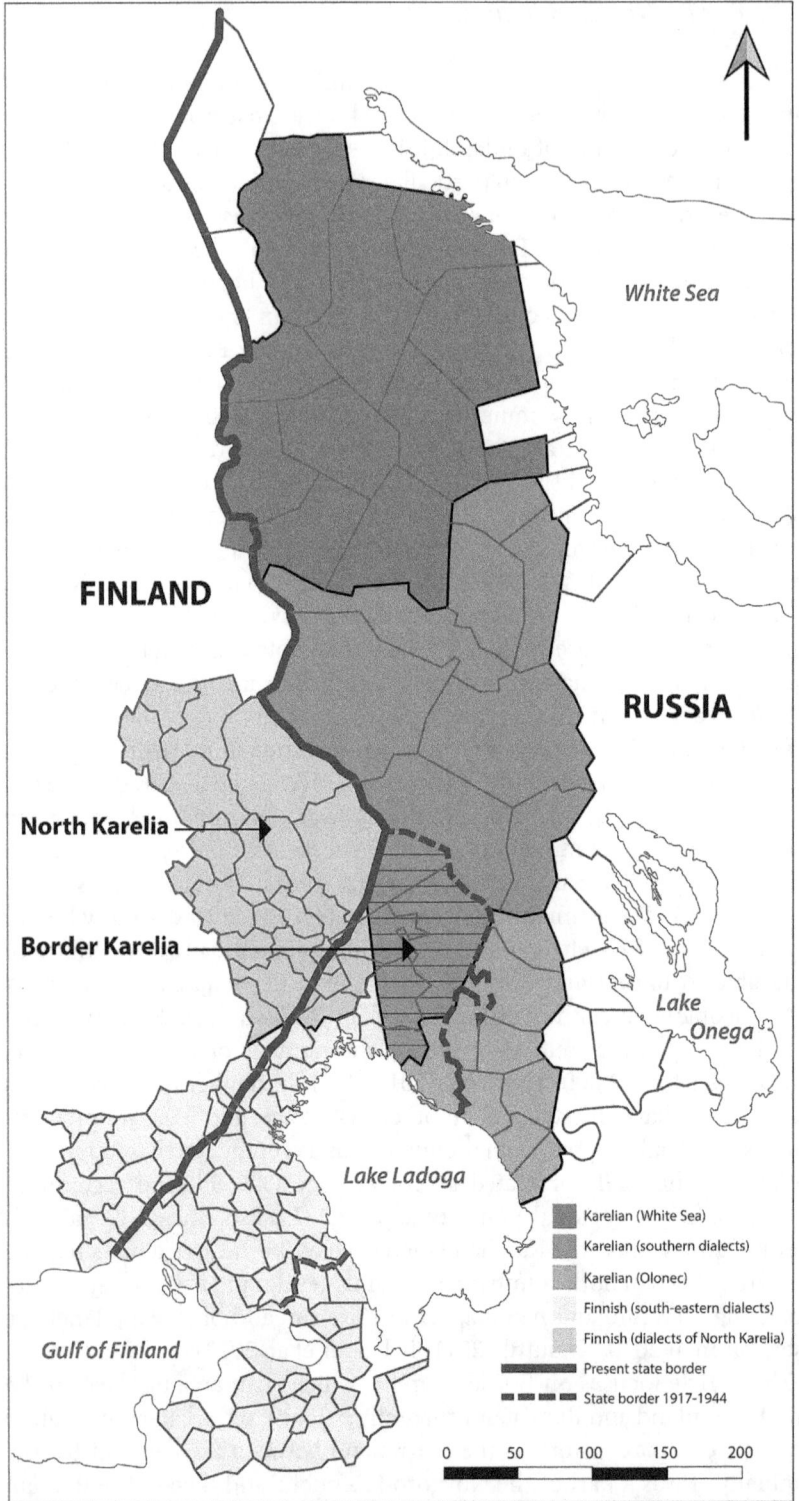

Map 1. The areas of the Karelian dialects and the Finnish dialects of North and South Karelia.

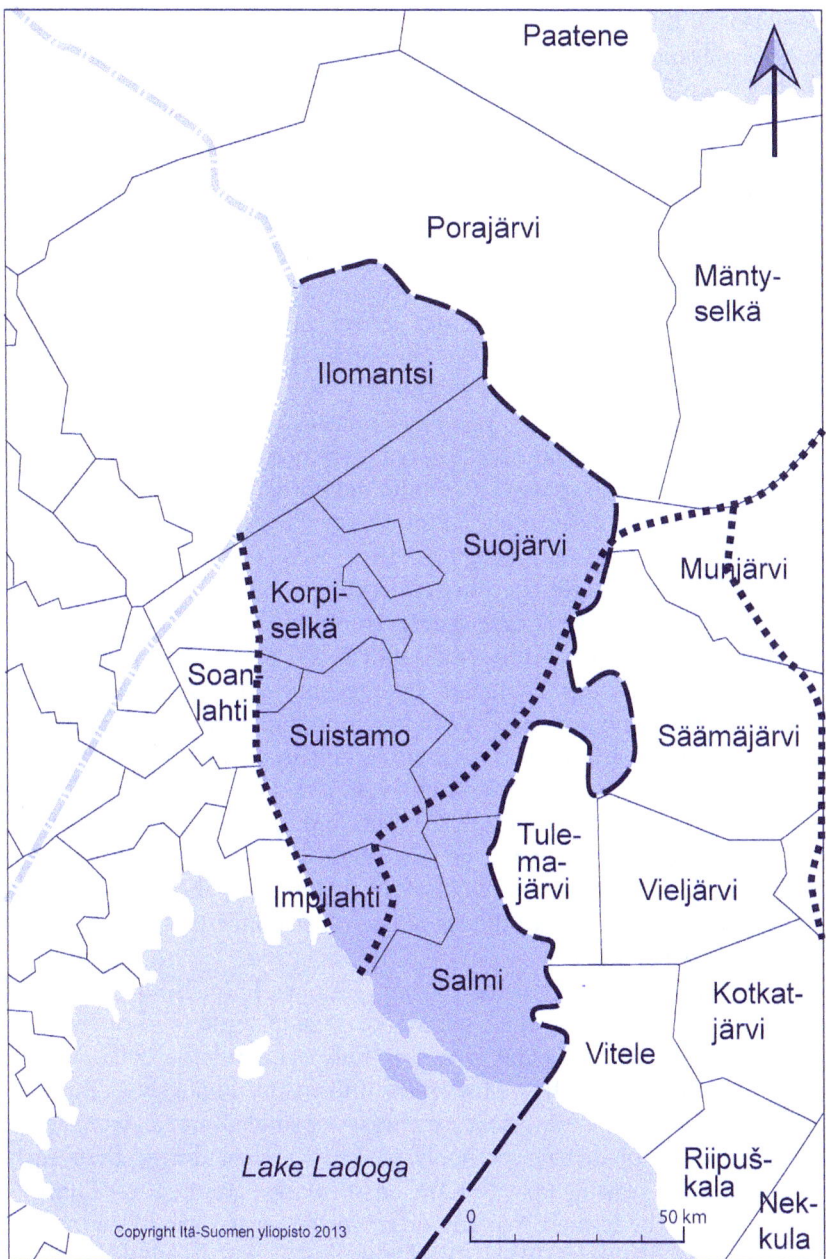

Map 2. The municipalities of Border Karelia.

independence and Border Karelia became part of the new country until the end of WWII. In 1944, Border Karelia was ceded to the Soviet Union, and its inhabitants were evacuated and resettled to other parts of Finland. Most of the 5,000–11,000 present-day Karelian speakers in Finland are either Border Karelian evacuees or their descendants.

The Karelian varieties spoken in Border Karelia were South Karelian in the western and northern parts and Olonets Karelian in the east and south (see Map 2). Karelian was not the only language spoken in this area, but, at the beginning of the 20th century in particular, growing industrialisation brought many Finnish-speaking Finns into Border Karelia. The two language groups were separated by religion as the Karelian speakers belonged to the Orthodox and the Finnish speakers to the Lutheran church. The religious and cultural barriers did not, however, prevent linguistic influence, and, in the Karelian varieties spoken in Border Karelia, Karelian and Finnish elements became intertwined. The Finnish influence was strengthened by elementary schools where only Finnish was used. Nevertheless, at the time of WWII, the Karelian varieties spoken in Border Karelia remained linguistically distinct from Finnish. (On Border Karelia and Border Karelian dialects, see also Koivisto in this volume.)

After the war, the Border Karelian evacuees were resettled into other parts of Finland, especially the eastern provinces of North Karelia and North Savo. During the post-war decades the Border Karelian people began to assimilate linguistically into the Finnish-speaking majority (even though they largely preserved their religion). There were several reasons for this process of language shift: the Karelian speakers lived scattered in several places and did not have a tight speech community, and the linguistically and religiously different groups met with social pressure and prejudices. Naturally, the shift was facilitated by the similarities between Eastern Finnish dialects and Karelian. Younger immigrants, in particular, faced negative attitudes at school, and their linguistic assimilation to Finnish dialects was rapid (Raninen-Siiskonen 1999, 174–175; Jeskanen 2005, 251–254; Kananen 2010, 89–90, 188–189). The middle-aged or elderly Border Karelians preserved their language much better. This development has led to the present situation where most of the Karelian speakers represent the oldest generation and where the language has seldom been transmitted to the younger generations.

This study investigates primarily the younger Finnish-Karelians who have heard Karelian from their parents or grandparents (and often other older relatives, too), but who have not fully acquired the language nor spoken it actively themselves. Most of the informants do not speak Karelian with the exception of a few discourse phrases or single Karelian words even though some of them have probably spoken Karelian during their early childhood when growing up with Karelian-speaking parents. These Finnish-Karelians could be termed "rememberers" in the sense introduced by, e.g., Campbell and Munzel (1989, 181), Craig (1997, 259), Holloway (1997, 12), Grinevald and Bert (2011, 51), Sallabank (2013, 14) and Thomason (2015, 56–57): they have never become fully competent in Karelian but can remember and reproduce fixed phrases and isolated words. Typically, they report being able to understand Karelian without difficulties and having good receptive skills, and, thus, they may be alternatively defined as *latent speakers*, defined as individuals "raised in an environment where a heritage language is spoken who did not become a fluent speaker of that language" (Basham and Fathman 2008, 578; see also Sallabank 2013, 14–15). There are, however, a couple of informants in our study who were able to switch to Karelian during the interview, albeit their Karelian contained abundantly Finnish features. These speakers have not had as much input from the previous generation as children growing up in a large language community, and, consequently, their Karelian differs from that spoken by the older generations. In the studies of language death, this kind of speaker is often called a *semi-speaker* (Dorian 1981, 115). In the present article, the more neutral term *heritage speaker* is preferred because, in its broad sense, this term covers a wide variety of language skills that range from highly proficient users to those who only have a cultural connection to the heritage language without productive linguistics skills (see, e.g., Montrul 2011).

3 Method, data, and the research questions

In this study, an imitation task was used to examine the control of Karelian language by informants with roots in Border Karelia. In folk linguistics, the term *imitation* refers to conscious use of a variety that is not the speaker's usual vernacular (Evans 2010, 379), and the term *control* is used when referring to the relative proficiency of the imitated variety (see, e.g., Niedzielski and Preston 2000, 23). Imitation has so far been rather seldom studied in linguistic research, but imitation tasks have been used in research on children's language acquisition (e.g., Snow 1998; Jones and Meakins 2013) in second-language acquisition research (Jessop et al. 2007; Wu 2013), and in research on speech pathology (Thoonen 1997; Seeff-Gabriel et al. 2010). One of the application areas of imitation is forensic linguistics where this method can be used for speaker recognition (Rogers 1998; Künzel 2000; Eriksson et al. 2010; Zetterholm 2010).

In the folk linguistic field, imitation has been used to investigate the perception of a variety that is not used by the respondents themselves: how conscious the informant is about the characteristics of this variety and in how detailed a manner (s)he can produce it. In these studies, imitations have mostly been reproduced in test settings. The method has been applied to examining, e.g., the differences between varieties of speech spoken by certain ethnic groups (Preston 1992), the perceptions of pronunciation by native and non-native speakers (Brunner 2010), and non-linguists' awareness of the typical features of regional dialects (Evans 2002; 2010, 383–387; Purschke 2010). In one application, imitating spoken dialect has been studied in so-called performance speech that is used when speaking to people who come from other areas or who perform in front of an audience (Schilling-Estes 1998; Farrús et al. 2007). Often the imitation research has involved a listening task for testing how authentic an imitated dialect is considered by the test subjects. In some studies, imitated speech is compared with a real sample of the variety in question in order to determine the most salient features.

In the present study, the research setting differs from the previous folk linguistic imitation studies in that the imitated variety is not unfamiliar for the test subjects but a familiar language that was spoken in their childhood families as a mother tongue. Later, the informants have shifted to Finnish and largely forgotten the Karelian they had learned at an early age. A central characteristic of this study is that the informants have a close and warm relationship to the imitated variety because the language also represents the homeland (Border Karelia) they have lost permanently (cf., Jeskanen 2005, 258–260; Palander 2015). The fragile and endangered status of Karelian also affects the attitudes towards Karelian by these people.

An additional difference is that the original variety, spoken by the Border Karelian people in their home region before WWII (or during the first decades after the war in Finland), has not been documented. This makes it difficult to assess the authenticity of the imitation. It is, however, possible to use some older studies and samples of Karelian Proper and Olonets Karelian as a baseline (Genetz 1884; Leskinen 1934; Ahtia 1936). In addition, some recent grammatical descriptions (Pyöli 2011; Zaikov 2013), a linguistic atlas of Karelian (Bubrih et al. 1997), and a large dictionary of Karelian (KKS 1968–2005) can be used as reference material.

The most recent and most important reference data is The Corpus of Border Karelia, compiled by the University of Eastern Finland[18] and based on recorded interviews made with Border Karelian evacuees in the 1960s and 1970s. The corpus contains approximately 120 hours of phonetically transcribed recordings of informants with roots in Border Karelia (in the municipalities of Ilomantsi, Korpiselkä, Suistamo, Suojärvi, Impilahti, and Salmi). The corpus contains recorded material from the older relatives of three of the informants in the present study (Ilomantsi 1917, Ilomantsi 1939 and Ilomantsi 1953) and presents the opportunity to compare the imitations with actual speech of the imitated speaker. On the grounds of the corpus, Finnish and Karelian elements have been mixed together, especially in Ilomantsi (the westernmost of the Border Karelia municipalities), but the speech of these speakers still contains abundantly typical phonetic features of Karelian language. When using this corpus, however, it is necessary to take into consideration the fact that this data was collected 20 or 30 years after the informants had been resettled in Finland. During the previous decades, when the Border Karelians lived among Finnish-speakers, the Karelian they spoke may have received strengthened influence from Finnish dialects.

The data consists of 31 tape-recorded folk linguistic theme interviews with 32 Finns whose families or, in one case, near acquaintances have roots in Border Karelia and who had heard Karelian in their childhood homes. The informants have lived in Eastern Finland in the county of North Karelia (see Map 1) in a linguistic environment where the local Finnish dialects share many features with the Karelian language. The interviewees were born between 1917 and 1969, and most of them represent the second immigrant generation: either they were in Border Karelia and were later evacuated into North Karelia as children, or they were born in Finland during or after WWII. One of the informants belongs to the first generation and was an adult at the time of evacuation. Three interviewees represent the third generation, and they remember how their grandparents spoke Karelian.

---

18 The corpus was compiled during the research project FINKA (funded by the Academy of Finland, Project Number 137479) in 2011–2014. The original recordings are archived at the Institute for the Languages in Finland (in Helsinki).

Two of the interviewees did not have Karelian roots. One of them was born in Suistamo and had lived there among Karelian speakers, but her own family was Finnish speaking. The other one lived during his childhood and part of his adulthood as a neighbor of an immigrant from Impilahti and observed the Karelian spoken by this immigrant. It was decided to include the interviews with these two informants in the study as the imitations, observations, and comments were very similar to those of the informants who were descendants of Border Karelians. Regionally, the informants represent all the municipalities of Border Karelia: Ilomantsi (8), Suojärvi (4), Suistamo (5), Suistamo/Suojärvi[19] (3), Impilahti (8), and Salmi (4).

The interviews were recorded in 2012–2013, mostly at the informants' homes and, in some cases, other family members were present during the interview. It should also be noted that two sisters from Salmi were interviewed together, which is why the number of informants is higher than that of the interviews. The language of the interview was Finnish in the sense that the interviewer spoke Finnish and most of the informants answered in Finnish. There was, however, one interviewee who only spoke Karelian during the interview. The interviews contained a discussion of the roots of the informant, experiences, and memories of the evacuation (with the oldest informants), and the present situation of Karelian language. The imitation task was conducted during the first half of the interview, and it was conducted by asking the interviewee to remember how their parents or grandparents had spoken. Thus, the informants imitated a language variety they had heard from their closest relatives. After the imitation task, a recognition task followed: a sample was plyed from The Corpus of Border Karelia recorded in 1970s, and the informant was requested to pick out words or features typical for Border Karelian dialects.

By using the imitation task described above the aim was to shed light on the linguistic memories of a childhood variety. The research questions were the following:

1. To what degree is Karelian produced? How long are the imitations that the informants are able to produce?
2. How detailed and authentic is the imitated Karelian? What kinds of linguistic features are mastered in a language that is not actively used?
3. On the methodological level, how is the imitation task applicable to research on a forgotten language or variety?

The first question will be dealt with in Section 4 where the interviewees are divided into several categories according to the imitated sequences. The second one will be treated in Sections 5 and 6 where the phonetic-phonological and grammatical accuracy of the imitations is analysed. Finally, the third question will be addressed in Section 7 together with the findings of the previous sections.

---

19 These interviewees had one parent from Suistamo and the other from Suojärvi.

4 The interviewees as imitators of Border Karelian dialects

The informants can be classified into five groups on the basis of their imitated performances, ranging from interviewees who did not produce any imitations to those who used Karelian or a Karelian-like variety in longer sequences or, in one case, throughout the whole interview. Between these two extremes, there were interviewees who imitated single words forms and longer phrases. Table 1 presents the imitator types and the number of informants who fall into each category. Most of the informants belong to the middle categories and the most common way to imitate is to produce phrases or short sentences. In the following subsections, the imitations and the metalinguistic descriptions about Karelian given by the interviewees will be analysed. The data excerpts have been transcribed by using a rough version of the Uralic Phonetic Alphabet notational system. The informants are referred to by a code that contains the municipality where the speaker or his/her parents or grandparents come from and the informant's year of birth.

Table 1. The types of imitations.

Type of imitations	N
No imitations	4
Single words imitated	6
Phrases or short sentences imitated	13
Long sequences imitated	8
Whole interview in Karelian	1
Total	32

4.1 Interviews with no imitations

Imitating a foreign variety in test conditions has proved to be a difficult task for non-linguists even though the manner or style of speaking of other people is often mimicked in casual everyday situations. Previous folk linguistic studies have shown that even producing linguistic features or giving examples from one's own regional dialect may be an insuperable task (see, e.g., Bolfek Radovani 2000, 62; Palander 2011, 167–168). In comparison with these observations, it is not surprising that in the present data there are four interviews where no imitations occurred. These interviewees were born in the 1930s–1950s and regionally represent the different municipalities of Border Karelia (Ilomantsi, Impilahti, Suojärvi, and Suistamo/Suojärvi). However, each of these informants was able to describe the linguistic features of Karelian or the whole variety on a general level. It is typical of the metalanguage used by non-linguists that because they do not use exact linguistic terminology, they may refer, by using the same colloquial term, to different phenomena or use several terms that reflect a single phenomenon (e.g., Preston 1998, 82–83; Mielikäinen and Palander 2014, 112–150).

One of the informants (Suojärvi 1954) mentioned *soinnilliset äänteet* 'voiced sounds' when describing the Karelian language, meaning most probably the voiced stops *b*, *d*, and *g*. These phonemes are non-existent in the Eastern Finnish dialects but form a characteristic feature of Karelian where their occurrence is a result of long-term Russian influence. The voiced stops are apparently also referred to by those descriptions according to which Karelian is *pehmosta* 'soft' (Ilomantsi 1938) or has a *pehmeämpi nuotti* 'softer tune or note' (Suojärvi 1954) (cf., Nupponen 2005, 169). Metalinguistically, the latter characterisations represent the description of the general impression of language or, in folk linguistic terms, *global* description, whereas the former is a description of *details*, i.e., single linguistic features (for the terms, see Preston 1996; 1998, 78–82). In the metalanguage used by Finnish non-linguists studied extensively by Mielikäinen and Palander (2014), the term *nuotti* 'note, tune' usually refers to intonation, but the term is also used more vaguely in expressing the general impression of speech.

The informants who did not produce any imitations (Suojärvi 1954, Suistamo/Suojärvi 1934) mentioned the Russian influence of "Russian words" when they described the differences between the Karelian language and Eastern Finnish dialects. Similar folk linguistic observations have been reported in other studies concerning Karelian evacuees (e.g., Nupponen 2005, 162, 192). Furthermore, it was pointed out that their older Karelian-speaking relatives had used different "words" for various tools used in agriculture, compared to the vocabulary of the Finnish dialects. The lay term *word* needs be interpreted with caution because in the Finnish non-linguists' metalanguage, the term "word" has larger referential scope than in linguistics, and the lay term "dialectal word" may refer to word forms that are not different lexemes but contain phonological or morphological features of areal dialects (Mielikäinen and Palander 2014, 131–132). In the case of speakers with Border Karelian roots, however, it is possible and even probable that these informants refer to actual foreign lexemes (e.g., Russian loan words that do not exist in Finnish). As the next section shows, the different vocabulary is one of the characteristics of Border Karelian and most of the informants of the present study were able to recall and reproduce these kinds of lexical items.

These general descriptions provided by the four informants (as well as the informants who will be dealt with in the next subsections) are in alignment with the actual features of Border Karelian dialects, and they, thus, show that these interviewees have some kind of conception of the way their relatives have spoken. They may not be able to describe the details, but they seem to be very aware of the difference between Karelian and Eastern Finnish dialects. When the views of Finns with roots in Border Karelia are compared with other Finns, it becomes evident that the Finnish-Karelians have a better conception of the existence of Karelian as a separate language different from Finnish dialects (Palander 2015).

4.2 Single words imitated

There were altogether six informants (Impilahti 1935a, Impilahti 1935b, Impilahti 1940, Impilahti 1946, Suistamo 1938, and Suistamo/Suojärvi 1936) who, when asked to speak as their parents or grandparents had spoken, could remember and produce single words but not longer sequences. Typically, they remembered Karelian lexemes that do not have a counterpart in present-day Eastern Finnish dialects, and, often, these words had originally been borrowed from the Russian language. The number of words produced by these informants varied from two to seven, and, thus, the imitation task proved to be very difficult for these speakers as well. It should be noted that the informants who belong to the next two groups (rememberers of phrases of longer segments) also listed several words in addition to longer stretches, but these words are not described in this section.

The words produced by these informants were mainly ordinary everyday words needed in agricultural contexts. Some of these referred to household activities (e.g., *mäčentää* 'to squash', *karzina* 'cellar', *riehtilä* 'frying pan' and *kartohka* 'potato'), others referred to different aspects of everyday life (*čihkattii* '[we] giggled', *kuplu* 'float' [< Kar. *kublu*], *näpläkkä* 'slippery' [< Kar. *ńäbläkkä*], *lotsku* 'hit, blow' [< Kar. *ločku*], *nareko* 'for a laugh', *puoskat* 'children', *läkkä* 'let's go'). Some informants were able to imitate the Karelian phonology and produce words containing non-Finnish phonemes, but often the Karelian words were pronounced in a Finnish-like form (for details, see Section 5).

In addition to these real Karelian lexemes, the informants mentioned "words" that do not actually represent distinct lexemes but contain phonological features that make them different from their Finnish counterparts. An example of this is the 2SG imperative form *kačo* 'look' (cf., *kato* or *kaho* in the eastern *Savo* dialect or *katso* in Standard Finnish). Interestingly, the informants also described the personal pronouns *mie* 'I' and *sie* 'you' as Karelian words even though the same pronouns are widely used in Eastern Finnish dialects. It is typical of Finnish non-linguists that, when describing Finnish dialects, they pay special attention to 1SG and 2SG pronouns. These pronouns are the most common and sometimes the only feature with which they distinguish dialects (Mielikäinen and Palander 2014, 185–195).

Furthermore, three informants (Impilahti 1935a, Impilahti 1935b, and Impilahti 1940) recalled the word *hospoti* used in Orthodox services, and some of them produced it in a longer form *haspodi pamiloi* ~ *hospoti pomiluinas*. This word originates from the Church Slavonic phrase *Господи помилуй* 'God have mercy' or *Господи помилуй нас* 'God have mercy on us'. The exact, original meaning of the expression has been fading and the informants did not mention it but said that their Karelian relatives had used the word as some kind of lament without a religious connotation. The phonological variation in these imitations is partly connected to the difference in the pronunciation of Church Slavonic [pomiluj] and Russian [pamiluj], partly to the fuzzy meaning and the foreignness of the expression.[20]

The single words that were imitated usually represented frequently occurring everyday vocabulary that differs from Standard Finnish and also from Finnish dialects. In the speech of some informants, the phonological

---

20 We are grateful to Professor Lea Siilin for explaining the background of the phrase.

shape of these words was Finnish-like, indicating that Finnish was the dominant language. Most of these informants could only remember a few words in the interview situation, and, often, they could not explain the exact meaning of the words (e.g., *čihkattii, nareko, hospoti pomiluinas*).

4.3 PHRASES OR SHORT CLAUSES IMITATED

Among the informants, the most usual way to imitate Karelian was to produce short clauses or phrases that had been frequently used by their family members. Imitations of this kind were given in thirteen interviews, and this group involves both older and younger interviewees, for example, not only the youngest one (Suojärvi 1969) but also the second oldest one (Impilahti 1923). In addition to phrases described in this section, many of these informants also mentioned single words or word forms that differ from Finnish.

The stretches that were recalled and imitated were often greetings and welcoming or farewell phrases (see examples 1), originally addressed to guests by the informants' relatives. Laments, too, were remembered, especially *a voi voi* 'oh dear', which is a multi-purpose expression and suitable for many kinds of situations (see examples 2). These phrases include many linguistic features typical of Karelian, even though the pronunciation is sometimes Finnish-like, and, thus, they demonstrate that in conventionalised formulas of this kind, the linguistic characteristics may be well preserved in the informants' memory. On the other hand, the Finnish-like pronunciation and some other modifications (such as *kuimba* pro Kar. *kuibo*, cf., Fin. *kuinka*) demonstrate the influence from the speaker's strongest language, Finnish.

(1) *Terveh tulkoa* 'welcome' (Ilomantsi 1929)
Tulkoa käymäh 'come for a visit' (Impilahti 1923)
Hyväst jiäkeä 'farewell' (Impilahti 1923)
Tulkah syömäh 'come and eat' (Ilomantsi 1944)
Tulgoahai perttih 'come in' (Ilomantsi 1944)
Kuimba olet jaksanu? 'how have you been keeping?' (Suistamo 1924)
Anna ku selätän 'let me hug' (Suistamo 1924)
Tulehan ota tsaijua ystäväin 'come and have tea my friend' (Impilahti 1949).

(2) *A voi voi mihi poika sai* 'dear dear where did the boy go' (Suistamo 1950)
A voi voi kun kivistää 'oh, it hurts a lot' (Suistamo 1950).

Interestingly, the youngest informant (Suojärvi 1969) recalled several scoldings (see examples 3). Originally, she had heard these sentences in her childhood, and they had been directed at the informant and other children by their grandmother. These expressions have a different tone compared to the previously mentioned, very polite and hearty phrases. What is common to all the phrases in (1–3) is that the expressions are affective and their affective nature is probably one factor that explains why these utterances have remained in the informants' mind. Actual curse words were not mentioned in the interviews with one exception: Suistamo 1950 brought up the expression *perhanan silakka* 'damn' (literally 'damn herring').

(3) *Mäne matkuah siit* 'get away with you';
Mitäbä lembua oletta ruatanu 'what the hell have you done';
Äijä töhlöi olloot 'they have really made a mess'.

Additionally, these interviewees remembered short discourse phrases, such as *a vot* 'well, good' (< Russian *a вот*), *kačo vai kačo* 'look' or *muga vai muga* 'yes it is', which are frequent in Karelian conversations. In the interviews, the informants reported that they still use these kinds of phrases in their everyday (Finnish) conversations when talking to their relatives, and these discourse phrases, thus, represent a kind of inside group language. A similar discourse-pragmatic element is the turn-initial particle *a* 'well; but' that occurs in the sequences imitated by nine informants (see examples 4). The whole data considered, this particle was used by 15 informants and it seems to be one of the most recognised features of Karelian language among lay people.

(4) *A mitäbä lembuo mie pagisen* 'well, what the hell should I say?' (Suojärvi 1969)
A ylen vaigie ruadoam mut miulen 'well, it's very difficult to do, I think' (Suojärvi 1961)
A mis om muila 'well, where is the soap?' (Suistamo 1950)
A kembo neče on 'but who is that?' (Impilahti 1923)
A mie tulen siul luokse 'well, I'll come to you' (Ilomantsi 1929).

Most of the expressions described in this section are phrases that have been used repeatedly in interactions among Karelian speakers, and they often have a clearly affective nature. This kind of linguistic expression represents a special form of language. For example, it has been shown that in child language acquisition, this kind of figure of speech is learned early and produced even at the stage where the child's own productively formed sentences are very short and immature (Kauppinen 1998). In language contact situations and bilingualism, it is very typical that code-switching involves discourse phrases or other discourse pragmatic elements (see, e.g., Matras 2009, 133; Verschik 2014), and, in the case of so-called semi-speakers (see, e.g., Dorian 2010, 108, Thomason 2015, 54) who have not fully acquired the dying language, the individuals may be able to communicate fluently thanks to fluent use of fixed expressions in appropriate conversational context. It is also interesting to compare the present case of language "rememberers" with individuals who are in the process of losing their language. Aphasia patients have been shown to preserve conversational structure even though their ability to produce speech has been impaired (Ulatowska et al.1992). Further, when studying dementia patients, it has been noticed that conventionalised welcoming and discourse practices are preserved relatively well even in the stage where communicating is difficult and language seems to have been forgotten (Obler and Gjerlow 1999, 100–103). Thus, it is probably not a coincidence that the discourse pragmatic elements are those that are best remembered in the present study.

4.4 Long sequences imitated

In this study, longer imitation sequences have been classified as those instances where the informant spontaneously switches from Finnish to Karelian, e.g., when (s)he is playing the role of a Karelian-speaking relative. These cases resemble code-switching, defined (for present purposes) as alternating the language used by a single person during the same conversation. Not all these Karelian stretches are imitations of other speakers, but, in some cases, the speaker has an active command of Karelian. Code-switches occurred in eight interviews, and, in four of them, the informants' roots were in the Ilomantsi municipality where the Karelian language seems to have been best preserved. This is probably connected with the fact that in the 1930s, Karelian speakers were still reported in several villages in Ilomantsi, which is also on the western side of the present state border (Turunen 1982, 69). The four interviewees mentioned above belong to the same, large Karelian family, but they are not closely related to each other. Other producers of longer sequences were from Salmi and Suistamo. Most of the informants of this group are pensioners, but two were born in the 1950s.

The following example is presented as an illustration of longer imitation (5) that consists of an improvised conversation where two sisters, A (Salmi 1933) and B (Salmi 1938), spontaneously decide to play the roles of their mother and grandmother; the interviewer (marked with I) has one turn in this conversation. The role-play was suggested by the interviewer at the end of the interview in which the two sisters participated together. In (5), the Karelian sequences are marked with italics and the Finnish ones are underlined. In the dialogue, the informants use Finnish as a metalanguage, i.e., for planning the situation or the next lines or indicating a self-repair after having produced a Finnish word form instead of Karelian. The conversation ended with B switching into Finnish in order to show that she wanted to end the Karelian dialogue.

(5) A: *Noh... ole sinä mamma.*
 'Well... you be the mother'.
 B: *Ahah.*
 'Okay'.
 A: *Ole sinä mamma nim minä olen... baba.*
 'You be the mother and I'll be... the grandmother'.
 I: <u>Hyvä.</u>
 'Good'.
 A: <u>Ja tuota kuvitellaampa tilanne.</u> <u>Että</u> *baba on tullut... käymäh... käymäh. Olen tullut käymäh ja...* <u>ja tuota... sitten... sinä</u>
 '<u>And er let's imagine a</u> situation. <u>So that</u> the grandmother has come... for a visit... for a visit. I have come for a visit <u>and... and er... then... you</u>'
 B: *No... kuiba nygöi piäsit tulemaa?*
 'Well... how did you get to come here now'?

A: *A... poigu toi. Hevosel... semmosta vauhtii kuule jotta... ei ku lumitierat vaa lens...* ei ku nyt, *lumitierat lendeli pitkin, tietä, ja tultih semmostu vauhtii jotta oli kova kyyti.*
'Well... the boy brought me. With a horse... so fast do you hear that... it sent the snow flying... no but, the snow flew along, the way, and we came so fast that we had a rough ride'.

B: *No... kunnebo Niilo jäi?*
'Well... where did you leave Niilo'?

A: *Tuloo... panoo hevosen kiini vai tuone... navetan eteh ni... sit tuloo tänne.*
'He will come... he'll just tie the horse there... in front of the cowshed... he will come here then'.

B: *Kače panen... hellah tulen da koufin tulemah.*
'Look, I'll kindle... the fire in the range and brew some coffee'.

A: *Pane vai koufi tulemah.* Pian... *raviese se siel tuloo.*
'You brew the coffee. Soon... quickly he'll come'.

B: *A nygöi lähen heti.*
'Well, I'm going straight away'.

A: *Kuimbo sinä... muka raviese läht?*
'How do you mean... you're going so soon'?

B: Ei... eikös mull oo semmone tyyli?
'Well... isn't that my style'?

A: Jotaki... *tagi pakoo lähet nyt.*
'Something... I think you are running away from something now'.

The conversation includes a set of phrase-like segments, probably memorised in the same way as the phrases discussed in the previous section, but the sisters also produced other kinds of turns that represent spontaneous speech. The performed dialogue clearly represents Olonets Karelian, spoken in Salmi where the two sisters were born. Karelianness is expressed with several Karelian words: *mamma* 'mother', *baba* 'grandmother', *kunne* 'where', *koufi* 'coffee', *muka* 'so' (in Karelian *muga*), *raviese* 'soon' (usually in the form *ravieh*, see KKS s.v. *ravie*), *tagi* 'probably'. However, some words are from Finnish, e.g., *navetta* 'cowshed' (in Karelian *liävä*) and *hevonen* 'horse' (in Karelian *heboińe*). Phonologically, the sample exhibits some distinctive features of Olonets Karelian, e.g., the word-final *u* in forms that end with *a* in Finnish and in Karelian Proper (*poigu* 'boy', cf., Fin. *poika*; *semmostu* 'such', cf., Fin. *semmosta*). Preservation of word-internal voiced stops (*poigu* 'boy', *lendeli* 'flew') makes the sisters' speech sound like Karelian.

With respect to morphophonological or phonological phenomena, the sample shows influence from Eastern Finnish dialects. The Finnish clitic *pa* has a Karelian equivalent, *bo*, and, in the sample, A uses the Karelian variant (*kunnebo* 'where', *kuimbo* 'how'), but, in the speech of B, the particle has a Finnish-like vowel (*kuiba* 'how'). The 3SG present tense forms produced by A end in a long vowel (*tuloo* '[he] comes', *panoo* '[he] puts') instead of the Karelian diphthong (Kar. *tulou*, *panou*). In the cases of consonant gradation (i.e., a set of consonant mutations typical of the Finnic languages) of the sequence *ht*, the weak grade follows the eastern Finnish pattern in the speech of both A and B: *lähen* 'I will go', *lähet* 'you will go' (in Olonets Karelian *lähten, lähtet*). In the illative forms, the Karelian suffix variant is *h* and its Finnish counterpart is *V(n)* (where *V* stands for lengthening the final vowel of the stem). In the speech of A and B, there is variation between Karelian and Finnish suffixes: *käymäh* 'for a visit', *eteh* 'in front of', *hellah* 'in the range', but *pakoo* '(run, get) away' (in Karelian *pagoh*).

Among the informants, there are a few speakers who switched from Finnish to Karelian without any prompting. One of these is Salmi 1953, whose speech is illustrated by example 6, in which he first uses Finnish but quickly switches to Karelian. He is telling a story about his grandfather, and, thus, the topic may be a factor that triggered codeswitching.

(6) Hän [isoisä] tuota, tykkäsi kirkos käyvä *häi, nägi että, valkie valo, valo sielä koivikos, näki semmosen ilmestyksen ni hän, koki sinnep pitää kirikkö luadie ja häi sitten teki tsasounan, rakendi siihen koivikon laitah sinne omal tilal ja. Ja, ja tuota, minäkin sitten, prihaččunnu kävin siellä, kirikös ja, kellojaki sai kokeilla soittaas sielä, Rautalammilla. Hän sinnek Koipiniemeh teki ku ei se, sinnes saatih oma kirikkö vasta, sinnek keskustah saatih, kuuskymmen yksi vasta valmistui sinne, sinnek kirikkö ja, sinne Koipiniemeh omah kyläh teki, teki tsasounan ja, häi sit sanoi, sanoi, kyläläsil "tulkoa tänne meil̮ on, tiäl̮ on, tiäl̮ oŋ kirikkö valmis". Ja, eiko nim muistanuh luboa kysyä nimih, rakennuslup(oa).*

'Well, he [the grandfather] liked to go to church. He saw that a white light [was] there in the birch grove, he saw such a vision so he felt that a church had to be built there and he built an Orthodox church there at the edge of the birch grove on his own farm. And, and well, also I went to the church as a boy and I was allowed to try to ring the bells there, in Rautalampi. He built there in Koipiniemi because they got their own church ready in the centre only in 1961. He built the Orthodox church there in Koipiniemi in his own village and then he said to the village people: "Come here, we have a church ready here". And he did not remember to ask any planning permission'.

The excerpt is basically Karelian, but it exhibits much influence from (Standard) Finnish, resulting in the varying use of Karelian and Finnish forms. For example, the word-internal stops are sometimes voiced as in Karelian (*luadie* 'to make'), but, often, they are pronounced by this speaker as voiceless, as in Finnish (*saatih* pro *soadih* '(they) got'). Similarly, the diphthongisation of long *a* and *ä* vowels, a feature common to both Karelian and Eastern Finnish dialects, occurs irregularly, and the informant produces forms with a long vowel, such as *saatih* (pro *soadih* 'they got'). The Karelian affricate *č* is sometimes pronounced correctly (*prihaččunnu* 'as a boy'), sometimes as a Finnish-like consonant cluster *ts* (*tsasounan* 'Orthodox church'). Phonetically, a striking non-Karelian feature is the lack of palatalisation in dental consonants (*nimih* pro *ńimih* 'any', *tilal* pro *t´ilal* 'on the farm'). The informant did, however, produce palatalised consonants during the interview when he listed forms that differ from Finnish, e.g., *tel'l'iämäh* 'to put', *älkää tel'l'ätkö* 'don't put'). Variation occurred also in lexicon, and the speaker used both Karelian and Finnish words: Kar. *luadie* 'to make' ~ Fin. *teki* 'he made'; Kr. *kirikös* ~ Fin. *kirkos* 'in the church'.

The same informant, Salmi 1953, frequently used short switches to Karelian that often comprised a few words or short sentences as in (7) (Karelian elements are marked with italics). One typical place for code-switching is those parts of conversation that are, for some reason, problematic for the speaker: for example, Finnish Romani people may switch from Romani to Finnish when speaking about things that are considered taboo in the Romani culture (Granqvist 2007, 217–218). In (7) the problematicity may be caused by the sensitive nature of the topic, and the code-switch may be an attempt to handle the situation. The switch seems to be non-intentional as the speaker then continues by commenting on the Karelian word *abuväline* 'aid' he had just used and points out the Karelian phoneme *b*, stating that he has "inherited" Karelian words from his father.

(7) Hän o invalidi kum pyörätuolilla ajaa. *Ei omil jalloil kule. Kulen nin tarviččee abu-, abuvälinee.* Niin tässähäm minäki sanoin "*abu-, abuvälineen*" tai, bee, beekirjain tulee, kielessä joskus nin tuota, kyllä sitä joskus käyttää tätä niin kun näitä, näitä, sitä, isän, isältä *perittyö,* sanoja.

'She is an invalid and drives a wheelchair. *She does not walk on her own feet, so she needs an aid.* So, I just said "abu-, abuvälineen ['an aid']" or b, the letter b comes in the language sometimes, so you sometimes use this, these words you have *inherited* from your father'.

The informants who were able to speak long sequences in Karelian also reported that they actually use Karelian with their relatives from time to time. Some of them have aimed at improving their language skills by taking courses in Karelian in Finland and in Russian Karelia. Many of them are active members of Karelian associations, and some have genealogy as a hobby and have visited the Border Karelian region (now situated in Russia) several times. Salmi 1953, quoted above, is an active Karelian enthusiast and even teaches Karelian in private (though he is not a professional language expert) and has created websites in Karelian. He reads Karelian books and newspapers and writes literary texts in Karelian. At the end of the interview, he read one of his texts aloud, and, when doing this, his pronunciation and grammar followed Olonets Karelian more accurately than in the sequences produced spontaneously. All in all, the informants that belong to this group clearly have vivid memories of the language use of their relatives, and some of them can be characterised as heritage speakers of Karelian, though their competence in Karelian is not as full as in the Finnish language. It is possible that at least some of these informants have learned to speak Karelian in their early childhood, but their Karelian has suffered from attrition at a later age when opportunities to use Karelian became scarce. Later, some of these interviewees began relearning their heritage language, and, in this language-learning process, Finnish, as the stronger language, has caused crosslinguistic influence.

4.5 THE WHOLE INTERVIEW IN KARELIAN

One of the informants spoke Karelian throughout the whole interview even though the interviewer posed her questions in Finnish. The informant was a male who was born in 1934 in Suistamo. His Karelian was very fluent and he spoke without the notable pauses or hesitations that were typical for most of the informants when they tried to speak Karelian. The interview lasted longer than an hour, and the interviewee did not have any difficulties in using Karelian the whole time. It seems that he had acquired Karelian in his childhood and has been maintaining his skills in Karelian so that he is now a bilingual Finnish-Karelian. Consequently, his linguistic memories of his relatives' languages are not imitations in the sense defined in this article: he did not imitate a variety that is somehow unfamiliar to him but rather used one of the languages of his linguistic repertoire. It was decided, however, to include his interview in the data because it offers valuable reference data to which the imitations of less fluent informants can be compared.

The informant's Karelian is illustrated here by example (8) where he tells about the situation when his family (together with other inhabitants of Border Karelia) were evacuated during the war and forced to leave their home. Prosodically and phonetically, the sample represents Karelian but contains Finnish traits in phonology, morphology, and lexicon. Influence from Eastern Finnish dialects can be seen for example in the vowel sequences *ia* and *iä* in the non-initial syllables: these are not always diphthongised as in Karelian but are represented as monophthongs (*miehii* 'men', cf., Kar. *miehie*). In the numeral '17th' there is variation between the Karelian affricate *čč* (*seiččemestoista*) and dialectal Finnish *tt* (*seittemästoista*). The passive forms, used by this speaker, were often morphologically Finnish-like, i.e., they did not contain the word-final phoneme *h*: *sanottii* '(they) said' (cf., Kar. *sanottih*), *luajittii* '(they) made' (cf., Kar. *luajittih*). Similarly, word-final *h* is missing in the illative forms in accordance with Finnish: *laitaan* 'to the edge' (cf., Ka. *laidah*), *pihaa* 'home' (cf., Kar. *pihah*). In this speaker's vocabulary, the verb *meinata* 'to be going to' has been borrowed from Finnish, and its Karelian counterpart would be *ainehtie*, *aiveltoa*, *konehtie*, etc. The word for 'December', *joulukuu*, is also from Finnish as in Karelian, the old name of this month is *raštavankuu*.

(8) *Hyvim muistan sen. Silloi. Meilhän ol' Leppäsyrjän kyläl laijas ol'i tämä, linnotustyöt mänös nim meilgi, ol'i tuba täys vaikka ol' pieni ni, niitä lat't'iel makai niitä linnotusmiehii silloj jo elokuuj jälkee. Ja ihan koko syksyn ne ol' Savosta ne mušikat. Aina sanottii Tuppuraista ja Tappuraista kun ne oli Liimataista ja semmosii sukuńimii ne ol' savolaisii. Linnotettii siihe kylän, laitaan tankkiesteitä luajittii ja muita ja. Sitten, elokuu ei kun joulukuu seiččemestoista päivä siin‿ ol' jo, sitä ennen ku se Koirinojal, sanon suoraa ryssä tul'i ni, ja niidä partioi tul'i nii ja yhen kerran ni, mamma jo, leibeä paisto ni meinai ämpärii panna‿ttei kergie paistoa pagoo pitää lähtie mut sit tul'igi että, ne partiot on suatu,*

pois, päiviltä että, viel̮ olimmo sitte ka-, kaks viikkoo seittemästoista päivä joulukuuta ni, iltasi ižä, tul'i, sieltä, linnotusporukoiss̮ ol'i, sielä ni, tuli, pihaa ja, sano että nyt, prihačut, nyt huo- yöl lähemmö. Tai jouvutta lähtemää että s- moinen o ukaasi tullu että.

'I remember it well. Then. We had fortifications underway on the edge of the village of Leppäsyrjä, so also we had the house although it was small, full of fortifiers. They were lying on the floor already after August. And the men from Savo were there all the autumn. They were always said to be Tuppurainen and Tappurainen because they were named like Liimatainen and such family names because they came from Savo. They were fortifying, making tank barriers and others on the edge of the village. Then, on the seventeenth of August, no, December, there was already, before that when – to tell the truth – the Russian came and the patrols came and once mother already baked bread and was going to put it into the bucket and she had no time to bake because she had to escape but then it happened that the patrols were eliminated and then we were for two weeks – on the seventeenth December in the evening father came from fortifying groups there, he came home and said that now, boys, we shall leave in the night. Or you must leave that such a *ukase* has come'.

Suistamo 1934 has a special interest in his roots, and, for years, he has been an enthusiastic recorder of Karelian culture. He has photographed, tape-recorded, and videoed Karelian events in Finnish and Russian Karelia. He does not read Karelian texts but listens to songs and says that he practices the language by speaking it alone at home. Like Salmi 1953 (see the previous section), Suistamo 1934 has been working in Karelian associations and has a close relationship with the present Border Karelia. It seems that he has preserved his heritage language despite living in a Finnish-speaking environment for most of his life. However, Finnish has probably been the dominant language in his daily life (and in the whole surrounding society) and has influenced his Karelian so that his speech shows a combination of Karelian and Finnish elements.

5 Imitated phonetic and phonological features

In this section, the phonetic or phonological Karelian features present in the imitations produced by the informants will be examined in detail. Throughout this section, it is important to keep in mind that some of these features were probably undergoing change in the speech of the persons the informants imitate, due to Finnish influence. The examination involves both short and long imitations, and a sample from the informant Suistamo 1934 (who spoke Karelian throughout the interview) is also included, which serves as a point of comparison to the imitations. Furthermore, a few words or phrases that were produced by the informants' close relatives who were present at the interview are included. All the most significant features that differentiate Karelian and Finnish are analysed. The findings are presented numerically in Tables 2 and 3, which show in how many interviews each feature occurs. The token frequencies of the features have not been calculated because the length of the imitations varies to a great extent. The statistical information should not be interpreted as an overall picture of the awareness of the features but as a rough general view of what Karelian phenomena have been best retained. In the next two subsections, the consonant features or phenomena will be presented first followed by features related to vowels.

5.1 Consonant features

The Karelian consonant features that occur in the imitations are presented in Table 2. The features are arranged in the table in the following order: First, there are Karelian phonemes that are entirely missing in the Finnish dialect phoneme system, and, second, there are a few phonemes and features that also occur in Finnish but which have a different distribution in Karelian. One phenomenon (word-boundary gemination) is a feature that is common in Finnish but is missing in Karelian. Finally, there is a set of morphophonological phenomena that differentiate Karelian from Finnish dialects. The numbers in the table indicate the number of informants whose imitations contain the feature in question and in this section, the features starting with the most common ones will be described, and then the more rarely occurring ones will be presented.

Table 2. Karelian consonant features in the imitations.

Features	N
Karelian phonemes	
voiced stops (*b*, *d*, *g*)	20
č (*iče*)	16
š (*tuošša*)	8
z (*toizel*)	5
f (*koufi*)	3
Phonemes with distribution different from Finnish	
word-final *h* (*käytih*)	14
palatalisation (*ol′*, *ńi*)	11
Lack of word-boundary gemination	17
Morphophonological phenomena	
gradation *st* : *ss* (*muissa*)	3
gradation *lk* : *ll*, *rk* : *rr* (*kullen, sarran*)	2
lack of gradation *ht* (*yhtes*)	1

The most common feature with which these speakers imitate Karelian are the voiced stops *b*, *d*, and *g*, which occur in imitations by 20 informants (see Table 2). Some interviewees name these phonemes "voiced consonants", but the examples given by them (e.g., *vaigie ruadoa* 'difficult to do', *libo* 'or') reveal that what they mean are the voiced stops, not voiced sibilants *z* or *ž*.

The phonological system of the Finnish dialects does not contain any voiced stops but only voiceless ones (*p*, *t*, *k*), and many informants describe the Finnish dialects as "hard" whereas Karelian is "soft". However, even though the existence of voiced stops is recognised by the informants, not all of them pronounce these consonants as voiced. In particular, those interviewees who produced only single words or word forms often replaced them with voiceless stops, e.g., *nyköi* (< *nygöi*) 'now', *kuplu* (< *kublu*) 'float', ***p**rihatsu* (< *brihaččų*) 'young man', and *hospoti* (< *hospod´i*) 'the Lord'. On the other hand, there are also a few instances of the hypercorrect use of voiced stops in cases where the Karelian stop is actually voiceless (e.g., ***b**irttih* (< *pert´t´ih*) 'to the house').

Word-boundary gemination (a phenomenon where the word-initial consonant is pronounced as a geminate when following certain inflectional endings) is characteristic to most Finnish dialects, including the dialects of North Karelia. Karelian, on the contrary, does not have this phenomenon at all. Even though word-boundary gemination is not a very conscious feature for non-linguists, the lack of it is clearly noticeable, and about the half of the informants (17 interviewees) imitate Karelian in a way in which gemination is lacking either altogether or at least occasionally: *a minne mänöyt* (pro *a minnem mänöyt*) 'well, where do they go', *elä hötvötä joutavoa* (pro *elä hötvötäj joutavoa*) 'don't waffle on'. In Finnish, using this gemination is an automatic process, and, for this reason, those informants who produced longer sequences in Karelian also from time to time pronounced forms with gemination (e.g., *miks et rubie**p** puhumah* 'why don't you begin to talk'). Interestingly, for some informants, the lack of word-boundary gemination seems to be a subconscious phenomenon probably acquired from their Karelian-speaking parents, and it is characteristic to their Finnish, too.

Another relatively frequently occurring consonant feature is the affricate *č*, which was found in the imitations by 16 informants. In the imitations, it usually occurs in the inflectional forms of the verb *kaččuo* 'look', such as *kačo, kačoha, kaččomah*. There are, however, a few other words in which the affricate was imitated, e.g., *neče* 'that', *päčil* 'on the stove', *kičakka* 'tight', *seiččemenitoist* 'seventeen', and *pilikkoloičimma* 'we chopped'. As the phoneme does not belong to Eastern Finnish dialects, many informants have replaced it with the Finnish-like consonant cluster *ts* (and often the word form then contains other Finnish-like features as well): *ka**ts**omaa* (< *kaččomah*) 'to look', *jäi**ts**ä* (< *jäiččä*) 'egg', *tarvi**ts**ee* (< *tarviččou*) 'needs', *lo**ts**ku* (< *ločku*) 'hit', *priha**ts**u* (< *brihaččų*) 'young man', and ***ts**aijul* (< *čuajul*) '(having) tea'. Again, there were also some cases of reverse phenomenon where the informant pronounced the affricate instead of the consonant *s*: *čintsoi* (< *senćoi*) 'hall', *čulččina* (< *sulččina*) 'Karelian pastry'.

A consonant feature very characteristic to Karelian but non-existent in Finnish is the occurrence of word-final *h* in certain inflectional morphemes; in Finnish, these morphemes end in the sequence *V(n)* (where V refers to the lengthening of the preceding vowel). This is clearly a consciously recognised Karelian feature among the non-linguists, and it was used in imitations by 14 informants. In the imitations, it occurs in the illative forms of nouns, e.g., *viäräh paikkah* 'to a wrong place', *perttih* ~ *pirttih* 'to the house', *saunah* 'to the sauna', *hellah* 'to the range', *stolah* 'to the table', but there are also illative forms grammaticalised as adverbs, e.g., *eteh* 'to the front of', *mukah* 'with', and *šekah* 'among'. In verb inflection, *h* occurs in 3rd infinitive forms, e.g., *pagisemah* 'to talk', *käymäh* 'to visit', *tulemah* 'to come', *kuolemah* 'to die', and in passive forms that are also used as 3PL forms in Karelian; e.g., *sanotah* 'is said' or '(they) say'. In addition to the previous forms, word-final *h* is typical in the past participles of Olonets Karelian, and these forms were imitated in a few cases: *tulluh* 'come', *muistanuh* 'remembered'. Furthermore, there is the greeting *terveh*, which was mentioned by only one informant, in the phrase *terveh tulkoa* even though this greeting is commonly used nowadays when Karelians meet each other. Word-final **h** is a well-known Karelian feature among the informants, and some of them use it hyperdialectally in word forms that do not contain *h* in Karelian, such as *čulččinah čupukkoah* (pro Kar. *sulččinoa čupukkoa*) 'Karelian pastry', *tulkah syömäh* (pro Kar. *tulgoa syömäh*) 'come and eat', and *olokah* (pro Kar. *olgoa*) 'be'.

Palatalisation of dental consonants occurred in the imitations of 11 informants. The phenomenon originally results from Russian influence and is characteristic to Eastern Finnic languages (Karelian, Ludian, and Veps) but also to the old Eastern Finnish dialects. There are, however, differences in the distribution of palatalisation: in Finnish dialects, dentals have only been palatalised before the phonemes *i* or *j* (and even though the phoneme *i* has often disappeared, the palatalisation of the preceding consonant has been maintained), but, in Karelian, palatalisation also occurs before any front vowels and sometimes even before a back vowel. In the imitations, the palatalisation usually follows the distribution of Finnish dialects, and it mostly occurs in the consonants *l*, *n* and *t*: *pol'issit arvel'* 'the police thought', *kävel'* '(s)he walked', *pal'joko mie ol'in* 'how old was I', *pokońńiekka* 'departed', *en ńi malda* 'I cannot', *ei ole ńimidä tapahtunut* 'nothing has happened', *t'iet'oin isä* 'grandfather's father', *ńälgävuojet* 'years of hunger', *rupes ńukuttamah* 'I began to be tired'. Sometimes palatalisation also occurs in new words, such as *ńäppäimistös* 'on the keyboard'. Palatalisation is a feature that is becoming less and less frequent in Finnish dialects, which may partly explain why it is imitated only by one third of the informants.

In the imitations, there are also some more rarely used Karelian consonant features, such as the sibilants *š* (eight informants) and *z* (five informants). Sibilant *š* is not only used in Russian loan words, such as *mušikku* 'man', *roša* 'cheek (of pike-perch)', *lešankku* 'fire place', *šarffu* 'scarf', but also in inherently Finnic words, e.g., *naimišiš* 'married' and *šekah* 'among'. In the dialects of Border Karelia *š* has apparently not been as regularly used as in White Sea Karelian, and this may be one reason for the fact that it is not imitated by many informants. It is also possible that the informants do not recognise the difference between *š* and Finnish *s* as the Finnish phoneme *s* may have many kinds of phonetic realisations. By contrast, it has been shown that the White Sea Karelians consider *š* as a feature typical to their own language (see Kunnas in this volume). Imitating the Karelian voiced *z* seems to require more phonetic skills, and most of the informants who use this phoneme have some kind of linguistic knowledge of Karelian acquired through their Karelian-related hobbies.

The other imitated consonant features are only occasional. Among them is the phoneme *f* in the loan words *koufi* 'coffee' and *šarffu* 'scarf' and a few cases where the imitations contain a word form that follows the Karelian morphophonological patterns. Three informants use the gradation of the cluster *st* (i.e., alternation between *st* and *ss*), e.g., [*ostoa* 'to buy':] *ossan* 'I buy', [*varustoa* 'to outfit' :] *varussin* 'I outfitted'. In Olonets Karelian, the clusters *lk* and *rk* are also susceptive to gradation, which is shown in two forms in the imitation data (*omil jalloil* 'with her own feet, cf., *jalka* 'foot'; *Sarras* 'in *Sarka* [a name]'). An opposite case is the cluster *ht*, which takes part in consonant gradation in Finnish but not in Olonets Karelian, and one informant (Salmi 1953) uses word forms with non-alternating *ht* (*lähtemmö* 'we will go').

5.2 Vowel features

The Karelian vowel features that occur in the imitation data are presented in Table 3 below, arranged according to the type of the phenomenon, and the numbers refer to the interviews in which the feature was imitated. In contrast to the consonant system, the Karelian vowel system does not contain phonemes different from Finnish, but the discrepancies are caused by differences in the realisation or the linguistic distribution of dialectal sound changes.

Table 3. Karelian vowel features in imitations.

Features	N
Diphthongisation	
diphthongisation of AA in 1st syllable (*hoaššettih, piässä*)	10
diphthongisation of AA in non-initial syllables (*poikoa, eneä*)	19
Apocope	
apocope of A (*tiäl*)	13
apocope of i (*olis*)	6
Changes in the vowel sequences	
non-initial *ie* < *eA* (*lähtie*)	6
non-initial *ie* < *iA* (*poikie*)	5
non-initial *UO* < *UA* (*istuo*)	3
non-initial *UO* < *OA* (*isuo*)	2
3SG person ending *u, y* (*pidäy*)	2
Nouns and particles ending in -*Oi* (*veroi*)	4
Word-final *U* (*piädy*)	2

The most frequently used Karelian vowel features, which occurred in the speech of 19 informants, were the diphthongised variants *oa* ~ *ua*, *eä* ~ *iä* in non-initial syllables, developed from long *a* and *ä* vowels, e.g., *karjaloa* 'Karelian', *matkuah* 'away', *jiäkeä* 'stay', *eläkiä* 'live'. In non-initial syllables, the diphthongised variants separate Karelian from Finnish, as in the eastern *Savo* dialects; the vowels *aa* and *ää* have, depending on the inflectional form in each case, either remained as long vowels (e.g., the illative case *matkaan*) or developed (through a diphthongised phase) into long *oo* and *öö* (e.g., the partitive case *karjaloo*) (see Kettunen 1940, Maps 179 and 182). A similar development of *AA* into diphthongs has happened in the first syllable: in the Finnish *Savo* dialects, the diphthongs *ua* and *iä* are used in most parts, and the variants *oa* and *eä* are used in a small area in the northern parts of the area (Kettunen 1940, Map 154). The Corpus of Border Karelia reveals that both sets of variants have been used by Border Karelian speakers in addition to the long vowels *aa* and *ää*, which follow the pattern of Olonets Karelian (see Bubrih et al. 1997, Maps 4–5; cf., Leskinen 1934, 103–145). Possibly this diverse realisation of diphthongisation is one reason for the fact that, in the imitations, only 10 informants used diphthongs in the first syllable. The ones who did, pronounced the diphthongs in a way typical to the Finnish *Savo* dialects: *rua*d*oa* 'to work', *vua*ssa 'beer', *hyväst jiäkeä* 'farewell', *piäsemmö* 'we will get'.

Apocope is a feature that is partly shared by Karelian and the *Savo* dialects and that partly differentiates the two. On the one hand, apocope of the vowels *a* and *ä* is a Karelian trait, and it occurs in the imitations of 13 informants, e.g., in the forms *mis* 'where' (in standard Finnish *missä*), *jot* 'that', *muilt* 'from the others', and *lat´t´iel* 'on the floor'. On the other hand, however, apocope of *i* is a frequent feature in the middle and southern parts of Finland's North Karelia, but it occurs in the imitations fairly rarely, only in the speech of 6 informants (e.g., *arvel´* '(he) thought', *pagisis* 'would talk', *veroiks* 'for the meal' ja *rupes* 'began'). It should be noted, though, that not all the imitations contain forms in which apocope is possible.

Another group of sound changes that differentiate Karelian from Eastern Finnish dialects are those that concern vowel sequences ending with *a* or *ä* in non-initial syllables (i.e., the combinations *ea*, *eä*, *ia*, *iä*, *ua*, *yä*, *oa*, and *öä*). In Karelian, these sequences have developed into diphthongs *ie*, *uo*, and *yö* whereas, in the Finnish *Savo* dialect, these sequences have become long vowels (e.g., *ee*, *ii*, *uu*, *yy*, *oo*, *öö*). The diphthongs are imitated infrequently (see Table 3) and most of the informants use, in addition to or instead of them, the monophthongs characteristic to Finnish dialects. The imitation data, thus, contains much variation of Karelian-like and Finnish-like forms: *vaigie* 'difficult', *valgie* 'white', *en ilkie lähtie* 'I don't dare to go', *monoloogie* 'monologue', *luadie* 'to do', *puhuo* 'to speak', *säilyö* 'to survive', *taluo* 'house', *lembuo* 'devil'; *vauhtii* 'speed', *savolaisii* 'Savo people', *housuu* 'trousers', *ripakeittoo* 'mushroom soup'. The Corpus of Border Karelia shows that this kind of variation between diphthongs and monophthongs is characteristic for the first generation of Karelian-speaking evacuees in Finland.

The rest of the features presented in Table 3 were used only by a few informants. One feature typical to Karelian but infrequent in the imitation data is the use of present tense 3SG personal forms ending in *u* or *y* (e.g., *pidäy* 'must' in Finnish, the 3SG forms are formed by lengthening the final vowel, e.g., *pitää*). Karelian-like 3SG forms are rare in the imitation data, and only two informants (Ilomantsi 1953 and Salmi 1953) use them: *häi lähtöy* 'he leaves', *kuka tulou* 'who comes'. Again, forms with a long *a* or *ä* (e.g., *pitää*) are found in The Corpus of Border Karelia together with forms ending with *y* (see Koivisto in this volume). Another Karelian phenomenon is the use of non-initial *oi* diphthongs in certain nouns and particles: *vero**i**ks* 'for the meal', *d´ied´**oi*** 'grandfather', *senčč**oi*** 'hall', *nyg**öi*** 'now', *rost**oi*** (< *prostoi*) 'bad, unskilled'. The final feature mentioned in the table is characteristic to Olonets Karelian (not Karelian Proper): in this variety, the word-final *a* and *ä* have been replaced with *u* or *y* in words with two or more syllables. This feature occurs in the imitations by two informants from Salmi (which belonged to the area of Olonets Karelian): *mel´l´iččäniekk**u*** 'miller', *sepp**y*** 'blacksmith', *semmost**u*** 'such', *piäd**y*** 'head'. In the Karelian of Salmi 1953, who often switched to Karelian during the interview, the use of word-final *u* and *y* was almost regular.

6. Imitated morphological and morpho-syntactic features

The previous section concentrated on the phonetic and phonological features that were present in both short and long imitations. In this section, the focus will shift from phonology to grammar and will examine some morphological and morpho-syntactic phenomena displayed in the imitated sequences. These grammatical features are noticeable only in longer imitation sequences, and they indicate that these informants master Karelian on a more profound level than those whose knowledge is restricted to single words and phonological characteristics. In what follows, the most commonly used morphological features will be presented along with some morpho-syntactic ones that occur in the imitation data.

One distinctively Karelian morphological feature, compared with the Finnish *Savo* dialects, is the 1PL personal ending *(m)ma, (m)mä* ~ *(m)mo, (m)mö* (e.g., *myö ole**mma*** 'we are', *myö oli**ma*** 'we were'). In Eastern Finnish dialects (and other colloquial varieties), this old personal ending has practically disappeared, and the verb is in the passive form (e.g., *myö ollaan* 'we are', *myö oltiin* 'we were'). The Karelian variant *(m)ma, (m)mä* has been characteristic to Karelian Proper and *mmo, mmö* to Olonets Karelian (Bubrih et al. 1997, Maps 140 and 144). The Karelian personal ending is present in seven interviews (see examples 9a-e below) and, in particular, the informants have imitated the variants ending with *o* or *ö*.

(9)   a.   *kalarruodoloi pilikkoloiči**mma*** 'we cut fish bones' (Ilomantsi 1953)
      b.   *malta**mmo** paista* 'we can talk' (Salmi 1930)
      c.   *pagise**mmo** toine toizel* 'we talk to each other' (Suistamo 1954)
      d.   *yöl lähe**mmö*** 'we'll leave in the night' (Suistamo 1934)
      e.   *nyt ku piäse**mmö** kot´ih keitä**mmö** put´in kahvit* 'when we now will go home we will make good coffee' (Salmi 1933)

Another morphological feature that differentiates Karelian from Finnish is the imperative marker that contains the geminate *kk* used in the 1PL and 2PL imperative forms of certain verbs (Pyöli 2011, 110–111; Zaikov 2013, 172–177). In the Finnish equivalents of these markers, there is a single *k*. The Karelian-like imperative forms were used by four imitators (see examples 10a-e):

(10) a. otta**kkoa** perunoa, kartohkoa mukah 'take potatoes with you' (Salmi 1933)
   b. lä**kkä** istummaan 'let's go to sit' (Impilahti 1946)
   c. kasva**kkua** ylöspäin 'grow up' (Ilomantsi 1931)
   d. ku että jaksane kantoa ku jättä**kkeä** siihe 'if you are not able to carry [the blanket], leave [it] there' (Suistamo 1934)
   e. kirjutta**kkoa**, kirjutta**kkoa** karjalasekse 'write, write in Karelian' (Suistamo 1934)

In Karelian dialects, the external locative cases (adessive, ablative, and allative) may be syncretic in the sense that a single case marker may correspond to several case functions. In Karelian Proper, adessive and allative cases have merged and resulted in the marker *lla, llä*, referred to as adessive-allative in Karelian grammar (Zaikov 2013, 96–98). Among the informants of the present study, those who use the adessive-allative are the ones who master Karelian better than the others, and these forms are found only in the speech of two informants (Ilomantsi 1931 and Suistamo 1934, see examples 11a-b). In Olonets Karelian, all the external case functions may be expressed with a single marker: usually *l*, rarely *la, lä* (Genetz 1884, 149–150; cf., Ahtia 1936, 44; Pyöli 2011, 45–46). In the imitation data, there are a few examples of this kind of syncretism as well (produced by Ilomantsi 1929, Ilomantsi 1939, Salmi 1933, and Suistamo 1934): in (12), the speaker first produces the ablative marker *lt* but then the ambiguous ending *l*, obviously in the ablative function, and, in (13), the marker *lä* has been used in the ablative function. Interestingly, both (12) and (13) are from speakers whose roots are in Ilomantsi, which is not in the traditional area of Olonets Karelian. On the basis of The Corpus of Border Karelia, however, it seems that adessive-ablative-allatives marked with *l* or *(l)la, (l)lä* have indeed been used in the Karelian variety spoken in Ilomantsi, and, thus, the imitations may well match the linguistic reality of the previous generation.

(11) a. *mi-tä   musika-**lla**   kuulu-u*
   what-PAR   man-ADE/ALL   be-PR.3SG
   'how are you, man' (Ilomantsi 1931)

   b. *män-i-mmö   Vesanno-**lla***
   go-PST-1PL   Vesanto-ADE/ALL
   'we went to Vesanto' (Suistamo 1934)

(12) *E-m   mie   mu-i-**lt**   kehto-o   osto-o*
   NEG-1SG   I   other-PL-ABL   feel.like-PR.3SG buy-INF1

   *siu-**l**   ossan.*
   you-ADE/ABL/ALL   buy-1SG

   'I don't feel like buying from others, I buy from you'. (Ilomantsi 1929)

(13) Sua   äkkiä   sie-**lä**   pois.
     come.IMP.2SG   quickly   there-ADE/ABL/ALL   away
     'Come at once away from there'. (Ilomantsi 1939)

Karelian personal inflection in verb forms differs from the Finnish one in 3PL, as in Karelian, the original 3PL forms have been replaced with the passive forms: *koululaiset leikitäh* 'the school children play', *pojat lähettih* 'the boys left' (Zaikov 2013, 146–171). In Finnish, the 3pl ending *vat, vät* is used: cf., Finnish *koululaiset leikkivät, pojat lähtivät*. Two of the informants used the passive together with plural subjects, as in examples (14) and (15), but it should be noted, however, that the passive forms in these examples (*ollaa* and *pagistii*) are morphologically Finnish-like as in Karelian, the corresponding passives would have the ending *h* (*ollah, pagistih*). The Corpus of Border Karelia reveals a great deal of variation in the use of the passive endings *h* and *V(n)* (i.e., Karelian and Finnish passive), and, thus, these imitations may be authentic reproductions of the language used by these speakers' older relatives. The use of the passive form in 3PL function is a well-known Karelian feature, and Karelian speakers are often imitated by using it (see, e.g., Räisänen 1986, 184–187, Punttila 1998, 92).

(14) Ka   ńiin=hä   ol-**laa**   vunuka-t   vielä hyvä-ssä   kunno-s.
     well   so=CLI   be-PAS   child-PL   still good-INE   condition-INE
     'Well, so the children are still in good condition'. (Ilomantsi 1931)

(15) Buabo   ja   d´ied´o,   ukki   ja   mummi   minu-n=ham
     grandma   and   grandpa,   grandpa   and   grandma   I-GEN=CLI

     pagis-**tii**   ihan   kuolema-a   asti   tällee.
     talk-PAS.PST   quite   death-ILL   until   in.this.way

'My grandma and grandpa, grandpa and grandma talked in this way until their death'. (Suistamo 1934)

One syntactic characteristic of Karelian is the use of the adessive case in experiencer constructions: in Karelian, an experiencer is marked with the adessive case whereas in Finnish, an experiencer is in the partitive case. (16) is the only example of the construction with adessive in the imitation data. The construction is common to Karelian and Russian, and it probably originated during the long-standing contact between Karelian and northern Russian dialects, and now a similar pattern exists in both languages. It seems, however, that the construction is inherent in both languages, and it is not possible to prove that it would have been directly borrowed from one language into the other (Sarhimaa 1990).

(16) Nyt   miu-**la**   väsyttä-ä.
     now   I-ADE   be.tired-3SG
     'Now I am tired'. (Ilomantsi 1917)

Furthermore, some differences in the case government of certain verbs are noticeable in the imitation data. For example, while in Finnish the construction *käydä tekemässä* (go-INF1 do-INF3-INE 'to go to do something') is found with the third infinitive in the inessive case, in Karelian, the same verb has an infinitive complement in the illative case (*käyvä ruadamah* go-INF1 do-INF3-ILL). In the imitation data, this pattern is used by Suistamo 1934, who spoke Karelian throughout the interview and had clearly acquired it as one of his native tongues (see examples 17–18).

(17) *Suistama-lla=ki   ni käy-tii,   joskus   miniä=ki*
     Suistamo-ADE=CLI so go-PAS.PST sometimes daughter.in.law=CLI

   *otta-**ma-a**   tiä-ltä   päi*
   take-INF3-ILL   this-ABL   from

   'Sometimes they went from here to Suistamo to take a daughter-in-law' (Suistamo 1934).

(18) *Isä   käv-i   se-n   kačč̌o-**ma-a**   sillon*
     father go-PST   it-ACC   see-INF3-ILL   then

   nel´jäkymmenyks   kevää-l
   forty.one   spring-ADE

   'Father went to see it then in the spring 1941' (Suistamo 1934).

The final examples of syntactic features characteristic to Karelian but different from Finnish are instances of the referentially open use of 2SG verb forms when the verb form does not refer to the hearer but to anyone who has the same kind of experience of the topic as the speaker. The open use of 2SG forms is not totally unknown in Finnish, but it is much more common to use the 3SG forms (so-called zero-person construction) in the same function. This use, too, is found in the data in the interview with Suistamo 1934, and it is exemplified in (19) and (20). In (20), the speaker uses the 2SG form to refer to anyone who lived in or visited the place in question. Example (20) shows alternating use of Finnish and Karelian constructions: first, in the subordinate clause, the verb is in 3SG form (*kirjottaa*), and, then, in the main clause, the verb is in 2SG imperative form (*eči*). In the Border Karelian dialects, the 2SG forms appear to have been used more often in eastern parts of the area, where the Finnish influence has been weaker and Russian influence stronger (Uusitupa 2017). The open use of 2SG in the Karelian language and in the Eastern Finnish dialect is probably caused by influence from Russian (see Leinonen 1983, 151, 159).

(19) *Siel=hän   **kuul-i-t**   ihaj   joka   paika-s,*
     there=CLI   hear-PST-2SG   quite   every   place-INE

nenkos-ta   tarino-a
such-PAR   speech-PAR

'There you heard such speech absolutely everywhere' (Suistamo 1934).

(20) Jos **kirjotta-a** kahe-l   sorme-l   vai   ni   sit
     if type-3SG   two-ADE   finger-ADE only   so   then

  eči   nii-tä,   siel   nii-tä,   merkki-löi
  look.for.IMP.2SG   they-PAR   there.ADE/ABL   these-PAR   symbol-PL.PAR

'If you type with two fingers you have to look for the symbols there' (Suistamo 1934).

All in all, using the grammatical features reviewed above, especially the morpho-syntactic constructions, requires more linguistic skills than reproducing single-word imitations or fixed phrases. Therefore, it is not surprising that the examples come from the interviews with those informants who could produce longer imitations and switch to Karelian. In this respect, informant Suistamo 1934 is noticeably different from all the others, and his Karelian includes many kinds of syntactic features that are not present in the other interviews. He acquired Karelian as a native language during his childhood and has managed to preserve it well. Another informant who often switched to Karelian during his interview is Salmi 1953, but he differs from Suistamo 1934 in that his Karelian (which was largely acquired at an adult age) is syntactically very Finnish-like.

7 Discussion

This article has presented the findings from an imitation task performed by 32 Finns who live in the province of North Karelia and, with the exception of one, have roots in Border Karelia, an area that was Karelian-speaking until 1944 and was then ceded to the Soviet Union. The informants had heard the Karelian language spoken during their childhood by their parents, grandparents, and other older people, but their own dominant language was Finnish and most of them spoke the dialect of North Karelia during the interview, although some informants used Standard Finnish. The data was collected in the context of a folk linguistic interview with a Finnish interviewer who spoke Finnish. Imitations were elicited by asking the informants to speak like their relatives. The imitations have been compared to the existing knowledge of Border Karelian dialects (The Corpus of Border Karelia, Dictionary of Karelian (KKS) and the previous studies). The analysis showed that there are considerable interindividual differences in the ability to imitate Karelian, ranging from four informants who did not provide any imitations to one interviewee who spoke Karelian throughout the interview. Most commonly, Karelian was imitated with discourse phrases and short clauses, familiar from everyday conversation; this kind of imitation was produced by 13 informants. Six informants listed single Karelian words and eight informants were capable of switching to Karelian and producing longer imitated sequences when remembering the way their older relatives had spoken.

The differences in the successfulness of the imitations can be roughly described as follows: the longer the imitation is, the more closely it follows the phonetic, phonological, morphological, and morpho-syntactic characteristics of Karelian. In some imitation studies, it has been found that syntactic features are more difficult to produce than phonological or morphological ones. On the level of phonetics and phonology, prosodic features (such as pitch, rate, and vocal quality) can be imitated even more systematically than segmental features (Preston 1992, 334–335). In the present data, the Karelian prosodic features (e.g., intonation, speech tempo, and speech rhythm) were imitated by only a few informants who produced longer imitation sequences (Ilomantsi 1931, Ilomantsi 1953, Salmi 1933, Salmi 1938, Suistamo 1934, and Suistamo 1954). Syntactic structures specific to Karelian were produced by those informants whose overall command of Karelian was the best.

Karelianness was most often imitated by voiced stops (in 20 interviews), diphthongisation of *aa/ää* in the non-initial syllables (19 interviews), lack of word boundary gemination (17 interviews), the afftricate *č* (16 interviews), word-final *h* (14 interviews), apocope of *a/ä* (13 interviews), palatalised dental consonants (11 interviews), and diphthongisation of *aa/ää* in the first syllable, all of which are typically Karelian features and differentiate Karelian from the Finnish *Savo* dialects, spoken in North Karelia where the informants lived. In a study concerning English, it has been shown that a non-native speaker can imitate an accent that is stronger than his/her own accent but not a weaker one (Rogers 1998). The present findings are in line with this observation as the informants with Border Karelian roots mostly imitated those Karelian features that differ from the dialect they use in their present place of residence. A prime example of this is the diphthongisation of *aa/ää*: diphthongisation has not occurred in the *Savo* dialects of North-Karelia in the non-initial syllables but only in the first syllable (where the quality of the diphthong is often slightly different from Karelian), and more often the informants imitated the non-initial diphthongs that differ from their Finnish dialect.

Some informants attempted to use actual Karelian features but applied these features incorrectly: Typically voiced stops or sometimes also affricates were pronounced in a context in which Karelian has a voiceless stop or another sibilant (e.g. **birttih** pro *pert't'ih* 'to the house', **čintsoi** pro *seńčoi* 'hall'). Word-final *h* seems to be a feature that many informants are aware of, but not all of them know the actual distribution of *h* in Karelian and produced it in wrong inflectional forms (e.g., *čulččinah čupukkoah* pro *čulččinoa čupukkoa* 'Karelian pastry', *tulkah* pro *tulgoa* 'come'). This kind of hypercorrect use of characteristically Karelian phonemes implies that these informants recognise and are aware that these sounds differ from Finnish even though their knowledge of Karelian is so vague that they cannot use them correctly. A similar phenomenon has been noticed in The Corpus of Border Karelia when Border Karelian speakers (recorded in the 1960s and 1970s) use Russian loanwords (Tavi 2015). In folk linguistic terms, this is called *accuracy* (or lack of accuracy): a non-linguist may be aware of a linguistic feature but not its distributional conditions (Preston 1996).

The above-mentioned features show knowledge of Karelian, but a contrary phenomenon was also seen in the data: the Karelian imitations reveal a broad crosslinguistic influence from Finnish that affects all the linguistic levels. Lexical, phonological, and grammatical influence is typical and probably inevitable in the contacts between closely-related languages (see, e.g., Riionheimo 2013, Riionheimo and Frick 2014). Furthermore, it should be kept in mind that the informants' dominant language is Finnish, and, thus, the Finnish influence resembles the transfer of the speakers' L1 in second-language acquisition. In the imitation data, the Finnish influence is most evident at the phonological level, as is the L1 transfer in language learning.

The Finnish influence is manifested, for example, in pronouncing the Karelian voiced stops as voiceless, in accordance with the Finnish phoneme system (*tulkoa* pro Kar. *tulgoa* 'come', *näpläkkä* pro Kar. *ńäbläkkä* 'slippery'). The affricate *č* was sometimes replaced with the Finnish cluster *ts* (*jäitsä* pro Kar. *jäiččä* 'egg') and palatalisation was used less in the imitations than in authentic Karelian. Word-boundary gemination, which is an automatic feature of Finnish, was realised in the Karelian sequences of some informants (*otap pois* pro Kar. *ota pois* 'take away') even though the lack of this gemination is a specific characteristic of Karelian. The word-final *h* may have disappeared and given way to the Finnish ending that is formed by lengthening the vowel (*ottamaa* pro Kar. *ottamah* 'to take', *sanottii* pro Kar. *sanottih* '(they) said; was said'). The long *aa/ää* was not diphthongised in the speech of all the informants (*saatih* pro Kar. *soadih* '(they) got', *soittaa* pro Kar. *soittoa* 'to ring') and the present tense 3SG form was often inflected with a long vowel characteristic to Finnish (*pitää* pro *pidäy* '(s/he) must').

Furthermore, it seems that those informants who have become estranged from Karelian did not separate Karelian from their local Eastern Finnish dialect in their imitations, which resulted in the production of Finnish dialectal features that do not have a counterpart in Karelian. For instance, some imitations contained schwa vowels that are common in Finnish dialects in certain consonant clusters (e.g., *olokah ihmisiks* 'behave yourselves', cf., Kar. *olgoa*) or the gemination of single consonants, also a wide-spread feature in Finnish dialects (e.g., *eihän täs mittää* 'there is nothing here', cf., Kar. *midäh*; *karjalloa* 'the Karelian language' pro Kar. *karjaloa*). Schwa vowels and gemination are foreign to Karelian, but, on the basis of The Corpus of Border Karelia, it has been shown that they may have occurred in some idiolects of Border Karelian evacuees who came from the western parts of Border Karelia. These features are probably the result of the earlier, longstanding contact between Karelian and Finnish speakers (Massinen 2012). The informants who (such as Salmi 1953 and Suistamo 1934) were able to produce longer Karelian stretches did not use these Eastern Finnish features. Salmi 1953 commented on the Eastern Finnish dialects of the area where he was currently living and brought out gemination as a feature that is, according to his observations, different from Karelian. Gemination was also mentioned by the oldest informant, Ilomantsi 1917, and she illustrated the difference between Karelian and the present Finnish dialect of Ilomantsi with examples that contained gemination: according to her, in Ilomantsi people would have said *tulu**kk**ee syö**mm**ään ja vä**ll**een* 'come soon to eat', but in Border Karelia people would have said *tulkoa lapset syömäh* 'come to eat, children'.

Even though Karelian is severely endangered in Finland, the present study suggests that the descendants of Border Karelian evacuees often have rather good recollections of Karelian and may be considered as latent speakers of Karelian (cf., Sallabank 2013, 14–15). Many of the informants report having a passive command of Karelian, and if they had the chance and the motivation, they could probably relearn Karelian with moderate effort (for similar relearning of Inari Saami, see Pasanen 2015). For example, Suistamo 1953 had been learning Karelian as an adult and apparently could have spoken more Karelian in the interview if the interviewer had been using Karelian. He considered the imitation task difficult because producing monologues in Karelian was not part of his everyday language use. The data also reveals that those informants who use Karelian when they meet their relatives also report recalling Karelian relatively easily. Suistamo 1934, who consistently spoke Karelian during his interview, reported that he uses Karelian whenever possible, for example in the meetings of a Karelian association and when meeting other Border Karelian evacuees. He even practices by speaking Karelian to himself and has managed to preserve the language: his Karelian contains diverse syntactic structures that were not found in the speech of other informants.

This study has applied the folk linguistic imitation method to the research of an endangered language, which is an innovative experiment with respect to both folk linguistics and contact linguistics. The method has brought out the most typical features that are used when imitating Karelian and given an overall picture of the knowledge of Karelian by second- and third-generation Karelian immigrants. Furthermore, it has shown how Finnish has influenced the Karelian spoken in Finland. The imitation task measured one kind of language ability, and, in the future, these results will be compared with findings produced using other methods, such as the observations elicited by a recognition task. It is obvious that different methods are needed to gain a multifaceted picture of how the heritage speakers of Karelian perceive the language spoken in their childhood home and how their possible perceptions differ from linguistic knowledge about Border Karelia dialects.

Glossing abbreviations

1PL	first person plural
1SG	first person singular
2PL	second person plural
2SG	second person singular
3PL	third person plural

3SG	third person singular
ABL	ablative
ACC	accusative
ADE	adessive
ALL	allative
CLI	clitic
GEN	genitive
ILL	illative
IMP	imperative
INE	inessive
INF1	first infinitive (A infinitive)
INF3	third inifinive (MA infinitive)
NEG	negation
PAR	partitive
PAS	passive
PL	plural
PR	present tense
PST	(simple) past tense
TRA	translative

References

Ahtia, E. V. 1936. *Karjalan kielioppi. Äänneoppi ja sanaoppi.* [Grammar of Karelian. Phonology and lexicology.] Suojärvi: Karjalan kansalaissseura.

Basham, Charjotte, and Aann K. Fathman. 2008. The latent speaker: attaining adult fluency in an endangered language. *International Journal of Bilingual Education and Bilingualism* 11:577–97.

Bolfek Radovani, Jasmine. 2000. *Attityder till svenska dialekter – en sociodialektologisk undersökning bland vuxna svenskar* [Attitudes towards Swedish dialects – a socio-dialectological study on Swedish adults]. SoLiD no. 13. FUMS Rapport no. 201, Uppsala: Uppsala universitet.

Brunner, Elizabeth Gentry. 2010. *Imitation, Awareness, and Folk Linguistic Artifacts.* Texas: Houston. Accessed January 1, 2015. https://scholarship.rice.edu/handle/1911/64394.

Bubrih, D. V., A. A. Beljakov, and A. V. Punžina. 1997. *Karjalan kielen murrekartasto* [Dialect atlas of the Karelian language]. Edited by Leena Sarvas. Helsinki: The Finno-Ugrian Society.

Campbell, Lyle, and Martha C. Muntzel. 1989. "The Structural Consequences of Language Death." In *Investigating Obsolescence. Studies in Language Contraction and Death*, edited by Nancy C. Dorian, 181–196. Cambridge: Cambridge University Press.

Craig, Colette Grinevald. 1997. "Language Contact and Language Degeneration." In *The Handbook of Sociolinguistics*, edited by Florian Coulmas, 257–270. Blackwell Handbooks in Linguistics 4. Oxford: Blackwell Publishers.

Dorian, Nancy C. 1981. *Language Death. The Life Cycle of a Scottish Gaelic Dialect.* Philadelphia: University of Pennsylvania Press.

Dorian, Nancy C. 2010. *Investigating Variation: the Effects of Social Organization and Social Setting.* Oxford: Oxford University Press.

Eriksson, Erik J., Kirk P. H. Sullivan, Elisabeth Zetterholm, Peter E. Czigler, James Green, Asa Skagerstrand, and Jan van Doorn. 2010. "Detection of Imitated Voices, Who Are Reliable Earwitnesses?" *The International Journal of Speech, Language and the Law* 17:1:25–44.

Evans, Betsy E. 2002. "An Acoustic and Perceptual Analysis of Imitation." In *Handbook of Perceptual Dialectology 2*, edited by Daniel Long and Dennis R. Preston, 95–112. Amsterdam: John Benjamins.

Evans, Betsy E. 2010. "Aspects of the Acoustic Analysis of Imitation." In *A Reader in Sociophonetics*, edited by Dennis R. Preston and Nancy Niedzielski, 379–392. New York: Walter de Gruyter.

Farrús, Mireia, Erik Eriksson, Kirk P. H. Sullivan, and Javier Hernando. 2007. "Dialect Imitations in Speaker Recognition." In *Proceedings of the Second European IAFL Conference on Forensic Liguistics / Language and the Law*, edited by M.Teresa Turell, Maria Spassova, and Jordi Cicres, 347–353. Barcelona: Institut Universitari de Lingüística Aplicada. Universitat Pompeu Fabra.

Genetz, Arvid. 1884. *Tutkimus Aunuksen kielestä. Kielennäytteitä, sanakirja ja kielioppi.* [Study on the Olonets language. Language samples, dictionary and grammar.] Helsinki: Finnish Literature Society.

Granqvist, Kimmo. 2007. "Mikä on erilaista romanikielen diskurssissa?" [What is different in discourse in the Romani language?]. In *Kielissä kulttuurien ääni* [*Language: the voice of cultures*], edited by Anna Idström and Sachiko Sosa, 206–222. Tietolipas 228. Helsinki: Finnish Literature Society.

Grinevald, Colette, and Michel Bert. 2011. "Speakers and communities." In *The Cambridge Handbook of Endangered Languages*, edited by Peter K. Austin and Julia Sallabank, 45–65. Cambridge: Cambridge University Press.

Grünthal, Riho. 2007. "Karjala kielten ja murteiden rajapintana" [Karelia as the interface of Languages and Dialects]. In *Rajalla. Tiede rajojaan etsimässä* [*On the border. Science looking for its borders*], edited by Kari Raivio, Jan Rydman, and Anssi Sinnemäki, 108–117. Helsinki: Gaudeamus.

Holloway, Charles E. 1997. *Dialect Death: The Case of Brule Spanish*. Amsterdam: John Benjamins.

Hämynen, Tapio. 2013. "Rajakarjalaisen kieliyhteisön rapautuminen ja karjalankielisten määrä Suomessa" [The attrition of the Border Karelian language community and the number of Karelian Speakers in Finland]. In *Karjala-kuvaa rakentamassa* [*Constructing the picture of Karelia*], edited by Pekka Suutari, 182–213. SKST 1389. Helsinki: Finnish Literature Society.

Jeskanen, Matti. 2005. "Karjalan kieli ja karjalankieliset Suomessa" [Karelian language and Karelian speakers in Finland]. In *Monenlaiset karjalaiset. Suomen karjalaisten kielellinen identiteetti* [*Karelians' many faces: The linguistic identity of Karelians in Finland*], edited by Marjatta Palander and Anne-Maria Nupponen, 215–285. Studia Carelica Humanistica 20. Joensuu: University of Joensuu.

Jessop, Lorena, Wataru Suzuki, and Yasuyo Tomita. 2007. "Elicited Imitation in Second Language Acquisition Research." *Canadian Modern Language Review* 64:1:215–220.

Jones, Caroline, and Felicity Meakins. 2013. "The Phonological Forms and Perceived Functions of Janyarrp, the Gurindji 'Baby Talk' Register." *Lingua* 134:170–193.

Kananen, Heli Kaarina. 2010. *Kontrolloitu sopeutuminen. Ortodoksinen siirtoväki sotien jälkeisessä Ylä-Savossa (1946–1959).* [*Controlled integration. The Orthodox evacuees in post-war Upper Savo (1946–1959).*] Jyväskylä Studies in Humanities 144. Jyväskylä: University of Jyväskylä.

Kauppinen, Anneli. 1998. *Puhekuviot, tilanteen ja rakenteen liitto* [Figures of speech, a union of situation and structure]. SKST 713. Helsinki: Finnish Literature Society.

Kettunen, Lauri. 1940. *Suomen murteet III A. Murrekartasto.* [The Finnish dialects III A. Dialect atlas.] SKST 118. Helsinki: Finnish Literature Society.

KKS = *Karjalan kielen sanakirja 1–6* [The Karelian dictionary 1–6]. Lexica Societatis Fenno-Ugricae XVI, 1–6. Helsinki: The Finno-Ugrian Society. 1968–2005.

Knuuttila, Sanna-Riikka. 2011. "Children – the Future of the Karelian Language? Case Study in a Karelian Village." *Journal of Estonian and Finno-Ugric Linguistics* 2:1:215–221.

Künzel, Hermann J. 2000. "Effects of Voice Disguise on Speaking Fundamental Frequency." *International Journal of Speech, Language, and the Law* 7(2): 149–179.

Laakso, Johanna, Anneli Sarhimaa, Sia Spiliopoulou Åkermark, and Reetta Toivanen. 2013. *Summary of the Research Project ELDIA (European Language Diversity for All). Abridged English-language version of the ELDIA Comparative Report.* Vienna: University of Vienna. Accessed April 3, 2015. https://phaidra.univie.ac.at/detail_object/o:304813.

Laakso, Johanna, Anneli Sarhimaa, Sia Spiliopoulou Åkermark, and Reetta Toivanen. 2015. *Towards Openly Multilingual Policies and Practices. Assessing Minority Language Maintenance Across Europe.* Linguistic Diversity and Language Rights 11. Bristol: Multilingual Matters.

Leinonen, Marja. 1983. "Generic Zero Subjects in Finnish and Russian." *Scando-Slavica. Tomus* 29:143–161. Copenhagen: Munksgaard.

Leskinen, Eino. 1934. *Karjalan kielen näytteitä II. Aunuksen ja Raja-Karjalan murteita.* [Samples of the Karelian Language II. Dialects of Olonets and Border Karelia.] Helsinki: Finnish Literature Society.

Lewis M. Paul, Gary F. Simons, and Charles D. Fennig, eds. 2015. *Ethnologue: Languages of the World, Eighteenth edition.* Dallas, Texas: SIL International. Accessed April 9, 2015. http://www.ethnologue.com.

Massinen, Henna. 2012. "*Yleis- ja erikoisgeminaatio Ilomantsin karjalankielisten siirtolaisten idiolekteissa*" [Primary and secondary gemination in the idiolects of the Karelian evacuees of Ilomantsi]. MA thesis. University of Eastern Finland.

Matras, Yaron. 2009. *Language Contact.* Cambridge Textbooks in Linguistics. Cambridge: Cambridge University Press.

Mielikäinen, Aila, and Marjatta Palander. 2014. *Miten suomalaiset puhuvat murteista? Kansanlingvistinen tutkimus metakielestä.* [How do Finns talk about dialects? Folk linguistic study on metalanguage.] Suomi 203. Helsinki: Finnish Literature Society.

Montrul, Silvina. 2011. "Introduction. The Linguistic Competence of Heritage Speakers." *Studies in Second Language Acquisition* 33:155–161.

Moseley, Christopher, ed. 2010. *Atlas of the World's Languages in Danger.* 3rd edn. Paris, UNESCO Publishing. Accessed April 9, 2015. http://www.unesco.org/culture/en/endangeredlanguages/atlas.

Niedzielski, Nancy A., and Dennis R. Preston. 2000. *Folk Linguistics.* Trends in Linguistics, Studies and Monographs 122. Berlin: Mouton de Gruyter.

Nupponen, Anne-Maria. 2005. "Iloisuus ja eloisa murre. Siirtokarjalaisten käsityksiä ja havaintoja murteista ja karjalaisuudesta." [Joyfulness and a vivid dialect. Conceptions and perceptions on dialects and karelianness by Karelian evacuees.] In *Monenlaiset karjalaiset. Suomen karjalaisten kielellinen identiteetti* [Karelians' many faces: The linguistic identity of Karelians in Finland], edited by Marjatta Palander and Anne-Maria Nupponen, 159–214. Studia Carelica Humanistica 20. Joensuu: University of Joensuu.

Obler, Loraine K., and Kris Gjerlow. 1999. *Language and the Brain.* Cambridge Approaches to Linguistics. Cambridge: Cambridge University Press.

Palander, Marjatta. 2011. *Itä- ja eteläsuomalaisten murrekäsitykset* [Dialect conceptions of eastern and southern Finns]. Suomi 200. Helsinki: Finnish Literature Society.

Palander, Marjatta. 2015. "Rajakarjalaistaustaisten ja muiden suomalaisten mielikuvia *karjalasta*" [How Border Karelians and other Finns view *Karelian*]. *Virittäjä* 119:34–66.

Palander, Marjatta, Pekka Zaikov, and Milla Uusitupa. 2013. "Karjalan kielen tutkimusta ja opetusta kahden puolen rajaa" [Research and education of Karelian on both sides of the border]. In *Karjala-kuvaa rakentamassa* [*Constructing the picture of Karelia*], edited by Pekka Suutari, 358–385. SKST 1389. Helsinki: Finnish Literature Society.

Pasanen, Annika. 2010. "Will Language Nests Change the Direction of Language Shifts? On the Language Nests of Inari Saamis and Karelians." *In Planning a New Standard Language. Finnic Minorities Meet the New Millennium*, edited by Helena Sulkala and Harri Mantila, 95–118. Studia Fennica Linguistica 15. Helsinki: Finnish Literature Society.

Pasanen, Annika. 2015. *Kuávsui já peeivičuovâ. 'Sarastus ja päivänvalo'. Inarinsaamen kielen revitalisaatio.* ['Dawn and daylight'. Revitalization of Inari Saami language.] Uralica Helsingiensia 9. Helsinki: Finno-Ugrian Society.

Preston, Dennis R. 1992. "Talking Black and Talking White: A Study in Variety Imitation." In *Old English and New. Studies in Language and Linguistics in Honor of Frederic G. Cassidy*, edited by Joan H. Hall, Nick Doane, and Dick Ringler, 327–355. New York: Garland Publishing.

Preston, Dennis R. 1996. "Whaddayaknow?: The Modes of Folk-Linguistic Awareness." *Language Awareness* 5:1:40–74.

Preston, Dennis R. 1998. "Folk Metalanguage." In *Metalanguage. Social and Ideological Perspectives*, edited by Adam Jaworski, Nikolas Coupland, and Darius Galasiński, 75–101. Cardiff Roundtable in Sociolinguistics 3. Language, Power and Social Process 11. Berlin: Mouton de Gruyter.

Punttila, Matti. 1998. *Haaskannäköinen tyttö. Kielikaskuista matkimuksiin.* [*Good-looking girl. From language jokes to imitations.*] Porvoo: WSOY.

Purschke, Christoph. 2010. "Imitation und Hörerurteil – Kognitive Dialekt-Prototypen am Beispiel des Hessischen" [Imitation and the view of a listener – cognitive dialect prototypes as an example of Hessian]. In *Perceptual Dialectology. Neue Wege der Dialektologie*, edited by Ada Christina Anders, Markus Hundt, and Alexander Lasch, 151–177. Berlin: De Gruyter.

Pyöli, Raija. 2011. *Livvinkarjalan kielioppi* [Grammar of Olonets Karelian]. Helsinki: Karjalan kielen seura.

Räisänen, Alpo. 1986. *Suomussalmen murrekirja* [Dialect book of Suomussalmi]. Helsinki: Finnish Literature Society.

Raninen-Siiskonen, Tarja. 1999. *Vieraana omalla maalla. Tutkimus karjalaisen siirtoväen muistelukerronnasta* [As a stranger in one's own land. A study in reminiscing narratives of Karelian evacuees.] Helsinki: Finnish Literature Society.

Riionheimo, Helka. 2013. "Multiple Roots of Innovations in Language Contact. Evidence from Morphological Intermingling in Contact between Ingrian Finnish and Estonian." *Studies in Language* 37:3:645–674.

Riionheimo, Helka, and Maria Frick. 2014. "The Emergence of Finnish-Estonian Bilingual Constructions in Two Contact Settings." *Sociolinguistic Studies* 8:3:409–447.

Rogers, Henry. 1998. "Foreign Accent in Voice Discrimination." *Forensic Linguistics* 5:2:203–208.

Sallabank, Julia. 2013. *Attitudes to Endangered Languages. Identities and Policies.* Cambridge: Cambridge University Press.

Salminen, Tapani 2009. *Endangered Languages*. Accessed January 10, 2015. http://www.helsinki.fi/~tasalmin/fu.html.

Sarhimaa, Anneli. 1990. "Karjalan kielen syntaksiin kohdistuneen venäjän interferenssin tutkimisesta" [On the study of Russian interference in Karelian syntax]. *Virittäjä* 94:438–455.

Sarhimaa, Anneli. 2016. *Karelian in Finland. ELDIA Case-Specific Report*. Studies in European Language Diversity 27. Accessed December 12, 2016. https://fedora.phaidra.univie.ac.at/fedora/get/o:471733/bdef:Content/get.

Schilling-Estes, Natalie. 1998. "Investigating 'Self-Conscious' Speech: the Performance Register in Ocracoke English." *Language in Society* 27:1:53–83.

Seeff-Gabriel, Belinda, Shula Chiat, and Barbara Dodd. 2010. "Sentence Imitation as a Tool in Identifying Expressive Morphosyntactic Difficulties in Children with Severe Speech Difficulties." *International Journal of Language & Communication Disorders* 45:6:691–702.

SKST = Suomalaisen Kirjallisuuden Seuran toimituksia [Editions of the Finnish Literature Society].

Snow, David. 1998. "Children's Imitations of Intonation Contours: Are Rising Tones More Difficult than Falling Tones?" *Journal of Speech, Language, and Hearing Research* 41:3:576–587.

Tavi, Susanna. 2015. "*Rajakarjalaismurteiden venäläiset lainasanat*" [Russian loanwords in the Border Karelian dialects]. MA thesis. University of Eastern Finland.

Thomason, Sarah G. 2015. *Endangered languages. An Introduction*. Cambridge Textbooks in Linguistics. Cambride: Cambridge University Press.

Thoonen, Geert. 1997. "Towards a Standardised Assessment Procedure for Developmental Apraxia of Speech." *European Journal of Disorders of Communication* 32:1:37–60.

Tsitsipis, Lukas D. 1989. "Skewed Performance and Full Performance in Language Obsolescence. The Case of an Albanian Variety." *Investigating Obsolescence. Studies in Language Contraction and Death*, edited by Nancy C. Dorian, 117–137. Cambridge: Cambridge University Press.

Turunen, Aimo. 1982. "Raja-Karjalan murteet" [The dialects of Border Karelia]. In *Karjala 2. Karjalan maisema ja luonto* [Karelia 2. The landscape and nature of Karelia], edited by Yrjö-Pekka Mäkinen and Ilmari Lehmusvaara, 65–89. Hämeenlinna: Arvi A. Karisto.

Ulatowska, Hanna K., Lee Allard, Belinda A. Reyes, Jean Ford, and Sandra Chapman. 1992. "Conversational Discourse in Aphasia." *Aphasiology* 6:3:325–330.

Uusitupa, Milla. 2017. *Rajakarjalaismurteiden avoimet persoonaviittaukset* [Open person constructions in Border Karelian dialects]. Publications of the University of Eastern Finland. Dissertations in Education, Humanities, and Theology 117. Joensuu: University of Eastern Finland.

Verschik, Anna. 2014. "Conjunctions in Early Yiddish-Lithuanian Bilingualism: Heritage Language and Contact Linguistic Perspectives." In *Language Contacts at the Crossroads of Disciplines*, edited by Heli Paulasto, Lea Meriläinen, Helka Riionheimo, and Maria Kok, 33–58. Newcastle upon Tyne: Cambridge Scholars Publishing.

Wu, Shu-Ling. 2013. "Applications of Elicited Imitation to Second Language Education." *Dialog on Language Instruction* 23:1–2:51–54.

Zaikov, Pekka. 2013. *Vienankarjalan kielioppi. Lisänä harjotukšie ta lukemisto*. [Grammar of White Sea Karelian. With exercises and readings.] Helsinki: Karjalan Sivistysseura ry.

NIINA KUNNAS
ⓘ http://orcid.org/0000-0002-2703-0600

Viena Karelians as Observers of Dialect Differences in Their Heritage Language

Abstract

This article deals with Viena Karelian laypeople's perceptions and evaluations of dialect. One aim was to determine which dialect features are discussed among laypeople and how laypeople perform in a listening task. The results show that the perceived dialect or language area of White Sea Karelian is smaller than the dialect area defined by professional linguists. Amongst the respondents, it was commonly thought that White Sea Karelian is spoken only in the Kalevala National District, and that Paanajärvi does not belong to the same dialect area. The listening task showed that the dialect awareness of Viena Karelians is not very high, as even their 'own' variety was sometimes incorrectly located. With respect to dialect perceptions, it can be said that differences in vocabulary are readily *available* and much discussed among Viena Karelians. Laypeople also commented on phonological differences but used colloquial terms such as *smooth* and *hard* to describe them. At a phonetic level, the variation between /s/ and /š/ was widely commented on by the informants. They noted that speakers of White Sea Karelian make more extensive use of /š/ whereas in the southern varieties of Karelian /s/ is more common. The speakers of White Sea Karelian were perceived to 'lisp' or 'speak with *š*', and speakers of other varieties were said to use a sharper /s/. According to this study, there is a perceptual connection between the form (extensive use of /š/) and the group identified as using it (speakers of White Sea Karelian).

1 Introduction

This article explores Viena Karelian laypeople's perceptions and evaluations of different varieties of Karelian. The article touches upon several kinds of borders: linguistic, geographic, and mental. The research questions are as follows:
1) How do Viena Karelian laypeople define the area of their 'own dialect' or 'own language'? Do they distinguish language borders between different Karelian varieties, and what kind of linguistic borders do they perceive between Finnish and their own variety?

2) Can laypeople recognize different varieties of Karelian and Ludian in a listening task?
3) Are Viena Karelians aware of dialect differences in their heritage language?
4) What kind of language features are discussed among laypeople?

The hypothesis is that the informants will make accurate observations about the variation in Karelian because White Sea Karelian itself has been found to include great variation (Kunnas 2007, 295). According to previous research (e.g., Juusela 1998, 72; Laurila 2008, 70), those laypeople whose dialect varies greatly are more aware of language variation than those laypeople whose dialect is more homogeneous.

Dialect perceptions and evaluations have not been researched extensively among Karelians. There are only two articles in which the perceptions of Viena Karelians have been studied (Kunnas and Arola 2010; Kunnas 2013). In addition, the dialect or language perceptions of Border Karelians, whose mother tongue is South or Olonets Karelian, have also been explored (Nupponen 2005; Palander 2015).

This article comprises eight sections. First, the data, theories, and methods used in this study are presented. Next, how Viena Karelian laypeople define the area of their 'own dialect' is examined. Section 6 relates the results of the listening task, and Section 7 presents the kinds of dialect differences Karelian laypeople are aware of and the types of language features that are discussed among the informants.

2 Research area and data

Traditionally, the Karelian spoken in the Republic of Karelia has been seen to be divided into three main dialects: 1) Karelian Proper, 2) Olonets Karelian, and 3) Ludian. Karelian Proper is further divided into: 1) White Sea Karelian[1], 2) Transitional dialect, and 3) South Karelian (Zaikov 2000, 27). Some researchers, as well as some of the Ludes themselves, regard Ludian as an independent language. However, amongst Russian researchers, it is still common to include Ludian as a dialect of Karelian. The opposite ends of the dialect continuum of Karelian are not mutually intelligible, and many researchers have debated whether these varieties should be treated as dialects or independent languages. (Kunnas 2007, 40–41; Karjalainen et al. 2013, 3–4; and sources mentioned.)

White Sea Karelian is spoken in northwest Russia, close to the Finnish border (see Map 2). It is the closest cognate language of Finnish, and Finns can quite easily understand White Sea Karelian dialects. White Sea Karelian is a highly endangered language. According to a 2010 census, there were some 25,000 speakers of Karelian in the Republic of Karelia, but this number only includes speakers of Olonets Karelian and Ludian (Ethnologue). Ten

---

1   Also called *North Karelian* and *Viena Karelian*.

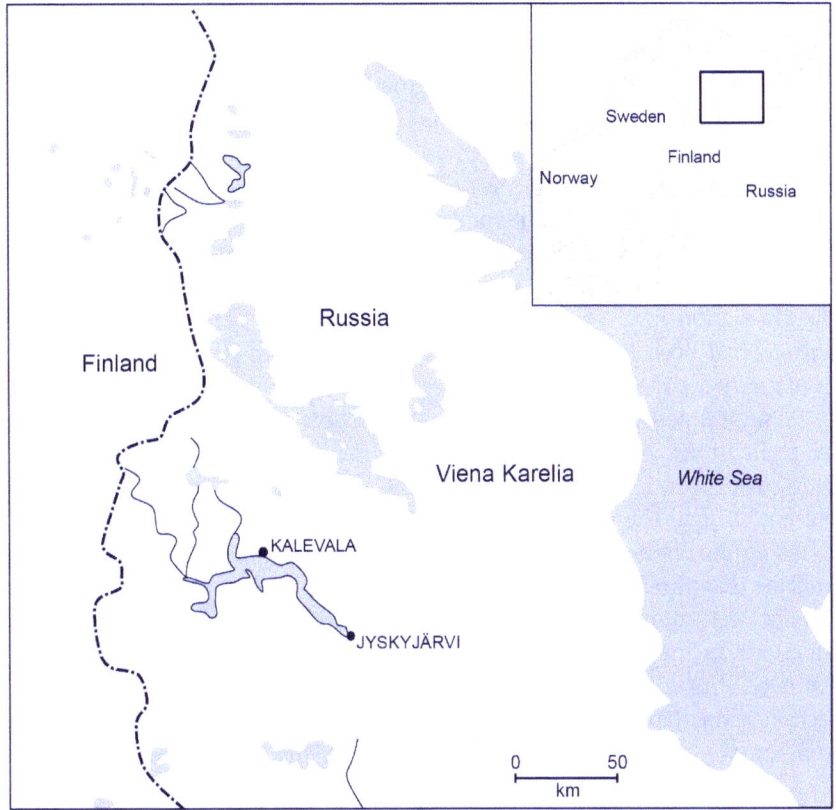

Map 1. The villages of Kalevala and Jyskyjärvi in Viena Karelia.

years ago the number of speakers of White Sea Karelian was estimated to be about 8,000 (Karelstat 2005, 12–17). The majority of speakers are over fifty, and most of the younger generations have a better command of Russian than Karelian. The situation in Karelia is generally diglossic: Russian is the language of society, education, and business, and the use of Karelian focuses on issues related to private life; it is used at home and in the sphere of personal interests and hobbies. Karelian is spoken mainly in small countryside parishes and is heard only very rarely in towns. (Kunnas 2009, 178.)

The fieldwork in the present study was conducted in two villages in Viena Karelia: Kalevala (previously called Uhtua) and Jyskyjärvi (Juškozero)[2] (see Map 1). Jyskyjärvi is a very small village with approximately 400–500 inhabitants. Kalevala is the administrative centre of the Kalevala National District (Kalevalski natsionalnyi rajon). The Municipality of Kalevala has approximately 5,000 inhabitants.

The data include theme interviews, group interviews, and listening tasks with 13 laypeople, and the data recordings represent approximately 7 hours (427 minutes). The data were collected using snowball sampling, and the Karelian language was used with the informants in interviews. The theme

---

2   The names of the Karelian municipalities and villages are written first in Karelian and after that (within parentheses) in Russian.

interviews were conducted at the informants' homes. One group interview was conducted at a library in Jyskyjärvi (with Agafia and Akuliina) and three took place in the informants' homes (with Maikki, Irina, and Polina, with Ortjo and Iivo, and with Olga and Tanja).

Both women and men are represented in the data, aged from 44 to 85 years old. The reason there are only older people in the data is that few young people can speak Karelian. Additionally, many young Karelians from Jyskyjärvi and Kalevala have moved to bigger cities to study or work. Most of the informants were born and had lived their whole lives (apart from the evacuation time[3]) in the core area of White Sea Karelia, although one woman had been born in the speaking area of Olonets Karelian but had lived many decades in Jyskyjärvi.

Assumed names are used for the informants, and they are introduced in detail in Appendix 1. Some of the informants had been interviewed previously (Kunnas 2007), and the same assumed names are used in the present study[4]. The examples selected from the data are presented using rough Uralic Phonetic Alphabet transliteration. Two successive dashes (- -) indicate that part of the turn has been left out. A hyphen shows that a word has not been completed. The periods and question marks have grammatical functions in the examples, whereas commas refer to a pause within the sentence. Proper nouns are written with initial capital letters. Excerpts from conversations have been transcribed in a similar fashion but include line numbers.

3 Theory and methods

This article represents a folk linguistics approach (e.g., Niedzielski and Preston 2000) but also employs aspects of language attitude research (e.g., Ryan and Giles 1982). The social psychological paradigm, which the latter represents, focuses on language evaluations, and the main interest in folk linguistics is on how people perceive linguistic similarities or differences. The interests within these approaches often overlap (Vaattovaara 2013), and these types of studies could widely be defined as language ideology studies (see Vilhula 2012, 2).

Woolard and Schieffelin (1994, 55) have defined language ideology as "cultural conceptions of language – its nature, structure, and use". The term language ideology covers both overt attitudes toward particular linguistic varieties and their speakers as well as underlying culturally defined notions of, for example, a hierarchical ranking of different dialects as well as the relationship between language and regional identities (Dickinson 2010, 55). Language ideologies are produced and processed through evaluations of linguistic behaviour (Bilaniuk 2005). According to Mäntynen et al. (2012), studies that observe language beliefs and valuations can also be

---

3 During WWII many Karelian speakers were evacuated to Komi Republic or to the Arkhangelsk area.
4 For more information about the informants, see Kunnas 2007, 359–371.

characterized as language ideology studies. They assert that conceptions concerning language boundaries are representative of language ideological processes (Mäntynen et al. 2012, 325–326).

This article uses both *direct* (group and theme interviews) and *indirect measures* (listening tasks) to discern people's language regard. The term *language regard* is used instead of *attitude* because not all beliefs are necessarily evaluative, and because both conscious and subconscious perceptions are under investigation (see Preston 2011, 10–11 and in this volume).

The metalanguage of laypeople is analysed in this study with a concentration mainly on *metalanguage one* which is, "talk about language" (Preston 1998, 75). *Metalanguage three* is also examined defined as "shared folk knowledge about language" (Preston 1998, 87) or "powerful underlying ideologies that lie behind folk beliefs" (Dennis Preston, e-mail message to author, 18 February 2015; cf., Niedzielski and Preston 2000, 308)[5]. The evaluations and perceptions of laypeople will be analysed using the method of content-oriented discourse analysis (see, e.g., Preston 1994; Liebscher and Dailey-O'Cain 2009).

In discourse analysis, language usage is not understood as mere transmission of information; rather, it is seen as revealing the speaker's reactions to the topic of discussion. Words that are chosen for the discourse reveal what kinds of feelings and attitudes a speaker has towards the theme. Every linguistic choice is connected to the speaker's evaluations as well as the underlying sociocultural ideology. (Fairclough 1989, 90–94; Kalliokoski 1995, 8, 14; Hodge and Kress 1996, 209–211.) This article not only investigates what laypeople say but also looks at how their opinions are constructed with certain words (see Liebscher and Dailey-O'Cain 2009, 198).

4 The perceived area of White Sea Karelian

During the theme and group interviews the informants were asked to delineate the area of their 'own language'. As Map 2 shows, professional linguists have defined the area of White Sea Karelian as quite large. However, laypeople in Jyskyjärvi and Kalevala commonly thought that White Sea Karelian is mainly spoken in Jyskyjärvi and Kalevala, perhaps also in the villages of Vuokkiniemi (Voknavolok), Vuonninen (Voinitsa), and Kontokki. The results are represented on Map 2.

It was common among the laypeople to think that their 'own language' is only spoken in the Kalevala National District (*Kalevalski natsionalnyi rajon*), which includes many old Karelian villages, e.g., Kalevala, Jyskyjärvi, Vuokkiniemi, Vuonninen, Pistojärvi (Tihtozero), Haikola (Haikolja), and Luusalmi:

---

5 *Metalanguage two* includes references to language itself in language use. *Bill whispered that he was leaving*, for example, is a sentence that refers to the linguistic fact of whispering, but "whispering" is not the topic of the discourse. (Preston 1998, 85; Dennis Preston, e-mail message to author, 18 February 2015.)

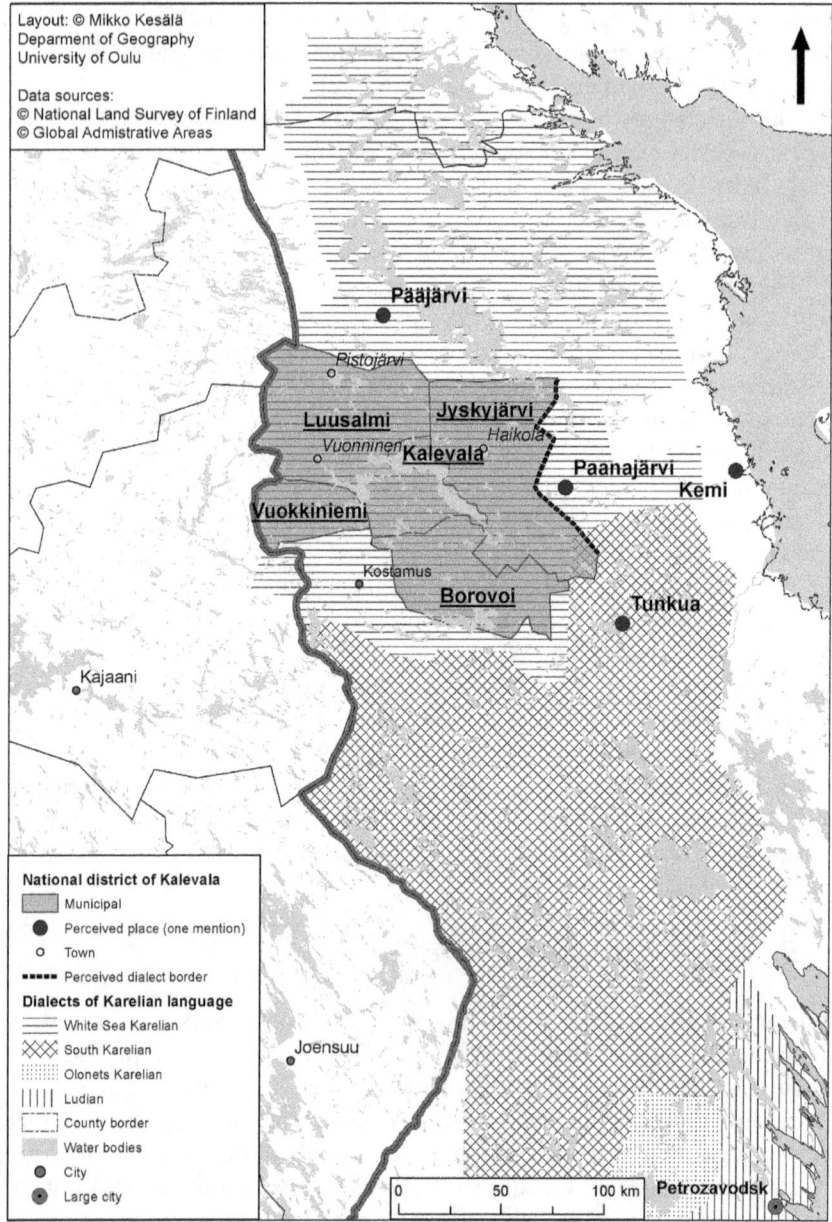

Map 2. The perceived dialect area of White Sea Karelian.

(1) *miäŋ* **karjalaŋ kieli** *Jyskyjärvessä, ja Uhtuolla* (Elviira)

[Our Karelian language (is spoken) in Jyskyjärvi and in Uhtua.]

(2) *niiŋku* **Jyskyjärven** *ta* **miän** *[pakinatapa] – – ei niis ole eruo ne ollah šamammoisie.* **Vuokkiniemi** *ta kaikki näm_ollah ihan* **yhemmoisie**. (Olga)

[There are no differences in the speech styles of people in Jyskyjärvi and Kalevala. Vuokkiniemi and all these are similar.]

(3) *no tiälä **Jyskyjärvessä, Uhtuossa, Vuokkiniemessä** ta tässä – – **Vuońnisešša** – – puhutaa yhennäkösesti. – – puhutah ihan **omua kieltä**. – – ihan oma **äitiŋkieli** se on. – – **Kalevalam piirissä** še on niiŋku meillä **oma, kieli**, – – ihan **oma kieli** šemmoni, **äitiŋkieli**, niiŋku **äitiŋkieli**.* (Akuliina)

[Here, in Jyskyjärvi, Uhtua, Vuokkiniemi, and in Vuonnini, people speak the same way. They speak their own language. It is an own mother tongue. In the Kalevala area we have our own language, a language completely our own, that kind of mother tongue, like a mother tongue.]

(4) *tässä vet **miäm** [Kalevalan] **piirissä** – – miän kielellä – – paistii nuo rajakylät kaikki – – **Koštamus, Kontokki** – – sekä Alajärvi – – Jyvyälakši – – Luušalmi, tuo, Nurmilakši, Uhtuo, ja V- Vuonnini Vuokkiniemi nehäŋ kaikki, ne on, niiŋku miäŋ kieli.* (Ortjo)

[In this our district, in our language, it was spoken in all those border villages, all – – Koštamus, Kontokki – – both Alajärvi – – Jyvyälakši – – Luušalmi, that, Nurmilakši, Uhtuo, and V- Vuonnini Vuokkiniemi which are all, like our language.]

(5) *varmast **Kalevalam piiri** kaikki, yhtä ja samua puhutah.* (Marina)

[Surely they speak the same way everywhere in the Kalevala area.]

The dialect of White Sea Karelian in the Kalevala District is seen as an *own language* and *mother tongue*. Among Finnish laypeople, it is also common to define some varieties of Finnish as *languages*, e.g., *Helsingin kieli* 'the language of Helsinki' (Mielikäinen and Palander 2014b, 33–39). It is interesting that Akuliina calls her own dialect *äitiŋkieli* 'mother tongue'. Does she want to emphasize the nature of White Sea Karelian *as a language of its own* rather than just a dialect of Karelian? According to previous research (Kunnas 2013), many Viena Karelians think that there is a language border between Olonets Karelian and their own language, but that the border is not as sharp between Finnish dialects and White Sea Karelian. Akuliina would seem to share this view.

The data also include other comments in which the informants draw language borders between Karelian varieties:

(6) *sielä kun on še, **Pieniseŋkä** [pro Pieniselkä], **Isošeŋkä** [pro Suuriselkä] šielä **eri kielellä** puhutaa.* (Polina)

[There are those, Pieniselkä (Malaja Selga), Isoselkä (Bolšaja Selga), they speak a different language there.]

Pieniselkä and Isoselkä, in the municipality of Kuittinen (Kuiteža), are villages where Olonets Karelian is spoken. According to Polina, Olonets Karelian is in fact a different *language* than White Sea Karelian.

Only one informant included the village of Paanajärvi (Panozero) in the dialect area of White Sea Karelian. The city of Kem, Pääjärvi (Pjaozero), and the village of Tunkua (Tunguda), which belongs to the South Karelian dialect area, were also mentioned. None of the informants included Kiestinki (Kestenga) in the area of their 'own language'. Akuliina, for example, related that in Kiestinki the dialect is already mixed and that people in Paanajärvi have a different language:

(7) *a vot - - Kiestiŋki tuolla, hyö voijjah jo sevottua, se on **ševot**. - - Puanajärvessä, siellä jo - - **toisemmoini kieli**.* (Akuliina)

[Well, In Kiestinki they may mix (the language); it is mixed. In Paanajärvi they have a different language.]

I would not go so far as to claim that the laypeople in Jyskyjärvi and Kalevala are wrong when they define the area of their own dialect differently from professional linguists. To my knowledge, there is no up-to-date research about Karelian language variation in Paanajärvi and Kiestinki, and the dialects spoken in these municipalities may actually differ greatly from dialects spoken in the Kalevala National District. In fact, non-linguists may be more sensitive to dialect boundaries than professional linguists, and they may be able to discern boundaries that linguists have not discovered (Preston 1993).

5 Perceptions about the dialects of Paanajärvi, Tunkua, and Rukajärvi

The village of Paanajärvi was mentioned many times when discussing dialect boundaries with the informants. Many people draw a strict line between the village of Paanajärvi and their own speech style. In the data, there are comments like:

(8) *Puanajärvi tuossa jo puhuu, toisel taval ku myö.* (Irina)

[In Paanajärvi, people speak differently from us.]

(9)

01 *tuošša **Puanajärvi** - - hyö jo toisel taval puhutaa.* (Irina)

02 *heil om **pehmie** šemmoini **kieli*** (Maikki)

[There in Paanajärvi, they speak in a different way. They have that kind of smooth language.]

(10) *Puanajärves on se, **snečoiŋ kieli** se, **puoli sanua sanotaa venyäheksi** ja paljon **venäjäŋ kieldä** - - Puanajärves käyttää* [!]. (Hilja)

[They have that 'the *snečoi* language' in the village of Paanajärvi. They say half of the words in Russian and they use much Russian language in Paanajärvi.]

Laypeople define the Paanajärvi dialect as *different* from their own, as *smooth* and heavily influenced by Russian, what they refer to as *snečoiŋ kieli* 'the snečoi language'.

Among Viena Karelians *snečoiŋ kieli* 'the *snečoi* language', or *snečku* 'the *snečku* language', is a commonly used pejorative designation for speakers of Olonets Karelian and other southern varieties of Karelian (Kunnas 2006, 242, 2013, 312–313; Pasanen 2003, 45). According to KKS (Dictionary of Karelian, s.v. *snetšku*), *snečku* is a nickname for those Karelians who live in the former province of Olonets and who speak *smoothly*.

Although it is clear that speakers of Olonets would be labelled *snečku*, in the former Olonets province, there are also villages in which South Karelian is spoken. For example, Rukajärvi (Rugozero), where South Karelian is still spoken, was formerly part of the Olonets province (Nevalainen 1998, 292–293). Therefore, for Viena Karelians, the designation *snečku* can refer to speakers of Olonets and South Karelian – and, as becomes clear from example 10, also speakers of White Sea Karelian outside the Kalevala District.

Throughout history, Viena Karelians have separated themselves linguistically as well as culturally from 'foreign' Olonets Karelians (Pöllä 1995, 313). It was not until the 19th century that the designation *Karelian* began to include speakers of Olonets Karelian and Ludian with speakers of Karelian Proper (Zaikov 1987, 13; Kunnas 2007, 45). The designation *snečku/snäčky* is probably also old: Irina, who was born in the beginning of the 20th century, said that her parents used the designation: *meilä vanhemmat on sanottu snäčkyŋ karjala* 'our parents used the name *Snäčky* Karelian' (Irina).

When I asked my informants about what kind of dialect was spoken in Tunkua and Rukajärvi (Rugozero), Agafia, Akuliina, and Ortjo defined the dialects as follows:

(11) *sielä on **nezeŋ** [pro nečen] kieli* (Agafia)

[They speak a *Neze* (pro *Nečče*) language there.]

(12) *heilä on – – niiŋko – – **Petroskoin ta** tämän **vienaŋkarjalaŋkieli**, še siitä on šekon siellä.* (Akuliina)

[They have a kind of a mixed (language). The languages of Petrozavodsk and White Sea Karelian have been mixed there.]

(13) *siellä puhutah kuule vain tätä, eiköhän enämbi jo venäjäŋ kielen šanoja ole **sevošša*** (Ortjo)

[There they speak this, I suppose they have more Russian words mixed in their language.]

Agafia referred to the dialect of Karelian spoken in Tunkua and Rukajärvi as *nezeŋ* (pro *nečen*) *kieli* '*Neze* (pro *Nečče*) language'. Pasanen (2003, 45) similarly found that many Viena Karelians used the designation *nečen kieli* '*Nečče* language' when they referred to Olonets Karelian. The designation *nečen* or *nečen kieli* '*Ne(č)če* language' is derived from the demonstrative pronoun *neče* 'that', which is used in Olonets Karelian (KKS, s.v. *netše*). The designation *nečen kieli* '*Nečče* language' is the same kind of expression as, for example, the *h-kieli* '*h*-language' or *miu-mau-murre* '*miu-mau* dialect' – expressions that Finnish laypeople use when they describe variety on the basis of dialect features (in this case, the consonant *h* in a non-initial syllable or inflected form *miun* 'my') (Mielikäinen and Palander 2014a, s.v. *h-kieli*, *miu-mau-kieli*). These kinds of pronoun-based labels are common among Finnish laypeople, but the Finns use personal pronouns only in these labels (Mielikäinen and Palander 2014b, 72–75). But why does Agafia use the designation *nezeŋ* (pro *nečen*) *kieli* '*Neze* (pro *Nečče*) language' when she describes South Karelian? As noted above, the demonstrative pronoun *neče* 'that' is only used in Olonets Karelian and, according to previous research, *neččen kieli* 'Nečče language' is used to refer to Olonets Karelian. It may be that by *neččen kieli* 'Nečče language' Agafia is referring to all dialects that were previously spoken in the Olonets province – similar to how the designation *snečku/snäčky* 'the *Snečku* ~ the *Snäčky* language' is used. Rukajärvi, where South Karelian is spoken, was previously part of the Olonets province (Nevalainen 1998, 292–293).

In the data, the dialects of Paanajärvi and Kiestinki as well as the varieties of South Karelian are described as *šekon* or *ševot* 'mixed' or 'hodgepodge' (*sevošša*) (examples 12 and 13). The implication is that the informant's own dialect is seen as pure and authentic (see Mielikäinen and Palander 2014b, 228–229). In Finland too, laypeople commonly use words that begin with the root *seka-* 'mixed' when they try to describe somehow problematic dialects (Mielikäinen and Palander 2014b, 230; see Palander 2015, 47). Professional linguists categorize the villages of Tunkua and Rukajärvi as within the speaking area of South Karelian. It is true, however, that, for example, the dialect of Rukajärvi has features of Olonets Karelian as well as White Sea Karelian: plosives are often voiced, but, on the other hand, the first and second person pronouns are of the same type as in White Sea Karelian (*mie* 'I', *sie* 'you' vs. Olonets Karelian *minä* 'I', *sinä* 'you'; KKS s.v. *mie*, *sie*, headword Rukajärvi).

6 Results of the listening task

The reaction test included three short (21–44 second) speech samples of Karelian and Ludian. The first was a sample of Olonets Karelian, which is mainly spoken in the southern parts of the republic. The second sample was Tver Karelian, which is spoken in Central Russia and is linguistically classified as a southern variety of Karelian Proper (for Tver Karelian, see Koivisto in this volume). The third sample was Ludian – a language that occupies an intermediate position between Olonets Karelian and the Veps language and is spoken near the Petrozavodsk area. The speakers in the samples of Olonets Karelian and Tver Karelian were women, and, in the Ludian sample, the speaker was a man. The sample of Olonets Karelian was recorded in 1996, the sample of Tver Karelian in 1957, and the sample of Ludian in 1958. Therefore, samples of Tver Karelian and Ludian represent older forms of the language than the sample of Olonets Karelian.

All the samples included dialect features that differ between White Sea Karelian and the dialect in question. The Olonets Karelian sample included a partitive form in which the partitive ending is *-du*: *suurdu* 'big-PAR' (cf., with White Sea Karelian *-ta*: *suurta* 'big-PAR'). There is also a first person plural form *pastamma* ('we roast') in which the second component of the *i*-ending diphthong has disappeared (cf., with White Sea Karelian *paistamma* 'we roast'). In general, the Olonets Karelian sample – as well as the other samples – featured many voiced plosives (e.g., *suurdu* 'big-PAR', *piiraidu* 'pie-PL-PAR') in the kinds of contexts in which the plosives are usually voiceless in White

Sea Karelian. The Ludian sample included a verb form typical of Ludian: *pyydab* ('fish.for-PR.3SG'; cf., White Sea Karelian *pyytäy* 'fish.for-PR.3SG') as well as *d´* in a context in which White Sea Karelian usually includes *j* (*d´oka* vs. *joka* 'every'). The speech samples were transcribed, and the excerpts can be found in Appendix 2.

The participants received no information about the samples before the listening task. After having listened to the speech samples, the respondents were asked: 'Where can you hear speech like this?' (see Vaattovaara 2012). The samples were played many times before the informants were able to suggest a location. The commentary about the samples as well as the discussions with the interviewer were recorded.

The following sections show how accurately the informants located the Olonets sample, Tver Karelian sample and Ludian sample, as well as how they described the varieties heard in the samples.

6.1 Reactions to the sample of Olonets Karelian

The first sample represented the speech style of Vitele – a small village in Southern Karelia. All the placements that the informants suggested are marked on Map 3. The dots on the maps are bigger in order of the number of times the place in question was mentioned by the respondents.

Two informants placed the sample quite close to its actual source. The speaker was said to come from *Petroskoin perältä* 'beyond Petrazavodsk' or *Petroskoin läheltä* 'near Petrozavodsk'. Three informants did not mention any specific place where the dialect in the sample might be from but labelled the dialect 'correctly'. From examples 14–16, it can be seen that the informants recognised the dialect of Vitele as Olonets Karelian (or South Karelian):

(14) *šnäčkyŋ kieli* (Irina)

[*Šnäčky* language]

(15) *näčkyn* [!] *niiŋkun* (Maikki)

[kind of *Näčky* language]

(16) *Oloṅet´s* (Hilja)

[Olonets Karelian].

Some speakers located the sample to the northern parts of the republic: Kalevala, Jyskyjärvi, and Paanajärvi were all suggested. Ortjo, who lives in Jyskyjärvi, guessed that the sample represented the dialect spoken in his own village. Interestingly, Agafia, who was born in the village of Tahtasovo quite close to the village of Vitele, supposed that the speaker came from Kalevala. As in many previous studies, it was also common in the data that the listeners failed to recognize not only those dialects they themselves were rarely exposed to but also the variety that was designed to represent their own local variety. Age, residence, life history, and mobility may all affect the placements that respondents make. (See, e.g., Williams et al. 1999, 351; Garret et al. 2003, 200–201; Palander and Nupponen 2005, 43–45; Laurila 2008, 70; Vaattovaara 2009, 139.)

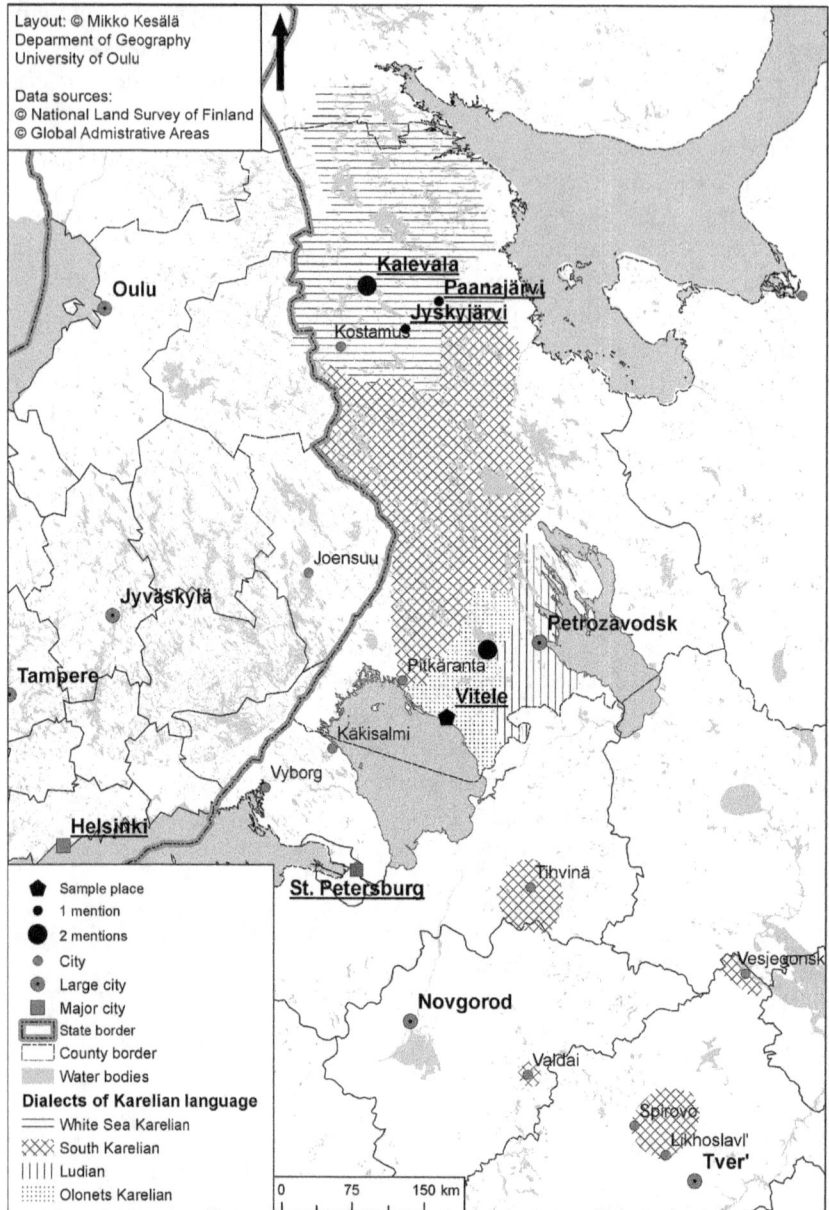

Map 3. Localizations of the Olonets Karelian sample.

Some informants took special note of the unfamiliar words they heard in the sample. For example, Olga guessed that the speech sample represented *eteläkieltä - - tätä karjalaŋ kieltä* 'south language, this Karelian language', by which she probably meant South Karelian, because the woman in the sample used the word *šipainiekat* 'pies'. It is true that the word does not belong to traditional White Sea Karelian, but according to the dictionary of Karelian[6]

6   KKS (Dictionary of Karelian) is a dialect dictionary. It contains examples from almost all dialects of Karelian Proper and Olonets Karelian.

(KKS, s.v. *šipanniekka*), it is only used in Olonets Karelian and not in South Karelian.

Akuliina and Palaka particularly noted the word *kartohka* 'potato'. The women mentioned that in their dialect the word for 'potato' is *potakka* or *peruna*. According to KKS (s.v. *kartohka*), the word *kartohka* is not only used mostly in Olonets Karelian but also in South Karelian.

Some answers were based on words that were not actually spoken in the sample. Agafia placed the sample in Kalevala because – according to her – the woman in the sample said *keitimpiirai* 'a pie baked in grease'. Another informant (Marina) heard the woman in the sample say *lättyö* 'pancake-PAR'. Laurila (2008, 44) and Vaattovaara (2009, 142–143) also found in their studies that sometimes people justified their answers based on words or dialect features that were not in the sample.

Irina and Maikki could not pinpoint any place the sample might be from. Rather, they simply placed the sample outside the Kalevala District:

(17) *ei se ollum me-* **miän** *näitä,* **piirii** (Irina)

[It wasn't from our district.]

(18) **miäm piiriin ei**, *myö niin emmä* [puhu] (Maikki)

[Not our district, we don't speak that way.]

The same kind of process of "drawing boundaries around oneself" has also been seen in the answers of Finnish laypeople when they performed listening tasks (Vaattovaara and Halonen 2015).

All in all, the reactions to the Olonets Karelian sample were, on the one hand, predictable and, on the other, surprising: many people were able to recognise the variety to be Olonets Karelian or a variety spoken in the southern parts of the republic. Others, however, placed the sample in the area of White Sea Karelian and even in their own or a nearby village. The interviewees' perceptions of their own dialect clearly are not as exact as would be expected (see Nupponen 2011, 3).

6.2 REACTIONS TO THE SAMPLE OF TVER KARELIAN

The second sample represented the speech style of Tver Karelian. The guesses that the informants made are marked on Map 4.

None of the informants placed the sample in the Tver area or in areas where South Karelian is spoken. Three informants located the sample near, beyond, or in the surroundings of Petrozavodsk. Three people, in fact, placed the sample in the village of Jyskyjärvi. When I asked the informants why they thought that the sample was from the Petrozavodsk area, they answered:

(19) **kuuluuhan** *tuosta pakinasta* (Elviira)

[You can hear it from the speech.]

(20) *pakinasta - -* **kuulee** *ttei ole me- meiän* [pakina], *se.* (Hilja)

[You can hear from the speech that this is not our speech.]

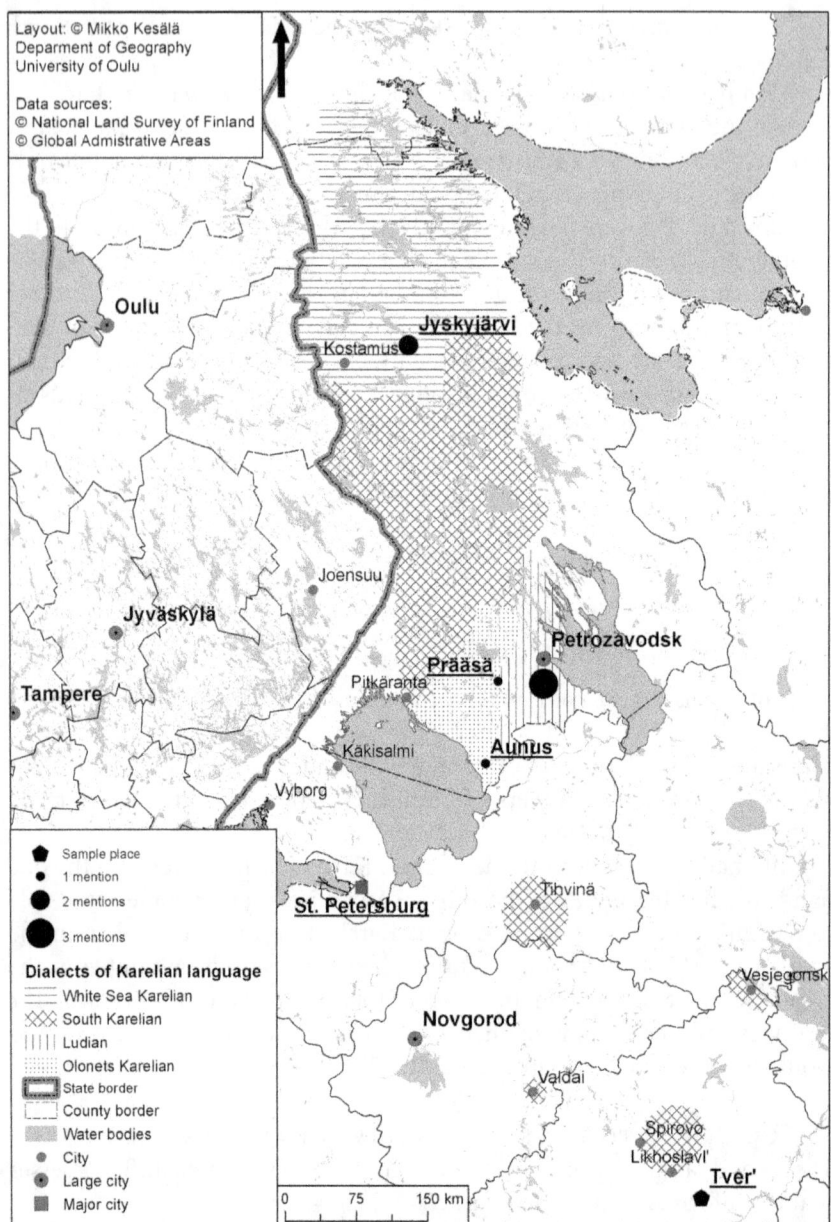

Map 4. Localizations of the Tver Karelian sample.

It is interesting to note that, in Finland, it is also common for laypeople to describe dialect differences with the verb *kuulua* 'hear' (Mielikäinen and Palander 2014b, 112).

Besides the Jyskyjärvi and Petrozavodsk areas, the sample was also located to the Olonets area, as three informants thought that the sample represented Olonets (or South) Karelian:

(21) *snečoi* (Hilja)

[the *Snečoi* language]

(22) *Aunuksen pakina* (Agafia)

[language of Olonets]

(23) *Oloṅets* (Polina)

[Olonets Karelian].

One informant said that the variety was like the Veps language and another thought that the sample represented the dialect of Prääsä (Prjaža), where Ludian is spoken.

It is not surprising that the Tver Karelian sample was not recognized. None of the informants had ever visited or stayed in the speaking area of Tver Karelian. On the radio and television, they hear the varieties of Olonets Karelian, White Sea Karelian, and South Karelian spoken in the Republic of Karelia. It may well be that they had never heard this variety of Karelian before.

6.3 Reactions to the sample of Ludian

The third sample was from the village of Kuujärvi (Mihailovskoje) where Ludian is spoken. The approximations that the informants offered are marked on Map 5.

Two informants located the sample correctly, guessing that it was from

(24) **Petroskoin** *sieltä* **alu̯eelta** *joštaki, oŋkse Jessoila vai* (Polina)

[From the district of Petrozavodsk somewhere, is it Jessoila or?]

(25) **Petroskoin alta** (Akuliina)

[In Petrozavodsk].

Ludian is spoken in the area surrounding of Petrozavodsk as well as in Jessoila (Essoila), which belongs to the district of Prääsä (Prjaža).

Two informants judged that the sample represented Olonets (or South) Karelian:

(26) *se niise samua snečoita* (Hilja)

[this is also the same *Snečoi* language]

(27) *Oloṅetskoita* (Lilja)

[Olonets Karelian].

Two informants located the sample to Olonets:

(28) *Aunuksen sillä kielellä* (Irina)

[language of Olonets]

(29) *Aunuksesta* (Marina)

[from Olonets].

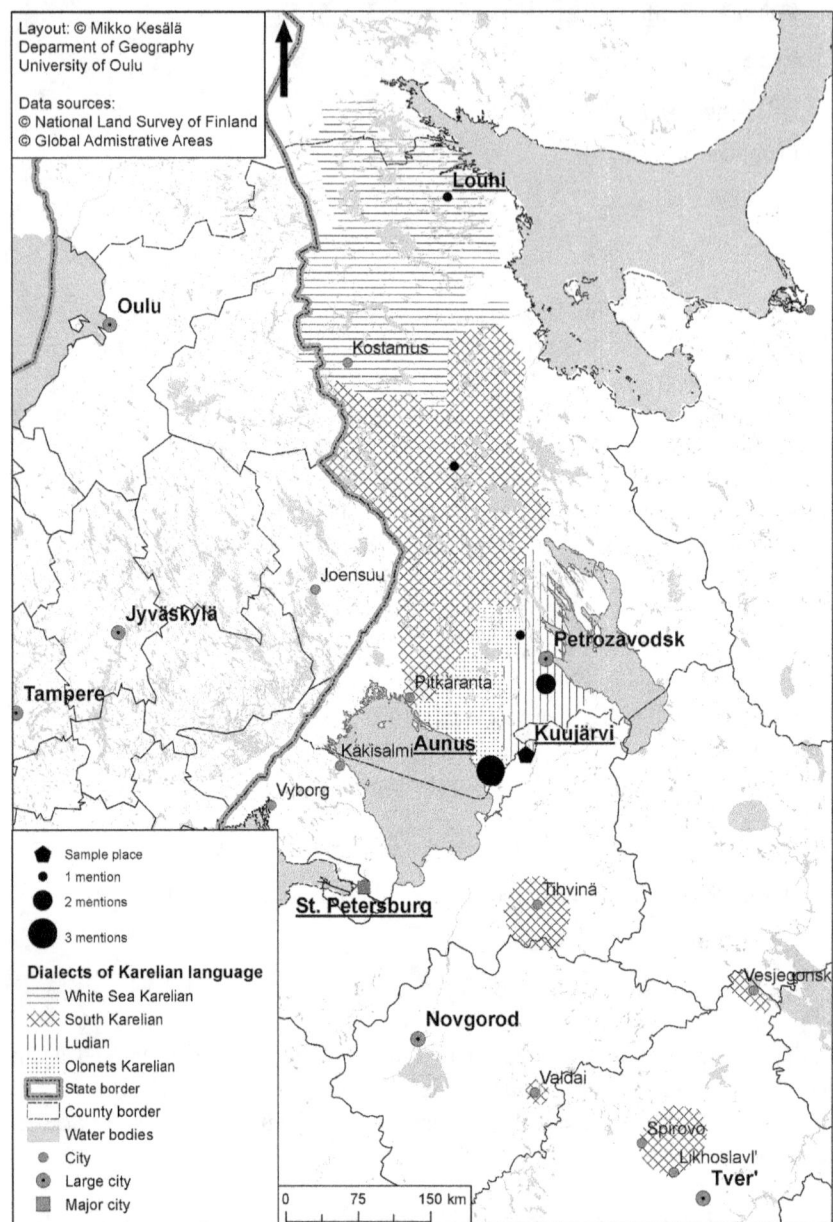

Map 5. Localizations of the Ludian sample.

Ortjo located the sample to the southern part of Karelia and thought that the speech represented the Veps language:

(30) *se on sielä eteläpuolel – – eiköhän ole še, ihan, se **vepšiŋ kieli*** (Ortjo)

[It's from the south; isn't it, it must be that Veps language?]

It is understandable that Ortjo thought that the sample was Veps. Of the varieties of Ludian, the dialect spoken in the village of Kuujärvi has been most affected by the Veps language (e.g., Kettunen 1960, 23–26).

Akuliina said that the sample is

(31) ***Petroskoin** alta, ili **Mujejärven** siinä vot, siinä välissä missä on ihan **šekon ne kielit** (!), ka- kaks kieltä y- yhteh - - ei sillä i nimie ole näemmä sillä šekokiellä.*

[In Petrozavodsk, or from Mujejärvi (Mujezerski), in the middle where the languages have been mixed. Two languages together; there isn't a name for this type of mixed language.]

Akuliina labels the sample a "mixed language" (*šekokieli*). However, according to Pahomov (2017), Ludian cannot be seen as such anymore. Similar to Akuliina, the name of the variety (Ludian) was completely unknown to most of the informants. Ortjo actually thought that I was speaking about the female name *Lyydi* when asked if the term Ludian was familiar to him.

The sample was also thought to represent South Karelian or the dialect of Louhi or, more broadly, a dialect different than the informants' own variety. A couple of people noted individual words they heard in the sample. Agafia, for instance, noticed that the sample included words from Russian (*siin on venäjän sanua* 'It includes Russian words'), and Maikki drew attention to the uniquely Veps relative pronoun *kudam*, which means 'which':

(32) ***koda**, tooše missä noim paissaa, missäk, missäkä noim paissaa* (Maikki)

[*koda*, there where they speak like that; where, wherever do they speak like that?]

The informants also justified their answers to this sample based on words that were not actually uttered. For example, when Agafia discussed the Ludian sample, she noted the speaker's use of: *hierussa* 'village-INE' even though the man in the sample twice said: *derevnjassa* 'village-INE'. (See Laurila 2008, 44; Vaattovaara 2009, 142–143.)

Marina located the Ludian sample outside of her own dialect area based on the cultural context of the sample:

(33)

01 *venehie laittai hoŋkast, eihän hoŋkast venehtä laiteta* (Marina)

[They built boats from pine? Boats aren't built from pine.]

02 *eikö?* (NK)

[Aren't they?]

03 *varmast ei, sehän heti happanou* [laughs] (Marina)

[No, certainly not, it would get mouldy immediately (laughs).]

04 [NK laughs]

05 - - ***eei se meidän se, hoŋkast ei laiteta, ei ole pakina** se myös* (Marina)

[No, it is not ours, we don't build from pine, the speech is not (ours) either.]

Marina did not think the sample could represent her own dialect because in her village boats are not built of pine. As in many previous studies among Finnish laypeople (e.g., Laurila 2008), it was common in this study that people took special note of the content of the samples. In some studies, very short samples (minimum one word) have been employed to prevent people from listening too carefully to the content of the samples (Vaattovaara 2009, 137; Vilhula 2012, 11–12). However, even if the speech sample is very short, there is no such thing as neutral content (Campbell-Kibler 2009, 138), and the content of the sample always influences the perceptions of the subjects (Campbell-Kibler 2007, 34–35).

To sum up, it is understandable that many of the informants thought the sample was from the Olonets area or represented the Veps language. Ludian is spoken in the District of Olonets and the dialect of Kuujärvi is heavily affected by Veps (Kettunen 1960). However, the data show that the label 'Ludian' was familiar to only a couple of the respondents, with most claiming that they had never heard of it.

7 Dialect differences in the Karelian language

One aim of the present study was to explore the kind of dialect differences speakers of White Sea Karelian were aware of. As expected, many of the interviewed were aware of lexical differences among Karelian dialects, but they also focused on phonetic differences.

Preston (2002, 50–51) divides language perceptions according to the following taxonomy:
1) *Availability*: Which language features are recognized, and how easily are they commented on?
2) *Accuracy*: How exact are the perceptions, and how do they represent linguistic facts?
3) *Detail*: How detailed are the perceptions (general awareness of a variety vs. specific details)?
4) *Control*: How well can the informant control or imitate the specific variety?

(See also Mielikäinen and Palander 2014b, 18; Palander 2015, 35–36.)

7.1 DIFFERENCES IN VOCABULARY

As previous research has shown (e.g., Mononen 2013, 138), the lexical aspect of dialect is a topic that is much discussed by laypeople. In this sense, it can be said that it is a feature that is readily *available* (Preston 2002, 50–51). The informants were well aware that their own dialect includes more loanwords from Finnish and vice versa, and that other Karelian varieties are more influenced by Russian. This closeness to the Finnish language was a topic that every informant touched on:

(34) *meiäŋ karjalaŋ kielihän se – – on – – šamammoista ku, šuomalaisetki puhutaa, paissaah.* (Hilja)

[Our Karelian language is similar to the language Finnish people speak.]

(35) *meil ol lähellä niiŋkun šuomeŋ kieldä* (Irina)

[Our Karelian language is close to the Finnish language.]

(36) *karjala še on šama šuomi – – on se melkein šama, no on niitä šanoja vähäni* [erilaisia] (Iivo)

[Karelian and Finnish: they are the same; it's almost the same. Well, there are some words that are different.]

(37) *meil oŋ karjalaŋ kieli ševotettuna šuomeŋ kieleh* (Lilja)

[We have a Karelian language that's mixed with the Finnish language.]

(38) *tämä miäŋ Kale- Kalevalan* [murre] *nii hän on oikeil lähel – – suomeŋ, kielellä* (Irina)

[This, our Kalevala dialect, is very close to the Finnish language.]

Ortjo, in fact, considers that his dialect is Finnish:

(39) *myö puhumma – – šuomeŋ kielellä vet*

[We speak the Finnish language.]

In a previous study (Kunnas 2013), it was shown that many Viena Karelian laypeople designate their own variety as *Finnish* and do not draw a language border between White Sea Karelian and Finnish. On the other hand, Viena Karelians may draw a language border between Olonets and White Sea Karelian (see Section 4 and Kunnas 2013).

According to the laypeople, the use of Finnish loanwords varies from village to village inside the speaking area of White Sea Karelian, and Finnish was not seen to have affected the dialect of Jyskyjärvi that much:

(40) *meillä* [Kalevalassa] *ta Vuokkiniemeš on paremmin, šitä šuomalaist enempi šanoja, šuomalaisie šanoja – – toizemmoini siellä heil* [Jyskyjärvellä] *on* (Olga)

[In the dialects of Kalevala and Vuokkiniemi, we have more Finnish words; the dialect of Jyskyjärvi is different.]

(41) [Jyskyjärvellä] *on semmosii karjalaisii* [sanoja] *jotta ei – – ole nikun, suomalaisi̯a sanoja* (Irina)

[In Jyskyjärvi, we have Karelian words, not really Finnish words.]

In previous research (Kunnas 2007, 43), Karelian laypeople have also commented on the fact that in the western villages of the Viena area the influence of the Finnish language is greater than in Jyskyjärvi.

According to Hilja, on the other hand, the heavy influence of Russian begins nearby, in the village of Paanajärvi. She claimed that

(42) *Puanajärves – – puoli sanua sanotaa venyäheksi ja paljon venäjäŋ kieldä – – Puanajärves käyttää. – – enemmäŋ käytössä se venäjäŋ kieli.*

[In the village of Paanajärvi they say half of the words in Russian and they use a lot of Russian. They use more Russian.]

Akuliina also said to Agafia, who was born in the speaking area of Olonets Karelian, that

(43) *teil* [livviläisillä] *on enemmän niiŋku venäjäŋ kieli*

[Your language is more like the Russian language.]

Some informants commented on single words that are different in Karelian varieties. Agafia drew attention to variation in the words for 'frog', 'curtain', and 'rubbish'. She had noticed that in White Sea Karelian 'frog' is *skokuna*, but in Olonets Karelian it is *slöppi*[7], and 'curtain' is *sanaveskad* in Olonets Karelian, but the people in Jyskyjärvi use the Finnish loanword *verho(t)*. Agafia had also found that in Jyskyjärvi, the commonly used word for 'rubbish' is *ruhka* whereas the word *toppa*, which is used in Olonets Karelian with the meaning 'rubbish', means 'flue' in White Sea Karelian dialects. Olga claimed that the word 'clean' is different in Jyskyjärvi and in her own dialect. According to Olga, people in Kalevala use the verb *siivota* 'to clean' whereas the people in Jyskyjärvi use the verb *rabiestoa* 'to clean'. Akuliina also had noticed that the word for 'door clasp' differs in Karelian varieties: she had not understood when a woman from the speaking area of Olonets Karelian had said *pane d´sokka se oveeh* 'Close the door clasp!' In White Sea Karelian, the word for 'door clasp' is *čäppi*.

7.2 Phonological differences

Viena Karelian laypeople are also aware of some phonological differences between different Karelian varieties. For example, the informants described other Karelian varieties spoken on the eastern or southern sides of their own language area as *smoother*. Comments like (44) are common in the data.

(44) *Petroskoil luo – – hyö nin, oikeim pehmi͜essa (!) paissaa, oikeim **pehmiesti**. Vot Agafia Petrovna* [Aunuksen alueelta kotoisin oleva], *hänel oma kieli on oikeim **pehmie** kieli. – – hyö paissah oikeim **pehmiesti** paissaa, heil om **pehmie** semmoni kieli.* (Akuliina)

[Around Petrozavodsk, they speak very smoothly, very smoothly, Agafia Petrovna (a speaker of Olonets Karelian) her own language is a very smooth language, they speak very smoothly, they have got that kind of smooth language.]

Olonets Karelian, in general, and the dialect of Paanajärvi were also described as *smoother* than the informants' own dialect, and the dialect of Olonets Karelian was labelled *pehmie pakina* 'smooth speech'. Added to that, Lilja defined her own dialect as *pure* and *hard*:

(45) *meil oli iham puhas karjalaŋ kieli, ko- niiŋku **kovalla*** (Lilja)

[We had a completely pure Karelian language, har- it's like hard.]

---

7   According to KKS, *šlöpöi*.

These comments have been interreted to mean that the respondents mean that in other varieties of Karelian there are more voiced plosives than in their own dialect, e.g., *pelto* vs. *peldo* 'field'. Many Finnish laypeople have also described Olonets and the South Karelian spoken in Border Karelia as *smooth* and commented that the plosives are often voiced, e.g., *buabo* 'grandmother' (Palander 2015, 49, 51; see Mielikäinen and Palander 2014a, s.v. *pehmeä, pehmyt*). It is not uncommon for laypeople to be able to separate voiced and voiceless consonants, typically using the terms *smooth* and *hard* (Mielikäinen and Palander 2014b, 221).

The data also contain one example that indicates that the informant had noticed differences in plosives between White Sea Karelian and southern varieties of Karelian:

(46) *Petroskoim perällä:* '*buaji **daa da**, šano **daa da**'* [nauraa]. *'Elä **buaji**'* – – *miän, miän ihmised* – – *paissah.* (Hilja)

[Beyond Petrozavodsk: speak daa da, say daa da (laughs). Don't speak. – – Our, our people speak.]

Hilja's mimicking includes the voiced plosives /b/ and /d/, and she gave the impression that Karelian speakers beyond or in the surroundings of Petrozavodsk use these phonemes extensively – or at least more than in her own dialect. In this imitation, Hilja cited the speakers of Karelian near Petrozavodsk. Among laypeople, imitation is commonly used to illustrate dialectal and often phonological differences (Mielikäinen and Palander 2014b, 26–27, 151). Hilja also claimed that speakers of Karelian near Petrozavodsk use the verb *buajie* 'to speak' whereas the speakers of White Sea Karelian use the verb *paissa* 'to speak' instead. This is interesting because, according to KKS (s.v. *poajie*), *poajie* or *puajie* 'to speak' is a verb used only in northern parts of Karelia and only in dialects of White Sea Karelian. Here, the folk knowledge on the dialect differences is not accurate compared with linguistic knowledge.

With respect to the phonological perceptions of laypeople, it can be stated that the quality of consonants is a language feature that is readily *available* and much commented on. However, the perceptions are not very *detailed*: the informants spoke only about *smooth* or *hard* consonants or speech styles. In the one example of imitation, the plosives were concretely pronounced (voiced), and, in that case, it can be said that the variety was well *controlled*. It is interesting to note that none of the Kalevala laypeople had noticed that the dialect of the nearby village of Jyskyjärvi already includes more voiced plosives than their own speech style and that none of the informants commented on the vowel differences between Karelian dialects.

7.3 Phonetic differences

At the phonetic level, there is one phone that was commented on very much: /s/. Many people had noted the variation in /s/ and /š/ in Karelian dialects.

Agafia, who was born in the speaking area of Olonets Karelian, said:

(47)

01 *tiälä* [Jyskyjärvessä] *oltih -s šše, a mie aina sanon ki**ss**a, lamma**s** - -.* (Agafia)

[Here (in Jyskyjärvi) was *šše*, but I always say *kissa* (a cat), *lammas* (a sheep).]

02 *oŋko se äš täälä erimoini ku siel?* (NK)

[Is the *š* here different from there (in the speaking area of Olonets Karelian)?]

03 *no še on tiäl enem- - - **šše, semmoine**, a meil on **ess** enemmä, pakinoissa, vop*

04 *pakinoissa ni jo samassa kuuluu semmoni sanaki* [pro *äännekin*.] (Agafia)

[Well, here it is more *šše*, that kind of, and we have more *ess* in our speech; in the word *pakinoissa* you can hear that kind of word (should be *sound*).]

Agafia had noticed that she uses a sharper /s/ whereas those people whose mother tongue is White Sea Karelian more extensively use /š/.

Akuliina compared Olonets Karelian with her own dialect and said:

(48) *meil on šemmoni jo **šššš, äššätämmä myö**, semmoni - - kieli on*

[We (Viena Karelians) have a kind of *š*, we speak with *š*, that kind of language.]

Polina, as well, drew attention to the phenomenon that speakers of White Sea Karelian use /š/ more extensively than Karelian speakers in the southern parts of the republic:

(49) *tiälä Pohjolassa* [Karjalan pohjoisosassa] *paremmin, šš, sössö-, **šöššötellää*** (Polina)

[Here in the North, more *šš*, lisp- maybe we're sort of lisping.]

(50) *meil on tässä niiŋku Kalevalam piirissä - - niiŋku Kaenuun* (!)*, tämä murre, tämä šöš-, šöššötelly, **šöššöttely, äššällä puhuta**, - - Kalevalam piirišsä, ašunto ei asunto kun ašunto ašunto.* (Polina)

[In the Kalevala District we have the same kind of dialect as in Kainuu (one area of Finland), this kind of lisping, lisping, we speak with *š* in the Kalevala District. We say *ašunto* ('apartment') not *asunto* ('apartment').]

It is clear that in examples 49 and 50 Polina is using the word *šöššöttely* 'lisping' to refer to the phenomenon that speakers of White Sea Karelian use /š/ extensively. What is interesting in this context is that other speaking areas of Karelian were also ascribed the label *šöššöttely* 'lisping' by the informants. Varieties of Karelian spoken in the Petrozavodsk area as well as in Paanajärvi were also described as marked by 'lisping':

(51)

01 *tuošša **Puanajärvi** - - hyö jo toisel taval puhutaa* (Irina)

[People in Paanajärvi speak differently than we do.]

02 *heil om pehmie šemmoini kieli* (Maikki)

[They have that kind of smooth language.]

03 *no ne **sössötetää** - - hyö toiseeh tapaah paissaa kum myö* (Irina)

[Well, they lisp, they speak differently than we do.]

(51)

01 *tuolla **Petroskoin** lähellä, siellä niikuin* - - (Polina)

[There near Petrozavodsk, they kind of...]

- -

02 ***sössöttämällä** paissaa* (Irina)

[lisp when they speak].

The various interpretations of 'lisping' may be due to laypeople finding it hard to describe linguistic phenomena. The colloquial language term 'lisping' can also mean different dialect features to different informants (see Niedzielski and Preston 2000, 4–5; Mielikäinen and Palander 2014b, 80).

During her student days, Akuliina had noted the speech style of a woman from the village of Mujejärvi, where South Karelian is spoken. Akuliina imitated the woman:

(52)

01 *niim pakasi jotta: 'sinä sano sinä vot* - - *si si', vot niin pakasi hän,*

02 *essätti, essätti. essätti niiŋku, essätti niin, hiän. hänel šemmone kieli oli.*

[She spoke like: 'You speak you, *si- si-*', well that was the way she spoke, she spoke with *s*, she had that kind of language.]

In example 52, in line 1, Akuliina articulates every sibilant in a very fronted position. In addition, Akuliina mentions that the woman from Mujejärvi *essätti* 'spoke with *s*'. In this context, the verb *essättää* 'to speak with *s*' probably means that the woman used a sharp, fronted /s/ instead of /š/. /s/ is transliterated into Russian as с and pronounced [es]. Pekka Zaikov (e-mail message, 10 June 2014) has posited that the designation *snečku* (pronounced with a sharp *s*) is also connected to the abundant use of sharp /s/ among speakers of Olonets Karelian.

It is clear that to laypeople these sibilants are somehow markers of separate varieties of Karelian. Despite the saliency and folk awareness of /s/ variation, sociolinguists have conducted little research on this variable. There are, however, a couple of studies in which the focus has been on the dialectal distribution of /s/ and /š/ in Karelian (e.g., Virtaranta 1946, 1984; Zaikov 2011).

All varieties of Karelian include the voiceless postalveolar sibilant /š/, but could it be that it is somehow acoustically different in different dialects? Virtaranta (1946, 38) argues that the noise of /š/ is more intense in Olonets Karelian, Veps, North Ludian, and the northern villages of the South Karelian speaking area than in the northern villages of the South Karelian speaking area. He (1946, 38) does not comment on the /š/ that is used in White Sea Karelian.

Even though the informants claim that speakers of White Sea Karelian use more /š/ (see also Zaikov 2013, 37), in certain contexts /š/ is more common in Olonets Karelian. For example, after a diphthong that ends in *i,* or in consonant clusters after *i,* there is no /š/ in White Sea Karelian, but in southern varieties of Karelian, /š/ occurs: *lašku* 'lazy', *mušta* 'black', *išköy* 'hits' (Virtaranta 1984, 269; KKM, maps 36, 78–82, 170). In this context, the folk findings on the distribution of /š/ are not accurate compared with linguistic knowledge. However, in word-initial contexts, /š/ is more common in Karelian Proper than in Olonets Karelian (*šada* vs. *sada* 'hundred', *šilmä* vs. *silmä* 'eye'; Virtaranta 1946, 5, 1984, 263–265; KKM, maps 74–76, 86, 93–95, 125). In specific cases, /š/ is also more common in word-internal positions in White Sea Karelian: *kešä* 'summer', *lapši* 'child', *kuuši* 'six' (Virtaranta 1984, 267; KKM, maps 77, 88, 89, 91, 96).

Zaikov (2011) supposes that North Russian dialects have affected White Sea Karelian such that the /š/ has become very common in White Sea Karelian. On the other hand, Virtaranta (1946, 39) has noticed that in some South Karelian dialects, which are very close to the Russian areas, /š/ is not very common. Virtaranta (1946, 36–39) has also found that /š/ is used more systematically in the northern villages of the South Karelian speaking area than in southern villages.

Ingrian Finnish, which is also spoken in Russia, also includes /š/. According to Mononen (2013), Ingrian Finn laypeople think that the 'shaa' sound (the Russian original /š/ pronounced [shaa]) is a typical feature of Ingrian Finnish. One informant noted that when young Ingrian Finns speak Finnish they absolutely try to avoid this 'stigmatized' sound. It is also suggested that the /š/ fades out of the idiolect when the speakers move to Finland. (Mononen 2013, 140–142.) As a matter of fact, Finnish laypeople are very accurate observers of sound differences: An informant who had moved to Finland from the speaking area of Olonets Karelian was identified as Karelian based on her/his sibilants. Finnish laypeople commented on the informant's speech: *sihahtaa niin kummasti* '(your speech) hisses so weirdly'. (Mielikäinen and Palander 2014b, 221.) Riionheimo and Palander (2017) have conducted listening tasks with Finnish laypeople, and, according to their data, it is common that laypeople notice /š/ when they hear a sample of Karelian language.

Variation in /s/ seems to be a phenomenon that laypeople universally recognize. In Finland, the fronted, sharp /s/, in particular, has been a point of much comment. For example, in recent folk linguistics studies outside the Helsinki area, the fronted, sharp /s/ was defined as a 'metropolitan' language feature, whereas laypeople in the Helsinki area defined a fronted, sharp /s/ as a feature of girls from East Helsinki. (E.g., Mielikäinen and Palander 2002, 97; Vaattovaara and Soininen-Stojanov 2006; Palander 2007, 43.) According to Aittokallio (2002, 80), the fronted sharp /s/ is a 'feminine' [s] in Finnish. In Sweden, there are similar areal and social differences in the *sj* sound. The fronted *sj* is regarded as 'more elegant', and it is associated with middle class norms about good social skills in the Stockholm area. In Sweden the fronted *sj* is also considered 'feminine' in nature. (Elert 1989, 77.)

The variation of /s/ is a marker of social identity in many speech communities (Vaattovaara and Halonen 2015; and sources mentioned). In Britain, the frontness of /s/ discloses the social class to which people belong (Levon and Holmes-Elliot 2012). Certain types of /s/ has been shown to be indexical of the *Pissis* speech style[8] of Helsinki Finnish (Vaattovaara 2013), gayness and femininity in 'modern Copenhagen speech' (e.g., Pharao et al. 2014), femininity and gayness in a man's voice in Afrikaans (Bekker and Levon 2016), and gayness as well as non-heteronormative identity in English (e.g., Campbell-Kipler 2011; Podesva and van Hofwegen 2014; Saigusa 2016). Based on the results presented in this section, it seems that in many speech communities the fronted /s/ has a higher status than the voiceless postalveolar sibilant /š/. In addition to Ingrian Finnish, in specific dialects of German, using /š/ is stigmatized (Mielikäinen and Palander 2014b, 222; and sources mentioned).

There are three semiotic processes by which people construct ideological representations of linguistic differences: 1) *iconization*, 2) *fractal recursivity*, and 3) *erasure* (Irvine and Gal 2000, 37–39; Kroskrity 2000, 22; Milani 2010, 120–121). In iconization, linguistic features are associated with the language user as if they were her/his natural features. One example of iconization is the connection between the fronted, sharp /s/ and teenage girls from (East) Helsinki. Erasure means that certain linguistic features are totally ignored or are isolated to the peculiarity of a single small group. In fact, erasure and iconization, as processes, are closely related to each other. (Mäntynen et al. 2012, 330–331.) In the present data, the process of iconization can be seen when laypeople connect extensive use of the voiceless postalveolar sibilant /š/ to speakers of White Sea Karelian. On the other hand, the same process could also qualify as erasure because extensive use of /š/ is represented as a peculiarity of one group of Karelian speakers, and laypeople do not seem to recognize that other speakers of Karelian also use it. Furthermore, we can talk about *enregisterment* (Agha 2005). Enregisterment is a language-ideological process, where, e.g., a certain type of sound becomes prominent in a language and begins to carry social meaning (Vaattovaara and Halonen 2015, 71). In northern parts of the Republic of Karelia, the voiceless postalveolar sibilant /š/ carries the meaning of being a speaker of White Sea Karelian.

Although this data set is small, and the study is more like a pilot in nature, it can be asserted that there is a perceptual connection between the form (extensive use of /š/) and the group identified as using it (speakers of White Sea Karelian). However, this /s/ vs. /š/ phenomenon needs additional study to find out what this is all about. Verbal guise tests with very short stimulus that emphasize different types of /s/ are needed as well as interviews with laypeople from all over Karelia. Dialectological as well as folk linguistic studies will be needed to deepen knowledge about the /s/ variation and its social nature.

8   *Pissis* or *Pissa-Liisa* 'Piss-Lisa' refers to ill-mannered, cider-drinking teenage girls who wear (tight-fitting) brand-name clothes (Paunonen 2006; Vaattovaara 2013, footnote 3; Lehtonen 2015, 142–144).

8 Conclusion

This article has examined dialect perceptions of Viena Karelian laypeople. It has also explored how these people evaluate and designate different varieties of Karelian. One aim has been to determine the dialect features that are discussed among laypeople, as well as the kinds of dialect differences they are aware of, and how well they can perform in the listening task.

The findings show that, according to the informants, the perceived dialect or language area of White Sea Karelian is much smaller than the dialect area defined by professional linguists. It was common to think that White Sea Karelian is spoken only in the Kalevala National District. Many informants also thought that Paanajärvi does not belong to the dialect area of White Sea Karelian, and that the dialect spoken there is different from the informants' own dialect. The dialect of Paanajärvi was described as *Snečoi language* and heavily influenced by Russian. The dialects spoken in Tunkua and Rukajärvi, in the speaking area of South Karelian, were described as *Nečče language* as well as mixed varieties.

In the listening task, the informants heard samples of Olonets Karelian, Tver Karelian, and Ludian. A few people recognized the Olonets sample as Olonets Karelian or a southern variety of Karelian, but it was also located to the speaking area of White Sea Karelian. The Tver Karelian sample was not located to Central Russia or the speaking area of South Karelian. The sample was mostly placed near Petrozavodsk or in the speaking area of Olonets Karelian. Many informants located the sample of Ludian quite close to the real place. The sample was thought to represent Olonets Karelian or the speech style that is spoken near Petrozavodsk. However, no one named the sample as Ludian, and this was a completely strange designation to most of the informants. The listening task showed that the dialect awareness of Viena Karelians is not very high, and even their 'own' variety was incorrectly located in one case.

When it comes to dialect perceptions, it can be said that differences in vocabulary are readily *available* and much discussed among Viena Karelians. The informants had accurate perceptions about Finnish origin words and their distribution as well as about the influence of Russian. At the phonological level, the quality of consonants, especially plosives, was also *available* amongst the informants. However, the perceptions of the informants were not very *accurate*, and it was common to describe the differences with colloquial terms like *smooth* and *hard*.

At the phonetic level, the variation in /s/ and /š/ was widely commented on by the informants. They had noticed the phenomenon that speakers of White Sea Karelian use /š/ extensively whereas in southern varieties of Karelian /s/ is more common. The speakers of White Sea Karelian were described to 'lisp' or 'speak with š', and speakers of other varieties were said to use the sharp /s/ more. According to the data, there is a perceptual connection between the form (extensive use of /š/) and the group identified as using it (speakers of White Sea Karelian). This connection could also be characterized as semiotic processes of iconization or erasure. By these processes, people construct ideological representations of linguistic differences.

This study raises many questions: What kind of variation is there in modern day dialects of White Sea Karelian outside the Kalevala National District? Are those dialects really as different from the Kalevala and Jyskyjärvi dialects as the informants suggest? At the phonetic level, it is clear that the abundant use of /š/ is an index of being a speaker of White Sea Karelian, but what is the larger picture? Sociolinguistic as well as sociophonetic methods are required to deepen knowledge of /s/ and /š/ variation in Karelian varieties as well as perceptions about their distribution. Nonetheless, this study has shown that, like many other language communities, this small endangered minority language community has built a social and linguistic identity around a particular type of sibilant.

Data

Recordings of laypeople in Jyskyjärvi and Kalevala: ONA IMS 225 – ONA IMS 238. Recording archive of Oulu. University of Oulu.
Sample of Olonets Karelian: ONA IMS 212: 2. Recording archive of Oulu. University of Oulu.
Sample of Tver Karelian: SKNA 87:1a. Archive of Finnish language. Institute for the Languages of Finland. Helsinki.
Sample of Ludian: SKNA 110:1. Archive of Finnish language. Institute for the Languages of Finland. Helsinki.

Glossing abbreviations

3SG	third person singular
INE	inessive
PAR	partitive
PL	plural
PR	present tense

References

Agha, Asif. 2005. "Voice, Footing and Enregisterment." *Journal of Linguistic Anthropology* 15:1:38–59.
Aittokallio, Kristiina. 2002. "Etinen, terävä [s] medioalveolaarisen /s/-äänteen varianttina" [Fronted, sharp [s] as a variant of media alveolar /s/]. MA thesis. University of Turku.
Bekker, Ian, and Erez Levon. 2016. "Perception in Contact: Evaluation of New Language Practices among Afrikaans-English Bilinguals in South Africa". Paper presented in Sociolinguistic Symposium 21 at the University of Murcia, June 16.
Bilaniuk, Laada. 2005. *Contested Tongues: Language Politics and Cultural Correction in Ukraine*. Ithaca: Cornell University Press.
Campbell-Kibler, Kathryn. 2007. "Accent, (ING), and the Social Logic of Listener Perceptions." *American Speech* 82:32–64.

Campbell-Kibler, Kathryn. 2009. "The Nature of Sociolinguistic Perception." *Language Variation and Change* 21:135–56.

Campbell-Kibler, Kathryn. 2011. "Intersecting Variables and Perceived Sexual Orientation in Men." *American Speech* 86:52–68.

Dickinson, Jennifer. 2010. "Languages for the Market, the Nation, or the Margins: Overlapping Ideologies of Language and Identity in Zakarpattia." *International Journal of Sociology of Language* 201:53–78.

Elert, Claes-Christian. 1989. *Allmän och svensk fonetik* [General and Swedish phonetics]. Stockholm: Norstedts.

Ethnologue = *Ethnologue. Languages of the World*. Accessed April 15, 2015. https://www.ethnologue.com/.

Fairclough, Norman. 1989. *Language and Power*. London: Longman.

Garret, Peter, Nikolas Coupland, and Angie Williams. 2003. *Investigating Language Attitudes. Social Meanings of Dialect, Ethnicity and Performance*. Cardiff: University of Wales Press.

Hodge, Robert, and Gunther Kress. 1996. *Language as Ideology*. London: Routledge.

Irvine, Judith T., and Susan Gal. 2000. "Language Ideology and Linguistic Differentiation." In *Regimes of Language. Ideologies, Polities, and Identities*, edited by Paul V. Kroskrity, 35–83. Santa Fe, New Mexico: School of American Research Press.

Juusela, Kaisu. 1998. "Yksilölliset poikkeamat morfologiassa" [Individual Divergences in Morphology]. In *Kirjoituksia muoto- ja merkitysopista* [Writings about morphology and semantics], edited by Urho Määttä and Klaus Laalo, Folia fennistica & linguistica 21, 51–75. Department of Finnish and General Linguistics. Tampere: Tampere University Press.

Kalliokoski, Jyrki. 1995. "Johdanto" [Introduction]. In *Teksti ja ideologia. Kieli ja valta julkisessa kielenkäytössä* [Text and ideology. Language and power in public language use], edited by Jyrki Kalliokoski, 8–36. Helsinki: University of Helsinki.

Karelstat 2005 = *Karelstat. Natsionalni sostav naselenija respubliki Karelija. Statistitseski sbornik N 5* [Karelstat. The National Composition of the Population in the Republic of Karelia. Statistic Collection No. 5]. Petrozavodsk.

Karjalainen, Heini, Ulriikka Puura, Riho Grünthal, and Svetlana Kovaleva 2013. *Karelian in Russian. ELDIA Case-Specific Report*. Studies in European Language Diversity 26.

Kettunen, Lauri. 1960. *Suomen lähisukukielten luonteenomaiset piirteet* [Typical features of cognate languages of Finnish]. Publications of the Finno-Ugrian Society 199. Helsinki.

KKM = Bubrih, D. V., A. A. Beljakov, and A. V. Punžina. 1997. *Karjalan kielen murrekartasto* [Dialect atlas of Karelian language] (edited by Leena Sarvas). Helsinki: Institute for the Languages of Finland and the Finno-Ugrian Society.

KKS = *Karjalan kielen sanakirja 1–6* [Dictionary of Karelian 1–6]. Lexica Societatis Fenno-Ugricae XVI,1–6. Helsinki: Finno-Ugrian Society. 1968–2005.

Kroskrity, Paul V. 2000. "Regimenting Languages: Language Ideological Perspectives." In *Regimes of Language. Ideologies, Polities, and Identities*, edited by Paul V. Kroskrity, 1–34. Santa Fe, New Mexico: School of American Research Press.

Kunnas, Niina. 2006. "Yksi, kaksi vai monta kirjakieltä? Vienankarjalaisten kanta kirjakielidebattiin" [How many literary forms of Karelian? A Viena Karelian viewpoint on the literary language debate]. *Virittäjä* 110:229–247.

Kunnas, Niina. 2007. *Miten muuttuu runokylien kieli. Reaaliaikatutkimus jälkitavujen A-loppuisten vokaalijonojen variaatiosta vienalaismurteissa* [Language change in Viena Karelian villages: A real-time study of phonological variation in dialects of Viena]. Acta Universitatis Ouluensis. Humaniora B 78. Oulu: University of Oulu.

Kunnas, Niina. 2009. "Ethnic Loyalty as an Explanatory Factor behind Individual Differences in Variation." *SKY Journal of Linguistics* 22:175–219.

Kunnas, Niina. 2013. "Vienankarjalaisten kielikäsityksiä" [Language conceptions of Viena Karelians]. In *Karjala-kuvaa rakentamassa* [Constructing the image of Karelia], edited by Pekka Suutari, 289–330. Helsinki: Finnish Literature Society.

Kunnas, Niina, and Laura Arola. 2010. "Perspectives on the Attitudes of Minority Language Speakers in Swedish Torne Valley and Viena Karelia." In *Planning a New Standard Language. Finnic Minority Languages Meet the New Millennium*, edited by Helena Sulkala and Harri Mantila, Studia Fennica Linguistica 15, 119–46. Helsinki: Finnish Literature Society.

Laurila, Anna-Leena. 2008. "Mielteitä omasta murteesta. Kansanlingvistinen tutkimus Lammilta" [Perceptions about own dialect. Folk linguistic study from Lammi]. MA thesis. University of Helsinki.

Lehtonen, Heini 2015. *Tyylitellen. Nuorten kielelliset resurssit ja kielen sosiaalinen indeksisyys monietnisessä Helsingissä* [Stylising. Linguistic resources of young people and social indexes of language in multi-ethnic Helsinki]. PhD diss., University of Helsinki, Department of Finnish, Finno-Ugrian and Scandinavian Studies. http://urn.fi/URN:ISBN:978-951-51-1333-7.

Levon, Erez, and Sophie Holmes-Elliot. 2012. "The Only Way is /s/. Doing Gender and Constructing Class in the Southeast of England." Paper presented in Sociolinguistic Symposium 19, Berlin, August 23.

Liebscher, Grit, and Jennifer Dailey-O'Cain. 2009. "Language Attitudes in Interaction." *Journal of Sociolinguistics* 13:195–222.

Mielikäinen, Aila, and Marjatta Palander. 2002. "Suomalaisten murreasenteista" [Finnish attitudes to dialects]. *Sananjalka* 44:86–109.

Mielikäinen, Aila, and Marjatta Palander. 2014a. *Miten murteista puhutaan? Kansanlingvistinen sanakirja* [How do people talk about dialects? Folk linguistic dictionary]. Accessed May 24, 2015. http://kielikampus.jyu.fi/mitenmurteistapuhutaan.

Mielikäinen, Aila, and Marjatta Palander. 2014b. *Miten suomalaiset puhuvat murteista. Kansanlingvistinen tutkimus metakielestä* [How Finns talk about dialects. Folk linguistic study on metalanguage]. Suomi 203. Helsinki: Finnish Literature Society.

Milani, Tommaso M. 2010. "What's in a Name? Language Ideology and Social Differentiation in a Swedish Print-Mediated Debate." *Journal of Sociolinguistics* 14:116–142.

Mononen, Kaarina. 2013. *Inkerinsuomalaisten suomen kielen käyttö Pietarissa ja sen lähialueella* [Use of Finnish among Ingrian-Finns in St Petersburg and its surroundings]. PhD diss., University of Helsinki, Department of Finnish, Fenno-Ugric and Nordic languages and literatures. helda.helsinki.fi/bitstream/handle/10138/38319/inkerins.pdf?sequence=1.

Mäntynen, Anne, Mia Halonen, Sari Pietikäinen, and Anna Solin. 2012. "Kieli-ideologioiden teoriaa ja käytäntöä" [Theory and practice in the analysis of language ideologies]. *Virittäjä* 116:325–348.

Nevalainen, Pekka. 1998. "Aunuksen Karjala" [Olonets Karelia]. In *Karjala. Historia, kansa, kulttuuri* [Karelia. History, folk, culture], edited by Pekka Nevalainen and Hannes Sihvo, 292–302. SKST 705. Helsinki: Finnish Literature Society.

Niedzielski, Nancy A., and Preston, Dennis R. 2000. *Folk Linguistics*. Trends in Linguistics: Studies and Monographs 122. Berlin: Mouton de Gruyter.

Nupponen, Anne-Maria. 2005. "Iloisuus ja eloisa murre. Siirtokarjalaisten käsityksiä ja havaintoja murteista ja karjalaisuudesta" [Joyfulness and a vivid dialect. Conceptions and perceptions on dialects and karelianness by Karelian evacuees.] In *Monenlaiset karjalaiset. Suomen karjalaisten kielellinen identiteetti* [Karelians' many faces: The linguistic identity of Karelians in Finland], edited by Marjatta Palander and Anne-Maria Nupponen, 15–55. Studia Carelica Humanistica 20. Joensuu: University of Joensuu.

Nupponen, Anne-Maria. 2011. "Savon murre savolaiskorvin. Kansa murteen havainnoijana" [The 'Savo dialect' according to Savo residents. Folk perceptions of dialectal speech], Paper presented in thesis defence at University of Eastern Finland April 4. *Virittäjä* 115. Web appendix.

Pahomov, Miikul. 2017. *Lyydiläiskysymys: kansa vai heimo, kieli vai murre* [Ludian question: nation or tribe, language or dialect]. Helsinki: University of Helsinki and the Ludian society.

Pharao Nicolai, Marie Maegaard, Janus Spindler Møller, and Tore Kristiansen. 2014. "Indexical meanings of [s+] among Copenhagen youth: Social Perception of a Phonetic Variant in Different Prosodic Contexts." *Language in Society* 43:1–31.

Palander, Marjatta. 2007. "Alueellisen taustan vaikutus murrekäsityksiin" [Regional variation in perceptions of Finnish dialects]. *Virittäjä* 111:24–55.

Palander, Marjatta. 2015. "Rajakarjalaistaustaisten ja muiden suomalaisten mielikuvia *karjalasta*" [How Border Karelians and other Finns view *Karelian*]. *Virittäjä* 119:34–66.

Palander, Marjatta, and Anne-Maria Nupponen. 2005. "Karjalaisten 'karjala'" ['Karelian' of Karelians]. In *Monenlaiset karjalaiset. Suomen karjalaisten kielellinen identiteetti* [Karelians' many faces: The linguistic identity of Karelians in Finland], edited by Marjatta Palander and Anne-Maria Nupponen, 15–55. Studia Carelica Humanistica 20. Joensuu: University of Joensuu.

Paunonen, Heikki. 2006. "Synonymia Helsingin slangissa" [Synonymity in Helsinki slang]. *Virittäjä* 110:336–364.

Pasanen, Annika. 2003. "Kielipesä ja revitalisaatio. Karjalaisten ja inarinsaamelaisten kielipesätoiminta" [Language nest and revitalisation. Language nest activity among Karelians and Inari Saami]. MA thesis. University of Helsinki.

Podesva, Robert J., and Janneke van Hofwegen. 2014. "How Conservatism and Normative Gender Constrain Variation in Inland California: The case of /s/." *University of Pennsylvania Working Papers in Linguistics* 20(2): 129–137.

Preston, Dennis. 1993. "The Uses of Folk Linguistics". *International Journal of Applied Linguistics* 3:181–259.

Preston, Dennis. 1994. "Content-Oriented Discourse Analysis and Folk Linguistics." *Language Sciences* 16:285–331.

Preston, Dennis. 1998. "Folk Metalanguage." In *Metalanguage. Social and Ideological Perspectives*, edited by Adam Jaworski, Nikolas Coupland, and Dariusz Galasiński, 75–101. Berlin: Mouton de Gruyter.

Preston, Dennis R. 2002. "Language with an Attitude." In *Handbook of Language Variation and Change*, edited by J. K. Chambers, Peter Trudgill, and Natalie Schilling-Estes, 40–66. Oxford: Blackwell.

Preston, Dennis. 2011. "The Power of Language Regard: Discrimination, Classification, Comprehension and Production." *Dialectologia*. Special issue II: 9–33.

Preston, Dennis R. 2015. "Does Language Regard Vary?" In *Responses to Language Varieties. Variability, Processes and Outcomes*, edited by Alexei Prikhodkine and Dennis R. Preston, 3–36. Amsterdam/Philadelphia: John Benjamins.

Pöllä, Matti. 1995. *Vienan Karjalan etnisen koostumuksen muutokset 1600–1800-luvulla* [Changes in the ethnic composition in Viena Karelia in 1600–1800's]. SKST 635. Helsinki: Finnish Literature Society.

Riionheimo, Helka, and Marjatta Palander. 2017. "Rajakarjalainen kuuntelutesti: havainnoijina suomen kielen yliopisto-opiskelijat" [Border Karelian recognition test: University students of Finnish language as observers]. *Lähivõrdlusi. Lähivertailuja* 27, 212–241.

Ryan, Ellen Bouchard, and Howard Giles (eds). 1982. *Attitudes towards Language Variation: Social and Applied Contexts*. London: Edward Arnold.

Saigusa, Julie. 2016. "Jane Lynch and /s/: The Effect of Addressee Sexuality on Fricative Realization." *Lifespans & Styles: Undergraduate Working Papers on Intraspeaker Variation* 2:1:10–16.

Vaattovaara, Johanna. 2009. *Meän tapa puhua. Tornionlaakso pellolaisnuorten subjektiivisena paikkana ja murrealueena* [Our way of talking – The Torne Valley as a perceptual space and dialect area]. SKST 1224. Helsinki: Finnish Literature Society.

Vaattovaara, Johanna. 2012. "Spatial Concerns for the Study of Social Meaning of Linguistic Variables – an Experimental Approach." In *Folkmålsstudier*, edited by Hanna Lehti-Eklund, Camilla Lindholm, and Gunilla Harling-Kranck, 175–209. *Meddelanden från Föreningen för Nordisk Filologi* 50. Helsingfors: Institutionen för nordiska språk och nordisk litteratur.

Vaattovaara, Johanna. 2013. "On the Dynamics of Non-linguists' Dialect Perceptions – the Perceived Spatiality of /s/ Variation in Finnish." In *Variation in Language and Language Use*, edited by Monika Reif, Justyna A. Robinson, and Martin Pütz, 131–60. Duisburg Papers on Research in Language and Culture. Frankfurt: Peter Lang.

Vaattovaara, Johanna, and Mia Halonen. 2015. "Missä on ässä? 'Stadilaisen *s*:n' helsinkiläisyydestä" [Where is 's'? About 'Stadi *s*' and its Helsinki origin]. In *Helsingissä puhuttavat suomet. Kielen indeksisyys ja sosiaaliset identiteetit* [Finnishes spoken in Helsinki. Indexicality of language and social identities], edited by Marja-Leena Sorjonen, Anu Rouhikoski, and Heini Lehtonen, 40–83. Helsinki: Finnish Literature Society.

Vaattovaara, Johanna, and Henna Soininen-Stojanov. 2006. "Pääkaupunkiseudulla kasvaneiden kotiseuturajaukset ja kielelliset asenteet" [Homeland definitions and language attitudes of people grown up in the capital region]. In *Helsinki Kieliyhteisönä* [Helsinki as a language community], edited by Kaisu Juusela and Katariina Nisula, 223–254. Department of Finnish Language and Literature. Helsinki: University of Helsinki.

Vilhula, Kaisa. 2012. "Pääkaupunkilainen puhekieli kahden paikallisen ryhmän kuulemana ja keskustelemana" [The spoken language of Helsinki as heard and discussed among two local groups]. MA thesis. University of Helsinki.

Williams, Angie, Peter Garret, and Nikolas Coupland. 1999. "Dialect Recognition." In *Handbook of Perceptual Dialectology, Vol I*, edited by Dennis R. Preston, 345–358. Amsterdam: John Benjamins.

Virtaranta, Pertti. 1946. *Eteläkarjalaisten murteiden s* [*s* in South Karelian dialects]. Offprint of Finnish-book 18. Helsinki: Finnish Literature Society.

Virtaranta, Pertti. 1984. "Über das *s* im Karelischen" [*s* in Karelian]. In *Studien zur phonologischen Beschreibung Uralischer Sprachen* [Studies on Phonological Description of Uralic Languages], edited by Péter Hajdú and László Honti, 259–274. Bibliotheca Uralica 7. Budapest: Akadémiai Kiadó.

Woolard, Kathryn, and Bambi Schieffelin. 1994. "Language Ideology." *Annual Review of Anthropology* 23:55–82.

Zaikov, Pekka. 1987. *Karjalan kielen murreoppia* [Dialects of Karelian]. State University of Petrozavodsk.

Zaikov, Pekka. 2000. *Glagol v karelskom jazyke. Grammatitšeskie kategorii litsa-tšisla, vremeni i naklonenija* [Verbs in Karelian. Grammatical categories of person, number, tense and moods]. State University of Petrozavodsk.

Zaikov, Pekka. 2011. "/s/:n ja /š/:n distribuutio karjalan kielen murteissa" [Distribution of /s/ and /š/ in the dialects of Karelian]. Paper presented in the Congress for Bubrih, Petrozavodsk, October 21.

Zaikov, Pekka. 2013. *Vienankarjalan kielioppi. Lisänä harjotuksie ta lukemisto* [Grammar of White Sea Karelian with practises and a reader]. Helsinki: Karelian Civilisation Society.

Appendix 1. The informants.

Informants in Jyskyjärvi

Agafia. At the time of the interview, a woman of 75 years of age. Agafia was born in the speaking area of Olonets Karelian but moved to Jyskyjärvi in 1950s. She has had eight years of school in Finnish language.

Akuliina. At the time of the interview, a woman of 50 years of age.

Hilja. At the time of the interview, a woman of 78 years of age. Hilja has relatives in Kalevala, in Paanajärvi, and in Finland, and she has visited Finland many times. In Karelia, she has travelled very little.

Iivo. Middle-aged son of Ortjo.

Irina. At the time of the interview, a woman of 79 years of age. Irina has many Finnish friends, and she has visited Finland, too. Irina has accommodated Finnish tourists.

Lilja. At the moment of the interview, a woman of 78 years of age.

Maikki. At the time of the interview, woman of 79 years of age. Maikki has not visited Finland and has not travelled a lot in Karelia either.

Marina. At the time of the interview, a woman of 72 years of age. Marina has lived in Petrozavodsk and in Vuokkiniemi, too. Marina belongs to the folklore group that performs dances and songs in Karelian and in Finnish. Marina has many friends in Finland, and she has visited Finland many times.

Ortjo. At the time of the interview, a man of 85 years of age.

Polina. Middle-aged daughter of Maikki. Polina lived in Finland at the time of the interview.

Informants in Kalevala

Olga. At the time of the interview, a woman of 72 years of age. Olga has lived in Petrozavodsk, in Borovoi, and in central Russia. Olga has accommodated Finnish tourists, and she has many Finnish friends.

Palaka. At the time of the interview, a woman of 78 years of age. Palaka has accommodated Finnish tourists, but she has not visited Finland and has not travelled a lot in Karelia either.

Tanja. At the time of the interview, a woman of 44 years of age. Tanja is the daughter of Olga. Tanja belongs to an amateur theatre group that uses White Sea Karelian in its performances.

Appendix 2. Transcribed samples of the listening task.

Sample of Olonets Karelian (41 seconds)

ylen puakšuh, pastammo piirua kaiken jyttymie rahtovatruskua, piiraidu, karjalampiirakak Suomes šanotah karjalampiirakad meil sanotah šipainiekad, vod niitä pastammo joka pyhiä päiviä, blinua suurdu blinua pienem bli- blinua, lolanjoa [!] kai- kaiken jyttymie pastus- ainos pastammo, a keitämme, kalarokkua, liharokkua, maimua toičči, kuorihes kuivattuu, kartohkua suorimme da kagriettua - - salaattua kaiken jyttymie.

[Very often we bake pies, all kinds of pies: quark pies, pastries, Karelian pastries, in Finland they say Karelian pastries but we say *šipainiekad* [a kind of pie]. Well those we bake in all days of feasts. Blinis too, we bake all the time: big blinis, smaller blinis, all kinds of blinis. And we boil [different things]: fish soup, meat soup, little fishes sometimes, dried smelts. We prepare potatoes and oats, all kinds of salads.]

Sample of Tver Karelian (21 seconds)

mi se on. yön itettäjäine, päivän pöllättäjäine annan mie šiula ruadua yöksi i päiväksi. Ombel sie, yö i päivä, oigei hengel pl´atenčcal, hot miun vunukkain käy yönitettäjän - - yö i päivä. plat'ťast, oigie hengie platenčcal on, yöksi i päiväksi oma upokojain.

[What is that? He who laments the night, frightens the day. I give you tasks for night and day. You should sew night and day, good spirit for newborn, even though my grandchild goes with lamenter of night. Night and day. Newborn has a good spirit. For night and day, my own deceased.]

Sample of Ludian (44 seconds)

d'oga ižand, d'erevnas kudamb eli, d'ärved vaste, hän, obižatelo pidi venehen, venehel täl no tol'ko ajel' piäliži, ehtade(t)i, vedi möta heinad, tošťa haugod tuu ve- venehel vedab, kalad pyydab, veneh om, d´oka taluož, kus oma d'ärved, a vot kel ii ole veneht, se pakičeb, tuleb velhe, andab veneht, mi gi(?), pidab ajada, piä(l)iči d'ärves, nu andab, konz om a veneh d'outai, konz ele d'outai, ei anda veneht, muga, ned mii-ed, poziiťes, venehed oli me(i)l hubaažed, ei suured venehed, miest yhesa, viiž, kest veneht ema, piä(li)či jaroštob ajada, a venehed vot kut sieteh(e), venehed sietii möl, siga d'ervňas om muasťer, ei voidu ka mii sieta veneht, a se sietab muaster, zakažib venehen, hän venehen zakazan ottab, sietab venehen, veneh sietaze hongažest lau-, veneh sietaze hongažest laudas-, hongain om puu, lujemb i paremb, - - ku kuuz.

[Every house holder in the village, who lived by the lake, he absolutely kept the boat. He just cruised across the lake. They crossed (the lake), shipped some hay. They carried wood by the boat, too. He fishes. There is a boat in every house that is situated by the lake. Well, and who hasn't got a boat, he asks for it. Somebody comes and gives a boat that has to be rowed across the lake. Well, he gives it if it is spare. When it is not spare, he does not give the boat, so. Those who - - in the villages. We had bad boats, not big boats. Nine men, five. - - cross the lake. And boats, how were they built? The boats were built in our area, there is a master in the village. And who could not build a boat then the master builds (it). Orders a boat. He (orders) a boat. Takes an order, builds a boat. The boat is built from Pine board. Pine wood is stronger and better than Spruce.]

Tamás Péter Szabó
http://orcid.org/0000-0001-5105-5202

Reflections on the Schoolscape: Teachers on Linguistic Diversity in Hungary and Finland

Abstract

This article[1] focuses on ideologies that pertain to linguistic diversity and multilingualism from a linguistic landscape approach to education. It is to be emphasised that ideologies pertaining to multilingualism and monolingualism have strong systematic resemblances. So-called monolingualist labeling, management, and control over linguistic varieties is something similar to multilingualism-related practices described in Nikula (et al. 2012). For example, dialects are often evaluated positively, but dialect users are generally criticized because they deviate from the so-called standard (cf., Milroy 2001; Kontra 2006).

In order to investigate a wide range of diversity-related ideologies, two communities with different social and historical backgrounds are compared: Hungarians who are considered standard-oriented (e.g., Kontra 2006) and Finns whose ideologies are generally not considered to be so standard-oriented (Laihonen 2010). This study investigates how teachers co-construct language ideologies in conversation with the researcher during co-exploratory walking tours through their school premises.

The results support theory building, and enhance further research on ideologies, e.g., in minority settings, where an adequate management of linguistic diversity and variability is essential for the maintenance of various indigenous languages. Other important fields of application are L1 and L2/L3 education.

---

1   This research was funded by the European Union's Research Executive Agency under Marie Curie Intra-European Fellowship for Career Development within the EU's Seventh Framework Programme for Research (grant nr. 626376) and the Kone Foundation in Finland (grant no. 44-9730). I am grateful to Petteri Laihonen and the anonymous reviewers for their insightful mentoring of earlier drafts.

1 Introduction

Many actors and sources contribute to the complexity of school interaction practices. Students and teachers, family members, peers, administrative personnel, political leaders, as well as textbooks, IT devices, and other objects influence interaction to various extents, through different modalities and media. 'Diversity', 'multilingualism', and related concepts may refer to what emerges interpersonally, in general, and in education, in particular. But how, in line with what terms and points of reference, do people speak about the heterogeneous and multi-layered sense-making that takes place in education? Examples in this article show different ways of speaking about 'diversity' or 'multilingualism' in educational research settings.

In order to investigate a wide range of diversity-related ideologies (Silverstein 1979), data sources from two countries with different social and historical backgrounds were built on: Hungary and Finland. In doing so, the point of departure is that Hungarian is generally described as a standard language culture (e.g., Kontra 2006; cf., Milroy 2001), while the current Finnish is often considered less standard-orientated (e.g., Laihonen 2010). As a focal point, the discursive reconstruction of school community members' linguistic repertoires were selected (e.g., Busch 2015). Concepts such as 'mother tongue', 'foreign language', 'normality', 'standard', 'acceptable', 'proper', 'formal', or 'informal' emerged in interaction and became distinguished, identified, labelled, and evaluated in relation to other persons and groups. In this data, interactants co-constructed linguistic boundaries – and boundaries between speakers of languages and varieties – while making accounts of linguistic and educational practices they were engaged in. In other words, the analysed discussions did not merely reconstruct persons' and groups' repertoires as inventories of codes they possessed; rather, in accordance with Busch's (2015, 14) definition of repertoire, participants reflected on the 'synchronic coexistence of different social spaces' and 'different levels of time' while reconstructing their lived experiences. Based on the idea that classroom interaction, socialisation and the material environment of formal teaching are closely connected elements of the same ecosystem (cf., Shohamy and Waksman 2009), teachers' accounts, which emerged during reflections on the material environment (i.e., the schoolscape; Brown 2012) of the schools in question, were worked with.

Speakers' perceptions, definitions, and evaluations of languages, varieties and societal groups are discussed in other articles of this volume as well (e.g., Preston, Palander and Riionheimo, Laakso, Koivisto, Kunnas). Most of these authors organize their studies along geographical borders vis-à-vis perceptions of dialects. This article elaborates on a spatial approach to language practices in educational settings, investigating how teachers establish relationships between languages, states, and speakers. The focus is on ways in which they co-construct geographical and political formations while reflecting on school spaces and institutional language policies in conversation with the researcher.

This study is based on fieldwork in eight schools, i.e., the goal was not to make comparisons of teachers' ideologies in Hungary and Finland, at a general level. The goal was to show different settings in the reconstruction of relationships between categories that emerged during the interviews. It is asserted in this study that different ways of constructing ideology can be associated with different explicit or hidden policies in education (cf., Shohamy 2006).

This article begins with a brief description of the cultural differences between Hungary and Finland that led the author to the idea of comparing emerging ideologies in these two school systems. Then the visual approach used in data collection and analysis is described in connection with related methodological and theoretical considerations. The subsequent section provides information about the corpus collected, and the research questions formulated. The microanalyses of examples (pictures and interview excerpts) are followed by Discussion and Conclusions in Sections 6 and 7. The conclusion contains proposed ideas for the application of the results in educational practice.

2 Hungary and Finland: different approaches

'Diversity', 'multilingualism', and other concepts appear in metadiscourses (discourses about language; e.g., Kroskrity 2000) in various forms. For example, in policy documents, these can be read as technical terms, accompanied by definitions, evaluations, and descriptions. However, policy documents may also be versatile in their practice of making relations between these terms and others, according to, for example, the purpose or the argumentation of the text. According to Nikula et al. (2010, 2012), 'diversity' and 'multilingualism' are often presented with a celebratory tone in the official documents of language policies in the European Union, but, at the same time, are conceptualised as threats to social cohesion. Further, Blommaert et al. (2012) have claimed that, from the individuals' and communities' point of view, there are many conflicts and difficulties in managing actual multilingual practices.

The idea of comparing ideologies in Hungarian and Finnish educational contexts came from the analysis of various texts. In the following paragraphs, characteristic descriptions of Hungarian and Finnish education culture will be briefly presented. Policy documents and a Eurobarometer survey will be built on while certain contrasts that can serve as a basis of comparison will be presented.

Kontra (2006) argues that Hungarian can be generally described as a standard language culture (Milroy 2001); that is, the so-called 'standard Hungarian' variety together with 'correct orthography' is at the centre of linguistic evaluation. Further, Kontra (2006, 97) argues that in Hungarian contexts, 'intralingual discrimination' is part of the metalinguistic traditions and social practices that influence education and lead to linguicism (e.g., Skutnabb-Kangas 1988). As part of practices linked to 'intralingual discrimination', the cult of 'correctness' is intertwined with the notions of 'mother tongue' and the 'native speaker' in Hungary (cf., Doerr 2009; Bonfiglio 2010), and these three are often referred to in metadiscourses circulating in and around the practice of 'language cultivation' (Hung. *nyelvművelés;* Sándor 2001). Although there are efforts to make 'standard language ideologies' visible and explicit in order to deconstruct them (e.g., Kontra 2006, 123), standard-oriented practices still play an important role in education. For example, competitions in orthography and 'proper speech' are equally common in elementary, secondary, and higher education (e.g., articles in Bozsik ed. 2005–2007).

In contrast, the role of the so-called 'standard' does not seem to be so influential in contemporary Finland. According to Laihonen (2010), the use of a 'standard' is expected mainly in writing: spoken language (Fin. *puhekieli*) is accepted in great variety, including urban dialects in teaching as well. Mantila (2010) further argues that destandardisation and counter-normative ideologies have spread throughout Finland in the last few decades.

At the level of education policy documents, both the Hungarian and the Finnish national core curricula contain statements concerning linguistic and cultural diversity. For example, the Hungarian National Core Curriculum (NAT 2012) emphasises the importance of 'intercultural competence' in connection with learning 'foreign languages', with the stated goal of shaping attitudes that include "the appreciation of cultural diversity and interest in and curiosity about communication across languages and cultures" (translated from Hungarian). However, the document refers only to the cultures of recognised national minorities and 'the universal culture' (in singular!). That is, NAT makes a distinction between Hungarian national culture (which includes the cultures of recognised national minorities) and a 'universal' culture, and treats them as stable and separate entities. What is lacking in this setting is a dynamic approach that considers contemporary migration trends as influential factors. This approach is present in the Finnish National Core Curriculum (eight years older than the Hungarian one), for example in the statement that "the instruction must also take into account the diversification of Finnish culture through the arrival of people from other cultures" (NCC 2004, 12).

Speakers' self-assessments of language proficiency also illuminate some differences in discourses on 'diversity' and 'multilingualism' in the two countries. According to the latest Eurobarometer results (EBS 2012), only 35% of the survey participants in Hungary responded that they "are able to speak at least one foreign language well enough to hold a conversation", while 75% of the respondents in Finland claimed so. Further, only 13% of respondents in Hungary indicated that they speak at least two languages "well enough to hold a conversation", while 48% of the participants in Finland answered this statement affirmatively. What seems to be the most relevant in this data set from the point of view of ideology studies is how people portray themselves as speakers (or non-speakers) of various languages. While the majority of respondents in Hungary projected the image of a monolingual person, the majority of participants in Finland constructed a bi- or multilingual self (cf., Leppänen et al. 2011). The fact that Hungary has one official national language while Finland has two (Finnish and Swedish) could also contribute to differences in the reconstruction of ideologies concerning 'diversity' and 'multilingualism'.

In summary: according to the literature, ideologies seem to be more pluralistic in Finland, in general, if we consider that (i) there are two national languages; (ii) variants in spoken Finnish are widely appreciated without stigmatisation in education, and, as Eurobarometer data suggest, (iii) Finnish inhabitants portray themselves as bi- or multilingual rather than as monolinguals.

3 A visual approach: principles and methods

An approach is proposed in this article that integrates visual semiotics and interaction analysis into the investigation of language ideologies. Some fundamental terms for the study will be defined in the following paragraphs, and the study will be placed in relation to previous ones.

In line with Silverstein's classical formulation (1979, 193), 'ideology' is defined herein as a set of explanations and descriptions that are predominantly made in order to rationalise and/or justify observed phenomena. That is, ideologies are often constructed in discussions on debated issues where the way of presenting and, thus, reconstructing some phenomena or social structures is relevant in evaluation and argumentation. In the consideration of the interpersonal and social context, the present study builds on Potter and Edwards' (2003, 93) discursive psychological views according to which 'mental phenomena' are both constructed and orientated towards in people's practices. It means that the 'borders' and 'categories' analysed may dynamically change in interaction, generally in negotiations between participants. This approach is in accordance with Laihonen's (2008, 668) findings that "interaction shapes and (re)constructs" language ideologies.

This author's previous studies on language ideologies (e.g., Szabó 2012, 2013) have been built on questionnaires, research interviews, and classroom observations, initiating dialogue between etic and emic perspectives on education. However, the combination of these data types still seemed insufficient in the exploration of complexities in education. Semiotically orientated studies on schools (e.g., Cohen 1971; Johnson 1980; Scollon and Wong Scollon 2004; Kress and van Leeuwen 2006; Brown 2012) have highlighted the significance of the material environment in education, and, further, visual methodologies (e.g., Rose 2012) have greatly enhanced the collection of education-related narratives and ideologies.

A brief review of previous research in the following paragraphs will help to explain why and how visual methodologies help ideology studies. Brown (2012, 282) has coined the term *schoolscape* in reference to the school-based material environment where text, sound, images, and artefacts "constitute, reproduce, and transform language ideologies". Her observations are in line with the earlier findings of Cohen (1971) and Johnson (1980), according to whom symbolisations play an important role in formal education. Further, as Scollon and Wong Scollon (2004) and Kress and van Leeuwen (2006) have demonstrated, students and teachers do not merely perceive the semiotic environment they are situated in, but, at the same time, they learn to interpret and reconstruct signs, such as texts and pictures on the wall, or the spatial organisation of desks. That is, recurring patterns in the display and arrangement of artefacts and furniture in the school space are connected with school practices: for example, the teacher-fronted arrangement of desks can be a sign of the dominance of lectures (e.g., instead of group work), or the overwhelming display of student art work may refer to efforts that promote student creativity (e.g., Szabó 2015; Laihonen and Szabó 2017).

The investigation of the schoolscape has many branches. First, Johnson (1980) recorded and analysed American schoolscapes without engaging in interaction with members of the school community. Similarly, Gorter and Cenoz (2014) built predominantly on their etic perspectives in their quantitative study. Making efforts towards the integration of emic accounts, Brown (2012) conducted research interviews while Dressler (2015) organised a post-hoc focus group discussion of some pictures she had taken during her fieldwork. Khan (2012) incorporated the topic of schoolscape into his multi-sited ethnography of Pakistani schools, using his observations and interviews in analyses. That is, in these three latter studies, community members helped the researchers to illuminate what was hidden or implicit for them (e.g., Shohamy 2006) and, in turn, they could gain insights into the ways researchers perceived and interpreted their working environment.

In accordance with the principles of involving research participants in the interpretation of the research site, I developed the 'tourist guide technique' as a method that enhances education-related discussions through the mobile co-exploration of school spaces. In practice, the 'tourist guide technique' means that I photo-documented the schoolscape while I was guided by a teacher from each school. The teachers were requested to comment on the choice of language and symbols on display as if they were tourist guides and I was a tourist. No list of questions was prepared beforehand, but, reflecting on the teachers' comments, questions were occasionally posed or further details were requested. This setting was easily accepted by the teachers because, in most cases, the tour gave me the very first occasion to enter a school building, and the tours often started at the entrance hall.

In its basic structure, the 'tourist guide technique' shares similarities with other mobile data collection methods, like the 'walking tour methodology' (Garvin 2010), 'narrated walking' (Stroud and Jegels 2014), or child-led 'tours' (Clark 2010), as the researcher and research participants co-explore the space in which their interaction is situated. What distinguishes the 'tourist guide technique' from other methods is the division of roles according to which the researcher acts as a tourist, equipped with a digital camera, who needs guidance for orientation. At the beginning of the tour, it was made explicit that the guide chose what to show and what to skip. Further, the length of the 'tour' was also greatly influenced by the guides. The teachers were asked beforehand, via e-mail, to be available for a tour of about 40–50 minutes, and they were informed, at the same time, that it was possible to deviate from this time frame and take shorter or longer tours. On several occasions, teachers became enthusiastic, explicitly noting that it was inspiring to have the opportunity to act as a 'guide'; in these cases, the tours became longer, a 135-minute tour was the longest. The interviewees were also physically in control of the voice recorder, thus adding their influence to the implementation of the interview.

The 'tourist guide technique' was designed in order to provide an alternative to the basic research interview format (ten Have 2004), positioning the guide as the more agentive participant in the interview; that is, the researcher's position is not of the 'conductor' or 'interviewer' in this setting. Although the guides were highly agentive and influenced the recorded interaction greatly, the collected materials still should be analysed as "local collaborative 'constructions', rather than purely individual expressions of 'mind' " (ten Have 2004, 76). That is, general statements such as 'this teacher thinks X' or 'that teacher stands for Y ideas' would be oversimplifying. Rather, the analysis highlights the dynamic nature of the co-construction of ideologies since the interviews were analysed as both data and topic (ten Have 2004), emphasising that the recorded utterances give evidence of both co-constructed language ideologies and interactional structures (Laihonen 2008). In order to illuminate these structures, ethnomethodological Conversation Analysis was applied to the data interpretation.

4 Data and research questions

The analysis is built on data from ongoing fieldwork in elementary and secondary schools in Hungary and Finland. This study includes approx. 2,100 pictures and more than 10 hours of voice recorded interviews from 8 schools. This data was collected in 2013 and 2014. The language of the interviews was Hungarian in Hungary, and English and partly Finnish in Finland. Informed consent was requested from and given by all the participants. Personal details such as names or addresses were altered in the transcription, and pseudonyms were used in the excerpts and the analyses. The initial 'T' in the excerpts refers to me, the researcher.

This article analyses how metadiscourses that reflect on the schoolscape may contribute to the co- or de-construction of notions about linguistic boundaries and categories. Micro-analyses provide examples of the complexity of meaning-making in interaction. Analyses are organised around the following questions:

1. What reconstructions of categories and boundaries emerge in metadiscourses on language teaching and language use in the school? Are there identifiable foci in the accounts?
2. How does the interactional setting contribute to the emergence of ideologies in the interviews?

5 Persons and communities with diverse repertoires: different approaches in the interviews

This section presents analyses that are based on the simultaneous investigation of the photographs and the audio recordings. Excerpts have been chosen that demonstrate contrasts between the co-construction of ideologies in different contexts.

The Hungarian examples come from a secondary school in Hungary. This choice was motivated by several considerations. First, the excerpts show the competitive and assessment-centred characteristics of Hungarian education, in general, and foreign language education, in particular (cf., Csapó et al. 2009; Nahalka 2011). Second, this interview was recorded with a teacher of English and Hungarian; that is, the guide was a local language expert who was experienced both in 'mother tongue' and 'foreign language' education. Finally, Exc. 2 shows the dynamics of ideology construction in a condensed way; that is, many different aspects of language teaching are discussed within a short time.

Two interviews from Finnish primary schools were selected. The excerpts show how the topic of 'international students' was discussed. Although students "who have another mother tongue than Hungarian" (Gabriella, teacher in Exc. 1–2) were mentioned in Hungary, as well, it was only in Finland that their role and position in the school community were discussed in detail. Further, one of the Finnish schools (see Exc. 4) had an English CLIL program (Content-and-Language Integrated Learning; Dalton-Puffer 2011) and an English-medium program so the inclusion of this school in the analysis can help to better understand institutional multilingualism.

Before the detailed analysis, it is important to emphasise that the interview interaction reflected on the very schoolscape that was co-explored. The design of the space and the use of the available surfaces were quite different in the example schools. For example, in the Hungarian school (Exc. 1–2), there were many certificates on display, announcing student success at local and nation-wide competitions in various school subjects, while such signs were absent from the visited Finnish schools (Exc. 3–4). These differences in the available and perceived material environment meant that, for example, 'competition' or 'good grades and scores' were not discussed in Finland in as much detail as in Hungary. At the same time, for example, the display of student art work was common to all of the schools, so it was one of the central topics of each interview.

Further differences in the discussions could be due to the fact that I was socialised in the Hungarian school system and speak Hungarian as a first language, while in Finland, I was a newcomer at the time of recording the interviews with limited proficiency in Finnish (that is why we chose to converse in English). That is, while I was mainly considered an 'expert' in Hungary, I was often addressed as a 'novice' in Finland. However, it was not only the teachers who addressed me differently: it was also the interpretation of my contribution in general that differed significantly. For example, if I asked a question in connection with any sign in Finland, it was generally taken as a simple request for information because I was not expected to understand the sign. Conversely, if I asked about the significance of a sign in Hungary, it was sometimes interpreted as a challenge on my behalf.

Figure 1. Flags of Italy, the United Kingdom, and Germany in a Hungarian classroom.

5.1 HUNGARY

The Hungarian example shows how the co-construction of strict distinction between 'mother tongue' and 'foreign language' as well as the focus on 'objectives' influence the emergence of language ideologies in an interview. These notions are regularly intertwined with the ideal monolingual speaker of the ethnolinguistic tradition (Blommaert et al. 2012): the 'native speaker' (Doerr 2009; Bonfiglio 2010). 'Natives' are generally linked to their countries (of origin); or, more precisely, it is languages and not speakers, personally, that are linked to certain states where those languages are spoken in their 'proper' way (cf., Gal 2007). As a consequence, visual references to nation states, such as flags (cf., Halonen et al. 2015), were common in the Hungarian school that was visited. For example, Figure 1 shows a scene from a classroom.

When entering the classroom depicted in Figure 1, Gabriella, the teacher guide, started to comment on it as follows (Jeffersonian [2004] notation is used):

(1) Hungary, secondary school. "Obvious"

```
1    G:  ez szin [tén egy]
         it's al [so a   ]
2    T:          [igen   ]
                 [yes    ]
3    G:  nyelvi előkészítős terem,=
         language preparatory class,=
4    T:  =ühm
         =mhm
```

```
5    G:   gondolom,
          I guess,
6         (.82)
7         ((nevet))   egyértelmű, hogy [milyen]
          ((laughs))  it's obvious    [what  ]
8    T:                                [hát én]
                                       [yeah I]
9    G:   nyelveket tanulnak
          languages they learn
10   T:   ez látszik, azt hiszem, igen, hogy ez egy
          it looks so, I think, yes, that it's a
11        ((nevet))   előkészítős terem
          ((laughs))  preparatory class
```

In this particular school, 'language preparatory' class means that students learn foreign languages intensively when they start their secondary studies (according to the teacher, they have 12 lessons of the first foreign language, and six of the second foreign language per week). In this excerpt, both the teacher and I constructed the ideology that languages are linked to (linguistically homogeneous) nation states: e.g., "it's obvious [what] languages they learn" (lines 7, 9). That is, on Gabriella's initiative, it was implied that the countries indexed by the flags could be associated with one language each – in this case, with English, German, and Italian. In line with this implication, the teacher and I did not start, for example, to explicate the languages in question, nor to discuss where these languages are spoken outside the indexed countries, nor mention more languages other than English, German, and Italian that are spoken in those countries. Thus, these languages were linked to states (i.e., geographical and political formations).

Differentiating between languages and varieties, that is, labelling and evaluating them, continued later in the same interview. After entering the classroom designated for the purposes of teaching English, I made a comparison between that very room and another I had visited in another school. I recalled my memories that in the other school, only the map of the UK was on display, while in the very room in which we both were standing, the UK map was accompanied by maps and tableaux of the US, Canada, New Zealand, and other countries that are often associated with 'inner circle' Englishes (Kachru 2008). When asked whether the display of these artefacts referred to a teaching practice that is aware of the differences between various Englishes around the globe, Gabriella responded that the textbooks they used sometimes provided information on some differences between the so-called British and American English, and she added that the students learnt about 'English-speaking countries' within the framework of a course called 'English civilisation'. That is, from the implication that geographical maps depicting states may refer to varieties of a language (which, again, establishes a relationship between state and language), we arrived at the formal curriculum of the preparatory class, which includes cultural studies. I then asked whether the students were aware of English varieties, but, without giving space for a reply at that point, I raised another question as follows. (I present the full excerpt in four parts in order to make the analysis easier to follow):

(2a) Hungary, secondary school. "American English picked up"

```
1    T:  és egyébként felfigyelnek ezekre a: a diákok,
         and, by the way, are the: the students aware of these
2        hogy mondjuk (- -)
         that, let's say,
3        (.38)
4        vagy egyáltalán mi mi mondjuk a központi nyelvváltozat?
         or, actually, what what is, let's say, the central variety?
5        hogy itt is a: (.) ez a BBC English, vagy inkább
         that here it's the: (.) this BBC English, too, or rather
6        (.47)
7        valamiféle=
         something=
8    G:  =már az iskolában?
         =you mean, in the school?
9    T:  igen, hogy      [a: a tanításban    ]
         yes, that in    [the: the teaching  ]
10   G:                  [hát igen, a     Bri]tish Englisht
                         [well, yes, it's Bri]tish English
11   T:  ühm
         mhm
12   G:  ö: szoktuk tanítani, .hh mivel
         e:r what we teach, .hh cause
13       ugye hát az Oxford University Press az maxi[máli]san
         you see, well, Oxford University Press maxi[mal ]ly
14   T:                                             [ühm ]
                                                    [mhm ]
15       (.25)
16   G:  teret hódított, azt gondolom, a leg[több    isko]lában,
         gained ground, I think, in the majo[rity of sch]ools,
17   T:                                     [ühm ühm     ]
                                            [mhm mhm     ]
18   G:  .hh és hát ők azt azt közvetítik↑
         .hh and, well, it's what they distribute↑
19   T:  ühm ühm
         mhm mhm
20   G:  ö: és azt gondolom egyébként, hogy hogy mi tanárok is
         and, by the way, I think that that we teachers also
21       az:zal találkoztunk leginkább [akár]
         encountered that the most     [even]
22   T:                                [ühm ]
                                       [mhm ]
23   G:  az egyetemen
         at the university
24   T:  ühm
         mhm
25       (.79)
26   G:  tehát nagyon-nagyon
         so very-very
27       (.35)
28       nekem volt egy skót ö: tanárom például az egyetemen,
         I had a Scottish e:r teacher, for example, at the university
29       .hh de:: (.) nem jellemző.
         .hh but:: (.) it's not usual
30   T:  ühm
         mhm
```

```
31        (.5)
32   G:   amerikaiak elvétve itt-ott. az amerikait (.) amerikai
          some Americans here and there. but the American (.) American
33        angolt viszont a gyerekek
          English is picked up
34        (.4)
35        n- nagyon gyorsan
          v- very quickly
36   T:   ühm
          mhm
37   G:   fölszedik magukra, hiszen
          by the children, because
38   T:   >ühm ühm<
          >mhm mhm<
39   G:   ha (.) ha: valaki veszi a fáradságot, hogy (.) angol
          if (.) if: somebody makes the effort to (.) watch a film
40        nyelven nézzen filmet [vagy]
          in English language   [or  ]
41   T:                         [ühm ]
                                [mhm ]
42   G:   z- hallgasson zenét, akkor mindenképpen=
          m- listen to music, then definitely=
43   T:   =igen=
          =yes=
44   G:   =az amerikaival fog találkozni.
          =s/he will encounter American.
```

In this excerpt, a complex set of categories was established in interaction. Talking about languages and varieties in connection with foreign language teaching, it was possible to appoint some coordinates according to which we positioned our practices and evaluations. First, I did not finish the initial question about the students' perceptions of language varieties (lines 1–2; consider the pause before repair in line 3); rather, I addressed the question of a so-called 'central variety' of English. By doing so, I implied that this latter topic was more relevant or important at this point of our discussion, and, further, that a 'central variety' might or should exist. I also referred to a candidate 'central variety', namely, 'BBC English' – using the name of the broadcasting company as an index of the UK. I did not use the word 'standard', but the term 'central variety', which can be associated with 'standard' as it also refers to a variety that has a distinguished position according to which language use can be evaluated. How I prefaced the term ("this BBC English", line 5) shows that I used it as a pre-set category that is presupposedly known by Gabriella. After negotiating that my question concerned the school context (lines 8–9), Gabriella said that it was 'British English' that she taught (relabelling the term, but keeping the reference to the same state). Gabriella justified this preference with two arguments. First, according to her, it is in line with the textbook publisher's influence on teaching practices because of its economic position in the Hungarian market (lines 13–14). Second, she linked the hegemony of 'British English' to her personal teacher training experience when she presented herself as a typical case (see "we teachers also encountered…" in lines 20–21). She added that her university teachers, too, mostly used what she called 'British English', with only a few exceptions (lines 20-32).

It is noteworthy that the analysed interaction emerged from a note on artefacts that referred to countries, and that the labelling of Englishes was predominantly based on indexes that pointed to countries (mainly to the UK and the US). Beyond the name of nations (British, American), the countries or regions of origin (in the case of university teachers), brands like the name of a broadcasting company (BBC) and a publishing house (Oxford University Press) can all be associated with countries. However, the mention of the latter two brands might also be associated with media contexts and global trends in content production and consumption. This 'media' line was taken further in the continuation of Gabriella's account. In line 32, she uttered the word 'American' three times, first in connection with university teachers, but in the second utterance, she switched back to my initial question in line 1 ("are the: the students aware of…") and reflected on the students' informal English learning habits. She said that students 'quickly pick up' (lines 35–37) 'American English'. This description implies that students learn 'American English' features in an effortless manner since media content is dominantly produced in that very variety (lines 42–44). According to Gabriella, the students needed extra effort to read or listen to English (lines 39–42).

With Gabriella, we labelled English varieties and distinguished some contexts that may influence language use (teacher training, classroom teaching, and media consumption – both in and out of school). What I initiated at this point was a comparison between the English the students 'pick up easily' and the English they learn formally in lessons. With my question in line 45, I strengthened the dichotomy between 'school English' and 'informal English':

(2b) Hungary, secondary school. "I'm lovin' it"

```
45  T:  >igen, és mondjuk van, amikor ez órán így< fel↑merül,
        >yes, and let's say does it happen that it ↑raises< in class
46      hogy (ezt hallottam egy filmben), hogy
        that (I heard this in a film), that
47      (.79)
48      [dalba máshogy mondják            ]
        [they say it differently in a song ]
49  G:  [ó persze, persze, ez ez          ] folyamatos harc, tehát=
        [oh of course, of course, it's it's] a constant fight, so=
50  T:  =aha
        =aha
51  G:  a a legjobb ez az I'm lovin' it, az a kedvencem,
        the the best is this I'm lovin' it, that's my favorite,
52  T:  ((nevet))  hahhahahaha
        ((laughs)) hahhahahaha
53  G:  ott ugye megtanítom a gyerekeknek, hogy oké, love,
        there, y'know, I teach the children that OK, love,
54      nincsen inges alakja,
        it has no -ing form,
55  T:  ((nevet))  hahaha
        ((laughs)) hahaha
```

```
56   G:   és akkor de, Tanárnő, hát a re- reklámban (.) hát, mondom
          and then, but Miss, wait, in the a- ads (.) well, I say,
57   T:   ((nevet))   haha
          ((laughs))  haha
58   G:   költői szabadság.
          poetic licence.
59   T:   ((nevet))   haha  [és akkor  ]
          ((laughs))  haha  [and then  ]
60   G:                     [mással nem] nem tudok    ((nevet))
                            [I can't   ] defend with  ((laughs))
61        védekezni.
          anything else.
```

In the form of a polar question, I initiated an iterative narrative (line 45: "does it happen?"; cf., Baynham 2011); that is, I asked Gabriella to say whether or not it happened regularly that her students contrasted the English they had learnt in a lesson and what they had encountered in the media. I also incorporated voicing (Hutchby and Wooffitt 1998, 225–228) into my question, mimicking an imagined student voice (line 46: "I heard this in a film", line 48: "they say it differently in a song"). Through voicing, I provided examples of potential contexts other than 'school English', recycling Gabriella's previous references to cinema and music (lines 39–42). Gabriella recalled that in her practice, such cases were natural ("of course, of course" in line 49), and, further, she re-established the relationship between these varieties. What I identified as 'difference' ("they say it differently"; line 48) became a constitutive element, a counterpoint in a 'constant fight' (line 49) in Gabriella's interpretation. This war metaphor interprets American English as offensive, and, together with the verb choice in line 60 ("defend"), strengthens the opposition of competing Englishes. Or, rather, the opposition of competing groups – students and teachers – who make their stances through debates on language use. With an example ("I'm lovin' it", line 51), Gabriella illustrated how English norms were usually negotiated in her lessons. She provided a short narrative (lines 51–58) in which she first voiced herself in her teacher position in a context where she gives grammatical explanations ("OK, love, it has no -ing form"; lines 53–54). She quoted an exclusive formulation of a rule from herself, claiming that the described case is the only possible and, thus, correct, rejecting any alternative usages. Next, Gabriella voiced a student who challenged the claimed general validity of the rule she had taught ("but Miss, wait, in the a- ads"; line 56 – the ads' refer to the McDonald's slogan ["I'm lovin' it"] that was widely advertised globally as well as locally, close to the research site). Gabriella finished the short narrative with self-voicing ("well, I say, poetic licence"; lines 56 and 58), claiming that, as a reaction to the opponent student's claims, she did not reformulate the exclusive rule but treated the student's example as an exceptional case. The term "poetic licence" is associated with restrictions (certain persons: poets, or genres: poetic works) that make some linguistic forms acceptable in certain circumstances, while the general validity of the basic rule (here, "love has no -ing form") still applies. As Gabriella recalled (lines 60–61) she could not make any other counter-argument. During

Gabriella's account, from the point where she mentioned "I'm lovin' it", I accompanied her narrative with laughter. This action can be interpreted as a display of sympathy on my part; that is, at this point, I did not challenge Gabriella's arguments. I challenged them later, as demonstrated in Exc. (2c).

In the interviews, either in Hungary or Finland, discussions about English varieties dominantly remained at the level of general terms and labels, lacking examples or references to empirical observations. Accordingly, in this interview, the example in (2b) was the only case in which a linguistic form illuminated differences between the established categories, "I'm lovin' it" being interpretable as both 'American' and 'informal' English. In the further course of the interview, we turned back to general terms while continuing our work with positioning and categorisation.

(2c) Hungary, secondary school. "That's how it should be"

```
62   T:   ((nevet))   hahah  (.)  egyébként szükségesnek tartod, hogy
          ((laughs))  hahah  (.)  by the way, do you find it necessary
63        ezt így meg- (.) védd úgymond a a a:: brit
          that you (.) defend it, so to speak, the the:: British
64        angolt, hogy
          English, that
65        (.79)
66   G:   nem önmagában azt, hogy a brit angolt és nem=
          not in itself that that the British English and not=
67   T:   =ühm=
          =mhm=
68   G:   =nem azért, mert nekem ez ö::
          =not cause cause for me it's e::r
69        (.65)
70        lelki szükségle[tem  ]
          my spiritual   [need ]
71   T:                  [aha  ]
                         [aha  ]
72   G:   vagy ilyesmi, hanem azért, mert a mindenféle vizsgákon
          or something like this, but because they expect this
73        ezt kérik tőlük.
          from them at all kinds of exams.
74   T:   ühm ühm
          mhm mhm
75   G:   ö: és hogyha:
          e:r and if:
76        (.43)
77        arra akarom felkészíteni, hogy neki, és sajnos ez a
          I want them to be prepared to, and unfortunately it's the
78        helyzet, hogy nem arra készítem fel, hogy
          case that I don't prepare them to {the case} that
79   T:   ühm
          mhm
80   G:   hogyha majd kiköltözik, akkor ö tudjon kommunikálni,
          if s/he moves abroad then er s/he should be able to communicate,
81   T:   ühm
          mhm
82   G:   hanem arra, hogy le tudjon érettségizni és esetleg
          but rather that s/he could pass the matriculation exam or
```

```
83          legyen egy nyelvvizsgája, nálunk az         [sem ]
            maybe to pass a language exam, at our place [it's]
84   T:                                                 [ühm ]
                                                        [mhm ]
85          (.47)
86   G:     jellemző, hogy mindenkinek van nyelvvizsgája,=
            not common either that everybody holds a language exam,=
87   T:     =ühm
            =mhm
88   G:     tehát (.) örülünk, hogyha egy osztályban olyan
            so (.) we're happy if about fifteen or twenty percent has
89          tizenöt, húsz százaléknak van
            a language exam in a class
90   T:     >ühm ühm<
            >mhm mhm<
91   G:     középfokú nyelvvizsgája valamelyik idegen nyelvből
            at mid-level, in one of the foreign languages
92   T:     >ühm ühm<
            >mhm mhm<
93          (1.35)
94   G:     ö: és hát sajnos erre kell felkészítenem.
            e:r and well, sadly, I need to prepare him/her for that.
95   T:     >ühm ühm< (.) igen.
            >mhm mhm< (.) yes.
96   G:     és akkor mindig megjegyzem, hogy igen, hogyha
            and then I always note that yes, if
97          (.63)
98          hallasz valakit beszélni, akkor elképzelhető, hogy
            you hear somebody speaking, it's possible that
99          nem így hallod, hanem úgy,
            you don't hear it this way but that way,
100  T:     ühm.
            mhm.
101  G:     de a vizsgán ezt így kell.
            but that's how it should be at the exam.
```

This section is first built on the dichotomy of 'British' vs. 'American' English that was established previously in the interview, and at this point I did not refer to the implicit distinction between 'school English' and 'informal English'. In my polar question (lines 62–64), I recycled the verb 'defend' (line 63) from Gabriella's previous turn (line 60) while challenging her stance. "Do you find it necessary" (line 62) might have implied the meaning 'it is not necessary', as Gabriella's defensive detailing (Drew 1998, 297) shows in lines 66–101. That is, she reframed the account of her professional practice in a way that she claimed was problematic, but, at the same time, she transferred responsibility to 'others' (i.e., external authorities, such as examiners or test makers). Gabriella argued that her preference for 'British English' was not based on a personal conviction (or, as she put it, "spiritual need"; line 70) but on external pressure ("they expect this…"; line 72). Thus, she repositioned herself from a highly agentive position ("I teach the children", line 53) to a position with very limited agency (see "not cause cause for me…", "but because they expect…"; lines 68, 72), claiming that one of her important tasks was to prepare the students for conforming to the expectations of testing authorities ("if: I want them to be prepared to..."; lines 75–83).

Gabriella elaborated on the implicit category of 'exam English' that differs from 'school English' in the sense that it is expected to be used only in exam situations. Stressing that she worked under pressure, she added that it was "unfortunate" (line 77) that her work focused on training the students to pass the exams rather than to communicate efficiently in real-life situations. Interestingly, in the context of establishing functional-situational categories like 'school' or 'exam English', she again reconstructed the ideology that 'foreign languages are spoken abroad': when she included a context in which English should be used in communication functionally, she mentioned "moving abroad" (line 80). That is, at this point the purpose of teaching English was not linked to the informal, actual everyday English use of the students. Rather, the use of English was future-orientated: to the moment when the students must pass exams (i.e., achieve 'objectives') or when they move to live abroad (as if English was not that relevant in Hungarian contexts).

In contrast with the language use of those who hold a certificate or live abroad, the students' actual, everyday English use appeared to be non-acceptable in the excerpt. Earlier, 'American' or 'informal' English was also labelled as problematic (consider the restrictions of "poetic licence" in line 58), but at this point, in relation to 'exam English', Gabriella voices a stronger opposition (e.g., "and then I always note..."; lines 96–101) that nothing but one variant is acceptable ("that's how it should be at the exam"; line 101). In line with the general practice, here she did not mention concrete examples either. What she did when making a contrast is pronominalisation ("this way" and "that way" in line 99).

To justify her preferences, Gabriella further emphasised the importance of her task as a pre-exam trainer in a side sequence (lines 83–91) in which she presented (unfavourable) statistics of their students who pass the state language exam. In Hungary, besides the matriculation exams, state language exam certificates are very important when applying to or graduating from a university, or when applying for a job. That is why a high percentage of students who hold a state language exam qualification make a secondary school very attractive in the highly selective Hungarian educational system. In this context, Gabriella joined widespread discourses circulating in the competitive Hungarian educational culture according to which the improvement of test results and the increasing number of Hungarian state language exam certificates are claimed to be priorities in foreign language education (e.g., Gál 2015).

Although an implicit 'proper English' category had already emerged in the previous excerpt (e.g., "that's how it should be at the exam"; line 101), next I initiated discussion about the relationship between 'exam English' and 'proper English'. Interestingly, the reconstruction of interplay between 'school English', 'exam English' and 'proper English' emerged in the course of the conversation:

(2d) Hungary, secondary school. "Scores"

```
102  T:  >ühm ühm< (.) igen. és hogyha valaki dolgozatban leír egy
         >mhm mhm< (.) yes. and if somebody writes such a form in
103      ö ilyen alakot, akkor azt
         a test, then that
104      (1.65)
105  G:  el [vileg hogyha]
         in [theory  if  ]
106  T:     [  (- - -)   ]
107  G:  hogyha az érettségi: javítási szempontjait
         if I follow the principles of correcting the
108      veszem figyelembe, akkor nem szabad elfogadnom.
         matriculation examination, I shouldn't accept that.
109  T:  ühm ühm
         mhm mhm
110  G:  én a dolgozatban alá szoktam húzni, el szoktam
         I usually underline that in the test, I accept that
111      fogadni és oda szoktam írni, hogy .hh de ugye tudod,
         and I comment that .hh don't you know that
112      hogy egy vizsgasztuáció[ban ez      ]
         in  an examination situa[tion this]
113  T:                         [aha         ]
                                 [aha         ]
114  G:  nem érne pontot?
         wouldn't score a point?
115  T:  >ühm ühm< igen, igen.
         >mhm mhm< yes, yes.
116  G:  és akkor általában nem olvassák el a megjegyzéseimet,
         and then they usually don't read my comments,
117      [tehát fogalma    ]
         [so s/he has no]
118  T:  [((nevet))        ]
         [((laughs))       ]
119  G:  sincs róla, hogy mi volt az üzenet mellé, csak azt érzékelte,
         idea what the comment was, what s/he perceived is that
120      hogy hát az úgy jó volt, mert kapott rá pontot.
         it was good as it was because s/he got the mark.
121  T:  aha, aha, aha.
         aha, aha, aha.
```

In my question, I did not mention concrete examples either; I followed Gabriella in keeping the construction of dichotomies at a general, abstract level. Thus, I initiated an iterative narrative on what happens in a case when "such a form" (line 102) is used in a test. It is clear from Gabriella's narrative that she interpreted "such a form" as 'unacceptable'. First, she referred to the "principles of correcting the matriculation examination", according to which – as Gabriella claimed – certain variants cannot be accepted (lines 105–108). Starting with "in theory" (line 105), she implied that something else can happen 'in practice'. Accordingly, as she narrated, she regularly differentiated between 'school English' and 'exam English' for the students in the form of explicit side notes. She voiced one of her potential side notes claiming that the evaluation of the answers in the lesson and the (matriculation and state) exams may differ (lines 110–114). In this part of Gabriella's account, earning a point (line 114) implied 'proper' language use. This equation was explicated in a comment in which she explained that it was not easy for her to make the students aware of the differences between 'school English' and 'exam English', because the students often ignored her side notes. According to Gabriella's critique, earning a point simply meant to the students that their performance "was good as it was" (line 120).

Table 1 summarises the categories and the contexts that were co-constructed in Excerpt 2.

Table 1. Categories and connections in Excerpt 2

Labels in the excerpts	'central variety' 'BBC English' 'British English'	'American English'
Labels/descriptions in the analysis	school English exam English proper English	informal English counter-English (cf., 'fight') unacceptable English
Media associated	textbook	films songs
Brands associated	BBC Oxford University Press	McDonald's
Users associated	teacher examiner	student
Locations associated	university (teacher training)	out of school (home)
	classroom foreign countries ('abroad')	

As Table 1 shows, a dichotomy of two opposed, more or less acceptable Englishes was reconstructed in different contexts. These Englishes were primarily labelled in accordance with references to two countries, the UK and the US. However, this localisation appeared at the level of general terms. In narratives on actual situations, global brands (such as Oxford University Press and McDonald's), societal roles (teacher, examiner, and student) and different physical locations were mentioned. University and out-of-school locations were associated with the dominance of 'British' and 'American' English, respectively, while both classroom and foreign countries were given a special role in the contextualisation of English usage. The classroom was reconstructed as an arena where competing Englishes are used and negotiated in regard to their acceptability both in the form of personal and mediated interaction (conversation and tests). Further, the classroom, in general, and as a location for exams, in particular, was opposed to (unnamed) foreign countries where a great diversity of Englishes can be found. That is, classroom negotiations on correctness were reconstructed as 'school problems', in relation to test scores. Out-of-school English use and the students' linguistic needs were mentioned only peripherally or with

Figure 2. Classroom scene from Finland.

negative evaluation. The appreciation of these two latter contexts appeared in the Finnish interviews analysed in the next subsection.

5.2 FINLAND

The following two excerpts come from Finnish elementary schools that are located in an officially monolingual Finnish-speaking municipality. The following examples are intended to demonstrate that making a distinction between 'mother tongue' and 'foreign language(s)' in parallel with keeping the focus on students' activities result in a significantly different construction of linguistic boundaries and categories than in the Hungarian example.

The first excerpt is from a tour led by Juho, the principal of an elementary school. During the tour, we spent time in a third-grader classroom, co-interpreting what was visible there. For example, we tried to make sense of the numerous references to the sea. As Figure 2 illustrates, there were fishing nets, paintings of sea scenes (e.g., sailboats on the sea), and models of lighthouses (see one in the table in Figure 2) on display.

At one point Eeva, the class teacher entered the room. Juho, taking the role of an interviewer, asked Eeva about the purpose of sea references. Eeva answered that currently the students were learning about the sea in an integrated way: for example, they dealt with this topic in geography and also in religious studies (e.g., symbolic lighthouse references in the Bible). Juho thanked Eeva, thus initiating the closure of the sequence, but Eeva continued and switched to the topic of English in a self-initiated way, as follows in Exc. (3a).

(3a) Finland, elementary school. "That's the point"

```
1    E:  we have that English s- er
2        (.98)
3        er theme also here (.) because I have many (.) children
4        from (.) who have English (they) other language
5    J:  [yeah, yeah I told]
6    E:  [(there was) so   ] that's the point we have the:se
```

The "English theme" was manifested in different ways. Among others, there were white cards attached to or placed next to objects, with their English names. For example, there was a sign that read "a clock" next to the clock in Figure 2. Further, there were cards that showed the name of the day, or a chart with English colour names. Pointing to these signs, Eeva named another thematic visual program in the classroom, besides the 'sea'. Eeva justified the presence of English with the composition of the class, claiming that many students "have English" as their "other language" (lines 3–4). First, she started to describe the students by localising their places of origin ("children from"; lines 3–4), but, then, through self-initiated self-repair (Schegloff, Jefferson and Sacks 1977), she switched to a possessive grammatical structure that implies that, according to Eeva, the students in question have a command of English, so that they understand the words on display. Eeva also claimed that the presence of English words was to the advantage of these children ("that's the point" line 6). Here, Juho negotiated with Eeva on how much detail was needed; that is, they both acted as my guides, and they elaborated on their roles in this situation (lines 5–6). In overlapping speech, Eeva repaired herself in line 6, transforming a candidate detailing ("there was") to a summarising statement.

What followed later was Eeva's account of the composition of the class (lines 7–22, not included in the excerpts). According to Eeva, there were students who spoke Spanish, Swedish, German, and Russian as their first languages. After providing these details, she continued that this school introduced English in first grade; that is, two years earlier than the norm in Finland. It is this early commencement of English teaching that she called useful in the following excerpt:

(3b) Finland, elementary school. "I'm including here"

```
23   E:  and it's it's helping
24       (.52)
25   J:  yeah=
26   T:  =yeah [yeah]
27   E:        [beca]use it's not only in third grade when it's
28       starting
29   T:  yeah
30       (.34)
31   E:  [so  ]
32   T:  [it's] a nice introduction[then]
33   E:                            [yeah] and so and so those
```

```
34      (.53)
35      those children
36      (.41)
37      who have
38      (1.25)
39      e::r
40      (.48)
41      both language in home,
42      (.36)
43      Finnish and English
44       (.3)
45  T:  [yeah    ]
46  E:  [or some ]
47      (.78)
48      children they have the whole day >they are only< speak
49      in English (at) home=
50  T:  =[yeah ]
51  J:  =[mhm  ]
52  E:  so it's
53      (.33)
54      I have noticed that it's
55      (.58)
56      when we are s- using English more than normally
57  T:  yeah
58      (.51)
59  E:  they feel that I'm inclu:ding here
60  T:  yeah [yeah] yeah
61  J:       [mhm ]
62  E:  it's it's my place
63  J:  yeah
64  E:  and it's normal to speak English
```

Eeva evaluated early English teaching as beneficial ("it's helping"; line 23), arguing that it enhanced the integration of those students who speak English in out-of-school contexts, for example at home: she portrayed these students as bi- or multilinguals (e.g., lines 41–43 or 48–49). According to her, creating and maintaining a multilingual classroom environment can enhance the inclusion of multilingual students. In her argumentation, she voiced a student ("I'm including here it's my place and it's normal to speak English"; lines 59, 62, 64) in support of the described practice. As Hutchby and Wooffitt write (1998, 226), voicing "can be used in a number of ways to warrant the factual status of claims and undermine the possibility of skeptical responses". The teacher further emphasised that the use of English was natural, and that it was part of the classroom interaction routine (line 64).

Eeva's arguments can be better understood if what she later says in other parts of the interview is taken into consideration. In line 56, "using English more than normally" referred to situations where English was used in other contexts than the English lesson (such cases in Hungarian schools were not mentioned). Eeva also mentioned (not included in the excerpt) that she sometimes asked the students in any kind of lesson to name something in English, or to answer a question in English. Further, it was not only English that was promoted through her practices. Eeva told me that she sometimes asked questions or counted in Spanish, German, or other languages, or asked the students to provide translations in their first language (e.g., she pointed to a helmet and asked a Spanish-speaking student, "what is this called in Spanish?"). She also recalled cases when she asked a Swedish-speaking student about Swedish. According to her, this action prepared the students' for Swedish studies and brought Swedish, the second national language, closer to them. Eeva also referred to the dynamically changing schoolscape, revealing that previously German or Spanish words were also on display, for example, the names of the days were on the blackboard for a period of time. What Eeva strongly emphasised was the socialising and integrating function of English as a lingua franca ("I'm including here" line 59). The inclusion of the other languages (e.g., German, Russian, Swedish, and Spanish) served similar integratory goals according to Eeva (implied in accounts that are not included in the excerpt).

It is noteworthy that the ideologies on the beneficial impact of multilingual practices were co-constructed with the continuous support of Juho and I. With continuers (e.g., "yeah" in lines 25–26, 29, 45, 50, 57, 60) or explicit positive evaluations (e.g., "it's a nice introduction then" in line 32), we encouraged Eeva to continue and elaborate on further details.

Eeva's account of her own practice can be associated with integration, but she did not use this term in the excerpt (see, e.g., "it's helping", "I'm including here" instead; lines 23, 59). Integration was mentioned in explicit terms in another Finnish elementary school where Maija guided me through the building. This tour was started as a standard research interview: we sat around a table and I conducted the interview according to pre-set questions. At the point we agreed that the pre-set questions had been answered, Maija offered to answer other, spontaneously emerging questions. I proposed "a short walk in the corridors" saying that "I very liked" the 'decorations on the wall' (I had visited lessons earlier, so I was familiar with the corridor). Maija agreed and started to guide me immediately. Initially I pointed to a board where some student artwork was posted.

(4a) Finland, elementary school. "You can see some English"

```
1    T:  er
2        (.31)
3    T:  these things ((door shut)) for example?
4    M:  yes there are some handicrafts work=
5    T:  =aha
6        (1.27)
7    M:  and then (.) usually we have the handicrafts work here and=
8    T:  ((chuckles)) =yeah yeah yeah
9    M:  then it seems that there's a
10       (.57)
11       sweets
12       (.32)
13       store a [candy store]
14   T:          [<yeah>     ] (.) yeah yeah yeah ((chuckles))
15   M:  and then here you can see some English
16       (.24)
```

```
17        that er
18        (.91)
19        that I'm not s- sure if they are the: English speaking classes
20        that have done the:se
21   T:   aha [aha]
22   M:       [but] it's it's very nice way of
23        (.62)
24        of integrating
25        (.47)
26        er also their work
27        (.27)
28   T:   aha
29   M:   that they do
30        (.25)
31        with with our kind of the normal
32        (.28)
33        classes that [we have here    ] so that we have English
34   T:               [((chuckles)) yeah]
35        (.67)
36   M:   er ((click of the tongue)) to be see:n here in the [coli-]
37   T:                                                      [yeah ]
38   M:   corridors [              as well so   ] good
39   T:             [((chuckles)) yeah yeah yeah]
40   M:   yeah that's really
41        (.99)
42   T:   yeah=
```

Maija, on my initiative, explained that the first collection of artwork we encountered was on the topic of 'candy store', noting that there are designated places for the display of student work (line 7). Immediately after the candy store board, she pointed to the next one that collected signs on the topic of 'good table manners'. She started her introduction by highlighting the language choice ("you can see some English" line 15). Since at another point in the interview she noted that the presence of English in the corridor can help the visitors to orientate themselves, it is possible that this formulation was due to the fact that in this situation I was a visitor from abroad (however, this could also be the use of 'you' as a general subject). The 'English' board in question (Figure 3) contained colour drawings depicting situations that should be avoided or, conversely, taken as a good example while eating in the company of others. Most of the works did not include any writing, but, in some cases, short sentences were added to the drawings, for example, "fork left hand knife right hand", "Never take food from your neighbour's plate" or "Too mutch" (above a drawing that shows a girl whose mouth is full of food). The board was headed by a card that could be interpreted as a title: "Good table manners".

Extending the topic of 'visible English', Maija started to speculate on the origin and purpose of the signs and their language choice. I call her explanations speculations since she claimed that she was not sure about this issue (line 19). Deciding that the signs were made by the English speaking class members, Maija explicitly stated that the presence of English served the goals of integrating two student groups: those who are members of the English speaking classes and those who study in the CLIL classes. She

Figure 3. "Good table manners" board in English in a Finnish school.

first called the latter group "normal" (line 30–31) probably because, as she told me in other parts of the interview, CLIL students are predominantly first language speakers of Finnish, while the English speaking classes were intended mainly for immigrant children with a good command of English. That is, speakers of Finnish were established as the unmarked or default group in the reconstruction of school multilingualism. Generally, Maija evaluated the assumed integrational efforts positively ("it's very nice way" line 22). It is noteworthy that her continuous positive adjectives could be indirectly recycled from my proposal for a "short walk"("I very much liked these decorations"; not included in the excerpt) and in connection with my status as a foreign visitor.

Further, Maija guided me to the doors of the English speaking classes:

(4b) Finland, elementary school. "They can come and read"

```
43   M: =and here (.) for instance here we have the two
44      (.3)
45      er English speaking classes here we have=
46   T: =aha=
47   M: =from one to six (.) and here's from (.) e:r three to four.
48      (.55)
49   T: aha
50      (.73)
51   M: and as you can see if you t- want to take a closer (.) picture
52      [here]
53   T: [yeah] yeah
```

```
54   M:  so you you can see that.
55       (.37)
56   T:  aha, yeah yeah the=
57   M:  =there are [the]
58   T:             [the] introductions and [er ]
59   M:                                     [pic]tures and
60       (.31)
61   T:  yeah=
62   M:  =things like that
63       (1.19)
64   T:  so [( - - -)         ]
65   M:     [so this is quite] nice so that the
66       (.27)
67       the other
68       (.32)
69       the the [kind of] the (.) normal classes where they
70   T:          [aha    ]
71   M:  have the clil teaching=
72   T:  =aha
73   M:  .hh they can come and rea:d
74       (.37)
75       [these sto:]ries so that [I'm sure] that they can they can
76   T:  [aha aha   ]             [ah hah  ]
77   M:  understand something that=
78   T:  =((chuckles)) hah hah hah [hah]
79   M:                            [is ] being said here.
```

This school had classes that predominantly used English as the language of instruction. These classes are meant for students with linguistic and cultural backgrounds other than Finnish. These classes have the official label *englanninkielinen luokka* 'English-speaking class' that appeared on the doors in an abbreviated form *EKL*.

This excerpt provides a complex example of co-exploration. First Maija pointed to the doors of the classrooms, thus, introducing the classes as topics for a detailed account ("here we have"; lines 43, 45 and pronominal reference also in line 47 – it is probably by accident that she said "one to six" instead of "one to two" when referring to the grades). Next, in reference to my photo documenting activity, she offered angles for my pictures ("if you want to take a closer picture"; lines 51–54). That is, she extended her role as a narrator or commentator guide to a guide who shares authority with the researcher in photo composition. After this point, the interpretation of the signs was closely collaborated on, including overlapping speech (lines 57–59).

As Figure 4 shows, there were self-introductory notes on the door together with a flag that indexed the home country of each student. Flags indexed countries and, in an indirect way, nationalities, but in this case, in contrast with Figure 1, these were not directly linked to classroom language policies. That is, in this context, the flags did not index the languages the students learnt but rather identified the students' country of origin while introducing them to an audience that uses English as a lingua franca. Accordingly, Maija portrayed the CLIL students as members of the target audience who are

Figure 4. Students' self-introductions on the door of the classroom in a Finnish school.

capable of reading and interpreting the texts on display (lines 75–77). She further constructed an active initiator role for the students, emphasising how they can find and use opportunities provided by the schoolscape ("they can come and read"; line 73). Again, she interpreted this practice as integratory, this time in an indirect way, mentioning the 'normal' CLIL students who could approach the spaces of the English speaking classes. Thus, the corridor was reconstructed as a space where students could move both physically and culturally-socially. Again, Maija evaluated such integratory practices positively ("quite nice"; line 65).

Table 2 summarises the categories and connections that emerged in Excerpts 3 and 4.

Table 2. Categories and connections in Excerpts 3 and 4

Labels/ descriptions in the analysis	(Spanish, Russian, German, Swedish + many other languages) English as a foreign language English as a mother tongue / 'home' language / 'other' language English as a lingua franca / integratory language	
Media associated	artwork on display	
Users associated	teacher	
	international students (who 'have English' / who are in the 'English speaking class') international students' family members	local students ('normal' / CLIL students)
Locations associated	home native country	
	classroom corridor	

As Table 2 summarises, various languages were mentioned as separate entities (especially in the interview in Exc. 3), and some functions of English in school activities were elaborated in detail in both schools. Otherwise, dichotomies were constructed between the users of English (and not between various Englishes); that is, mainly two student groups, the 'locals' and the 'international' students were in opposition in connection with their needs for integration. As a consequence, spaces, where these student groups meet (i.e., the classroom and the corridor), were constructed as spaces of integration. The out-of-school (home and native country) context was highlighted only in the case of 'international' students, both in terms of reference to their daily language use habits (Exc. 3) and their self-introductions on the classroom door (Exc. 4).

6 Discussion

In this article, I have analysed different types of co-construction of ideologies on diversity and multilingualism. I investigated reconstructions of linguistic borders and categories as well as the interactional contexts in which these were co-constructed. The contexts differed at various levels: the interviews were recorded in two countries, both in elementary and secondary schools, and, of course, local characteristics of the school communities also had an impact on the course of interactions. Further, and this was the focus of my analyses, the interaction during the "guided tours" was shaped by continuous reflections on the schoolscape and by negotiations between the participants of the interactions. The following paragraphs summarise some consequences of the applied methodology, and the discussion is followed by examples in relation to some major discourses that circulate in Hungarian and Finnish education.

Both the Hungarian and the Finnish examples departed from reflections on the actual space that was co-explored, often leading to detailed discussions on current school practices. That is, the method was successful in addressing social meanings through the discussion of visual elements (cf., Rose 2012). Since I analysed interaction at a micro level, some basic comments on the interactional organisation are necessary. First, as there were no pre-set questions during the guided tours, the participants chose what to talk about. This is one of the reasons why I analysed and compared the data at a micro level: the point of the investigation was not to make systematic cross-cultural or cross-country case-to-case analyses; it was instead based on continuously emerging reflections. What is systematically observable in the data is the interactional organisation. The findings include the fact that there were continuous negotiations in the interviews that contributed to the re-positioning of all participants. For example, guides often initiated a topic by themselves (e.g., in Exc. 1, 3), but there were cases in which the conversation returned to a more traditional, interview-like setup with researcher questions and respondent answers (e.g., Exc. 2). In general, the guiding teachers made use of the position that was offered to them; that is, not only the route and the length of the tour was their choice, but they were also free to involve others in the tour. As a consequence, the guide frequently directed the voice recorder towards students or colleagues, asking them about certain issues and acting as an interviewer (e.g., Exc. 3). What I controlled in my 'tourist' role was the photo documentation of the environment (cf., Clark 2010). However, as Exc. 4 shows, sometimes I was instructed by the guide to take pictures of particular scenes and from certain angles.

From the point of view of co-construction, some comments on the nature of my contribution are needed because it is especially important to make the researcher's position explicit in ideology studies (e.g., Dallyn 2014). As a professional linguist, I work with models that do not separate languages into isolated entities but conceptualise 'language' as the interactive, dynamic, and multimodal use of semiotic resources that often show signs of hybridisation (e.g., Dufva, Aro, and Suni 2014). I also aim to promote linguistic diversity and multilingualism through my professional activities; that is why I tended to challenge some monolinguistic and monoculturalist ideologies in the interviews, for example in Exc. 2c. However, as the examples show (e.g., Exc. 1, 2b) I sometimes appear to agree with explanations or justifications that are not compatible with the above mentioned professional principles. Thus, the analysis of the materials provides opportunities for researcher self-reflection as well.

As pertains to the linguistic boundaries and categories that emerged during the conversations, I will compare how languages, persons, loci of language use, and school places were discursively reconstructed in different settings.

The labelling of languages and varieties in the Hungarian example was based on the distinction between two Englishes (labelled variedly), keeping these varieties and the contexts of their use apart. In Exc. 2, language learning was primarily portrayed as a way of preparing for something in the future; that is, it targets potential future events, such as 'passing an exam' or 'moving abroad'. Varieties of English were separated in line with a distinction between their typical users: 'British English' was mainly linked to teachers and examiners while 'American English' was linked to students. As the latter variety was evaluated as less acceptable, this parallel dichotomy implied that the students' English proficiency was not desirable in light of school expectations (claims about test scores and exam certificates strengthen this implication).

Discussions about the 'central' variety of English, acceptability, and some tensions between teachers' and students' norms (see the 'fight' metaphor) linked the discussions to standard language ideology (Kontra 2006; Milroy 2001) and the notion of deficit. That is, what students were actually capable of doing in English (e.g., watching films, listening to songs) was elaborated on less, implying that their existing skills are less relevant than others that, according to the teacher, are to be developed (e.g., conforming their language to the norms of tests, passing exams). Although there were maps and tableaux of countries other than the UK in the co-observed classroom space, the classroom was discursively reconstructed in a way that strengthened the hegemony of learning and teaching British English. This reconstruction was enhanced by the teacher's short narratives of classroom scenes.

In the Finnish examples, linguistic forms or varieties were not the focus of discussion but distinct languages and their users together with the contexts of usage in and outside the school. The emerging accounts were closely connected to the co-explored sites, which brings me to the discussion of the discursive reconstructions of school spaces. Classrooms (Exc. 3) and corridors (Exc. 4) were constructed as spaces in which and with which students could interact both directly (in classroom interaction) or through media (reading the words or artefacts on display). Consequently, students were portrayed as persons who already had resources that they used in interaction and when interpreting the schoolscape (e.g., "children [...] who have English" in Exc. 3; "they can come and read" in Exc. 4) and, thus, took opportunities to establish relationships with others. That is, the students were taken as functionally bi- or multilingual persons. As part of the students' repertoire, English was constructed as a lingua franca, as a language of integration that bridges local ("normal" Exc. 4) students and those students who have "other languages". In the interviews, "other" meant 'other than Finnish'.

This way of creating the category of 'other' languages and their speakers through English raises some issues. First, it was clear from the analysis of Exc. 3 that the role of English was dominant in the construction of a multilingual classroom that served as a space for a multilingual community. In the condition that we co-explored, only English (and Finnish) signs were on display in the classroom even though the teacher mentioned that 'other' languages were also previously represented. The integratory role of English was also complex in Exc. 4. The teacher presented the use of English as a lingua franca as a successful practice in the integration of the 'English speaking' (EKL) students into the school community. However, while the first language of the majority of the 'normal' (CLIL) students was apparently and visibly Finnish (as was revealed during the tour of the school), not all of the EKL students' languages appeared. In other words, through the English-medium self-introductions and the English-medium signs on "good table manners" some languages that the EKL students spoke were erased from the schoolscape (for the notion of ideological erasure, see Irvine and Gal 2000). That is, the reconstruction of linguistic diversity was predominantly carried out through the creation of oppositions between 'normal' students who learn English as a foreign language and 'other' students who can be integrated through their higher than average level command of English. In summary, the Finnish examples relate to efforts in implementing integratory tools both at the levels of designing classroom interaction and the schoolscape. That is, the students' proficiency in different languages was treated as a resource (Nikula et al. 2012) in formulating the answers to the ever-growing challenge of educating students with diverse cultural and linguistic background in Finnish schools (e.g., Voipio-Huovinen and Martin 2012; Suni and Latomaa 2012).

7 Conclusions

With a focus on labelling and boundary-making practices, this study showed how the integration of visual methodologies into ideology research can be used in a complex interpretation of educational practices. The interaction between the participants in reflections on the schoolscape enhanced the construction of evaluations of, and narratives and explanations about education. In general, it was the discursively reconstructed context of notions such as 'mother tongue' and 'foreign language(s)' that made a difference in the presented examples.

The results of the study can be adapted in educational contexts in which an adequate management of diversity is essential. For example, similar 'guided tours' can be led with the participation of several school community members, providing space for them to discuss their own interpretations of the spaces they collectively use. Separate or joint tours can be organised for students (cf., Clark 2010), teachers, principals (cf., Shohamy 2014), optionally requesting the contribution of a researcher or other 'foreigner' whose outsider perspective can add to the articulation of potential problems, difficulties, or special needs. That is, 'guided tours' can contribute to the local management of diversity and, hopefully, to the utilisation of the diverse repertoires of school community members as resources.

Transcript symbols (cf., Jefferson, 2004)

[	the point of overlap onset
]	the point at which two overlapping utterances end
=	no break between the two lines
(1.21)	elapsed time by hundredth of seconds
(.)	a brief interval (shorter than 0.2 seconds)
::	prolongation of the immediately prior sound (the longer the colon row, the longer the prolongation)
-	cut-off
word	stress via pitch and/or amplitude
↑ ↓	shifts into especially high or low pitch
.hh	inbreath
> <	talk speeded up compared to the surrounding talk
< >	talk slowed down compared to the surrounding talk
(( ))	transcriber's description
(- -)	the transcriber could not get what was said

References

Baynham, Mike. 2011. "Stance, Positioning, and Alignment in Narratives of Professional Experience." *Language in Society* 40:63–74.

Blommaert, Jan, Sirpa Leppänen, and Massimiliano Spotti. 2012. "Endangering Multilingualism." In *Dangerous Multilingualism*, edited by Jan Blommaert, Sirpa Leppänen, Päivi Pahta, and Tiina Räisänen, 1–21. Basingstoke: Macmillan.

Bonfiglio, Thomas P. 2010. *Mother Tongues and Nations: The Invention of the Native Speaker*. New York: De Gruyter.

Bozsik, Gabriella, ed. 2005–2007. *Két évtized a helyesírásért*. [Two decades for orthography]. Eger: EKF Líceum.

Brown, Kara D. 2012. "The Linguistic Landscape of Educational Spaces." In *Minority Languages in the Linguistic Landscape*, edited by Durk Gorter, Heiko F. Marten, and Luk Van Mensel, 281–298. New York: Palgrave.

Busch, Brigitta. 2015. *Linguistic Repertoire and Spracherleben, the Lived Experience of Language*. Working Papers in Urban Language & Literacies 148. London: King's College.

Clark, Alison. 2010. *Transforming Children's Spaces*. New York: Routledge.

Cohen, Yehudi A. 1971. "The Shaping of Men's Minds: Adaptations to Imperatives of Culture." In *Anthropological Perspectives on Education*, edited by Murray Lionel Wax, Stanley Diamond, and Fred O. Gearing, 19–50. New York: Basic Books.

Csapó, Benő, Gyöngyvér Molnár, and László Kinyó. 2009. "A magyar oktatási rendszer szelektivitása a nemzetközi összehasonlító vizsgálatok eredményeinek tükrében" [The selectivity of Hungarian educational system in the light of international comparative studies]. *Iskolakultúra* 3–4:3–13.

Dallyn, Sam. 2014. "Naming the Ideological Reflexively." *Organization* 21:244–265.

Dalton-Puffer, Christiane. 2011. "Content-and-Language Integrated Learning: From Practice to Principles?" *Annual Review of Applied Linguistics* 31:182–204.

Doerr, Neriko Musha, ed. 2009. *The Native Speaker Concept. Ethnographic Investigations of Native Speaker Effects*. New York: De Gruyter.

Dressler, Roswita. 2015. "Sign*geist*: Promoting Bilingualism through the Linguistic Landscape of School Signage." *International Journal of Multilingualism* 12:128–145.
Drew, Paul. 1998. "Complaints about Transgressions and Misconduct." *Research on Language and Social Interaction* 31:295–325.
Dufva, Hannele, Mari Aro, and Minna Suni. 2014. "Language Learning as Appropriation: How Linguistic Resources Are Recycled and Regenerated." *AFinLA-e Soveltavan kielitieteen tutkimuksia* 6:20–31.
EBS. 2012. *Europeans and Their Languages. Report*. Special Eurobarometer 386. Accessed December 4, 2016. http://ec.europa.eu/public_opinion/archives/ebs/ebs_386_en.pdf.
Gal, Susan. 2007. "Multilingualism." In *The Routledge Companion to Sociolinguistics*, edited by Carmen Llamas, Louise Mullany, and Peter Stockwell, 149–156. Abingdon: Routledge.
Gál, Lilla. 2015. "Nyelvtanítás, nyelvtudás és media." [Language teaching, language proficiency and media] *Taní-tani*. Accessed December 4, 2016. http://www.tani-tani.info/nyelvtanitas_nyelvtudas_media.
Garvin, Rebecca Todd. 2010. "Responses to the Linguistic Landscape in Memphis, Tennessee: An Urban Space in Transition." In *Linguistic Landscape in the City*, edited by Elana Shohamy, Eliezer Ben-Rafael, and Monica Barni, 252–271. Bristol: Multilingual Matters.
Gorter, Durk, and Jasone Cenoz. 2014. "Linguistic Landscapes inside Multilingual Schools." In *Challenges for Language Education and Policy: Making Space for People*, edited by Bernard Spolsky, Ofra Inbar-Lourie, and Michal Tannenbaum, 151–169. New York: Routledge.
Halonen, Mia, Tarja Nikula, Taina Saarinen, and Mirja Tarnanen. 2015. " 'Listen, There'll Be a Pause After Each Question': A Swedish Lesson as a Nexus for Multi-Sited Language Education Policies." In *Language Policies in Finland and Sweden*, edited by Mia Halonen, Pasi Ihalainen, and Taina Saarinen, 220–243. Bristol: Multilingual Matters.
Hutchby, Ian, and Robin Wooffitt. 1998. *Conversation Analysis*. Cambridge: Polity.
Irvine, Judith T., and Susan Gal. 2000. "Language Ideology and Linguistic Differentiation." In *Regimes of Language: Ideologies, Polities, and Identities*, edited by Paul V. Kroskrity, 35–84. Santa Fe: School of American Research Press.
Jefferson, Gail. 2004. "Glossary of Transcript Symbols with an Introduction." In *Conversation Analysis: Studies From the First Generation*, edited by Gene H. Lerner, 13–31. Philadelphia, PA: John Benjamins.
Johnson, Norris Brock. 1980. "The Material Culture of Public School Classroom: The Symbolic Integration of Local Schools and National Culture." *Anthropology and Education Quarterly* 11:173–190.
Kachru, Braj B. 2008. "World Englishes in World Contexts." In *A Companion to the History of the English Language*, edited by Haruko Momma, and Michael Matto, 567–580. Chichester, UK: Wiley-Blackwell.
Khan, Muhammad Ali. 2012. "Social Meanings of Language Policy and Practices: A Critical, Linguistic Ethnographic Study of four Schools in Pakistan." PhD diss., Lancaster University.
Kontra, Miklós. 2006. "Sustainable Linguicism." In *Language Variation – European Perspectives*, edited by Frans Hinskens, 97–126. Amsterdam: John Benjamins.
Kress, Günther, and Theo van Leeuwen 2006. *Reading images*. New York: Routledge.
Kroskrity, Paul V. 2000. "Regimenting Language." In *Regimes of Language: Ideologies, Polities, and Identities*, edited by Paul V. Kroskrity, 1–34. Santa Fe: School of American Research Press.
Laihonen, Petteri. 2008. "Language Ideologies in Interviews: A Conversation Analysis Approach." *Journal of Sociolinguistics* 12:668–693.
Laihonen, Petteri. 2010. "A finn nyelv korpusztervezése, korpuszpolitikája." [The

corpus planning and corpus policy of the Finnish language] *Magyar Nyelvjárások* 48:169–190.

Laihonen, Petteri, and Tamás Péter Szabó. 2017. "Investigating Visual Practices in Educational Settings: Schoolscapes, Language Ideologies and Organizational Cultures." In *Researching Multilingualism: Critical and Ethnographic Approaches,* edited by Marilyn Martin-Jones and Deirdre Martin, 121–138. London: Routledge.

Leppänen, Sirpa et al. 2011. *National Survey on the English Language in Finland: Uses, Meanings and Attitudes.* Studies in Variation, Contacts and Change in English 5. Accessed December 4, 2016. http://www.helsinki.fi/varieng/series/volumes/05/.

Mantila, Harri. 2010. "Suomalaisen kielenhuollon periaatekeskustelu 1990- ja 2000-luvulla." [The discussion on the principles of language planning in Finland in the 1990's and the 2000's] In *Kielellä on merkitystä,* edited by Hanna Lappalainen, Marja-Leena Sorjonen, and Maria Vilkuna, 179–205. Helsinki: Finnish Literature Society.

Milroy, James. 2001. "Language Ideologies and the Consequences of Standardization." *Journal of Sociolinguistics* 5:530–555.

Nahalka, István. 2011. "Az iskolai esélyegyenlőtlenségről vallott kisebb és nagyobb tévhiteink." [Our minor and big misconceptions concerning inequalities in the school] *Taní-tani.* Accessed December 4, 2016. www.tani-tani.info/kisebb_es_nagyobb_tevhiteink.

NAT. 2012. "Nemzeti Alaptanterv." [National Core Curriculum] *Magyar Közlöny* 66:10639–10847.

NCC. 2004. *National Core Curriculum for Basic Education.* Helsinki: National Board of Education. Accessed December 4, 2016. http://www.oph.fi/english/curricula_and_qualifications/basic_education.

Nikula, Tarja, Sari Pöyhönen, Ari Huhta, and Raili Hildén. 2010. "When MT + 2 Is Not Enough. Tensions with Foreign Language Education in Finland." *Sociolinguistica* 24:25–42.

Nikula, Tarja, Taina Saarinen, Sari Pöyhönen, and Teija Kangasvieri. 2012. "Linguistic Diversity as a Problem and a Resource." *Dangerous Multilingualism,* edited by Jan Blommaert, Sirpa Leppänen, Päivi Pahta, and Tiina Räisänen, 41–66. Basingstoke: Macmillan.

Potter, Jonathan, and Derek Edwards. 2003. "Sociolinguistics, Cognitivism, and Discursive Psychology." *International Journal of English Studies* 1:93–109.

Rose, Gillian. 2012. *Visual Methodologies. An Introduction to Researching with Visual Materials.* (3rd ed.) London: Sage.

Sándor, Klára. 2001. "Language Cultivation in Hungary: Further Data." In *Issues on Language Cultivation,* edited by Klára Sándor, 43–61. Szeged: JGYTF Kiadó.

Schegloff, Emanuel A., Gail Jefferson, and Harvey Sacks. 1977. "The Preference for Self-Correction in the Organization of Repair in Conversation." *Language* 53:361–382.

Scollon, Ron, and Suzie Wong Scollon. 2004. *Nexus Analysis: Discourse and the Emerging Internet.* New York: Routledge.

Shohamy, Elana. 2006. *Language Policy: Hidden Agendas and New Approaches.* New York: Routledge.

Shohamy, Elana. 2014. "School Principals as Makers of School Language Policy." Paper presented at the University of South Australia, August 20.

Shohamy, Elena, and Shoshi Waksman. 2009. "Linguistic Landscape as an Ecological Arena: Modalities, Meanings, Negotiations, Education." In *Linguistic Landscape. Expanding the Scenery,* edited by Elana Shohamy and Durk Gorter, 313–331. New York and London: Routledge.

Silverstein, Michael. 1979. "Language Structure and Linguistic Ideology". In *The Elements: A Parasession on Linguistic Units and Levels,* edited by Paul R. Clyne, William F. Hanks, and Carol L. Hofbauer, 193–248. Chicago: Chicago Linguistic Society.

Skutnabb-Kangas, Tove. 1988. "Multilingualism and the Education of Minority Children." In *Minority Education: from Shame to Struggle*, edited by Tove Skutnabb-Kangas and Jim Cummins, 9–44. Clevedon: Multilingual Matters.

Stroud, Christopher, and Dmitri Jegels. 2014. "Semiotic Landscapes and Mobile Narrations of Place: Performing the Local." *International Journal of the Sociology of Language* 228:179–199.

Suni, Minna, and Sirkku Latomaa. 2012. "Dealing with Increasing Linguistic Diversity in Schools – the Finnish Example." In *Dangerous Multilingualism*, edited by Jan Blommaert, Sirpa Leppänen, Päivi Pahta, and Tiina Räisänen, 67–95. Basingstoke: Macmillan.

Szabó, Tamás Péter. 2012. *"Kirakunk táblákat, hogy csúnyán beszélni tilos". A javítás mint gyakorlat és mint téma diákok és tanáraik metanyelvében* [Repair as communication practice – repair as discourse topic. A multi-faceted investigation of Hungarian school metalanguage]. Dunajská Streda: Gramma.

Szabó, Tamás Péter. 2013. "A Corpus-Based Analysis of Language Ideologies in Hungarian School Metalanguage." *Research in Corpus Linguistics* 1:65–79.

Szabó, Tamás Péter. 2015. "The Management of Diversity in Schoolscapes: an Analysis of Hungarian Practices." *Apples – Journal of Applied Language Studies* 1:23–51.

ten Have, Paul. 2004. *Understanding Qualitative Research and Ethnomethodology*. London: Sage.

Voipio-Huovinen, Sanna, and Maisa Martin. 2012. "Problematic Plurilingualism – Teachers' Views." In *Dangerous Multilingualism*, edited by Jan Blommaert, Sirpa Leppänen, Päivi Pahta, and Tiina Räisänen, 96–118. Basingstoke: Macmillan.

Anna-Riitta Lindgren
http://orcid.org/0000-0001-8315-8206

Leena Niiranen
http://orcid.org/0000-0001-9488-0130

The Morphological Integration of Scandinavian and Saami Verbal Borrowings in Kven and Their Impact on Contact-Induced Language Change

Abstract

This article describes contact-induced changes in the morphology and vocabulary of Kven verbs. It examines how matter and pattern replication (Matras 2009) differ in contact with a relative language compared to a non-relative language. The Kven language in northern Norway is a language connected to both Saami, a language related to Kven, as well as Norwegian and Swedish, Scandinavian languages that belong to a different language group. The lexical, derivational, and inflectional influences of these contacts on Kven verbs are described. The data consists of both oral and written Kven material.

The Kven are a national minority in northernmost Norway. Their language was previously considered a Far North dialect of Finnish, but it was recognized as an autonomous language in 2005. During the rapid modernization of the 20th century, the borders between the nation-states Finland and Norway influenced linguistic divergence between dialects on several different linguistic levels. This article deals with lexical and inflectional phenomena that lead to linguistic divergence.

There are differences between the matter and pattern replication in Scandinavian languages as opposed to Saami. There are no pattern replications from Norwegian or Swedish, while matter replications are basically integrated into one inflectional type. The impact from Saami is more multifaceted, as the Saami loans are integrated into many inflectional and derivational types, leading to a variety of pattern replications. This result is due to the similarity between the morphological structures of Saami and Kven.

Verbal borrowings have been analysed as to whether they represent a direct or indirect integration into the recipient language. Most of the examples represent indirect integration, but there are also some borrowings, especially from Saami, that are presumably examples of direct insertion.

1 Introduction

Does the outcome of contact-induced language changes depend on the linguistic similarities and differences of the recipient and donor languages? What kinds of influence do extra linguistic contexts, such as borders and the sociolinguistics of multilingual situations, have? This study examines verbal borrowings in Kven from different donor languages, namely the Scandinavian and Saami languages. Kven is a relative language of Finnish, and is spoken as a minority language in northern Norway. Scandinavian languages are typologically different from Kven, as they belong to a different language family. In contrast, Saami and Kven, which belong to the same language group, share more similarities. For example, they both have a rich morphology and many derivatives. This raises several interesting questions. First, how are the verbal borrowings from these donor languages morphologically integrated into the recipient language of Kven? Second, what is the outcome of these language contacts on verbal inflection? The replication of sound-meaning pairs – matter replication – and the replication of linguistic patterns – pattern replication – of verbal borrowings in Kven have been studied. Is there a difference in how matter replications or verbal loans from Scandinavian versus Saami languages are integrated into Kven? What kind of pattern replication can be found in Kven morphology, and is it an outcome of contact with Scandinavian or Saami languages?

Section 2 presents a discussion of the influence of political borders on multilingual communities, and presents the development of Kven from a dialect to a minority language in Norway. Section 3 addresses the theoretical considerations of language contact and borrowing. Section 4 lays out the data and methods. Section 5 describes matter replications in Kven from two types of donor languages. Section 6 details the different types of pattern replications. Lastly, Section 7 presents the conclusions.

2 Kven: a language variety in a multilingual border region

2.1 Dialect or language?

Traditionally, language varieties spoken by Tornedalians in the northernmost part of Sweden and by the Kven in North Norway were considered to be Finnish dialects, more specifically the Far North dialects (Fin. *peräpohjalaismurteet*) also spoken in the Lapland Province in Finland. The northernmost branches of the Far North dialects were the northernmost dialects of Finnish. Today, Kven is the northernmost language of the Finnic language and dialect continuum.

During the 20th century, the Far North dialects diverged linguistically. As a consequence of modernization in these Arctic parts of Norway, Sweden and Finland, the nation-state borders acquired a much stronger influence on language varieties than ever before. In many ways and on many levels, the Arctic regions of the Nordic countries became more closely integrated with the central parts of the countries – the Kven got closer to Oslo, the Tornedalians to Stockholm, and the Far North Finns (Fin. *peräpohjalaiset*) to Helsinki. Linguistic changes continued in Finland, in dialects of the majority language of the country, and in Sweden and Norway, in unofficial minority languages.

Dialects in northern Finland were influenced by standard language, especially the vocabulary in those domains that became important through modernization, such as new technologies, administration, media, and formal education, as well as by the main destandardized spoken language in the entire country. This resulted in new regional spoken language varieties in the province. On the other side of the nation-state borders, the active and passive use of the majority languages among the minorities expanded very quickly, and the expanding flow of modern vocabulary was integrated as loanwords from the majority languages. In addition to vocabulary differences, the grammar of the Kven, as well as the Jällivaara dialect of the *Meänkieli* – the language of the Tornedalians – has been in the process of diverging from the grammar of the Far North dialects through morphological innovations.

Because of this divergence, the linguistic varieties of the Tornedalians and the Kven have sometimes been characterized by Finns as old Finnish and sometimes as a mixed language. Many Kven have interpreted the differences between their variety of spoken language and the Finnish spoken in Finland to mean that their language was bad Finnish and that the latter was real Finnish – without taking into account the different variations of Finnish within Finland.

As Chambers and Trudgill (1998, 3–12) have pointed out, relative languages and dialects can be considered as a continuum, in which pure linguistic criteria are not decisive for what is a language and what is a dialect. The criterion of mutual comprehension is not even definitive. For example, within some languages – like Chinese and Arabic – there is enough difference within the language itself that varieties of the language are not mutually understandable. On the other hand, some languages – like Swedish and Norwegian – although recognized as different languages, are similar enough that a speaker of one can be understood by a speaker of the other. Certainly, the nation-state borders have a great influence, and it is often a political question as to whether a variety on a continuum is considered to be a dialect or a language.

During the last two decades, several European languages that were previously considered to be dialects have officially achieved the status of a language, e.g., Low German in Germany and in the Netherlands, Limburger in the Netherlands, Scots in the United Kingdom, Võru in Estonia, and Meänkieli in Sweden; Kven was recognized as an official language in Norway in 2005. The European Charter of Regional and Minority Languages played an important role in this development.

The linguistic differences between Kven and standard Finnish are similar to the differences between Swedish and Norwegian. It is possible to consider Kven a dialect of Finnish or Meänkieli; alternately, there are enough linguistic differences between Kven and these varieties to be able to define Kven as an autonomous language. This was the conclusion drawn by Hyltenstam and Milani (2003) who recommended that its recognition as a language support its revitalization because a language has a higher status than a dialect. This recognition has liberated Kven from the stigma of bad Finnish, and, today, an improvement in attitudes towards Kven can be seen taking place, both among the Kven minority and among other people.

As usual, there are different opinions among the Kven themselves. Some consider their language to be Norwegian Finnish, a variety of Finnish, whereas others, particularly those who have been actively revitalizing the language, consider Kven to be a separate and unique language.

2.2 Sociolinguistic periods of the Kven

Kven is traditionally spoken in multilingual villages along the coast of the northernmost part of Norway in Finnmark and Troms Counties. The expansion of the Finns to the northernmost areas of the North Calotte brought them to the Norwegian coast, particularly during the 18th and 19th centuries. Most of them came from the region that is today the Lapland Province in Finland and the Torne Valley in Sweden (Niemi 1978). This is the region of the former Far North dialects before the divergence of Kven and Meänkieli.

Through marriages with the Saami, the descendants of the Finns who settled in the inland Saami municipalities of Kautokeino, Karasjok, and Tana, were Saamified (Niemi 1978). In the coastal areas, at the end of the 19th and in the beginning of the 20th century, the ethnic and linguistic profiles of the Kven villages varied. Some of the villages were nearly monolingual Kven speaking villages, others were bilingual Kven-Saami or Kven-Norwegian villages, and some were even trilingual. In the multilingual villages, individual bi- and trilingualism was common, but there were also monolingual individuals. Every summer, reindeer-herding Saami families from the inland villages came to the coastal villages for approximately three–five months. It was not unusual for the Saami to also speak Kven; consequently, the Kven language, although primarily spoken only by the Kven, was also spoken by many Saami as their second or third language, as well as by a few Norwegians (Lindgren 2009).

Because of a combination of an assimilation policy and rapid modernization, there was a language shift among the Kven to Norwegian during the 20th century. The most used language of the Kven gradually changed from that of Kven to Norwegian. Multilingualism was not rewarded because it was considered to deter the learning of the majority language, Norwegian. By the 1960s, Kven was no longer being transferred from parents to children. This language shift among both the Kven and the coastal Saami made Norwegian the dominant language all over the coastal villages. Kven became seriously threatened and is now only spoken among the Kven by the elderly. Although many other Kven do have a competence in the language, they mostly use it in communicating with Finns, and speak Norwegian with other Kven. There has not been a language shift among the Saami in the inland villages, so the reindeer-herding families still speak Saami with each other (Lindgren 2009; 1993, 262–265).

Starting in the 1980s, there have been revitalization movements, particularly among the Saami, but also among the Kven. The Kven people were officially recognized as a national minority in 1998. Oral and written Kven and Finnish are used today in the media, they are subjects in schools, and they are used in a growing number of cultural activities. During the last few years, a language council has been working to create a standardized language variety of Kven suitable for the production of teaching materials. Based on these efforts, teaching materials and a grammar have been published (Eriksen 2014; Söderholm 2014).

3 Theoretical background

Linguistic borrowing is a well-known phenomenon, especially in intensive language contact, where most language speakers are bilinguals – like in many Kven communities – and where communication, therefore, most often occurs between bilinguals. In this article, the term *borrowing* is used to refer to a permanent language change in a speaker's native language (Thomason and Kaufman 1988, 21). Bilinguals make use of resources from their total linguistic repertoire, and because they consciously or even unconsciously use elements from both languages in speech production, they may introduce spontaneous innovations (Matras 2009, 5; Riionheimo 2013, 647). Innovations created in bilingual language use become permanent borrowings only if the language community as a whole accepts them (Haspelmath 2009, 41).

The term *donor language* is used to refer to the immediate model language for borrowing, and *ultimate donor language* refers to an original source language in cases where more than two languages are involved in a borrowing process. *Recipient language* refers to a language that receives borrowings. *Model word* or *model verb* refers to the original entity in the donor language that is used as a model to form a loanword or a replica word in the recipient language. *Model* can even refer to a larger entity than a word in the donor language used as a model for replication. For example a syntactic, semantic, or morphological pattern in the donor language can form a model for replication.

The usual motivations of borrowing, often suggested in the literature of language contact, are the prestige of the donor language, gaps in the recipient language, and cognitive motivation, all of which are based on a bilingual communicative setting (Matras 2009, 149–153). The prestige hypothesis suggests that recipient language speakers can gain a higher status by using loanwords. In such a case, the concept that a borrowed word refers to has already been lexicalized in the recipient language. However, when a replication is a near synonym to an inherited word, it can still refer to the specific referent, and the desire to communicate accurately can be the motivation for borrowing.

Cultural loans are borrowed to fill gaps in the recipient language. For example, concepts that are used when referring to technical innovations are often borrowed when those innovations are introduced. In Kven, terms that refer to modern society are often borrowed from Norwegian. Utvik (1996) studied Norwegian noun loans in Kven and found many words that refer to society, school, or other institutions. Cultural loans can also be terms that belong to a specific Arctic livelihood that Kvens learned in Norway. Andreassen (2003), who studied the names of fish and marine animals in Kven, found that both Saami and Norwegian loanwords were used, particularly in relation to animals in the Barents Sea.

Borrowing can also be linked to bilingual language processing. When it is not possible to find the same accurate expressions in both languages, borrowing can be used to fill a gap, though this does not necessarily mean that the receiving language has any shortcomings. It might simply indicate the difficulty of activating a specific word in a bilingual conversation, or that some element of the donor language is used unconsciously, among other things. When the motivation for borrowing is to fill gaps, there will be no parallel expression in the recipient language before the replication takes place (Matras 2009, 150).

Changes induced by contact can be divided into two basic categories. One of them concerns the replication of sound-meaning pairs in the recipient language. Most often, such replications are loanwords, but even morphemes are sometimes replicated from one language to another. Another type of replication is the import of a syntactic, morphological, or semantic pattern. Different terms are used in literature to refer to these two basic categories. For example, Haugen (1950) stresses the difference between importation versus calque, and Haspelmath (2009) stresses the difference between material borrowing versus structural borrowing. The terms used by Matras (2009), namely *matter replication*, are used herein to refer to the replication of sound-meaning pairs and *pattern replication* is used to refer to the transferring of linguistic patterns. The terms *borrowing, replication, loan,* and *loanword* are used as synonyms.

Three important criteria are used to define how to identify matter replications. These are phonological, semantic, and geographic criteria (Häkkinen 1997a, 24–27). Loanwords are integrated into a recipient language using different types of phonological adaptations. Old loanwords are integrated better than younger ones, which have specific phonological features that often do not occur in the inherited vocabulary of a language.

Moreover, verbal replications are morphologically adapted. It is normal that some of the inflection types of the recipient language are used to adapt loanwords. For example, in Finnish, both some of the Old German loan verbs and most of the younger verb loans – among them Swedish loan verbs – are replicated into the so-called contracted verb type (Häkkinen 1997b, 47, see also Section 5.1.1).

Swedish words were borrowed in Finnish during the centuries when Finnish was a minority language in the Kingdom of Sweden, and in the 19th century when Finland was a grand duchy under the Russian emperor. There was a diglossic situation in which upper classes and public sectors used Swedish, except for the church, which used both Swedish and Finnish, while the peasantry used Finnish, except for the coastal areas, which used Swedish. During the period from 1863 to1902, Finnish was made an official language, equal with Swedish, through several language decrees. During the same period, Finnish was introduced in all public domains and as a family language in all social groups (Tommila and Pohls 1989). At the same time and up until the middle of the 20th century, nationalistic language planning was engaged to eliminate the Swedish influence. Because Kven existed outside the influence of the language planning in Finland, more borrowings from Swedish are used in Kven than in the most current varieties of Finnish. When the Kven settlers moved to Norway, they had these Swedish loans as well as a pattern in their dialects to replicate verbs from a Scandinavian language.

The Finnish language has received loanwords, especially from Indo-European languages, and most investigations of loanwords in Finnish have concentrated on these, although there are also loanwords from Saami in Finnish. There are more Saami loanwords to be found in the Far North Finnish dialects, which continues to have contact with the Saami in modern times. Äimä (1908) studied Saami loanwords in these northernmost Finnish dialects, and he presented 101 etymologies. Aikio (2009) presents 300 Saami loanwords in the Far North dialects collected from etymological dictionaries. Aikio believes that there must be even more Saami loan words in the Far North dialects that are unrecognized currently because the etymological dictionaries do not include all dialect words. Additionally, there are old Saami loans with a distribution in other Finnish dialects based on the contact with the Saami languages that were still spoken in the more southern parts of Finland in the Middle and Early Middle Ages (Aikio 2007). Aikio (2009) presents etymologies of several Saami substrate loanwords in Finnish and Karelian. Häkkinen (2007) gives an overview of Saami loans in standard Finnish, which were often conveyed through writers who had come from or had contact with northern Finland.

Besides the Swedish loanwords, the Kvens had Saami loanwords when they arrived in Norway, and the number of Saami loans increased in Norway, so there are also new Saami loans in Kven. Because there has not been much of a focus on Saami loanwords in Finnish, it is not very clear how loan verbs from Saami are morphologically integrated into Finnish, i.e., whether they are adapted in the same inflectional type of contracted verbs as the Swedish loan verbs are. It is typical for both Kven and Saami to contain a large number of derivational suffixes. In both languages, verbal derivations are used not only to express morpho-syntactic means, such as causativity or anti-causativity, but also to express aspect, or how verbal acts relate to the flow of time. These are the basic categories of verbal derivations, and they can be divided into several subtypes (ISK § 303–310). Nickel and Sammallahti (2011, 541) refer to verbal derivations in Saami as aspectual and grammatical, with the latter including both causative and anti-causative derivations.

Because Kven and Saami share many corresponding linguistic elements, it follows that it is easier for language users to create mental or cognitive links that connect the elements of these languages and to make comparisons between such elements (Aikio 2007, 21; Riionheimo 2013, 647). Bybee (2003) describes language as a network in which lexemes have stronger or weaker connections to each other depending on their lexical strength, which means that frequent forms of paradigms resist regularizing change. Paradigms that are highly frequent keep their irregularities, while paradigms that are less frequent more easily regularize. So, in usage-based theories, such as Bybee's, the way language is actually used is thought to have an impact on how mental lexicons are organized, and indeed, even how language is structured. Because phonetic and semantic similarity creates stronger networks between linguistic elements, connections can be created – even between a bilingual's different languages – more easily when they share similar elements. (Bybee 2003, 5, 22, 113, cf., also Koivisto in this volume.)

There have been different answers to the question of how a donor language effects the morphological replication of loan verbs in the recipient language. Recently, Wohlgemuth (2009) has studied this question from a typological point of view, arguing against the view that the complexity of verbal morphology in the receiving language makes borrowing difficult (2009, 9, 251–255, 296). Moravcsik (1975) has defended the view that verbs cannot be borrowed as verbs, but they must first be reverbalized in the receiving language by derivation. However, according to Tadmor (2009, 61), Moravcsik does not take into account that verbs can be borrowed into isolating languages without making any adaptation. Tadmor concludes (2009, 63) that morphosyntactic adaptation may still be needed when borrowings are inserted into a synthetic language.

Wohlgemuth (2009) argues that the need for grammatical and typological compatibility between the recipient and donor languages is not a relevant factor for the borrowability of verbs. According to him, both direct insertion and indirect insertion can be found in a synthetic language, such as Finnish (2009, 208–213). Direct insertion means that a loan verb is directly incorporated into a verb inflectional class in a recipient language without any overt marking, whereas indirect insertion means that a loan verb is incorporated using a morpheme that overtly marks the replication. Causative derivational morphemes are often used in indirect insertion. However, other derivatives may also be used, and it is possible that both direct and indirect insertion have subtypes.

In this article, borrowing into Kven from Scandinavian languages, (which are typologically different from Kven), and from Saami, (a language typologically more similar to Kven) is compared, and the differences between replications that come from Scandinavian languages and Saami are discussed. Whether there are matter and pattern replications from the donor languages will be examined along with whether it is possible to find both a direct and an indirect insertion of loan verbs, and whether loans from Scandinavian languages and Saami are incorporated into the same or different inflectional types.

4 Data and method

The data represent both oral and written Kven. The oral corpus consists of material collected by Lindgren between 1967 and 1985, as presented in Lindgren (1974, 1993), in addition to her unpublished material, the data was collected from the areas of Raisi/Nordreisa[1] in North Troms, Pyssyjoki/Børselv in Porsanki/Porsanger, a central part of Finnmark County, and Annijoki/Vestre-Jakobselv in eastern Finnmark. The material collected is from the time just before the ethnic renaissance and represents the language used by the elderly people from that time: people who were from the last generation that spoke Kven on a daily basis with each other in the Kven villages. The informants were chosen using specific criteria, such that the so-called semi-speakers were excluded from the data (Lindgren 1993, 31–32). Some of the informants were also trilingual and spoke Saami as their second or third language.

Even though the Kven language mainly survived as an oral language, there are also some written sources available. The most important of these are studies written by Johan Beronka (1885–1965), who was born in Vesisaari/Vadsø and whose mother tongue was Kven. He was a vicar in Porsanki in 1916–1920 and in Vesisaari from 1920 to 1930. He released a syntactic study in 1922 and a study of derivation and morphology in 1925. His corpus was collected from 1916 to 1920 in Porsanki, and from a seemingly earlier period in Vesisaari. Beronka's material represents Kven dialects from the time before Norwegianization, when many Kven did not yet speak Norwegian.

Another written source used herein is the first novel written in Kven, called *Kuosuvaaran takana* 'Behind Kuosuvaara'. The author of this novel is Alf Nilsen-Børsskog (1928–2014), who was born in Pyssyjoki and whose mother tongue was Kven. The novel tells about a group of people from Pyssyjoki who refused to follow the orders from the German occupation forces to evacuate to southern Norway during the Second World War; instead, they escaped to the mountains. Nilsen-Børsskog also published two other novels and several collections of poems in Kven. The books of Nilsen-Børsskog contributed to the revitalization of the Kven language. However, Nilsen-Børsskog wrote his books before standardization and his written language was not influenced by the language council, as he created his own written standard before the council did. The council has used his writings as part of their written sources, secondary to the oral materials from the various Kven dialects.

Both Scandinavian and Saami have had an impact on the Kven verbs that belong to borrowing because they seem to have permanently affected Kven. As early as the 1920s, Beronka described some of the same features that will be presented below. Only the influence on the dominant language of speakers will be described, as all informants were genuine speakers of Kven. Examples from Nilsen-Børsskog's novel represent an idiolect of Kven

---

1 In northern Norway, many place names can be found in all three languages spoken in the area. This article presents place names in Kven first and then in Norwegian.

because he was a creative writer. Nevertheless, the written language can be assumed to represent a more stable use of language than the oral one does.

An important methodological question is how to identify the loanwords from the Scandinavian or Saami languages in the material. For this purpose, loanwords have been defined using phonological, semantic, and geographic criteria as described by Häkkinen (1997a). It is presumed that typical features for young loanwords in Kven are the same as in Finnish (see ibid, 261), but allow for the possibility of phonetic substitutions. When Saami loanwords are incorporated into Kven and Finnish, the substitutions of Saami vowels and consonants follow a specific substitution pattern. An overview of this pattern is presented in Korhonen (1981) and Aikio (2007 and 2009). A phonetic substitution, or the use of the most phonetically similar inherited phoneme as a substitute, is also possible in young Saami loan words. However, so-called etymological nativization can be a reason why even young loanwords look older than they actually are. Etymological nativization means that there is a pattern for phonetic substitutions based on the substitutions of older loanwords. Even young loanwords can follow such an established pattern (Aikio 2007, 21, 43).

Loans in a recipient language can keep the same basic meaning that they have in the donor language, but it is also possible that the lexical meaning changes. Although young loanwords have preserved their original meaning better than old loanwords, both types may have lost their original basic meaning, e.g., the concrete meaning may have become abstract. Lexical interference between words with a similar phonetic shape from donor and recipient language may also have created a new meaning (Häkkinen 1997a, 42–51; Weinreich 1974, 48–49).

In addition to phonetic and semantic criteria, geographic distribution is also used to determine the Scandinavian donor language. It is not always easy to separate loans from the near relative donor languages of Swedish and Norwegian. In some cases, parallel borrowing processes must be considered. Many Saami loans in Kven can be found in Far North Finnish dialects. In these instances, they often resemble inherited Finnish words and are identified because they are rarely known in standard Finnish. There are also unique borrowings from Saami found in Kven. Most often, Saami loanwords in Kven are from the Northern Saami, but loanwords with a distribution in Finnish dialects, in particular, may have some other Saami language as the donor language (Häkkinen 2007).

The etymologies of loanwords are not given here, since the focus is on the morphological integration of verbal replications in Kven. The possible model word is checked in Norwegian in *Bokmålsordbok* (BO), and in Saami in the following dictionaries: Sammallahti's *Sámi-suoma-sámi sátnegirji* (SSS), Svonni's *Davvisámegiela-ruoŧagiela, ruoŧagiela-davvisámegiela sátnegirji* (DR), and *Neahttadigisánit* (NDS). Where the dictionary is not mentioned, the BO has been used for the Norwegian model word, and the SSS for the Saami model word. The Internet dictionary of the Swedish Academy, *Svenska akademiens ordbok* (SAOB), has been used to look for the possible Swedish model verb, and the Finnish etymological dictionary *Suomen sanojen alkuperä* (SSA) to identify older Scandinavian or Saami loanwords in the material. The Finnish dictionary *Nykysuomen sanakirja* (NS) has been used to check for words in modern Finnish, and Lönnrot's dictionary *Suomalais-ruotsalainen sanakirja* (SRS), was consulted for words and word meanings possibly lost in modern Finnish. The Meänkieli dictionary *Meänkielen sanakirja* (MKS) and the dictionary of Finnish dialects, *Suomen murteiden sanakirja* (SMS), have been used to determine geographical distribution. Swedish loanwords from the Turku dialect in Grönholm's study (1988) have been compared to our Scandinavian loans, and Saami loans into Finnish as presented by Aikio (2009) have been compared to our Saami loans. A great help in identifying loanwords in the novel by Nilsen-Børsskog has been Pyykkö's *Sana-aitta* (Pyykkö 2008).

5 Matter replication

The following is a discussion of whether the integration strategies that were found represent a direct or indirect insertion (see Wolgemuth 2009) and the subtypes that eventually occur. In a replication in which a derivational suffix is used, but no root word can be found in Kven, the derivational suffix is called a verbalizer (VBL), and in cases in which there is an affix that can only be found in borrowed verbs, it is called a loan verb marker (LVM) (see Wohlgemuth 2009, 95, 98). Only the phonetic substitutions of replications have been considered if they have relevance to the analyses of morphological incorporation or if they can help to identify the donor language.

5.1 MATTER REPLICATION FROM SCANDINAVIAN LANGUAGES

5.1.1 Contracted verbs in Kven

One set of Scandinavian verbs has been assimilated into Kven as a verb type called contracted verbs (cf., Jarva and Mikkonen in this volume). This type was originally a derivation type, but the derivational suffix and verb stem have been conflated together. According to traditional analyses of Finnish, the so-called first infinitive[2] has an ending *A*; however, the infinitive suffix is morphologically restructured to be *tA* (Karlsson 1983, 297). The same has happened in Kven. The derivational suffix *A* can be seen in the 1SG form. Norwegian loanwords seem to follow the pattern of Swedish loanwords (see Section 3), and are integrated into this verb type:

> *striikka-a-n* 'I knit' : *striika-ta* 'to knit' < Norw *strikke* id.
> knit-VBL-1SG : knit-INF
> *pestilla-a-n* 'I order' : *pestilla-ta* 'to order' < Norw *bestille* id.
> order-VBL-1SG : order-INF
> *tägnä-ä-n* 'I draw' : *tägnä-tä* 'to draw' < Norw *tegne* id.
> draw-VBL-1SG : draw-INF

---

2   There are many infinitives in Finnish and Kven. In Kven, you can find three types of infinitives, which are refered to as first, second, and third infinitive. (Söderholm 2014, 232–237.)

The difficulty with Norwegian loans is separating them from earlier Swedish loans. *Striikata* seems to have been replicated from Norwegian, because in Swedish *sticka* is used to mean 'to knit' (SAOB). A phonetic criterion shows that the Kven verb *pestillata* 'to order' is a replication from a Norwegian verb since there is a vowel *i* in the second syllable like in Norwegian, and not a vowel *e* like in Swedish (*beställa* /bestella/).

Beronka (1925, 77) presents the verb *tägnätä* 'to draw', which is also based on a Norwegian model verb. In addition, Beronka presents *riitata* 'to draw' < Swe *rita*. These two verbs have the same meaning, but they are replicated from different donor languages. *Riitata* most obviously belonged to the language of the Kvens before they moved to Norway, while the new word *tägnätä* came into use in Norway. Therefore, this could be an example of prestige motivation (see Matras 2009, 150). Nevertheless, *tägnätä* can also refer to a specific activity at school, namely drawing. For instance, *tängninki* is a noun replicated in Kven from Norwegian, which means: 1) 'drawing, a picture', 2) 'drawing, a school subject' (Utvik 1996, 213). Here, the motivation for borrowing seems to be the need to refer to a specific referent.

Many Scandinavian loans in Kven are old loanwords from Swedish, e.g., *freistata, reistata* 'to try' < Swe *fresta, freista* (SSA s.v. *reistata*), *hoksata* 'to get the message' < Swe (dial.) *håkks(a)*, Old Swe *hoxa, hughsa* (SSA s.v. *hoksata*), *piisata* 'to be enough' < Old Swe *spisa* (SSA s.v. *piisata*), *pärjätä* 'to manage, get on, get along' < Swe *bärga* (SSA s.v. *pärjätä*). These verbs are used in western Finnish dialects, and some of them even have a larger distribution in Finnish dialects. *Hoksata, piisata* and *pärjätä* are also known in modern Finnish. Based on the time when these verbs were borrowed into Finnish and their distribution in Finnish dialects, it is obvious that these loanwords were already a part of the language of the Kven settlers by the time they moved to Norway.

The examples above, as well as many other examples, demonstrate that the replication model of Norwegian loans into Kven in the contracted verb type is based on the replication model of Swedish loan verbs into Finnish. Even in verbs that must have been replicated from Norwegian, the vowel *e* at the end of the Norwegian infinitive form[3] is substituted, using the vowel *a* at the end of the verb stem in Kven (*raakata* < Norw *rake*). Therefore, the replication model for Norwegian loans in Kven is based on etymological nativization (see Aikio 2007), meaning that new loans have been integrated using an already existing model. Nummila (2013) presents a parallel case of etymological nativization of the agent noun derivative in Finnish.

Wohlgemuth (2009, 209) classifies the integration of Finnish verbs in the contracted verb type as direct insertion because there is no derivational suffix visible in the integration. Nevertheless, contracted verbs have historically been verbal derivations (Lehtinen 2007, 100). Traditionally, Finnish grammarians have presented contracted verbs as including a derivational suffix *A* (ISK § 304). There is a variation between *A* and *t* in the verb stem,

---

3   Infinitives in Norwegian dialects can end in *e* or *a*; however, in Northern Norwegian dialects infinitives end in *e* (Jahr and Skare 1996, 14).

striikat-a (infinitive), *striikkaa-n* (present tense1SG). That the consonant *t* is a part of verb stem is seen also in 2PL imperative forms, which in both the Kven and Far North Finnish dialects is *striikak-kaa* < *striikat-kaa* (Lindgren 1993, 132). In Kven, the 2PL imperative suffix is also restructured from *kAA* to *kkAA* (Lindgren 1993, 60).

The derivational suffix *A* used in contracted verbs is semantically empty, and its function is to be a verbalizer, i.e., to form verbs from nouns. Semantic openness is the reason the contracted verb type is productive (Räisänen 1987, 496). Because the contracted verb type actually includes a derivational suffix, the contracted verb type can be interpreted to represent indirect insertion.

5.1.2 eera verbs

One subtype of the contracted verb consists of those in which a verb stem and a suffix element *eera* are replicated from the model verb. This verb type is also used in the standard Finnish language, and has been borrowed from Swedish. In all Nordic languages, there are verbs that are formed with the suffix *era*. This suffix is based on an Old Nordic suffix, which has been replicated through Low German, and ultimately from Roman sources (Wohlgemuth 2009, 228–229). According to Wohlgemuth, the suffix *eera* is used in Finnish as a complex loan verb marker (2009, 208–209). This loan verb type was already used in the old Finnish written language, but it gradually lost its productivity, starting in early 19th century, as a result of language planning (Häkkinen 1994, 517; Räsänen 2005). In the standard Finnish language, many loan verbs, which were previously replicated from Swedish using the *eera* suffix, are replicated today using another suffix, *Oi*, originating from Finnish.

In the material, many verbs have been replicated using the suffix *eera*, which in Kven is used as a loan verb marker to replicate verbs that in Norwegian end in *ere*:

> *spant-eera-ta* 'to pay for' < Norw *spand-ere* id.
> pay.for-LVM-INF

Most of the verbs that have been replicated in the *eera* type seem to be new cultural loans from Norwegian, which are used to describe phenomena in society in the late 20th century, such as *spanteerata*. Similar cultural loans are *evakkueerata* 'to evacuate' < Norw *evakuere*, and *pansyneerata* < *pensjonere seg* 'to retire on a pension'. These verbs come from oral material, and, therefore, they have been integrated into Kven phonetically, in contrast to the verbs of Nilsen-Børsskog. The verbs used by that author, e.g., *kommenteerata* 'to comment' and *kapituleerata* 'to capitulate', are not in obvious use in Meänkieli, even though there are Swedish verbs similar (see SAOB, s.v. *kommentera*, *kapitulera*) to the Norwegian model verbs. Therefore, these verbs in Kven seem to have been replicated from Norwegian. *Kapituleerata* is also directly connected to the historical period of the Second World War, which Nilsen-Børsskog describes in his novel.

In the verb *hunteerata* 'to ponder' < Swe *fundera*, *f* is replaced with *h*, which was previously a typical substitution for the Swedish *f* in Finnish dialects (Grönholm 1988, 217–219). This verb demonstrates that Kvens knew this loan verb model when they arrived in Norway. *Hunteerata* has a distribution in many western Finnish dialects (SSA, s.v. *funteerata*). The *eera* verb type is also known from earlier translations of the Finnish Bible, which was read by Kvens. Many verbs that belong to the *eera* type have been replicated from Norwegian, but integrated according to an already existing Swedish model, like other contracted verbs.

It is also notable that the donor language plays an important role in determining which verbs are accommodated in this type, since all the examples of *eera* verb loans were loanwords based on Norwegian or Swedish model verbs that either ended in *ere* or *era*. The phonological shape of the input form is also an important factor, as pointed out by Wohlgemuth (2009, 215–216). A loan verb marker, even though it has been borrowed from a donor language, means that the borrowed stem is marked to be a verb, and, therefore, represents an indirect insertion (Wohlgemuth 2009, 209).

5.1.3 Oi(tte) *verbs*

The derivational suffix *Oi* is used to form denominal derivatives in Finnish from trisyllabic nouns in addition to being used as a verbalizer of borrowed verbs (ISK § 331). In Kven dialects, the first infinitive form in the *Oi(tte)* verb type varies like *piikaroita* 'to spike' ~ *piikaroiđa* ~ *piikaroija*~ *piikaroittea(t)*, and is conjugated in the 1SG *piikaroitten* (see Beronka 1925, 33; Lindgren 1993, 156–158; Söderholm 2014, 192–193).

Below follows a discussion of whether the suffix *Oi* can be used as a verbalizer of borrowed verb stems in Kven or if it only appears as a denominal derivational suffix:

a) *feeri-öi-jä* 'to have a holiday' < Norw *feri-ere* id.
   have.a.holiday-VBL-INF
b) *feeri-öi-jä* 'to have a holiday' < *feeriä* 'holiday' < Norw *ferie* id.
   holiday-ESS-INF

The verb *feeriöijä* is possibly replicated from the Norwegian verb *feriere*, in a similar way as foreign verbs in Finnish are replicated using the suffix *Oi* (Hakulinen 1978, 284). Yet, the Kven noun *feeriä* could also be the root word for the verb *feeriöijä*. Beronka (1925, 33) presents a similar verb derivation process with *harava* 'a rake' > *haravoija* ~ *haravoiđa* 'to rake hay', in which the root word *harava* is also a trisyllabic word. Because many of the *Oi(tte)* verbs are denominal derivatives of inherited words in Kven, it is most likely that the verb *feriere* is actually an essentiative derivative from a noun (see ISK § 303) and not based on a Norwegian model verb in Kven.

The verbs *fiskaroija* 'to be a fisher' and *piikaroija* 'to spike' are also verbal derivatives of borrowed trisyllabic nouns in Kven. In these examples, the root words have borrowed nouns ending in *Ari* (see Utvik 1996, 102, 168 *fiskari, piikari*). *Oi(tte)* verbs in Kven are most often denominal derivatives in which the root word is either a loan word or an inherited word. It follows that, unlike Finnish, which uses this derivational suffix both as a verbalizer of nouns and a verbalizer of foreign verbs (ISK § 331), the derivational suffix *Oi* is only used as a verbalizer of nouns in Kven. This is also expected, because Kven has not been an object for language planning like Finnish.

5.1.4 Other insertion types

In Finnish, there are two inflection types in addition to contracted verbs and *Oi(tte)* verbs that have previously been used to replicate loan verbs. These are verbs with an *i* stem and verbs with a suffix *ile*, both of which are also used as a derivational suffix (ISK § 303). Today, these verb types are less productive than the contracted verbs and *Oi(tte)* verbs, and according to Grönholm (1988, 274–276) they are losing their productivity (cf., also Jarva and Mikkonen in this volume). An examples of *i* stems is presented below:

kraappi-it 'to rake hay' < Swe *skrapa* id. (SSA, s.v. *raapia*)
rake-INF

The verb *kraappiit* is used in both Meänkieli and Finnish dialects, indicating that it was most likely not replicated from the Norwegian donor language (Norw *skrape*). Verbs such as *praattia, raatia* 'to talk' < Swe *prata* / Norw *prate* or *pryyttiä* < Swe *bryta* / Norw *bryte* 'to break' could have been replicated from either Swedish or Norwegian, although this subtype is not very frequent. Some Swedish loans in the Turku dialect have been integrated in the same way, and, according to Grönholm (1988, 275–276), such verbs are incorporated directly into an existing inflection class, even though *i* is also a derivational suffix. According to such a view, this type represents direct insertion, although it is possible to argue that even in this case the foreign verb has been integrated using the continuative derivational suffix *i* (Hakulinen 1978, 282).

The following example includes a frequentative derivational suffix *ile* (ISK § 303):

praama-il-la < *praama-ta* 'to boast' < Swe *bramma, brama* (dial.) (SSA, s.v. *pramea*)
boast-FREQ-INF

Nilsen-Børsskog uses the verbs *praamaila : praamailen* and *mooraila : moorailen*, which are verbs that have a frequentative derivational suffix *ile* in the verb stem. The verb *praamaila* is a derivative of *praamata*; both of these verbs are also known not only in Kven, but also in Meänkieli and in Finnish dialects. *Mooraila* means 'to say good morning', and is likely a derivative of *moora* 'good morning' < Norw *morn* (Pyykkö 2008). There is no verb in Norwegian that can be used as a model verb for *mooraila*. This derivation represents a quotative derivation because the root noun refers to speaking. This frequentative type is used in a similar way also in Finnish (Kytömäki 1990, 56). Many frequentative derivatives of this type have a contractive verb as a root verb: *fästäillä* < *fästätä* 'to have a party'< Norw *feste*.

Some of the complex verb types also contain verbs that are unique replications in which the verbalizer is a derivational suffix in Kven. For example:

triives-ty-ä < 'to enjoy oneself' < Norw *trives* id.
enjoy-VBL-INF

This replication is an example of phonological conditioning (Wohgemuth 2009, 215), as the replication follows the Norwegian model verb phonetically. The verbalizer is a derivational suffix that expresses reflexivity, something that is inherent in the meaning of the Norwegian model verb. In the Torne Valley, the same verb has been replicated from Swedish: *triivastua* < Sve *trivas* (MKS).

5.2 Matter replication from Saami

5.2.1 Disyllabic basic verbs (taajoa)

Verbs that belong to the basic verb type in Kven have only one stem (a vowel stem). This inflectional type is the largest, compared to all other types, if based on the number of verb lexemes. Verbs in this inflectional type have two or more syllables. The verb stem ends in *A, U, o, i,* or *e,* and the infinitive morpheme is either *A* or the same vowel as the vowel at the end of the verb stem. In addition, this infinitive type can end in *t* < **k* (see Hakulinen 1978, 51) in some Kven dialects. Basic verb type corresponds to Söderholm's (2014, 189) *verbityyppi 2*, and to *kertoa-TYYPPI* in ISK (§ 102–103). Many borrowings from Saami have been integrated within this inflection type of disyllabic verbs in Kven.

naakki-a ~ naakki-i(t) 'to sneak' < SaN *njáhkat* id.
sneak-INF   (DR, see also SSS, s.v. *hiipiä,* SSA, s.v. *naakia*)
jaukku-a ~ jaukku-u(t) 'to disappear' < SaN *jávkat* id. (SMS, s.v. *jaukkua*)
disappear-INF
taajo-a ~ taajo-o(t) 'to play' < SaN *dádjut* id. (SSA, s.v. *taajoa*)
play-INF
kurppa-at 'to bind, tie' cf., SaN *gurpet, gurpat* id. (DR, SSA, s.v. *kurppa*)
bind-INF

These verbs have two syllables in both the Kven and Saami languages, and, particularly in those Kven dialects in which the infinitive ends in *t*, these verbs in Kven and Saami are remarkably similar. Lindgren (1993, 169) points out that the conservation of *t* at the end of the infinitive form in some Kven dialects has probably been reinforced by Saami contact.

The verb *kurppaat* is possibly a derivation of the noun *kurppa* 'bundle, small pack' < SaN *gurpi,* which can also be found in SSA (see also Beronka 1925, 76 and Aikio 2009, 258). *Kurpata*, which belongs to the contracted verb type, occurs in the Finnish etymological dictionary (SSA, s.v. *kurppa*) and in the Finnish dialect dictionary (SMS, s.v. *kurpata*), but not in the present material. Nevertheless, especially when the verb stem ends in *A*, an alternation with the contracted verb type can be found in Kven (*jatkaa* ~ *jatkaat* / *jatkata* 'to go on, continue', cf., Jarva and Mikkonen in this volume).

Most of these verbs are used in the Far North Finnish dialects. In Aikio (2009), the verbs *naakkia* and *taajoa* are presented, and *jaukkua* can be found in the Finnish dialect dictionary (SMS). Some of these verbs are also mentioned in written Finnish sources, e.g., the verb *naakia* is found as early as in the 17th century (Häkkinen 2007). The distribution of these verbs demonstrates that many of them already belonged to the Kven vocabulary when the people moved to Norway, and they are, perhaps, significantly older. Even though the Saami form is given in Northern Saami in the examples, it is possible that some other Saami language is the real donor language, since many of these verbs have a distribution in other Saami languages. Possible donor languages could be those Saami languages that were previously spoken in Finland or Sweden (cf., Häkkinen 2007; Aikio 2009).

The present study does not have any examples of *e* stems among the Saami borrowings, and the example including the *a* stem (*kurppaat*) is possibly a denominal derivative. The other borrowings could be interpreted to represent direct insertion if the last vowel (*i, o, u*) in the verb stem is analysed as a stem vowel. Yet, the vowels *i, o,* and *u* can all be found among verbal derivational suffixes, and disyllabic words that include these vowels are considered to be old derivatives (Hakulinen 1978, 47). Verbal derivatives that include the derivational suffix *i* or *o* are often continuatives (Hakulinen 1978, 275, 282), like the verbs *naakia* and *taajoa*. Verbal derivatives that include the suffix *U* are anti-causative derivatives in Finnish (see ISK § 334), like the verb *jaukkua*. This would indicate that these verbs could also represent an indirect insertion type if they have been integrated within a certain type of derivation.

5.2.2 Trisyllabic basic verbs

Trisyllabic basic verbs in Kven include a causative derivational suffix *(ttA* or *stA)* used as a verbalizer. An example of *ttA* verbs are presented first:

ruka-tta-a(t) < 'to hasten' < SaN *rohkkáhit* id.
hasten-VBL-INF

The causative suffix *ttA* can be used in Kven, like in *kastuttaat* 'to pour water' < *kastuut* 'to become wet' (Pyykkö 2008). This derivational suffix is also known in Finnish, in which it can be used to derive both denominal and deverbal verbs (ISK § 318). Since there is no root word for the verb *rukattaat*, it seems that the causative suffix *ttA* is used as a verbalizer in this case, with the verb being an example of indirect insertion. *Rukattaat* is also used in the Far North Finnish dialects.

In the following examples the Kven verb has been integrated using the causative derivational suffix *stA*:

njuaru-sta-at 'to cast a (Saami) lasso' < SaN *njoarostit* id.
cast.a.lasso-VBL-INF
henka-sta-at 'to hang tr.' < *hengata* 'to hang intr.', comp. SaN *heaŋggastit* tr. id.
hang-CAUS-INF

In these examples, the model verb in Saami has a derivational suffix *stit*, which is used in Sami in many derivational types. Deverbal *stit* can refer to a momentary inchoative or diminutive act (Nickel and Sammallahti 2011, 545, 557, 559).

The suffix *stA* can be used to form verbs from nouns in Kven, like the word *saustaa(t)* 'to smoke (e.g., to smoke fish)' < *sau* 'smoke' (Beronka 1925, 30). In Finnish, *stA* is most often used to derive denominal verbs; even so, it can sometimes be used to derive deverbal verbs, as with *asustaa* 'live' < *asua* 'to live'. According to ISK (§ 326), the *stA* derivative as a deverbal derivational type is not very productive in Finnish anymore.

For the verb *njuarustaat*, there is no root word in Kven; therefore, the causative suffix has a function as a verbalizer, and the verb has been integrated into Kven using indirect insertion. The verb *karistaat* 'to run, rush after' < *garistit* (SaN), also appears to be an indirect insertion from the Saami model. Aikio (2009, 265) also presents similar Saami loan verbs in the Far North dialects, commenting that the Finnish loan verbs, including those with the *stA* suffix, indicate that the Saami model verb includes a momentative suffix.

In contrast, the verb *henkastaat* has a root verb, *henkastaat* (tr.) < *hengata* (itr.), and is, therefore, a causative derivation in Kven. For instance, Alf Nilsen-Børsskog uses *hengata* as an intransitive verb and *henkastaat* as a transitive verb (see Pyykkö, 2008). The root verb *hengata* seems to be a loan from Swedish because it is found in Meänkieli (MKS, s.v. *hengata*), while the causative derivation of this verb is based on the Saami model. Nonetheless, there are not many examples in Kven where the derivational suffix *stA* is used as a causative suffix of deverbal derivatives; instead, it is used in pattern replication. This type is discussed further in Section 6.3.

5.2.3 Contracted verbs

Some verbs from Saami are replicated in the contracted verb type. Many verbs replicated in this type have not been found as they are verbs that fall into the disyllabic basic verb type (see Section 5.2.1). The 1SG form is presented here, including the verbalizer:

näskä-ä-n 'I scrape' : *näskä-tä* 'to scrape the membrane off' < SaN *neaskit* id.
scrape-VBL-1SG : scrape-INF
kuoraa-n 'I follow a footprint' : *kuora-ta* 'to follow a footprint' < SaN *guorradit* id.
follow-VBL-1SG : follow-INF   (SMS, s.v. *kuor(r)ata*)

Both the verb *näskätä*, which refers to the preparing of skins, and *kuorata* occur in the Far North Finnish dialects, and are found in Aikio (2009, 257, 267). Another contracted verb, *fierata*, is not found in either Torne Valley

Finnish or in the Finnish dialects, but the noun *fiera* 'a shoe grass ball' is mentioned in the Finnish dialect dictionary (SMS, s.v. *fiera*). *Fierata* 'to skein up shoe grass into a ball' could be a derivation of *fiera*, or the other way around (see Kulonen 1996, 28 for similar examples). All the loans in the contracted verb type in Saami have been integrated using an indirect insertion (see contracted verb type in Section 5.1.1).

5.2.4 Oi(tte) *verbs*

In the material, there are some verbs that have been replicated to *Oi(tte)* verbs from Saami.

> *suokkar-oi-đa* 'to investigate, study' < SaN *suokkardit* id.
> study-VBL-INF

There is no root word in Kven from which to derive *suokkaroiđa*, so this verb has actually been replicated from the Saami model. The Saami verb *suokkardit* consists of the verb stem *suokkar* and a derivational suffix *dit*. The root word *suokkar* does not occur as an independent word, and its meaning is unclear (information provided by Kjell Kemi). It seems that the element *ar* at the end of the Saami verb stem is the motivation for using this verbalizing suffix (cf., *piikari* > *piikaroija*, Section 5.1.3). There is also a denominal verb derivative of a similar type, *naakkaroiđa* 'to argue', in which the root word is a loan from the Saami *naakkari* 'stubborn' < SaN *nággár*.

5.2.5 tele, skele, ile *verbs*

There are many examples of Saami verbs that have been replicated into different frequentative derivational types. These derivatives have many variants, but all derivatives include a suffix element *(e)le* (see ISK § 358):

> *raima-tel-la* 'to become very scared' < SaN *ráimmahallat* id.
> become.scared-VBL-INF
> *villi-tel-lä* 'to be fooled' < SaN *fillehallat* id.
> fool-VBL-INF
> *riuđu-skel-la* 'to drive in water' < SaN *rievdat* id.
> drive-VBL-INF
> *muijo-il-a* 'to smile' < SaN *mojohallat* id.
> smile-VBL-INF

Raimatella is a replication from Saami as there is no root verb or root noun that can be used in a derivation. *Villitellä* can also be analyzed in different ways. In Beronka (1922, 46), it is presented as a loanword from Saami, but it could also be a derivation from the inherited root word *villi* 'wild, false' (SSA s.v. villi). This is because *villitellä* can be found in Lönnrot's dictionary (SRS s.v. *villitellä*), meaning 'to fool someone', but this verb seems not to belong to Modern Finnish, e.g., it is not found in the NS. In any case, the passive meaning of this verb has been replicated from Saami.

In the verb *riuđuskella*, the frequentative derivational suffix *skele* seems to have been used as a verbalizer. In the same way, the derivational suffix *ile* in the verb *mujoila* is used as a verbalizer. According to Aikio (2009, 264), there is a noun, *muju* 'smile', and a verb, *mujuta* 'to smile', and a verb, *riutua* (ibid. 273), which means the same as *riuđuskella* in Far North Finnish dialects. Consequently, the verb *muijoila* is likely a parallel loan from Saami. Alternately, the verb *riuđuskella* in the material can also be a derivative of the verb *riutua*; however, *riutua* does not occur in the material.

The verbalizer in these examples is a frequentative derivational suffix. Kven and Saami suffixes often share a phonetic similarity, e.g., the consonant *l* occurs in suffixes of both languages. This phonetic similarity may be one reason why Saami verbs have been inserted into these frequentative derivational types. The impression is that these derivatives are used more frequently in Kven than in Finnish, and contact with Saami might explain the increased use in Kven.

6 Pattern replication from Saami

Pattern replication means that different syntactic, semantic, or morphological patterns form a model, which is replicated from the donor language even though sound-meaning pairs have not been borrowed. In the Kven corpus herein, there are examples of lexicalization, an innovative use of frequentative derivatives, a semantic change in derivational suffixes, and a change in inflection.

6.1 LEXICALIZATION OF *MUISTELA* 'TO TELL'

The deverbal derivative *muistela* has been lexicalized to mean 'to tell' in Kven and is a *frequentative* derivative from the verb *muistaa* 'to remember'. In Finnish, *muistela* means 'to remember, look back', which is actually related to the meaning of 'to tell', even though the Saami model for the lexicalization of the verb *muistela* seems obvious. The root verb *muistaa* 'to remember' still has the same meaning in Kven as it has in Finnish today:

> muist-el-a 'to tell' cf., SaN *muihtalit* id.
> tell-FREQ-INF

The Saami model verb is also phonetically close to the Kven verb, as it is originally a loan from Finnish (SSA, s.v. *muistaa*). There are many examples of the lexicalization of frequentative derivatives occuring both in Kven and Finnish, such as *ajatella* 'to think' < *ajaa* 'to drive, pursue' (Häkkinen 1997a, 132).

6.2 REPLICATION USING A FREQUENTATIVE DERIVATIVE (S)TEL(E) IN KVEN

Examples in which Saami patterns have been replicated using a frequentative derivative in Kven can be found in denominal verbal derivatives of the disyllabic nouns *talo* 'house', *kaffi* 'coffee' and *herra* 'gentleman'. Similar derivatives are also found in Finnish (see ISK § 358):

> *talo-stel-la* 'to keep a house, live' cf., SaN *dálostallat* id.
> house-FREQ-INF
> *kaffi-stel-la* 'to make and drink coffee' cf., SaN *káfestallat* id.
> coffee-FREQ-INF
> *herru-stel-la* 'to strut, live like a lord' cf., SaN *hearrástallat* id.
> gentleman-FREQ-INF

Saami and Kven verbs share both semantic and phonologic similarities in these examples as the derivational suffixes (in Kven *(s)tel(e)* and in Saami *stallat* or *hallat*) have the consonant *l* in both languages and often a frequentative meaning. In many cases, Saami seems to be a model for specific derivatives in Kven of this word type, e.g., *valkistella* 'to make a campfire', *polvistella* 'to kneel', *sokkastella* 'to play blind man's bluff', *kylästellä* 'to make a visit' and *unistella* 'to dream'.

Some frequentative derivatives in Kven have obtained a passive meaning, like *tartutella* 'to be taken'. This is a pattern replication from the Saami derivational suffix *hallat*, which is also used to refer to 'an injurious act' (see Nickel and Sammallahti 2011, 565; Lindgren 1993, 188).

According to Kytömäki (1990, 59–62), some of the denominal derivatives have a specific semantic use in Finnish, with one central use being to express the properties of the agent of the derivation verb, like the verb *herrustella* in the material. These derivatives are also productive in Finnish. Many of these examples are used in northern Finland in the Saami contact areas (Lindgren 1993, 187–188).

6.3 A NEW DIMINUTIVE DERIVATIONAL TYPE STA

Many deverbal derivatives with the suffix *stA* in Kven have borrowed a diminutive meaning from the Saami model. The Saami model verb has a derivational suffix *stit*, like *riŋgestit* 'to phone quickly' (SSS, s.v. *soittaa*). Section 5.2.2 describes how this Saami verb type is replicated using a matter replication in Kven.

A derivational type of *(A)is(e)* verbs is probably the link between the Saami model and the new derivational type in Kven. Some of the *A(i)se* derivatives have a momentane meaning, which refers to 'doing something only once, or for a short period of time' (ISK § 368).

> *kys-äis-tä* 'to ask once, ask shortly' < *kysy-ä* 'to ask' (Beronka 1925, 33).
> ask-MOME-INF

There is a semantic similarity between *A(i)se* derivatives in Kven and Saami *stit* derivatives because the Saami derivational suffix *stit* has the meaning 'to do something a little', so they both refer to a short duration of action. In addition, *A(i)se* derivatives also share structural (three syllables) and phonetic (the consonant combination *st*) similarities with the Saami *stit* derivatives. Because of these phonetic and semantic similarities, verbs that belong to this derivational type have strong connections to the Saami *stit* derivatives (cf., Bybee 2003).

There is also a tendency that momentane *A(i)se* derivatives get mixed with *stA* derivatives and therefore, get even closer to the Saami *stit* derivatives in many conjugation forms (see Section 6.4). In addition, the border between the verb stem and the infinitive ending is restructured.

rink-as-ta 'to phone quickly'
ring-MOME-INF
ringa-sta-a < SaN *riŋgestit* 'to phone quickly, for a little time' (SSS, s.v. *soittaa*)
ring-DIM-INF

When there are both semantic and phonetic similarities between a model word and a replica word, the language users create associative links between such words, and a change in meaning is often a result (Häkkinen 1997, 47; Weinreich 1974, 48–49). In this case, the associative links are created between two derivational suffixes. Because *stA* derivatives are not very frequently used in deverbal derivatives (see Section 5.2.2), it is easier to introduce a new semantic meaning to the *stA* suffix. Moreover, *A(i)se* derivatives have had a function as a link between the model verb and the new Kven derivational type.

Some of these derivatives can be found in the bilingual Saami–Finnish area, but there are no parallels to these derivatives in other Finnish dialects, e.g., *Suomen murteiden sanakirja* (SMS, the dictionary of Finnish dialects) presents an example of this derivational type only from Enontekiö in northern Finland (see SMS, s.v. *ajastaa*).

The following examples are from Kven:

korja-sta-at 'to clean, clear quickly' < *korja-ta*, cf., SaN *čorgestit* id.
clean/clear-DIM-INF
oota-sta-a 'to wait for a short time' < *ootta-a* 'wait' (Kven)
wait-DIM-INF
cf., *vuordde-stit* 'to wait for a short time' < *vuord-it* 'wait' (SaN)
wait-DIM-INF

The Kven derivation *korjastaat* resembles the Saami model verb, but because there is an inherited root, *korjata* 'clean, clear' (Beronka 1925), this is a derivation based on a Saami pattern. The Kven verb with this derivational suffix does not always have a clear phonetic model in Saami, although there are many examples of pairs of verbs that can be formed using this derivational type in both Kven and Saami. Nevertheless, it is possible to explain that bilinguals in Kven and Saami have found a 'gap' in Kven when it comes to expressing a diminutive act. As a result, they have replicated the means of expression from Saami (cf., Matras 2009, 149–150).

This derivational type is used frequently in Kven, both in the oral material from Raisi and Pyssyjoki, and in the written material from Nilsen-Børsskog's novel. Beronka also has examples of this derivational type. It seems to be quite an ordinary derivational type in Kven, which is used to deriving verbs that have a diminutive meaning like in Saami. It is possible to find verb derivatives of this type from many different categories of verbs, e.g., *laulastaa* 'to sing a little' < *laulaa* 'to sing', *panestaa* 'to put a little' < *panna* 'to put', *kuorsastaa* 'to snore for a little time' < *kuorsata* 'to snore'. Even the Scandinavian loans can be derived by sometimes using this derivational suffix (*praatastaa* 'to talk a little' < *praatata* 'to talk').

6.4 Inflectional influence of Saami verbs

All inflection types in Finnish and Kven have a vowel stem, i.e., the stem ends with a vowel. However, some Finnish and Kven verb and noun inflection types have a stem allomorph called a consonant stem and ending with a consonant. This means that there are inflection types with a vowel stem only, as well as types with vowel and consonant stems in a complementary distribution in the paradigm. In the most western Kven dialects, located in Troms County, there are a lot of innovations with vowel stems. The process is quite complicated, presented in Lindgren (1993) and (1999), but there are two main trends. In the first one, some inflection types with consonant stems are in the process of assimilating to the basic verb type (see Section 5.2.1) that has only vowel stems. In the second type, forms with a consonant stem are substituted with forms based on the vowel stems of the same inflection type. Assimilation to the basic verb type, among other trends, is typical for the derivative *(A)ise* verbs, resulting in variations with both traditional and new forms. For example, the traditional forms: infinitive and present 1SG, 2SG, and 3SG *aukasta* 'to open': *aukasen : aukaset : aukasee*, and new forms: *aukastaa : aukastan : aukastat : aukastaa*; cf., basic conjugation type *varastaa* 'to steal': *varastan : varastat : varastaa*. The expansion of the vowel stem into the entire paradigm is typical for the derivative *tele, skele,* and *ile* verbs, so that there are variations between traditional and new forms, as shown in the following examples (traditional followed by new form): infinitive *työtel-ä ~ työtele-ä* 'to work', passive present and past tense *muistel-han ~ muistele-than : muistel-thiin ~ muistele-thiin* of the verb *muistela* 'to tell', and active past participle *kylästel-ly ~ kylästele-nny* of the verb *kylästellä* 'to visit'.

As discussed in Section 5, there are Kven derivative verbs that seem to have been associated with Saami: *(A)ise* and *tele, skele* and *ile* verbs. Because the Saami verbs do not have consonant stems, it is possible that this connection with the Saami verbs has also influenced the expansion of vowel stems; cf., corresponding forms of the verb 'to open' in Saami *rabastit : rabastan : rabastat : rabasta*. The verb derivatives like *ootastaa(t)* (see Section 6.3) in Kven are conjugated like verbs in the basic verb type (e.g., *varastaat*), so these verbs also create a network of both phonetic and semantic associations between the *stit* derivational type in Saami; and the *(A)ise* and basic verb types in Kven, propably affecting the paradigmatic change of *(A)ise* verbs towards the basic verb type. These verbs also have three syllables in both Kven and Saami, so there is also a similarity in word structure between Kven and Saami verbs.

The model from Saami seems to have also affected a paradigmatic change in the derivative types of *tele, skele,* and *ile* verbs in Kven, shifting them away from having both consonant and vowel stems to having only vowel stems. The Saami influence is likely here as such an alternation between two stems is not known in Saami. Verb derivatives with the suffixes *tele, skele,* and *ile* seem to be productive in Kven (cf., the verb derivatives in Nilsen-Børsskog's novel), and the Saami language has probably influenced their productivity (see Section 6.2).

The Kven verb type with consonant stems includes three kinds of verbs: *A(i)se* derivatives that have three syllables (in the vowel stem and in the infinitive); *tele, skele,* and *ile* derivatives that have three or four syllables; and shorter verbs with two syllables, e.g., *juosta* 'to spring', *kuula* 'to hear', *mennä* 'to go', *nousta* 'to rise', *olla* 'to be', *tulla* 'to come'. The expansion of vowel stems only concerns the three- and four-syllable verbs. Verbs that originally had consonant stems have developed differently; long verbs have shifted towards the verbs that only have vowel stems, while disyllabic verbs have maintained consonant stems. The different development of these verb groups also proves that a change from consonant to vowel stems is a result of contact with Saami since only the verbs with three or four syllables have parallels with verbs in Saami.

However, the frequency of these verb types also plays a role in the expansion of the vowel stem. Disyllabic verbs are a small group of verbs that have a high textual frequency[4] (see examples above), meaning that they are used often in oral production. In contrast, verb derivatives with *(A)ise* or *tele, skele,* and *ile* have a higher lexical frequency – meaning that there are more lexemes that belong to one inflectional type – although their textual frequency is lower. The short verbs with high textual frequency are most likely to be remembered as such, stored in the mental lexicon as whole entities, while the longer verbs with low textual frequency are produced through morphological processing. This difference explains why the shorter verbs maintain their complicated paradigm, but the longer verbs change their inflectional type. (Lindgren 1993, 56–58, 263–243.)

In Finnish, diminishing the number of inflection forms with consonant stems is a development that has been taking place slowly for hundreds of years (Bussenius 1939; Hakulinen 1978, 69–73; Paunonen 1976). In Kven North Troms dialects, the expansion of the vowel stem has clearly accelerated. From the point of view of the morphological naturalness theory[5], this development can be seen as a trend towards a more natural inflection system with vowel stems only and with fewer inflection types (Lindgren 1993, 1999). In addition to those changes effected by language contact with Saami, there are also other innovations in the conjugation of verbs in Kven dialects that show a tendency towards a more natural morphological system. The expansion of the vowel stems is typical for the dialects in North Troms, whereas in the Pyssyjoki dialect, the innovations have taken place in other

4 Bybee's (2003) concept of type frequency is the same as lexical frequency, and she uses the concept of token frequency to refer to textual frequency.
5 Natural morphology is a relative, gradual concept. The most natural type of morphology is fully transparent, in the sense that every morpheme has one form and one meaning. Researchers of natural morphology have investigated, inter alia, what kind of structures are widely distributed, are relatively resistant to language change, or develop frequently due to language change. Natural morphology can be considered a part of cognitive linguistics (Dannemark 2010, 30–40).

ways (ibid.). Thus, the development towards a more natural conjugation system is not automatic, but can take different directions because there are many different possibilities in the structures of the language.

In Raisi, folk linguistic concepts developed of 'deep' Finnish and 'easy' Finnish – 'deep' meaning a variety that is closer to the 'real' Finnish used in Finland, and 'easy' being the variety that most of the Kven in Raisi speak. The connection between these concepts and morphological innovations is examined in Lindgren (1974) through a combination of quantitative material and qualitative interviews. The informants with the highest frequencies of traditional forms in the quantitative material were characterized by other Kven as speakers of the 'deep' language. The qualitative interviews confirmed that the traditional forms were associated with 'deep', with the conclusion that the concepts of 'deep' and 'easy' have a connection to these morphological changes. The idiolectal linguistic differences were compared with the multilingual biographies of the informants. The idiolects of 'deep' language reflect the relevant factors in the language shift process favouring the use of Kven and conservatism in relation to Norwegianization, e.g., gender, age, generation after immigration, dwelling place in Raisi, etc. (Lindgren 1974, 121–137).

At the level of dialects and multilingual communities, the phenomenon of the accelerated development of natural morphological changes is seen in some Kven dialects and in the Jällivaara dialect of Meänkieli. In the Far North dialects in Finland, it is found only in the northernmost Saami–Finnish bilingual area in the dialect used as the second language of older Saami born before WWII (Lindgren 1993, 254–255). There are marked differences in the amount of the new forms in these dialects: the highest number of innovations was in Jällivaara, the next in Raisi, fewer in Pyssyjoki and the fewest in Annijoki. The amount of new forms correlates with the multilingual profiles of the Kven communities and the history of the multilingualism in them, so that most of the accelerated development has occurred in the communities where the Kven-speaking part of the population is the smallest and where there has been intensive multilingualism over time (Lindgren 1993, 244–255, 262–265; 1993b, 31–33; 1999). Therefore, both quantitative variation in the idiolects and differences in the amount of morphological changes in the dialects indicate that the morphological development has a connection with multilingualism. Tendencies towards grammatical simplification in special multilingual settings have been previously discussed, e.g., see Itkonen (1964, 188–193) and Dorian (1981).

Riionheimo (2007) points out that certain language changes have multiple causes. This is the case for the expansion of vowel stems in certain Kven dialects. The process is influenced by: 1) the contact with a relative language, a pattern borrowing; 2) an internal language tendency towards a more simple inflection, 3) intensive multilingualism in the language communities, and 4) the lexical and textual frequency of verb groups.

7 Conclusions

Verbal borrowings from Scandinavian and Saami languages have been integrated in different ways into Kven. Verbs from Scandinavian donor languages have been replicated in the verb type of contracted verbs and their subtype *eera* verbs with only a few exceptions. In addition, some verbal borrowings from Scandinavian languages can be found among disyllabic *i* stems. Only a few individual borrowings have been integrated into a category of complex verbs.

There are only a few verbs borrowed from Saami that have been integrated into the contracted verb type in Kven. Others have been integrated into the disyllabic basic verb type, and they represent *i, a, o,* and *u* stems. Most of these loanwords can also be found in the Far North Finnish dialects. There are many verbs that have been integrated using different types of complex verbs. For example, causative derivational suffixes can function as a verbalizer in some cases although the frequentative derivational suffixes are used in this function most often.

A clear difference between these two donor languages is that Saami alone is the donor language for morphological pattern replication, i.e., a model, in many cases, for the innovative use of derivational suffixes. The lexicalized use of a frequentative verb can be found, new ways to create frequentative derivatives, and a new diminutive derivational type in Kven (see Section 6). Contact with Saami also seems to have increased the use of verbal derivatives, as frequentative derivatives in particular, and the innovative diminutive type based on the Saami model are used often. Saami has also influenced the inflection in certain dialects; this is a process with multiple causation, in which pattern borrowing from Saami is but one aspect.

The difference between the impact from Scandinavian languages and Saami is often based on phonetic and semantic similarities as Kven and Saami derivational suffixes share many common features. All the languages of multilinguals are included in their mental language networks (Matras 2009), and networks between linguistic forms, materialized in lexemes, become stronger when these elements share phonetic or semantic similarities (Bybee 2003).

Borrowings from both model languages were most often integrated using indirect insertion, which is understandable because Kven is a synthetic language (see Tadmor 2009, 63). Integration in the contracted verb type was analysed, which is used to integrate verbs from both Scandinavian and Saami into Kven as an indirect integration strategy. This verb type includes a derivational suffix although this suffix is incorporated into the verb stem (Räisänen 1987, 496).

There are more subtypes of verbs that have been integrated from Saami using indirect insertion than borrowings from Scandinavian languages. They not only consist of the contracted verb type, but also two types of causative derivatives as well as different frequentative derivational types that are used in the indirect integration of Saami verbs. This indicates that similarities between the donor and recipient language have an impact on how verbal borrowings are integrated within the recipient language Kven.

It is more difficult to explain whether the loans integrated into disyllabic stems (e.g., *taajoa*) have been integrated using direct or indirect integration. Verbs in this subgroup have been well integrated into the Kven language system. Because the last vowel of these verb stems is also used as a derivational suffix, it has likely also functioned as a verbalizer in these verbs. Most often, disyllabic verbs are loans from Saami to Kven, with the exception of some *i* stems, which are borrowings from Scandinavian languages.

The largest group of verbal borrowings in the material is cultural loanwords from Scandinavian languages integrated into the contracted verb type. There are many borrowings from Norwegian in the *eera* verb type. These two groups of Scandinavian loans are bigger than all the other groups combined, which reflects the need for vocabulary that the Kvens met in the modernization process. Many verbal borrowings from both Swedish and Saami can be found also distributed in the Far North Finnish dialects. Many Saami verbal borrowings are connected to the means of Arctic livelihood, which the Kven shared with their Saami neighbours.

In Finnish investigations of loanwords, the focus has been on Indo-European loanwords. It was demonstrated in this study that the donor language matters in terms of replication, and that the comparison of the impact on Kven from different donor languages increases the understanding of the integration of verbal borrowings in a recipient language.

Matter replications from Scandinavian languages, the preservation of more Swedish loans than there are in Finnish, new Norwegian loans, and both matter and pattern borrowings from Saami, all have the effect of diverging Kven from Finnish dialects and the Finnish standard language. These phenomena have been aspects of the development that has led to the autonomization of Kven. The divergence at different levels shows the remarkable influence of a nation-state border on a language.

Abbreviations

1SG	1st person singular
2SG	2nd person singular
2PL	2nd person plural
3SG	3rd person singular
CAUS	causative derivative
DIM	diminutive derivative
ESS	essentiative derivative
FRE	frequentative derivative
INF	(first) infinitive (A infinitive)
LVM	loan verb marker
MOME	momentane derivative
VBL	verbalizer
tr.	transitive
intr.	intransitive

Norw   Norwegian
SaN   Northern Saami
Swe   Swedish

Data

Dialect material from Kven dialects collected in 1967–1971 and in 1983–1985 by Lindgren. Part of the material is presented in Lindgren 1974 and 1993. The material can be found in the Institute for the Languages of Finland and in Tromsø University Museum.

Nilsen-Børsskog, Alf. 2004. *Kuosuvaaran takana. Elämän jatko 1*. Indre Billedfjord: Iđut.

References

Aikio, Ante. 2007. "Etymological Nativization of Loanwords: A Case Study of Sámi and Finnish." In *Sámi Linguistics*, edited by Ida Toivonen and Diane Nelson, 17–52. Amsterdam: John Benjamins.

Aikio, Ante. 2009. "The Sámi Loanwords in Finnish and Karelian." PhD diss., University of Oulu.

Andreassen, Irene. 2003. "Tainariksi kuttuthaan se steimpiitti täälä: en studie av kvenske fiske- og sjødyrnavn i Varanger, Porsanger og Alta" [A study of Kven fish and shellfish names in Varanger, Porsanger and Alta]. PhD diss., University of Tromsø.

Beronka, Johan. 1922. *Syntaktiske iagttagelser fra de finske dialekter i Vadsø og Porsanger* [Syntactical observations of the Finnish dialects in Vadsø and Porsanger]. Kristiania: Jacob Dybwad.

Beronka, Johan. 1925. *Iagttagelser fra orddannelses- og formlæren i de finske dialekter i Vadsø og Porsanger* [Observations of word formation and morphology in the Finnish dialects in Vadsø and Porsanger]. Oslo: Jacob Dybwad.

BO = *Bokmålsordbok. Bokmålsordbok: definisjons- og rettskrivningsordbok*. [Bokmål dictionary.] Universitetet i Oslo i samarbeid med Språkrådet. 2010. Accessed May 5, 2015. http://www.nobordbok.uio.no/perl/ordbok.cgi?OPP=&bokmaal=+&ordbok=bokmaal.

Bussenius, Arno. 1939. *Zur Ostseefinnischen Morphologie: Stammesalternation im Ostseefinnischen*. [About the morphology in the Finnic languages: stem alternations in the Finnic languages.] Berlin: Walter de Gruyter.

Bybee, Joan. 2003. *Phonology and Language Use*. Cambridge: Cambridge University Press.

Chambers, J. K., and Peter Trudgill. 1998. *Dialectology*, 2nd ed. Cambridge: Cambridge University Press. First published 1980.

Dannemark, Nils I. S. 2010. "Variasjon og mønster. Drag ved det norske talemålet til ein del barn i Guovdageaidnu" [Variation and pattern. Features in the Norwegian spoken language in Guovdageaidnu]. PhD diss., University of Tromsø.

Dorian, Nancy. 1981. *Language death: The life cycle of a Scottish Gaelic dialect*. Philadelphia: University of Pennsylvania Press.

DR = Svonni, Mikael. 2013. *Davvisámegiela-ruotagiela, ruotagiela-davvisámegiela sátnegirji. Nordsamisk-svensk, svensk-nordsamisk ordbok*. [Northern Saami–Swedish, Swedish–Northern Saami dictionary.] Karasjok: ČálliidLágádus.

Eriksen, Agnes. 2014. *Minun kieli. Minun aaret.* [My language. My treasure.] Porsanger: Porsanger kommune.

Grönholm, Maija. 1988. *Ruotsalaiset lainasanat Turun murteessa* [Swedish loanwords in Turku dialect]. Åbo: Åbo Academy Press.

Hakulinen, Lauri. 1978. *Suomen kielen rakenne ja kehitys* [The structure and development of the Finnish language]. Helsinki: Otava.

Haspelmath, Martin. 2009. "Lexical Borrowing: Concepts and Issues." In *Loanwords in the World's Languages*, edited by Martin Haspelmath and Uri Tadmor, 35–54. Berlin: De Gruyter Mouton.

Haugen, Einar. 1950. "The Analysis of Linguistic Borrowing." *Language* 26:210–231.

Hyltenstam, Kenneth, and Tomaso Milani. 2003. *Kvensk – språk eller dialekt?* [Kven – a language or a dialect?] Report for Kultur- og kirkedepartmenet and Kommunal- og regionaldepartementet in Norway, publication number V–0982 SE.

Häkkinen, Kaisa. 1994. *Agricolasta nykykieleen. Suomen kirjakielen historia.* [From Agricola to Modern Finnish. A history of Finnish written language.] Helsinki: WSOY.

Häkkinen, Kaisa. 1997a. *Mistä sanat tulevat: suomalaista etymologiaa* [Where do words come from: Finnish etymologies]. Tietolipas 117. 2nd ed. Helsinki: Finnish Literature Society.

Häkkinen, Kaisa. 1997b. "Kuinka ruotsin kieli on vaikuttanut suomeen" [What kind of impact has Swedish had on Finnish]? *Sananjalka* 39:31–53.

Häkkinen, Kaisa. 2007. "Suomen kirjakielen saamelaiset lainat" [Saami loans in Finnish written language]. In *Sámit, sánit, sátnehámit. Riepmočála Pekka Sammallahtii miessemánu 21. beaivve 2007,* edited by Jussi Ylikoski and Ante Aikio, 161–182. Mémoires de la Société Finno-Ougrienne 253. Helsinki: Finno-Ugrian Society.

ISK= *Iso suomen kielioppi* [Descriptive Grammar of Finnish], edited by Auli Hakulinen, Maria Vilkuna, Riitta Korhonen, Vesa Koivisto, Tarja Riitta Heinonen, and Irja Alho. 2004. Helsinki: Finnish Literature Society.

Itkonen, Terho. 1964. *Proto-Finnic Final Consonants. Their History in the Finnic Languages with Particular Reference to the Finnish Dialects I:1.* Helsinki: Finnish Literature Society.

Jahr, Ernst Håkon, and Olav Skare. 1996. "Oversyn over nordnorske dialektar – kart og målprøver" [An overview of Northern Norwegian dialects – a map and dialect excerpts]. In *Nordnorske dialekter,* edited by Ernst Håkon Jahr and Olav Skare, 9–77. Oslo: Novus forlag.

Karlsson, Fred. 1983. *Suomen kielen äänne- ja muotorakenne* [The structure of Finnish phonology and morphology]. Porvoo: Söderström.

Korhonen, Mikko. 1981. *Johdatus lapin kielen historiaan* [An introduction to the history of Saami language]. Helsinki: Finnish Literature Society.

Kulonen, Ulla-Maija. 1996. *Sanojen alkuperä ja sen selittäminen. Etymologista leksikografiaa.* [Origins of words and their explanations.] Suomi 181. Helsinki: Finnish Literature Society.

Kytömäki, Leena. 1990. "Nominikantaisten verbinjohdosten rakennemalleja" [Structural models for verbs derived from nouns]. *Sananjalka* 32:49–73.

Lehtinen, Tapani. 2007. *Kielen vuosituhannet. Suomen kielen kehitys kantauralista varhaissuomeen.* [Thousands of years of language. The development of Finnish from Proto Uralic to Early Finnish.] Tietolipas 215. Helsinki: Finnish Literature Society.

Lindgren, Anna-Riitta. 1974. "Konsonanttivartaloiset verbimuodot Raisin murteessa" [Verbs with consonant stems in Raisi dialect]. MA thesis, University of Helsinki.

Lindgren, Anna-Riitta. 1993. "Miten muodot muuttuvat. Ruijan murteiden verbitaivutus Raisin, Pyssyjoen ja Annijoen kveeniyhteisöissä" [How forms change. Verbal inflection in the Far North Dialects from the Kven communities in Raisi, Pyssyjoki and Annijoki]. With English Summary. PhD diss., University of Tromsø.

Lindgren, Anna-Riitta. 1999. "Linguistic Variation and the Historical Sociology of Multilingualism in Kven Communities". In *Language Change. Advances in Historical Sociolinguistics*, edited by Ernst Håkon Jahr, 141–166. Berlin, New York: Mouton de Gruyter.

Lindgren, Anna-Riitta. 2009. "Kvensk i Norge" [Kven in Norway]. In *De mange språk i Norge. Flerspråklighet på norsk*, edited by Tove Bull and Anna-Riitta Lindgren, 107–124. Oslo: Novus forlag.

Matras, Yaron. 2009. *Language Contact*. Cambridge: Cambridge University Press.

Moravcsik, Edith. 1975. "Verb Borrowing." *Wiener Linguistische Gazette* 8:3–30.

MKS = *Meänkielen sanakirja* [The dictionary of Meänkieli]. Accessed May 5, 2015. http://meankielensanakirja.com/about.

NDS = *Neahttadigisánit* [The Internet dictionary]. Accessed May 5, 2015. http://sanit.oahpa.no/sme/nob/.

Nickel, Klaus Peter, and Pekka Sammallahti. 2011. *Nordsamisk grammatikk.* [Northern Saami Grammar.] Karasjok: Davvi Girji AS.

Niemi, Einar. 1978. "Den finske kolonisasjon av Nordkalotten – forløp og årsaker" [The Finnish colonization of the Northern Hemisphere – progress and motivations]. *Ottar* 103:49–70.

NS = *Nykysuomen sanakirja. Lyhentämätön kansanpainos.* [Modern Finnish Dictionary.] Porvoo: Söderström, 1987–1991.

Nummila, Kirsi-Maria. 2013. "Keskialasaksalaiset tekijännimet vanhassa kirjasuomessa ja vanhassa kirjavirossa" [Middle Low German agent nouns in Old Literary Finnish and Old Literary Estonian]. *Lähivõrdlusi. Lähivertailuja* 23:265–284.

Paunonen, Heikki. 1976. "Sunna juoksi suuret korvet. Arkaistisia konsonanttivartaloisia essiivejä kansanrunoissa". [Archaic consonant stems in the essive case in folk poems.] In *Kielitieteellisiä lehtiä*, edited by Raija Lehtinen, Tapani Lehtinen, Pirkko Nuolijärvi, and Heikki Paunonen, 111–122. Helsinki: Finnish Literature Society.

Pyykkö, Vappu. 2008. *Sana-aitta* [Word storehouse]. Accessed April 2, 2015. http://www.kvenskinstitutt.no/sprak/sana-aitta-ordliste-til-borsskogs-romaner.

Riionheimo, Helka. 2007. *Muutoksen monet juuret. Oman ja vieraan risteytyminen Viron inkerinsuomalaisten imperfektinmuodostuksessa.* [The multiple roots of change. Mixing native and borrowed influence in the past tense formation by Ingrian Finns.] Helsinki: Finnish Literature Society.

Riionheimo, Helka. 2013. "Multiple roots of innovations in language contact". *Studies in language* 37:3:645–674.

Räisänen, Alpo. 1987. "Miten uudet *aa, ää* -loppuiset supistumaverbit tulevat nykysuomeen?" [How do contracted verbs ending in *aa, ää* enter into Modern Finnish?] *Virittäjä* 91:491–502.

Räsänen, Matti. 2005. "Kritisoida vai kritikoida? Eräs vierassanaryväs". [*Kritisoida* or *kritikoida*? A group of loanwords in Finnish.] *Kielikello* 1/2005:23–26.

SAOB = *Svenska akademiens ordbok.* [The dictionary of Swedish Akademy.] Accessed May 5, 2015. http://g3.spraakdata.gu.se/saob/s.

SMS = *Suomen murteiden sanakirja 1–8.* [Finnish dialect dictionary 1–8.] Helsinki: Institute for the Languages of Finland. 1985–2008.

SRS = Lönnrot, Elias. 1958 [1874–1880]. *Suomalais-ruotsalainen sanakirja. Finsktsvenskt lexicon.* [Finnish-Swedish dictionary.] 3rd edition. Porvoo. Helsinki: WSOY.

SSA = *Suomen sanojen alkuperä. Etymologinen sanakirja.* [The origin of Finnish words. Etymological dictionary.] Helsinki: Institute for the Languages of Finland & Finnish Literature Society. 1992–2000.

SSS = Sammallahti, Pekka. 1994. *Sámi-suoma-sámi sátnegirji. Saamelais-suomalaissaamelainen sanakirja.* [Sámi-Finnish-Sámi dictionary.] Vaasa: Girjegiisá.

Söderholm, Eira. 2014. *Kainun kielen grammatikki* [The Kven Grammar]. Helsinki: Finnish Literature Society.

Tadmor, Uri. 2009. "Loanwords in the World's Languages: Findings and Results." In *Loanwords in the World´s Languages*, edited by Martin Haspelmath and Uri Tadmor, 55–75. Berlin: De Gruyter Mouton.

Thomason, Sarah Grey, and Terrence Kaufman. 1988. *Language Contact, Creolization, and Genetic Linguistics*. Berkeley: University of California Press.

Tommila, Päiviö, and Maritta Pohls, eds. 1989. *Herää Suomi: suomalaisuusliikkeen historia* [Wake up Finland: the history of Finnish national movement]. Kuopio: Kustannuskiila.

Utvik, Hanne Elin. 1996. "Norske ord i finsk språkdrakt: en studie av nyere skandinaviske substantivlån i kvensk/ruijafinsk tekstmateriale med hovedvekt på norske lån" [Norwegian words formed in the Finnish language: a study of newer scandinavian noun loanwords in Kven/Ruija Finnish texts with the main focus on Norwegian loanwords]. MA thesis. University of Tromsø.

Weinreich, Uriel. 1974 [1953]. *Languages in Contact. Findings and Problems*. Hague: Mouton.

Wohlgemuth, Jan. 2009. *A Typology of Verbal Borrowings*. Berlin: Mouton de Gruyter.

Äimä, Frans. 1908. "Lappalaisia lainasanoja suomen murteissa" [Saami loan words in Finnish dialects]. *Suomalais-ugrilaisen seuran aikakauskirja* 25:3–64.

Vesa Jarva
http://orcid.org/0000-0001-7965-9083

Jenni Mikkonen
http://orcid.org/0000-0002-9737-1136

Lexical Mixing in a Conversation between Old Helsinki Slang Speakers

Abstract

In this article, a conversation between Old Helsinki Slang (OHS) speakers recorded in 1965 is examined. A notable feature of OHS is the heavy use of Swedish-based or otherwise un-Finnish words although it mostly follows the grammar of colloquial Finnish. The sample that is analyzed consists of free speech, and it lasts 65 minutes. If uncertain items are taken into account, then the proportion of borrowed lexical items in the data is 29–32%. Function and content words in OHS differ markedly in their etymological origin as the function words are overwhelmingly Finnish.

Although OHS has some phonological and phonotactical features that are strikingly "un-Finnish," it is apparent that these features have been adopted along with loanwords. While some morpho-syntactical features in OHS differ from those of Standard Finnish, they are widely known in Finnish dialects and colloquial Finnish and, therefore, cannot be interpreted as innovations in OHS. Morpho-syntactically, the sample can easily be interpreted as a variant of Finnish.

While the proportion of borrowed words in OHS is not exceptional among the world's languages, it is in any case notable; furthermore, core borrowing is common and even basic vocabulary is the product of borrowing. Roughly 40% of the vocabulary of OHS can be defined as slang, a proportion unknown in Finnish dialects or in Standard Finnish. This slang vocabulary is overwhelmingly borrowed, and it can be seen as the most apparent contact feature of OHS. It has made this variety of urban speech virtually incomprehensible to contemporary dialectal or Standard Finnish speakers.

1 Introduction

Old Helsinki Slang (OHS) is a linguistic variety that was spoken in the working-class quarters of Helsinki at the beginning of the last century. By the 1950s, it had gradually developed into its modern form. A notable feature of OHS is the heavy use of Swedish-based or otherwise un-Finnish words although it mostly follows the grammar of colloquial Finnish. In brief, OHS mixes Finnish morpho-syntax and Swedish vocabulary. This is illustrated in the following example from the data:

(1) *faija*   *skiia-s*   et   *starbi*   ol-is   alasti   ellei
    father   say-PST   that   man   be-CON   naked   if.not
    sil   oo   *hugari-i*   *messi-ssä*
    he-ADE   have   knife-PAR   with-INE
    'father said that a man would be naked if he did not have a knife with him'

The words in italics are loan words which were apparently unknown in Finnish dialects and the standard language of the time. *Faija, skiias, hugari,* and *messissä* derive from Swedish, but they have been changed both phonologically and semantically: for example, *skiiaa* 'to say, to speak' is based on the Swedish dialectal word *skissa* 'speak untrue, false,' which is derived from *skit* 'shit' (Liuttu 1951; Mikkonen 2014, 84). *Starbi* '(old) man' comes from the Russian *stáryj* 'old.' All the function words, e.g., the conjunctions *et* and *ellei*, pronoun *sil* and copula *olis ~ oo*, are Finnish.

Grammatically, this sentence follows Finnish grammar with both the loanwords and Finnish words followed by Finnish suffixes, e.g., the illative case ending *-ssä* in *messi-ssä* (< Sw. *med sig* 'with her/himself'). The sentence also shows several morpho-phonological features characteristic of Finnish dialects or colloquial speech, such as apocope in the conjunction *et* (< Standard Finnish *että*) and in the pronoun *sil* (< Standard Finnish *sillä*).

Researchers agree that Swedish influence on the vocabulary of OHS is significant, but estimates of the proportion of Swedish or un-Finnish words vary. Paunonen (2006, 51) has claimed that "almost 80 percent" of OHS vocabulary is Swedish. Jarva (2008, 66; see also Meakins 2013, 166) views this figure with scepticism and is fairly certain that 80% is an overestimate.

OHS has also been subject to contrasting treatment by researchers, depending on whether it is seen as a variant of Finnish or as a mixed language. Paunonen (2006) seems to consider OHS a separate language. Jarva (2008, 65, 76) compares OHS with mixed languages, and Meakins (2013, 166) offers OHS as an example of a mixed language. On the other hand, Kallio (2007) supports the view that OHS is a variant of Finnish, while for de Smit (2010), "if it is to be considered a mixed language at all, then it is 'a marginal case.' " These contrasting views are at least partly due to the fact that OHS is an unstandardized speech form that has varied both diachronically and synchronically and has not been systematically documented.

This article examines a conversation between OHS speakers recorded in 1965. To the knowledge of the authors, the recording is a unique sample of free speech in OHS. Some of the recorded material was used by Paunonen (2000) in compiling his dictionary of Helsinki slang, but it had not been systematically examined until Mikkonen (2014) investigated its Swedish-based vocabulary.

The primary focus is lexical, however, some phonological and morpho-syntactic features of the language will also be commented and exemplified. The proportion of loanwords will be estimated, the different sources of the vocabulary of OHS will be described, and the adaptation of un-Finnish words to the structure and grammar of Finnish words will be investigated. In addition to Swedish-based and Finnish words there are also loanwords from Russian and other languages, as well as heavily manipulated words whose origin is contested or impossible to determine.

The sample is also compared with contemporary Finnish, both the dialectical and standard language, with the aim of finding out which features of OHS are based on Finnish and which features can be understood as foreign influence, either as borrowings or as contact-based innovations in OHS. The more OHS has in common with different variants of Finnish, the more reasonable it would be to interpret it as a variant of Finnish rather than as a mixed speech form or separate language.

The structure of the article is as follows. Section 2 provides a survey of written records and previous research relating to OHS. Section 3 deals with the socio-historical background of OHS and the different language forms that have influenced it. The data and methods of the survey are discussed in Section 4. In Section 5, the lexical, phonological, and morpho-syntactic features of the data are described. Section 6 concludes the article.

2 Written records and previous research on OHS

The first mention of the slang used in Helsinki dates from the late 19th century. Around the beginning of the 20th century, the Finnish humor magazines *Kurikka* and *Tuulispää* published stories containing OHS words, sometimes even whole sentences and short texts. OHS was termed *sakilaisten kieli* 'gang members' language,' *sakin kieli* 'gang language,' or just *saki*. (Jarva 2008, 56, 60–61.)

In 1914, Kurikka published a list of about 400 OHS words under the title *Sakilainen sanakirja* (Dictionary of *Saki*). In 1915, the alias *Sakinkielen professori*, 'professor of the *Saki* language,' described OHS as follows: "As in big foreign cities, in Helsinki the *Saki* people also have a language of their own. It is not in fact a language in its own right, but has to be spoken in conjunction with either Finnish or Swedish." In the 1910s and 1920s, several novels were published that incorporated OHS words in their dialogue. Since then, OHS and modern Helsinki slang have commonly been used in fiction and memoirs. (Paunonen 2000, 39–40, 2006, 51; Jarva 2008, 60–62.)

Old Helsinki Slang has been widely investigated lexically, and collections of its words have been compiled since the early 20th century. The most remarkable collections of OHS are those of T. Kaiponen, K. Linna, and K. Stenvall, each containing about 3,000 words in use from 1915 to the 1940s. Heikki Paunonen has co-edited (with Marjatta Paunonen) a dictionary of Helsinki slang (Paunonen 2000). The dictionary utilizes practically all the available OHS source materials. It has 33,000 entries, and it also provides plenty of examples. The dictionary contains both OHS and modern slang words, provides references to sources, and states the period when each word was used. Thus, it provides a clear picture of the vocabulary of OHS. (Jarva 2008, 62.)

Very few recordings or notations of free speech were made in Old Helsinki Slang, and literary sources are not a guide to authentic speech. Even when such sources include samples of OHS, the grammar in them has obviously been "improved" by adapting Standard Finnish rules. (Kallio 2007, 180; Jarva 2008, 61.) The recording explored in this study is apparently the closest to free speech that is extant. It comprises a discussion between five OHS speakers and was made by M. A. Numminen in 1965. Although the recording was made after the shift from OHS to modern slang, the informants were born in 1890–1910 and undoubtedly would have spoken OHS in its "golden age." (See Section 5.)

The overwhelming majority of OHS material was collected by laypersons, as linguistic research in Finland traditionally focussed on rural dialects. Despite making his recording of OHS, Numminen was not allowed to discuss it in his *cum laude* thesis, produced for the University of Helsinki, on the grounds that while dialects were fit topics for theses, "slang was not a dialect". (Kallio 2007, 182; Numminen, e-mail message to Jenni Mikkonen, March 22, 2015.) Urban speech forms were ignored by Finnish linguists until the 1970s when sociolinguistic research got underway in Finland. The scholar who has conducted the most intensive academic research on OHS is Professor Heikki Paunonen, co-editor of the above-mentioned dictionary of Helsinki slang. Paunonen participated from its outset, in 1972, in a project to research colloquial Finnish speech in Helsinki (the results are reported in Paunonen (1995)), and has written several articles on OHS that cast much light on its background (e.g., Paunonen 1993, 2006).

At first glance, the most prominent feature of OHS is its Swedish or otherwise un-Finnish vocabulary, which in consequence has often been the focus of linguistic attention. Researchers agree that the influence of Swedish on OHS vocabulary is significant, but estimates of the proportion of words of Swedish origin vary. In his MA thesis, Liuttu (1951) claims that 51% of OHS words are of Swedish origin, a figure cited by Paunonen (1995, 22). Later, however, Paunonen revised his estimate upwards, stating that: "at a conservative estimate, three quarters" (2000, 28) or "almost 80 percent" (2006, 51) of OHS vocabulary is of Swedish origin. Jarva (2008, 66) views these figures with scepticism and suggests that they are meaningful only if words that do not exist in Standard Finnish or Finnish dialects are not counted.

Attention has also been drawn to the borrowings in the basic vocabulary of OHS. Wälchli (2005) gives the OHS equivalents of the 207-word Swadesh list and finds almost 60 words of Swedish origin. After omitting all function words, Kallio (2007) lists 150 examples of "borrowed 'basic vocabulary' items." Jarva (2008, 68) concludes that about 80% of the verbs, adjectives, and nouns in the Swadesh list have un-Finnish equivalents in OHS.

It is not evident which words qualify as OHS vocabulary; it is even questionable if the vocabulary of OHS can be distinguished from the vocabularies of Finnish and Swedish. Forsskåhl (2006, 63) writes about "words used as slang" and says that OHS speakers might use: "any Swedish words they knew;" that is to say, there was no discrete OHS vocabulary but any Swedish words could be used as slang. Paunonen has stated (in an e-mail message to Jenni Mikkonen, April 10, 2015) that he distinguishes 'slang words' from 'matrix language,' and that only the former are included in his dictionary; the rather startling figure of 80 percent of Swedish words is also estimated from the slang vocabulary. On the other hand, Wälchli (2005) points out that Swedish-based words have not necessarily displaced Finnish ones but co-exist with them; in this sense borrowing in OHS may be referred to as 'paralexification' or a 'lexical reservoir' (Jarva 2008, 78–79; Meakins 2013, 166).

Jarva (2008, 66, 68) criticizes Wälchli and Kallio for including words of different ages in their word lists, since OHS and modern Helsinki slang are different forms of speech, and their vocabularies are subject to variation over time. Paunonen (2000, 17), however, describes OHS and modern slang as a "linguistic continuum" and states that some words from the beginning of the 20th century continue to represent "everyday reality" in modern slang.

In the 2000s, OHS has been discussed from the perspective of language contact, and as such it has been subject to contrasting treatment by researchers, depending on whether it is seen as a variant of Finnish or a mixed language. It has also been compared to intertwining mixed languages, of which the best known cases are Media Lengua and Ma'á. (Jarva 2008, 62–66.)

Paunonen stresses in several articles that OHS is an independent form of speech, and it should not be considered a Finnish slang variant. He uses the Finnish word *sekakieli* (which may be translated as 'mixed language') and uses the term "matrix language," stating that dialectal Finnish was the matrix language in which "vocabulary adopted from Swedish was inserted" (Paunonen 2006, 52, 57). Wälchli (2005) discusses OHS in the context of contact linguistics and concludes that while OHS does not completely fit the prototype of an intertwining mixed language variety, it comes close to it. Kallio admits that OHS has a lot in common with Media Lengua and Ma'á, but he also says that none of these three languages can be considered a mixed language, and that OHS is "genetically" a Finnic language or dialect of Finnish (Kallio 2007, 178–180). This is based on his position that "genetic relatedness should always be based on grammatical rather than lexical evidence." Kallio also likens OHS to pidgins, a view that has been critically discussed by Jarva (2008, 76) and de Smit (2010, 12).

Forsskåhl (2006) discusses OHS as a variant of Finnish, but notes that Finnish and Swedish slang words developed in parallel, and she makes observations that suggest code-switching between Finnish and Swedish. Jarva (2008, 65, 76) concludes that OHS is a "distinct code" that can be either "a register of Finnish or a language symbiotic with Finnish;" however, he compares OHS with mixed languages. Meakins (2013, 166) sees OHS as an example of a mixed language constructed from the grammar of one language and the lexicon of another. This view is by no means established: de Smit (2010) measures OHS against Peter Auer's code-switching model and concludes that OHS is not genetically mixed and that if it is to be considered a mixed language at all, then it can only be as "a marginal case."

3 Linguistic and socio-historical background

3.1 The Finnish and Swedish languages in Helsinki

The city of Helsinki was founded in 1550 on the Swedish-speaking south coast of Finland. It remained a small town during Swedish rule as the cultural and administrative centre of Finland was then in Turku. At the beginning of the 19th century, Finland became part of the Russian empire. Helsinki was named the capital city in 1812, and the university was relocated there from Turku in 1828.

According to Paunonen (1993, 53), the Swedish language was at its strongest in Helsinki in the 1840s and 1850s. The upper and middle class spoke mostly Swedish, and the social and cultural life of the city was dominated by Swedish speakers. The majority of the working class came from neighboring Swedish-speaking rural areas. In 1850, Helsinki had only 20,000 inhabitants, of whom 10% were Finnish-speaking. The Swedish language had high status, and people moving to the city from Finnish-speaking areas commonly switched to Swedish. (Jarva 2008, 54.)

The situation began to change in the 1860s with industrialization and the increasing number of people who moved to Helsinki from elsewhere in the country. The newcomers came from both Swedish- and Finnish-speaking areas, but as the attraction of the growing city spread to more distant areas, more and more of the newcomers were Finnish-speaking. The population of Helsinki grew fourfold, an increase of more than 100,000, between 1870 and 1910. At the same time, the proportion of Finnish-speaking inhabitants grew from 26% to 59%. (See statistics in Paunonen 1993, 54.) Bilingualism was common in the city between both language groups, with 35% of people declaring themselves able to speak both Finnish and Swedish in the 1900 census (Paunonen 1995, 11). Although the Finnish- and Swedish-speaking populations were at that time equal in numbers, Swedish had much higher status. It continued to be dominant in the upper classes, and had hegemony in cultural, economic, and municipal affairs. (Paunonen 1995, 5–7, Forsskåhl 2006, 53–54; Jarva 2008, 55.)

The official status of Finnish changed in the second half of the 19th century when the Finnish language was granted the status of an official language and a language of instruction. At the same time, the first cultured families began to use Finnish as a language of discussion, even if they did not speak it properly, and to send their children to the new Finnish-speaking schools. Others, however, wanted to retain Swedish as the national language of Finland. "The language struggle" continued into the 1930s, although the position of Finnish strengthened after the independence of Finland in 1917, when both Finnish and Swedish were established as official languages of the city. (Paunonen 1993, 54–55; Jarva 2008, 54–55.) Meanwhile the proportion of the population that was Finnish-speaking steadily rose in Helsinki, to 69% in 1930 and 80% in 1950. (See statistics in Paunonen 2006, 24.)

3.2 The birth of Old Helsinki Slang in the bilingual working-class community

During a time of rapid industrialization, new working-class quarters emerged to the north of the old town, along a road called Itäinen Viertotie (Sw. Östra Chaussén, 'Eastern Highway'). It was separated from the city center by a narrow strait, over which a bridge called Pitkäsilta ('Long Bridge') was built. Around the year 1900, there were more than 29 factories and workshops with over 2,500 workers in the area, which also included a large harbor with its own railway line and sawmill. (Waris 1973, 53.) Cheap apartments for the workers were built in the vicinity of this expanding industrial area, in Kallio, Sörnäinen, Hermanni, and Vallila (Sw. Berghäll, Sörnäs, Hermanstad, and Vallgård). By 1900, 20,000 people lived in these northern districts (Waris 1973, 62; Jarva 2008, 56); over 80% of them were working class (Waris 1973, 110). The birth rate was high in the area; children born out of wedlock were common, and 24% of the population was under the age of ten. This clearly affected the standard of living in the area. Almost one third of the workers were unskilled, and for this group in particular there was little security during an era of economic change, and most of them worked on temporary contracts. (Ibid., 118–119.) Living conditions were cramped and unhealthy, with an average population density of more than four persons per single-room apartment (ibid., 160).

The majority of the inhabitants had moved from rural areas. According to the 1900 census, two thirds of the population in the northern suburbs had been born outside Helsinki, and of the city-born, 80% were under 20 years old. (Waris 1973, 87.) The incomers had moved from neighbouring regions, particularly from western Uusimaa. Other significant sources of migration were around the southern shores of Lake Päijänne (the Lahti area) and central Ostrobothnia (around Kokkola). Since many of the newcomers had come from Swedish-speaking areas, one third of the population in the northern suburbs was Swedish speaking. (Ibid., 68, 98.)

Among the working class, there was no boundary between the language groups. Finnish and Swedish workers had to communicate, even if they had only a limited knowledge of each other's language. Their families lived side by side in the same buildings and apartments, and marriages between the two language groups were common. It has been estimated that about one fifth of marriages were bilingual. It was also common to take sub-tenants irrespective of their language. (Waris 1973, 99–101.) On the community level, functional blingualism was common, with people using Finnish and Swedish. First generation immigrants were mostly monolingual and learned the other language only passably, while their children grew up to be bilingual. (Forsskåhl 2006, 54; Paunonen 2006, 51–52; Jarva 2008, 55–56.)

As there was no compulsory education system and homes were small and crowded, working-class children spent most of their time outdoors, outside the linguistic models and control of grown-ups (Forsskåhl 2006, 63). They were the first urban generation, and it was among them that Old Helsinki Slang came into being. Boys and young men gathered in gangs whose identity was based on their own street or part of the city and not on their native language; thus there were both Finnish- and Swedish-speaking boys in the same gangs. The Finnish word for these gangs was *saki* 'gang, mob, group,' and OHS was dubbed *sakilaisten kieli* 'gang members' language' or just *saki*. (Jarva 2008, 56.)

The *Saki* language had low status, and it was socially stigmatized as the language of street boys. It also violated the national romantic idea of a pure language, as it mixed Finnish and Swedish and did not follow the rules of Standard Finnish. School teachers, therefore, took a rather critical attitude toward OHS. It was neither spoken nor even acceptable in all working-class families, although it implied a strong working-class identity. (Paunonen 2000, 42–43; Jarva 2008, 57.)

As more and more people moved from Finnish-speaking areas to Helsinki, OHS lost its role as an intermediate language between Finnish and Swedish speakers and gradually developed into a modern slang, at the latest during the 1950s. As is true of slang in general, modern Helsinki slang is not associated with a particular street or part of the town but with a whole generation, youth culture, lifestyle, or field of interest. (Jarva 2008, 60.) Paunonen (2000, 17) distinguishes between Old Helsinki Slang and Modern Helsinki Slang, and he divides OHS into two stages: the stage of emergence (1890–1919) and the "golden age" (1920–1949).

3.3 THE LANGUAGE FORMS THAT AFFECTED OHS

It is commonly said that OHS employed Finnish grammar or had Finnish as the matrix language. However, it was not based on Standard Finnish but on the dialects spoken by the migrants to the city. At the beginning of the 20th century, the Standard Finnish used by the upper class was based on a literary tradition and differed sharply from the rural dialects spoken by Finnish working-class people. Standard Finnish had not yet established its status as an official language, and, thus, it had only a limited influence on uneducated Finnish speakers. Almost all Finnish speakers spoke a rural dialect as their native language, and this holds true for those who moved to Helsinki. (Jarva 2008, 55, 58.)

Finnish dialects can be divided into two groups: western and eastern. The majority of the Finnish speakers who moved to Helsinki spoke a western dialect, in particular a Tavastian (Häme) dialect. Although Helsinki was located in a Swedish-speaking region, the nearest Finnish-speaking areas, in Tuusula and Nurmijärvi, were only about 20 kilometers from the city. Many features of OHS can be traced to the dialect of these areas. On the other hand, the dialectal background of the newcomers was not uniform but included many different dialects that were at that time all used alongside each other. The identity of OHS speakers was not based on their native language or on any single rural area or dialect; according to Waris (1973, 102–103), the difference between an urban citizen and a newcomer was more important than differences between language groups. Citizens were hostile towards newcomers, as the latter competed for jobs and, thereby, reduced wages. Rural immigrants were unskilled and had low living standards (ibid., 122). For these reasons, OHS and urban identity were not founded on any single dialect (Jarva 2008, 58).

As Finnish speakers were in the majority in the northern suburbs, it may be surprising that Swedish had such a strong influence on OHS. However, Swedish was still the main language of economic life in the early 20th century. Supervisors, master builders, and engineers all spoke Swedish, and housemaids and servants worked in Swedish-speaking households. Swedish-speaking workers had more contacts with Swedish-speaking supervisors and better opportunities to enter skilled professions. Thus Swedish-speaking workers often had a better professional and economic position than their Finnish-speaking counterparts. For the first urban generation, knowledge of Swedish opened the door to social advancement. (Waris 1973, 105, 102.)

There are no significant differences in the way standard Swedish is written in Sweden and Finland, but there are substantial differences in pronunciation, and it can be argued that some of the features of the Swedish spoken in Finland are due to contact with Finnish. Such language contact has brought some degree of convergence between Finnish and Swedish pronunciation and made it easier for Finnish and Swedish to mix in OHS. Moreover, the Swedish-speaking migrants spoke various Finland-Swedish dialects that might have been very different from the Finland-Swedish spoken in Helsinki. Many lexical items in OHS can be traced back to Swedish dialects, mostly to those spoken in the region around the capital. One example dialect comes from a rural Swedish-speaking area just east of Helsinki, Sibbo (Fi. Sipoo), the phonology of which fits well into the Finnish system. (Forsskåhl 2006, 65; Jarva 2008, 58–59.)

Swedish slang or other colloquial variants of Swedish spoken in Helsinki can also be detected in OHS, as demonstrated by Forsskåhl (2006, 59), who lists several Swedish inner city slang words that are used in OHS. Paunonen (2006, 52) also assumes that the OHS vocabulary was absorbed from older "street boy" slang or a dialect of Swedish.

The Russian language also had an impact on OHS as, until 1917, Finland was a part of the Russian empire and many Russian civil servants and soldiers lived in Helsinki. Many Russians followed the army or came as seamen or traders. (Forsskåhl 2006, 54–55.) The Cossacks and their horses were a great attraction for many boys living in the city, who followed the soldiers around and visited their garrisons. Russian soldiers sold food, especially bread, to civilians. As many Russian families also lived in working-class areas, it is natural that the *saki* gangs had contact with Russian children. (Paunonen 2005, 53.)

4 Data and methods

4.1 THE RECORDING

This study examines a conversation between five OHS speakers, recorded by M. A. Numminen in 1965. The recording lasts five hours, of which 65 minutes are free speech. The sample analysed consists of free speech only, and it comprises 1,272 lexemes and 8,607 tokens.

All the informants are men, and four of them are known by name. They were born between 1899 and 1905 and lived in Kallio and Sörnäinen. The identity of the fifth man is unknown. It can only be deduced that he lived in Kallio and was around the same age as the other informants. (Paunonen, e-mail message to Jenni Mikkonen, April 10, 2015.) Thus it can be said that all the informants were living in the area where OHS originated, and that they were boys or young men at that time. Paunonen (2000, 17) defines the emergence stage of OHS as the years 1890–1919. Although the recording dates from 1965, the men's speech can be considered to be OHS because the informants mostly recall their childhood and speak in a relaxed and natural way. They mention a lot of dates, locations, and people that were associated with Helsinki in the early 20th century. It is also demonstrated (see Section 6) that the speech in the recording matches linguistic features known to be typical of OHS.

The informants are aware that they are speaking OHS, as they use the terms *slangi* ('slang') and *slangikieli* ('slang language'). One of them even talks about a boy who was fifteen years older than the speaker, who says that he was, "in the gang where the guys were creating this slang language" (this is also mentioned by Paunonen 2000, 14). On the other hand, the informants say regretfully that they have forgotten some slang words and that the recording should have been made 40 years earlier. One of the men says that he remembers almost all the words but finds them hard to use. As the discussion is lively and features a lot of overlapping speech, it is not always easy to identify who is speaking at any given moment.

Numminen (e-mail message to Jenni Mikkonen, March 22, 2015) has reported that one of the informants was a sailor and spoke only OHS while the others "slipped" occasionally into "common" Helsinki speech. In some cases, there is apparent code switching to Standard or colloquial Finnish, and sometimes the speech of someone in an official position, such as a teacher or manager, is cited in Standard Finnish. The fact that such uses must be intentional suggests that the informants see OHS and Standard Finnish as different speech forms or distinct codes. There is also one code switch to Swedish:

(2) se   sano   et   *svara*   *på*   *svensk-a*
    he   say.PST   that   answer   in   Swedish-DEF
    'He [the teacher] said that "answer in Swedish"'

Here the citation *svara på svenska* is in Swedish while the reporting clause is colloquial Finnish.

The speaker narrates that although his home was Swedish-speaking, he attended a Finnish school because his father, although more fluent in Swedish, was "Finnish-minded." The speaker also reports that he had to fight other pupils on account of his mother tongue and that they called him *svenkollo* 'stupid Swede.' Otherwise the informants view Finnish and Swedish as equal and make clear that both languages were used in parallel among children and at work. Another informant reports that Swedish and Finnish were spoken together in his home, and a third one regrets that he cannot speak Swedish although, "half of the boys were speaking Swedish in their homes." In sum, it is clear that the speakers have a positive attitude to Swedish, that they lived in a bilingual community and that at least two of them grew up in bilingual families. Nevertheless, only Finnish is used as a matrix language in the data in which Swedish manifests itself only in the form of borrowed vocabulary, with the exception of the above-mentioned single three-word code switch.

4.2 Transcription and lexemes

The recording was transcribed lexically, i.e., un-lexical sounds, errors, and hesitation were omitted. This is because the focus of the study is on vocabulary and morpho-phonological features to which only lexical items are relevant. The conventions of Standard Finnish are followed in spelling; phonological quantity is marked with one or two letters, a dental affricate with *tš*, and so on. Therefore Swedish loans are transcribed differently from Standard Swedish spelling, for example, *tšöraa* 'to drive' (< Sw. *köra*) and *rookaa* 'to happen' (< Sw. *råka*). Finnish spelling is considered the better choice in this context since the Swedish words are accommodated into Finnish grammar, thus making the data comparable with, e.g., Paunonen's dictionary (2000).

As already mentioned (Section 4.1), the recording is regarded as a plausible representation of the language used by OHS speakers in the early 20th century. There is some apparent code switching to Standard Finnish (and in one case to Swedish), but, on the whole, such cases are rare. Therefore the whole sample is treated as an example of one form of speech, and every lexical item is counted in the data as an OHS word; OHS is not seen as a separate slang vocabulary. Contrary to, e.g., Paunonen's dictionary, proper nouns are excluded, such as place and person names, from the data. However, when a proper noun is used as a common noun, e.g., *vagemikko* 'doorman' which is a compound of *vage* 'guard, watchman' (cf., Finn. *vahti* and Sw. *vakt*) and the Finnish male name *Mikko*, it is included in the data.

Phonological variants, such as *döftää* ~ *döftaa* 'to smell, stink,' *kliffa* ~ *liffa* 'nice, fun' or *böbi* ~ *pöpi* 'stupid, crazy,' are counted as one lexical item, but where words have different slang suffixes or derivational elements, e.g., *bygga* 'building' and *byggari* 'builder,' they are counted as separate items. The same goes for words that belong to different word classes, such as *bygga* 'building' and *byggaa* 'to build' or *brekkaa* 'to break' and *breggis* 'broken.' In the quantitative analysis, compound words are counted as two lexical items, as there may well be both a Finnish and a loan component in one word, e.g., *himakieli* 'home language' where *hima* comes from Swedish (cf., *hem* 'home,' *hemma* 'at home') and *kieli* is Finnish. (Mikkonen 2014, 28–29.)

4.3 Defining a loanword

When defining loanwords, the criteria commonly used in etymological research has been applied, i.e., that there must be an equivalence both in the phonological shape and meaning of the loanword and in its origin in the donor language. In most cases, it is easy to identify the source word as the words have only recently been borrowed, and, therefore, the source word is semantically and phonologically almost identical. Several etymologies are also mentioned in the literature (see Appendix in Mikkonen 2014).

However, OHS presents two particular problems: unexpected phonological variation and recent borrowings from Swedish to Finnish. In the first case, as there is notable phonological variation in the vocabulary of OHS and words are sometimes heavily manipulated and accommodated to Finnish grammar, phonological resemblance to the source word is often blurred. For example, the OHS word *kliffa* 'nice, fun' looks quite different from its probable source word, Swedish *livfull* 'compelling, gripping.' To understand this, it should be noted that words are commonly manipulated in OHS by adding un-Finnish phonological elements to them; in this case the etymologically inexplicable consonant cluster *kl-*. Furthermore, *kliffa* varies with *liffa*, the latter being closer to the source word. Another example is *karra* 'ice cream.' To define this as a loanword from Russian, first of all you must know that Russian ice cream vendors shouted *horošoe moroženoe* 'good ice cream.' OHS speakers adopted this slogan first as *karossi-marossi*, from which *karra* developed.

Second, as the Finnish language has borrowed numerous words from Swedish, there are often no criteria to determine whether OHS borrowed the word directly from Swedish or just applied a Finnish word that had already been borrowed from Swedish. For example, *hampuusi* 'dockworker' (< Sw. *hamnbuse*), *kanaali* 'canal'(< Sw. *kanal*) and *knalli* 'bowler hat' (< Sw. *knall*) have been borrowed from Swedish to Finnish, but they may well be separate loans in OHS. Such cases have been counted as loanwords in OHS. However, this does not apply to words that clearly differ from their Swedish origin but occur in Standard Finnish, such as *ankkuri* 'anchor' (cf., Sw. *ankare*) and *kasarmi* 'garrison' (cf., Sw. *kasern*). There are also several Swedish or German loanwords in Finnish that were clearly borrowed long before OHS emerged, such as *markka* 'mark, a currency unit,' *saippua* 'soap,' *peli* 'play,' and *helvetti* 'hell.' They are not counted as Swedish loanwords in the survey.

If OHS were interpreted simply as a variant of Finnish, there would be no reason to read any word borrowed from Swedish to Finnish as a 'native' word. However, in this context, it can be understood that OHS, as a separate form of speech, developed on the basis of Finnish dialects, and, consequently, the view that OHS inherited both native Finnish words and Swedish loanwords from the Finnish dialects from which it was descended must be adopted.

There are also some lexical items the origin of which cannot be proven with certainty. Such cases are, e.g., *jeesaa* 'to help,' which could only with difficulty be interpreted as a variant of *jelppiä* and *helppaa* (< Swedish *hjälpa* 'to help'), and *gartša* 'street,' which has the apparently un-etymological slang suffix *-tša* and could be connected with the Russian word *gorod* 'city' or with the Swedish word *gata* 'street.' There are altogether 38 uncertain words, which comprise 3% of the data.

4.4 Content and function words

Content words have a referential meaning and are typically nouns, verbs, and adjectives. Function words have a grammatical or discursive function, and they are typically particles, pronouns, and auxiliary verbs.

In the Word Loanword Database (WOLD), lexical items are classified into one of the following categories: nouns, verbs, adjectives, adverbs, and function words (Tadmor 2009, 59). This study aims to follow the WOLD classification as far as possible so that the findings can be compared with universal tendencies in the borrowing of content and function words. Nonetheless, WOLD does not treat lexical items as such but gives universal meanings that can be lexicalized with words that belong to different word classes in different languages. Thus there are various cases in which the semantic classification of word classes in WOLD has not been followed.

First of all, Finnish *olla* 'to be, to have' and *ei* 'no, not' are verbs and, thus, following the WOLD definition, should be classified as content words. However, they have been classified as function words as they have no referential meaning; both are used as auxiliary verbs, and the latter comes close to a particle. In WOLD, the meaning 'no' is classified as a function word; the meaning 'to be' falls into the semantic category 'verb' but its semantic field is "miscellaneous function words."

Second, Finnish adverbs are particularly ambiguous with respect to their classification into content and function words. According to WOLD, adverbs should be content words, but the database has only classified the meanings 'near,' 'far,' 'fast' (= 'quickly'), and 'slow' as adverbs. Many of the meanings in the semantic category of 'function words' in WOLD are lexicalized as adverbs in Finnish: *ales* 'down,' *läpi* 'through,' *enemmän* 'more,' *heti* 'immediately,' *joskus* 'sometimes,' *myöhään* 'late,' *siellä* 'there.' Clearly, many of the Finnish adverbs that occur in the data should not be classified as content but as function words. This is the case with all adverbs that have the same kind of syntactical function as conjunctions, adpositions, and particles. They also often have the same stem as adpositions and pronouns.

Content words herein include adverbs that are morphologically transparent derivatives or inflected forms of adjectives and nouns, such as *kiva-sti* 'nicely' (*kiva*-ADV 'nice'), *snadi-sti* 'a little, slightly,' *kova-sti* 'hard,' *aiko-i-na-an* 'once, at one time' (time-PL-ESS-POS.3PL), and *miele-llä-än* 'gladly, with pleasure' (mind-ADE-POS.3SG). Furthermore, some adverbs are included among content words as their meanings are classified as adverbs or adjectives in WOLD: *hiljalleen* 'slow' and *alasti* 'naked.'

As Finnish swear words can be used syntactically rather freely, their word class is hard to define. Swear words have been counted as content words because they basically have referential meaning, e.g., *perkele, piru* 'the devil,' *helvetti* 'hell.'

5 Analysis

This section describes lexical, phonological, and morpho-syntactic features of the data. Vocabulary is discussed in Section 5.1, in which the proportion of loan words is estimated and the etymological origin of the function and content words is discussed (5.1.2). Among the loanwords, there are many so-called core borrowings that do not designate a new concept but coexist with a Finnish word with the same meaning. The proportion of loanwords is especially high in the slang vocabulary, i.e., among the words that are not known in Standard Finnish or any of its dialects.

Section 5.2 presents a discussion of how the loanwords were adapted to Finnish word structure so that they could be inflected following the rules of (dialectal) Finnish. Loanwords may be adapted to Finnish grammar and their structure made more uniform by the use of slang suffixes, which are discussed in Section 5.3.

Section 5.4 covers phonological features, which, in addition to vocabulary, are the most obvious contact-induced features in OHS. The data contains several phonemes and word-initial consonant clusters that are either rare or totally unknown in Finnish dialects.

The morpho-syntax of OHS is discussed in Section 5.5. It seems clearly to be Finnish; even where the morpho-syntactic features in the data deviate from Standard Finnish, they are known widely in Finnish dialects and colloquial Finnish. However, the conjugation of OHS verbs and interrogative suffixes are discussed in more detail. As they have no direct parallel in Finnish dialects, it is possible that they have developed independently in OHS, at least in part.

5.1 Vocabulary

5.1.1 Proportion of loanwords

The data comprises 1,272 lexical items, of which 340, or 26.7%, are of Swedish origin. A further 22 lexical items have been borrowed from Russian, 2 from English, and 2 from German. This makes a total of 366 loanwords, that is, 28.8% of the entire data set. The rest, 868 lexical items, or 68.2% of the data, are from the Finnish language. A further 38 lexical items could not be placed in any of the previously mentioned groups, owing to their uncertain provenance. (Mikkonen 2014, 68–69.) If the uncertain items are taken into account, then the proportion of borrowed lexical items in the data is 29–32%.

As far as tokens are concerned, the proportion of loanwords is considerably smaller. This is a result of the frequently used Finnish-based function words, such as *se* 'it, that,' *ja* 'and,' *niin* 'so, then.' The proportion of loanword tokens is about 15%. The 20 most frequently used words in the data, their word classes, and the frequency of their tokens are presented in Table 1.

Table 1. The 20 most frequently used words in the data, and their tokens (Mikkonen 2014, 57–58).

	lexical item	word class	English translation	tokens
1	*se*	pronoun	'it, that, s/he'	625
2	*olla*	verb	'to be, to have'	581
3	*ja*	conjunction	'and'	430
4	*niin*	adv/conj	'so, then'	355
5	*minä/mä*	pronoun	'I'	216
6	*kun*	conjunction	'when; as, than'	211
7	*ne*	pronoun	'they'	161
8	*että*	conjunction	'that, so'	157
9	*ei*	verb/particle	'no'	154
10	*sitten*	adverb	'then; next, after'	148
11	*siellä*	adverb	'there'	132
12	*siinä*	adverb	'there'	130
13	*me*	pronoun	'we'	129
14	*no*	particle	'well, so'	129
15	*joo*	particle	'well, yes'	118
16	*kundi*	noun	'boy, young man'	106
17	*mutta*	conjunction	'but'	102
18	*silloin*	adverb	'then'	97
19	*perkele*	noun	'damn', swear word	97
20	*tulla*	verb	'to come'	75

Of the 20 most used tokens in the sample, 19 originate in the Finnish language. The most frequent Swedish-based word in the sample is *kundi* 'boy, young man,' which occurs 106 times. Function words are the most frequently used words, as in any other Finnish variant. For example, of the 20 most frequently used Finnish words in the frequency dictionary of Finnish (Saukkonen et al. 1979), 10 also appear in the data: *se, olla, ja, niin, kun, ne, että, ei, mutta,* and *tulla*. The data is compared with a frequency dictionary of Finnish dialects (Jussila et al. 1992) in Section 5.1.4.

5.1.2 Function and content words

Function and content words in OHS differ markedly in their etymological origin. The function words, which are also the most frequent items (see Table 1), are overwhelmingly Finnish. Included as function words are conjunctions, adpositions, particles, pronouns, and numerals. All of the words in the foregoing groups are Finnish; the only exception is the Swedish preposition *på* (see Example 2). Because the data is from free speech, there are a lot of fillers and discourse markers (*ai* 'oh,' *no* 'well,' *niinku* 'like,' *tuota* 'er'). The pronouns in the sample are either Standard or colloquial Finnish, as are the cardinal numbers. There are also nouns in the sample that are derived from Swedish numerals, such as *fima* 'a five pence coin,' *tisika* 'a ten pence coin,' and *trettika* 'thirty,' which refers to a house number. These are all counted as content words. (Mikkonen 2014, 54–55.)

The adverbs in the data are also mostly Finnish; the only apparent loan adverbs are *hatkaan* 'away' (< Russian *hodko* 'quickly, eagerly'), *snadisti* 'a little' (< Sw. *snad*), *messissä* 'along, with' (< Sw. *med sig*), and *veke* 'away, off' (cf., German *Weg* or Swedish *väg* 'road'). In this context, *messissä* and *veke* are counted as function words (see Section 4.4).

Nouns, verbs, and adjectives are counted as content words. The only two exceptions are the verbs *olla* and *ei*, which are used as auxiliary verbs. The proportion of loanwords varies across the different word classes: 43–45% of nouns, 38–40% of verbs, and 25% of adjectives. When all of the adverbs treated as content words are included, loanwords account for 35–38% of the content words in the data whereas, with the function words, the proportion of loanwords is less than 1%. The dichotomy between Finnish function words and Swedish content words in OHS is well known and has been exemplified by, e.g., Jarva (2008, 67).

5.1.3 Core borrowings and basic vocabulary

Many of the loanwords in the data are so-called core borrowings (Haspelmath 2009, 48) that do not designate a new concept but coexist with a Finnish word with the same meaning. Therefore, many synonymous expressions have been found, both Finnish and borrowed: e.g., *hyppää – hoppaa* 'to jump,' *kävellä – steppaa* 'to walk,' *seisoa – staijaa* 'to stand,' *jalka – klabbi* 'leg,' *kallio – bärtši* 'rock,' *mies – gubbe* 'man,' *vesi – voda* 'water,' *vanha – gamla* 'old,' *rödis – punainen* 'red,' and *iso – buli* 'big.' The word 'nose' is an interesting example of the various coexisting synonymous variants found even in this relatively small data set: it has two Finnish variants, *nenu* and *nokka*, and three Swedish variants, *knesa*, *knevde*, and *klyyvari*. The Standard Finnish word *nenä* does not occur in the data. (Mikkonen 2014, 56–57.) In many cases, only a borrowed word occurs in the data despite the fact that a common Finnish word was accessible to the OHS speakers. For example, the loanword *nykla* 'key' occurs in the data but the Finnish word *avain* does not. Several words for 'girl' are present, such as *friidu*, *gimma*, and *jentta*, but not the Finnish word *tyttö*. The same phenomenon occurs with *šagga* 'food,' *griinaa* 'to laugh,' *delaa* 'to die,' and *skeidanen ~ skiti* 'dirty.'

Core borrowings make up most of the borrowed items in the data. Alongside these are a number of cultural loans, which "designate a new concept coming from outside" (Haspelmath 2009, 46). Among these are *bilika* 'car,' *spora* 'street car,' *dispari* 'house manager,' *mašunisti* 'machinist,' and *slaagi* '(football) team.' Although Standard Finnish words for these urban or modern concepts existed, they were probably unknown to Finnish dialect speakers in the early 20th century.

It is clear from the discussion above that many loanwords in OHS are drawn from basic vocabulary, which is thought to be resistant to borrowing although the concept is vague and there is no agreement on which words are included in a basic vocabulary. A well-known example is Swadesh's non-cultural vocabulary, which is not based on systematic research but has been described as the author's "best guess" (Haspelmath 2009, 36).

On the basis of the results of the WOLD project, Tadmor (2009, 68–71) has produced a new basic vocabulary list called the Leipzig-Jakarta list. 64 of the 100 words (or meanings) on the Leipzig-Jakarta basic vocabulary list also appear in the data, 29 (45%) of them with a word of Swedish origin. As already mentioned, in many cases, both Swedish and Finnish variants occur with the same meaning. Synonymous basic vocabulary pairs include *eldis – tuli* 'fire,' *blude – veri* 'blood,' *staijaa – seisoa* 'to stand,' *duunaa – tehdä* 'to do/ make,' and *kantraa – kaatua* 'to fall.' However, there are several meanings that are only expressed in the data with loanwords, such as *flatari* 'louse,' *blosis* 'a wind,' *ögari* 'eye,' *flygaa* 'to fly,' *griinaa* 'to laugh,' and *skruutaa* 'to eat.'

5.1.4 Defining slang vocabulary

As mentioned in Section 5.1.1, the list of the 20 most frequently used words in the data (see Table 1) consists mostly of function words that are common in any variant of Finnish. A comparison of this list with a frequency list compiled for Finnish dialects (Jussila et al. 1992) reveals that the two are surprisingly similar. For the 20 most frequent lexemes in OHS, no less than 14 are among the 20 most frequent in Finnish dialects, and the four most common lexemes are ranked in the same order in both lists. The most notable exceptions are *kundi* and *perkele*, which are common in the data but do not occur at all in the database of the frequency dictionary of Finnish dialects. *Kundi* 'a boy, (young) male' originates from the Swedish *kund* 'customer' and is almost unknown in most Finnish dialects; the massive vocabulary of Finnish dialects contains only sporadic references to the word *kunti ~ kynti* 'customer, regular guest' (SMS s.v. *kundi*). Unlike *kundi*, *perkele* 'damn' (literally 'the devil') is an old and commonly used word in Finnish, but as the dialect speakers interviewed by the researchers were relatively reserved and conservative, they presumably considered it inappropriate to swear during an interview. Sivula (1995) has examined the avoidance of swearing in recordings of Finnish dialects. According to him (1995, 241), interviewees control their speech, whether consciously or not. The informal slang speakers in the present recordings did not experience any similar restraint when interviewed by a university student in his twenties. However, it is possible that, in reality, swearing is more common in slang than in rural dialects.

Given that the most frequent words in the data and in the frequency dictionary of Finnish dialects are identical, OHS would appear to be a variant of spoken Finnish. However, a different impression is gained when all the lexical items in the data are taken into consideration. The vocabulary in the data will now be compared with the contents of two dictionaries, one a dictionary of Finnish dialects (SMS) and the other a dictionary of Standard Finnish (NS). As the volumes of the SMS published to date only cover words beginning with the letters A–K, the data will be limited to this vocabulary segment.

The SMS utilizes a massive database that covers all the rural dialects of Finnish. Therefore, if a given word is not included in the dictionary, it can be assumed to be unknown in any Finnish dialect. However, a word may be omitted from the SMS if it is interpreted as a loanword from the standard language, i.e., if it is not a genuine dialectal word. This may be the case with words occurring in the data that refer to concepts of modern society, such as *ehdonalainen* 'parole, probation,' *johtokunta* '(school) board,' and *kansanedustaja* 'member of parliament.' They have apparently been incorporated into OHS from Standard Finnish. The data is also compared with what is in the NS, which was published in 1951 and describes the Standard Finnish used in the 1930s and 1940s. 'Slang' is defined herein by using these two sources as a benchmark: if a given word in the data does not occur in either the SMS or the NS, it is deemed a slang word.

The data includes 473 lexemes that begin with a letter from A to K. Of these, 269 are known in Finnish dialects or Standard Finnish (according to the SMS and NS, respectively). Furthermore, the SMS makes occasional references to 29 words that in OHS can be interpreted as independent loanwords or phonetic variants, however, the possibility that they are based on some variant of Finnish cannot be completely excluded.

Thus, 37–43% of the lexical items in the data can be classed as slang. These words are unknown in either Finnish dialects or Standard Finnish and must, therefore, be interpreted as innovations in OHS. The proportion is surprisingly high and reflects the significant difference between the vocabulary of OHS and the vocabulary of any other variant of Finnish. The vast majority of the slang words in the vocabulary of OHS are loanwords or words of unknown origin. Only a handful can clearly be traced to Finnish. Such words include *ildis* 'a free evening' (< *iltaloma*), *kassu* 'garrison' (< *kasarmi*), *keglu* 'knife' (< *kekäle*, lit.'cinder'). Of the 175 most definitely slang words, 144 are unquestionably loanwords, most of them of Swedish origin. The proportion of loanwords is thus 83%, which is in line with the "almost 80%" estimated by Paunonen (2006, 51).

5.2 Adaptation of loanwords

As already mentioned, all the words in OHS are inflected following the rules of (dialectal) Finnish. As Finnish is an agglutinative language, case endings or other suffixes often have to be added to the noun stems, which typically end with a vowel and comprise two syllables. If a loanword already has these same features, it can be used in OHS without any adaptation just by adding to it the suffixes demanded by the rules of Finnish grammar, e.g., from Swedish (*bastu* 'sauna,' *flikka* 'girlfriend,' *fylla* 'drunkenness,' *smedja* 'smithy,' *gubbe* '(old)man, boy') and from Russian (*lafka* 'shop, firm,' *mesta* 'place,' and *voda* 'water').

When a loanword ends with a consonant, Finnish suffixes cannot be directly added to it. Thus a common strategy in Standard Finnish is to insert an extra vowel between the loanword and the suffix. The same occurs in the data: frequently occurring extra vowels in the data are *-i* and *-u*, as in *ööli* 'beer' < *öl*, *hesti* 'horse' < *häst*, *blaadi* 'tobacco, cigarette' < *blad*, *friski* 'healthy' < *frisk*, *groussi* 'strong' (< German *gross*), *botu* 'boat' < *båt*, *fiksu* 'smart' < *fix*, *fisu* 'fish' < *fisk*, *futu* 'foot' < *fot*, and *vedu* '(fire)wood' < *ved*. Many of the loanwords that end with a consonant end with the vowel *e* in OHS, but this may derive from the Swedish affix *-en/-et*, used to code definiteness, as in *dörre* 'door' (< *dörr-en* door-DEF), *blude* 'blood' < *blod-et*, *lande* 'country' < *land-et*, *šöte* 'meat' < *kött-et*. Words ending in *-a* may reflect Swedish definite or plural forms, as in *gamla* 'old' (< *gamla* old.DEF) and *nykla* 'key' (< *nycklar* key.PL).

In addition to adding extra vowels, loanwords ending with a consonant may be adapted to Finnish stems by adding a slang suffix; this is discussed in Section 5.3.

Swedish verbs, which typically have two syllables and end with a vowel, fall naturally into what is called in many text books the fourth conjugation of Finnish verbs (e.g., White 2001, 159; the verbs of this conjugation are traditionally called *supistumaverbit* 'contracted verbs,' e.g., in Itkonen 1964 188–192). However, there are some peculiarities in the OHS data that give reason to postulate a distinct 'OHS conjugation.' (Jarva 2008, 73–74; verb conjugations are further discussed in Section 5.5.1.) Several verb stems have been borrowed from Swedish without any adaptation: *skrivaa* 'to write,' *luktaa* 'to stink,' *byggaa* 'to build,' *kantraa* 'to fall (over), to tumble,' and *hoppaa* 'to jump.' The same is true of the verb *bonjaa* 'to understand' (< Russian *ponja-*).

When a verb in the donor language has only one syllable, it must be expanded with an extra syllable in OHS. The data exhibits only a few examples of this: *flytaa* 'to flee, escape' < *fly*, *rutsaa* ~ *ruddaa* 'to row' < *ro*, and *draisaa* 'to draw' < *dra*. In addition to two-syllable verb stems, two loan verbs consisting of three syllables also occur in the data: *kaveeraa* 'to speak, talk' originates from the Russian verb *govorit* but has possibly been associated with the Finnish word *kaveri* 'friend, mate' and with the Swedish derivative verb suffix *era*. *Brassailla* 'to play (games)' (< Sw. *brassa*) has a Finnish frequentative suffix. There are two variants to the way in which the Swedish *hjälpa* 'to help' has been borrowed: *jelppaa* and *jelppiä*. The latter is unique in the data since it is a loanword but ends with the vowel *i*; all the other verbs of this type are Finnish, such as *hankkia* 'to buy, acquire,' *juhlia* 'to celebrate,' and *oppia* 'to learn.'

5.3 SLANG SUFFIXES

In OHS, it is common to manipulate words by means of specific enlargements known as 'slang suffixes,' of which the most common are *ari* and *is*. These slang suffixes have no semantic content and do not express any grammatical relation, but they are stylistic or affective devices. Thus the term 'suffix' is somewhat inadequate. It is, nevertheless, used here for traditional reasons. In Finnish, the terms *slangijohdin* 'slang suffix, derivative affix' and *slangijohdos* 'slang derivative' are commonly used (Nahkola 1999, ISK § 214); Wälchli (1995) calls slang suffixes 'enlargements.'

The data contain over one hundred lexemes with a slang suffix. These are mostly loanwords or words of uncertain origin; only a few of them are Finnish.

The slang suffix *ari* derives from the Swedish agent suffix *are* and is used in many Swedish loanwords both in Standard Finnish and in OHS. In the data, this source of *ari* is present in such words as *brotari* 'wrestler' < *brottare*, *byggari* 'builder' < *byggare*, and *hugari* 'knife'< *huggare* 'sword, sabre.' Nevertheless, there are many cases in which *ari* is neither an agent suffix nor a loan but can only be interpreted as a non-etymological slang suffix. Sometimes it follows a one-syllable word: *gravari* 'grave' < *grav*, *munnari* 'mouth' < *mun*, or *ögari* 'eye' < *öga*. More commonly, however, the source word has two or more syllables: *bilari* 'ticket' < *biljett*; *bysarit* 'trousers' < *byxor*, and *tšeggari* 'chain' < *kätting*. It is noteworthy that in many cases the original Swedish word is a compound or otherwise complex word: *daggari* 'earthworm' < *daggmask*, *flatari* 'louse'< *flatlus*, *dispari* 'house manager' < *disponent*, and *smörgari* 'sandwich' < *smörgås*.

The slang suffix *is* has apparently come into OHS along with Swedish slang words (Jarva 2008, 70). In the data, the suffix is used, for example, in the following words: *golvis* 'floor' < *golv*, *rödis* 'red' < *röd*, *falskis* 'secret, hidden' < *falsk*, and *branttis* 'bank, steep hill' < *brant*. Sometimes a noun with the slang suffix *is* can be traced to a Swedish verb, e.g., *breggis* 'broken (arm)' < *bräcka* 'to break,' *simmis* 'swimming pool' < *simma* 'to swim,' and *strittis* 'urinal' < *stritta* 'splash, splatter.' The words *safkis* 'canteen', *dorkis* 'nuthouse,' and *skeidis* 'waste dump' are apparently derived from *safka* 'food' (< Russian *zavtrak* 'breakfast'), *dorka* 'crazy' (< Sw. *dåke, dåre*), and *skeida* 'shit' (< Sw. *skit*).

The third slang suffix commonly found in the data is *tši ~ tsi ~ tšu ~ tsu*, which is of unknown origin. It is used, for example, in the following words: *bärtši* 'cliff' < *berg*, *mutši* 'mother' < *mor, moder*, *tortši* 'square, market' < *torg*, *frötši* 'mistress' < *fröken* 'miss', and *goitšu* 'hut' < *koja*.

Each one of these slang suffixes often occurs with words whose etymology is difficult to establish; these words are phonetically manipulated or otherwise unexpected. For example, the following words may have originated either from Finnish or from Swedish: *pollari* 'policeman' (< Finn. *poliisi* or Sw. *polis*), *maijari* '(male) teacher' (< Finn. *maisteri* or Sw. *magister*), *trabari* 'staircase' (< Finn. *rappu* or Sw. *trappa*), and *glitšu* 'shed, cellar' (< Finn. *liiteri* or Sw. *lider*). The following words bear only a slight resemblance to a possible source word: *disarit* 'tits' (cf., Finn. *tissi*), *glenuri ~ klenuri* 'child, boy' (cf., *klen* 'weak'), and *gönkkis* 'toilet, outhouse' (cf., *gödsel* 'excrement'). Some words are of unknown origin, such as *glitšari* 'hit, clip (round the ear),' *janari* 'countryboy,' and *slurkkis* 'police station.'

The data include only a few examples of apparently Finnish words that have been manipulated with a slang suffix: *rindis* 'breast' < *rinta*, *ildis* 'a free evening' < *iltaloma*, *romis* 'junkyard' < *romukauppa*, and *rantši ~ rantšu* 'beach' < *ranta*. This suggests that slang suffixes were originally used for the purpose of adapting loanwords to Finnish grammar and making their structure more uniform. In modern colloquial Finnish, slang suffixes are commonly used with Finnish words (Nahkola 1999; ISK § 214).

As already mentioned, the slang suffixes have no semantic content, and they should not be compared with derivative affixes. However, to some extent, they diverge semantically from each other: words with *ari* often refer to agents or living creatures while words with *is* refer to places or locations, but there are also exceptions, as the examples above illustrate.

5.4 Phonological features

In addition to vocabulary, the most obvious linguistic outcomes of language contact in OHS are phonological. In the first place, OHS contains phonemes that are unknown or rare in Finnish dialects. They include the voiced stops [b], [d], and [g], a voiceless palato-alveolar sibilant [š], an affricate [tš], and a voiceless labiodental fricative [f]. Examples include *bastu* 'sauna' (< *bastu*), *gamla* 'old' (< *gammal*), *hugari* 'knife' (< *huggare*), *dörre* 'door' (< *dörr*), *voda* 'water' (< Russ. *voda*), *šellaa* (< *skälla*) 'to scold, fault,' *mašunisti* 'machinist' (< *maskin*), *tšennaa* 'to know' (< *känna*), *tšyrkka* 'church' (< *kyrka*), *faija* 'father' (< *far, fader*), and *safka* 'food' (< Russ. *zavtrak*). Among these 'foreign' consonants, [b], [g], and [f] can be geminated – [bb], [gg] and [ff]: *gubbe* '(old) man' (< *gubbe*), *byggaa* 'to build' (< *bygga*), and *buffeli* 'bumper' (< *buffert*). The voiced dental stop [d] can also be geminated, as in the verb *ruddaa* 'to row' (< *ro*). However, in this case, [dd] does not derive from the source word.

Second, OHS has many word-initial consonant clusters, which are also unknown in Finnish dialects: *blaija* 'prostitute' (< Russ. *bljad'*), *brotari* 'wrestler' (< *brottare*), *draisaa* 'to draw' (< *dra*), *groussi* 'strong' (< Germ. *gross* 'big'), *skola ~ skole* 'school' (< *skola*), *sleepaa* (< *släppa*) 'to let go, let loose', *smörgari* 'sandwich' (< *smörgås*), *snöge* 'snow' (< *snö*), *stara* 'old (man)' (< Russ. *stáryj*), *svenska* 'Swedish (language)' < *svenska*, *tvettaa* 'to wash' (< *tvätta*), and so on. Three-consonant clusters are also possible in OHS, but rare: *skriigaa ~ skriikaa* 'to shout, scream' (< *skrika*), *skvalraa* 'to tell (tales)' (< *skvallra*), and *strittis* 'urinal' (< *stritta* 'to splash').

Third, OHS violates vowel harmony, which is a constraint strictly adhered to in Standard Finnish. According to the rules, the front vowels [ä], [ö], and [y] cannot be used in the same word as the back vowels [a], [o], and [u]. However, the data includes the following three combinations of front and back vowels: *ö–a* in *röökaa* 'to smoke' (< *röka*) and *sökaa* 'to look for, search for' (< *söka*), *y–a* in *fylla* 'drunkenness' (< *fylla*) and *dyykkaa* 'to dive,' and *ä–u* in *järkku* 'iron' (< *järn*).

In all the above examples, the foreign phonemes in OHS can be traced to the source words, but there are also several hypercorrect forms that do not derive from the source word. For example, there is an unetymological voiced stop in the following words: *bonjaa* 'to understand' (< Russ. *ponja-*), *blokkaa* 'to pick (up), gather' (< *plocka*), *goisaa* 'to sleep' < *koja*, *skagaa* 'to shake, shudder' (< *skaka*), *skeida* 'shit' (< Sw. dial. *skita, skeita*), and *faidaa* 'to make love' (< *fajtas* 'to fight'). There are also hypercorrect word-initial consonant clusters, as in *klabbi* 'foot' (< *lab* 'paw') and *knesa* 'nose' (< *näsa*). Although hypercorrect forms are mostly based on loanwords, the verb *dallaa* 'to step, tramp' derives from the Finnish verb *tallata*.

Hypercorrect forms are also commonly manipulated, e.g., with slang suffixes. Examples in the data are *trabari* 'staircase' (< Finn. *rappu* or Sw. *trappa*), *botlari* 'potato' (< Finn. *pottu* or Sw. *potatis*), *breggis* 'broken' (< *bräcka* 'to break'), *ildis* 'a free evening' (< Finn. *iltaloma*), *glitšu* 'shed, cellar' (< Finn. *liiteri* or Sw. *lider*), *šubu* 'soup' (< Finn. *soppa*, Sw. *soppa* or Russ. *sup*), and there are many others. In addition, it is not uncommon to find manipulated words or variants that originate from the same source word: *gönkkä ~ göntsä ~ göna* 'excrement,' *gönkkis* 'toilet,' and *gönaa ~ gönkkaa* 'to defecate' (cf., *gödsel* 'excrement), and *kraga ~ krageli ~ kraisu* 'collar,' and *kragaus ~ kragninki* 'fight' (cf., *krage* 'collar'). Since the same source word can have as many as five variants in this relatively small data set, it is clear that variation is very common in OHS and that it can sever words from their origins in such a way that they can no longer be connected with a source word except via more regular variants. For example, *dövää* 'to stink' is a variant of *döftää ~ döftaa*, which apparently derives from the Swedish *dofta*, and *šagga* 'food' cannot be connected with the Russian word *zavtrak* 'breakfast' without the etymologically more regular *safka*.

Although the phonological and phonotactic features mentioned above are strikingly un-Finnish and have equivalents in Swedish, they are known in Standard Finnish and not all of them are alien, even in dialects. The fricative [f] and some word-initial consonant clusters are known in many southern and western Finnish dialects, including those in the districts bordering on Helsinki. They are particularly common in recent loanwords and sound-symbolic words. Itkonen (1989, 350–351) states that [f] and the word-initial clusters *kl, kr, kn, pl, pr, tr, fl,* and *fr* are known in the dialect of Nurmijärvi, 20 kilometers north of Helsinki. According to him, they may have been adopted along with Swedish loans, but they also have "apparent affective color," and they can be used hypercorrectly in both native and loanwords: *färeet* 'shivering' (< Finn. *väreet*), *kriipee* 'to climb' (< Finn. *kiipe-*), and *koofärtti* 'envelope' (< Sw. *kuvert*). There is, then, an apparent resemblance between OHS and the Nurmijärvi dialect, however, what might be seen as foreign elements in native words are only infrequently applied in OHS.

Nevertheless, these foreign features are far more common in OHS than in any Finnish dialect, and some of them are known only in Standard Finnish; such cases are [b], [g], and [š] and many word-initial consonant clusters. The affricate [tš] is unknown even in Standard Finnish, where only the consonant cluster [ts] is used.

The voiced dental stop [d] is unknown in Finnish dialects, but it occurs in Standard Finnish. According to Paunonen (1993, 57), it was replaced in the working class areas of Helsinki with the western dialect [r], but no examples of this occur in the data. In eastern dialects, instead of [d] or [r], the sound is lost: for example, the Finnish word for 'eight' is pronounced *kahdeksan* (Standard Finnish) ~ *kahreksan* (western dialects) ~ *kaheksan* (eastern dialects). The same goes for the consonant cluster [ts], which is pronounced [tt] in western dialects but as [ht] in eastern dialects, e.g., *metsä ~ mettä ~ mehtä* 'forest.'

The data shows variation between standard and dialectal variants. First of all, [d] is often pronounced as in Standard Finnish: *käde-ssä* (hand-INE), *tiedä-tte* (know-2PL), *joudu-i-n* (have.to-PST-1SG), but it can be lost, particularly in the cluster *hd*: *yhdeksän* ~ *yheksän* 'nine,' *kaheksan* ('eight;' in Standard Finnish *kahdeksan*), *kahe-lle* (two-ADE; in Standard Finnish *kahdelle*). The examples below illustrate this variation. In Example (3), [d] occurs in the Finnish words *meidän* and *yhdellä*, as well as in the loanword *kundeilla* (< Sw. *kund*). In Example (4), [d] is not present in the word *meijän* (cf., *meidän*).

(3) meidä-n kunde-i-l ol-i yhde-llä haglari
    we-GEN boy-PL-ADE have-PST one-ADE shotgun
    'one of us boys had a shotgun'

(4) meijä-n talo-n jenta-t ol-i kivo-i
    we-GEN house-GEN girl-PL be-PST nice-PL.PAR
    'the girls in our house were nice'

Second, the standard variant [ts] varies with dialectal [tt] ~ [t]: *seitsemässä* (seven-INE), *ratsu* 'mount,' *ruotsi* 'Swedish language,' *kato* ~ *katos* (look. IMP.2SG), *itte* 'self' (in Standard Finnish *itse*), *viitti* (bother.NEG, in Standard Finnish *viitsi*). Example (5) illustrates the dialectal form *ittemme* instead of the Standard Finnish *itsemme*.

(5) me duuna-ttiin monta kundi-i itte-mme
    we make-PAS.PST many boy-PAR self-POS.1PL
    maijari-ks
    magister-TRA
    'many of us boys completed a (swimming) diploma'

The above examples suggest that the matrix language in OHS is neither Standard Finnish nor any given dialect but instead reflects an "unofficial colloquial language" (Paunonen 1993, 58–59). In this kind of urban and antinormative speech, people do not use variants that can be stigmatized as rural, nor do they use overly formal or official forms. When this colloquial speech differs from Standard Finnish, it displays features that are widely distributed across Finnish dialects; in other words, these features are not characteristic of any one specific dialect. What is of special interest in this context is that this type of colloquial speech was said to be evolving "among young people" in Paunonen's data, which was collected from 1972 to 1974 (Paunonen 1993, 57). However, the present data demonstrates that similar speech patterns were used as the matrix language of OHS by elderly men in the 1960s.

5.5 Morpho-syntactic features

The morpho-syntax of OHS seems clearly to be Finnish. Not only the native Finnish words but also the Swedish and other loanwords, as well as words heavily manipulated – whether with slang suffixes or by other means – all follow the rules of Finnish grammar. The only apparent exception is the code-switching to Swedish in Example (2).

Even where the morpho-syntactic features in the data differ from Standard Finnish, they are known widely in Finnish dialects and colloquial Finnish, and therefore cannot be interpreted as innovations in OHS. For example, in Standard Finnish, verbs must agree in person and number with their subjects, but it is common in free speech for 3PL forms to ignore this rule. This is illustrated in Example (4) in which the subject *jentat* is in the plural while the verb *oli* is in the singular. It is also common to use passive forms instead of 1PL forms, as is shown in Example (5), in which the subject is the 1PL pronoun *me*, but the verb *duunattiin* is in the passive form.

These kinds of morpho-syntactic differences between OHS and Standard Finnish should not, then, be interpreted as innovations in OHS. However, a number of peculiarities remain that have been noted in the literature. Among these are the OHS verb conjugation (Paunonen 2000, 22–23; Jarva 2008, 73–74) and the interrogative suffix *ks ~ ts* (Paunonen 2000, 23–24; Jarva 2008, 75–76), which will be discussed in this section. As they have no direct parallel in any Finnish dialect it is possible that they have developed, at least in part, independently in OHS.

Research has also focused on the choice of the object case (Paunonen 2000, 25; Jarva 2008, 74), although in the data, this invariably follows Standard Finnish grammar. There are some examples of the use of a personal pronoun in the genitive case (*mu-n*) in utterances in which it should be in the accusative (*mu-t*), according to the rules of Standard Finnish. This is a western dialectal feature also mentioned by Paunonen (2000, 24).

5.5.1. OHS conjugation

Many verbs in OHS follow an idiosyncratic verb conjugation, which is a simplified form of the Finnish fourth conjugation with an infinitive ending *ta/tä* (White 2001, 159; Jarva 2008, 72–74). In Standard Finnish, there is a difference between verbs in the first and fourth conjugations, as illustrated in the following table with the verbs *kastaa* 'to dip, dunk' and *vastata* 'to answer' (Itkonen 1989, 362; Jarva 2008, 73).

Table 2. The first and fourth verb conjunction.

	1st conjugation	4th conjugation
INF	kasta-a	vastat-a
1SG	kasta-n	vastaa-n
3SG	kasta-a	vastaa
PST.3SG	kasto-i	vastas-i
PP	kasta-nut	vastan-nut
IMP.2PL	kasta-kaa	vastat-kaa
NEG.IMP.2PL	älkää kasta-ko	älkää vastat-ko

In the first conjugation, the verb stem (*kasta-*) is not altered, only in the past tense the final vowel changes before the past tense suffix /i/ (*kasta + i > kastoi*). The fourth conjugation features two possible verb stems: one ending with a consonant (*vastat-a ~ vastan-nut*) and the other ending with a long vowel (*vastaa-*). Furthermore, the A infinitive (*kastaa*) and 3SG in the present tense (*kastaa*) are similar in the 1st conjugation, while they differ in the 4th conjugation (*vastata* and *vastaa*, respectively). Thus, the 1st conjugation is simpler in that it has only one verb stem, and the 4th conjugation is simpler in that the verb stem is not altered in the past tense.

In OHS, most loan verbs are conjugated in a way that combines the Standard Finnish 1st and 4th conjugation paradigms: they have only one stem as in the 1st conjugation, but they follow the 4th conjugation in that the verb stem ends with a long vowel (*aa/ää*), and the past tense forms end with the suffix *s(i)*. In the following examples, (6) and (9), the A infinitive forms are *draisaa* 'to pull, withdraw, drag,' and *tšiigaa ~ tsiigaa* 'to look,' and the negative imperative forms are (*älkää*) *draisako* (7) and *tšiigako* (11). They follow the 1st conjugation. In contrast, the past tense forms are *draisas* (8) and *tsiigasi* (10), and the participle form is *tsiigannu* (12), all of which follow the 4th conjugation.

(6) me   yrite-tään   draisa-a   sitä   vek
    we   try-PAS   pull-INF   it-PAR off
    'we're trying to pull it [= fish-hook] off [the nose]'

(7) älkää   ny   draisa-ko   kundi-t
    NEG.IMP.2PL   now   pull-NEG.IMP.2PL boy-PL
    'don't pull it [fish-hook] now, boys'

(8) ne   draisa-s   oikein   flintti-in
    they pull-PST   really   face-ILL
    'they [= policemen] really hit [us] in the face'

(9) se-n   täyty   kolme   kerta-a   päivä-s   tšiiga-a
    he-GEN   have.to.PST   three   time-PAR   day-INE   look.out-INF
    'you had to look out three times a day [so that the bigger boys would not find you]'

(10) Mä   aukas-i-n   ove-n   ja   tšiiga-si
     I   open-PST-1SG   door-GEN   and   look-PST
     'I opened the door and looked'

(11) älkää   tšiiga-ko   tänne
     NEG.IMP.2PL   look-NEG.IMP.2PL here
     'don't look over here!'

(12) ne   ei   tsiiga-nnu   yhtään
     they NEG.3SG   look-PP   at.all
     'they [= policemen] didn't care at all [when they hit us]'

The Finnish dialects spoken near Helsinki also mix the 1st and 4th conjugations, a practice that has been interpreted as a contact-induced feature. The area of this "morphological disturbance" in Finnish dialects borders directly on a Swedish-speaking area. (See map in Itkonen 1964, 192.) However, the examples put forward by Itkonen (1989, 362–365) appear more random than those in OHS since both the native and borrowed verb paradigms are mixed. In the data, every verb unknown in Standard Finnish or the Finnish dialects follows the OHS conjugation; in contrast, every Finnish verb of the 1st or the 4th conjugation follows Standard Finnish grammar. This marked dichotomy suggests that the primary function of the OHS conjugation is to easily adapt borrowed verbs to Finnish grammar.

5.5.2. The interrogative suffix ks ~ ts

In OHS, the Finnish interrogative suffix *ko ~ kö* is extended with the suffix *s* and then reduced to *ks*. In questions, the personal pronoun immediately follows the verb (Jarva 2008, 75). This is also seen in the data, in which most of the cases are in 3SG:

(13) ol-i-ks se jurris vai selvä
 be-PST-Q he drunk or sober
 'was he drunk or sober?'

As the 3rd person pronoun *se* 's/he, it' occurs after the interrogative suffix, it is hard to determine whether the suffix ends with *s* or whether it has merely lost its final vowel and fused with the pronoun, e.g., (Standard Finnish) *oliko se* > **olik se* > *olikse*. However, the final *s* of the suffix is clearly present when it is followed by a word that does not begin with *s*, as in Example (14). There is also one example of 1SG (15) in which the suffix *ks* is evident.

(14) vielä-ks Eetu elä-ä
 still-Q Eetu live-PR.3SG
 'is Eetu [A male's name] still alive?'

(15) saa-n-ks mä tul-ta
 get-1SG-Q I light-PAR
 'can I have a light?'

In most cases of 2SG, the personal suffix *t* is retained but with no interrogative suffix used at all; thus, questions are marked only by the inversion in word order (Example 16). However, one example occurs of 2SG without a personal ending (17).

(16) muista-t sä ne stenusoda-t
 remember-2SG you those stone.fight-PL
 'do you remember the stone fights?'

(17) muista-ks sä si-tä Snelli-n kundi-a
 remember-Q you that-PAR Snell-GEN guy-PAR
 'do you remember that guy Snell [last name]?'

As plural forms do not occur in the data, it is not possibe to describe the system of question forms without personal endings in OHS suggested by Jarva (2008, 75–76). Omitting the ending *t* in 2SG is natural as it avoids the complicated consonant cluster **tks*: e.g., *muista-ks* 'do you remember' instead of **muistat-ks*. However, there is no evidence of the omission of personal endings in general.

The OHS question forms in the data can be explained by reference to Finnish dialects, in which the interrogative suffix *ks* and the *ko ~ kö*, known in Standard Finnish, are both widely used. However, the omission of the suffix in 2SG (as in Example 16) is exceptional in Finnish dialects, with most examples occurring in the dialects of South Eastern Finland. (Forsberg 1994, 60–61.) It is debatable how much these dialects have influenced the colloquial Finnish spoken in Helsinki. According to Forsberg (1994, 65), the omission may have been triggered by bilingual native Swedish speakers, as there is no interrogative suffix in Swedish.

6 Discussion

According to the data, the proportion of words of Swedish origin in OHS is 29–32%. This is significantly fewer than the estimates presented in the literature. These former estimates were not based on systematically collected data or recordings, and they focused exclusively on the slang vocabulary of OHS, whereas the present study treats the whole sample as an example of one form of speech and counts every lexical item in the data as an OHS word. However, in Section 5.1.4, all the words known in Finnish dialects or Standard Finnish have been excluded from the so-called slang vocabulary of OHS. In this sample, the proportion of loanwords and those of uncertain provenance amounts to 90%. This supports Paunonen's (2006, 51) claim that "almost 80 percent" of the vocabulary of OHS is of Swedish origin.

The results of this study may be compared with data collected in the LWT project (*Loanwords in the World's Languages*; see Tadmor 2009). Tadmor (2009, 56–57) divides languages into four categories according to their rate of borrowing, i.e., the proportion of loanwords in the lexicon. Based on this criterion, OHS would be placed in the category of high borrowers (languages with a borrowing rate of 25–50%), and, out of the total of 41 languages in the list, it would be ranked in 10th–15th place for lexical borrowing rates. This demonstrates that the proportion of borrowed words in OHS is not exceptional in world languages.

Function and content words in OHS differ markedly from each other in their etymological origin. Loanwords account for 35–38% of the content words in the data whereas the proportion of function words that are loanwords is less than 1%. A difference of this order is rarely seen anywhere as the average borrowing rate of function words in the LWT project is 12.1%. However, some other languages in LWT have also borrowed only a few function words, if any, and there are languages with a similar relation between borrowed content and function words as that found for OHS. For example, in Imbabura Quechua, 32.5% of the content words are loanwords compared to only 2.3% of the function words (Tadmor 2009, 55).

Borrowing rates can also be estimated for word classes. In the LWT project, the average borrowing rate is 31.2% for nouns, 15.2% for adjectives and adverbs, and 14.0% for verbs (Tadmor 2009, 61). In the data, the corresponding rates are 43–45%, 16% and 38–40%. The striking borrowing rate for verbs in OHS can be explained by the high numbers of synonymical verbs that refer to fighting, running, playing, and other outdoor activities, while the LWT project focuses on semantically basic verbs. There may be several verbs in the data that correspond to just one semantic verb in the LWT project. However, two languages in LWT have borrowed even more verbs than nouns. An interesting parallel with OHS is Saramaccan, in which as many as 44% of the verbs are borrowed, compared to 37.1% of the nouns (Tadmor 2009, 66). Whereas Saramaccan has undergone partial relexification by Portuguese, in the case of OHS, it might be more appropriate to define borrowing as paralexification as the loanwords often coexist with a Finnish word with the same meaning. This kind of core borrowing (see Section 5.1.3) can be explained by the prestige of the donor language, and it is also common in situations of extensive bilingualism (Haspelmath 2009, 48). This would be in line with the sociohistorical and linguistic background of OHS.

Many of the loanwords in OHS have been drawn from basic vocabulary, which is thought to be resistant to borrowing. In this study, OHS loanwords were compared with the Leipzig-Jakarta list introduced by Tadmor (2009, 68–71). 64 of the 100 words (or meanings) on the list also appear in the data, of which 29 (45%) are characterised by a word of Swedish origin. The data may also be compared to the 100 most borrowing-resistant items on the LWT meaning list (Tadmor 2009, 67). A comparison reveals 58 equivalent meanings in OHS, of which 17 (29%) are loanwords. The numbers are relatively high, even if some previous estimates have been even higher; up to about 80% of the verbs, adjectives, and nouns in the Swadesh list (Jarva 2008, 68).

The phonological and morpho-syntactic features of the data are largely in agreement with previous findings, but some observations can be made.

Although OHS has some phonological and phonotactic features that are strikingly un-Finnish and have equivalents in Swedish, not all of them are unknown in all Finnish dialects. The fricative [f] and some word-initial consonant clusters are known in many western Finnish dialects, also in those around Helsinki. It is apparent that these features have been adopted along with loanwords, and both in dialects and in OHS they can be used hypercorrectly, i.e., they cannot be traced to a source word. However, OHS applies foreign elements to native words only on rare occasions. Also the use of slang suffixes is more common with borrowed than with native words. This suggests that the slang suffixes were originally used to adapt loanwords to Finnish grammar and render their structure more uniform.

While some morpho-syntactic features of OHS differ from those of Standard Finnish, they are widely known in Finnish dialects and colloquial

Finnish and, therefore, cannot be interpreted as innovations in OHS. Many verbs in OHS follow an idiosyncratic OHS conjugation, which combines the Standard Finnish 1st and 4th conjugation paradigms. This has been interpreted as an outcome of language contact, as a similar mixing of Finnish verb conjugations is also known in Finnish dialects close to the language border with Swedish. However, the data shows that the OHS conjugation is used only with borrowed stems; Finnish verbs are conjugated according to the rules of Finnish grammar. This suggests that the primary function of the OHS conjugation is to facilitate the adaptation of borrowed verbs to Finnish grammar. On the basis of the examples in Paunonen's dictionary (Paunonen 2000, 23; see also Jarva 2008, 77–78), more radical morpho-syntactic changes in OHS may have occurred around the beginning of the 20th century, but they are not detectable in the data, which were recorded in 1965.

It can be concluded that the grammatical differences between OHS and other Finnish variants have no particular significance. Morpho-syntactically, the sample herein can easily be interpreted as a variant of Finnish. It is neither Standard Finnish nor any given dialect, but it is an example of an "unofficial colloquial language" (Paunonen 1993, 58–59). In phonology and phonotactics, contact-induced features are more apparent, but mostly parallel those in neighboring Finnish dialects. In addition, foreign features and slang suffixes are mostly applied to borrowed or heavily manipulated words; native words mostly remain the same.

While the proportion of borrowed words in OHS is not exceptional among world languages, it is nevertheless remarkable. Furthermore, core borrowing is common and even basic vocabulary has been borrowed. Such massive borrowing has led to paralexification, i.e., the occurrence of both Swedish and Finnish variants that express the same meaning. Roughly 40% of the vocabulary of OHS can be defined as slang, a proportion unknown in Finnish dialects or in Standard Finnish. This slang vocabulary is overwhelmingly borrowed, and it can be seen as the most apparent contact-induced feature of OHS. It is this that has made this variety of urban speech virtually incomprehensible to contemporary dialectal or Standard Finnish speakers.

Glossing abbreviations

1PL	first person plural
1SG	first person singular
2PL	second person plural
2SG	second person singular
3PL	third person plural
3SG	third person singular
ADE	adessive
ADV	adverb
CON	conditional
DEF	definitive

ESS	essive
GEN	genitive
ILL	illative
IMP	imperative
INE	inessive
INF	A infinitive
NEG	negation
PAR	partitive
PAS	passive
PL	plural
POS	possessive
PP	past participle
PR	present tense
PST	(simple) past tense
Q	question
TRA	translative

References

de Smit, Merlijn. 2010. "Modelling Mixed Languages: Some Remarks on the Case of Old Helsinki Slang." *Journal of Language Contact – VARIA* 3:1–19.

Forsberg, Hannele. 1994. "Havaintoja kysymystyypistä *otat sie ~ sä*." [Observations on the question type *otat sie ~ sä*.] *Virittäjä* 101:60–68.

Forsskåhl, Mona. 2006. "Helsinki Slang around 1900: a New Slang Variety Is Born." *Revue d'Études françaises* 11:53–67.

Haspelmath, Martin. 2009. "Lexical Borrowing: Concepts and Issues." In *Loanwords in the World's Languages. A Comparative Handbook*, edited by Martin Haspelmath and Uri Tadmor, 35–54. Berlin: Mouton de Gruyter.

ISK= *Iso suomen kielioppi* [Descriptive Grammar of Finnish], by Auli Hakulinen, Maria Vilkuna, Riitta Korhonen, Vesa Koivisto, Tarja Riitta Heinonen, and Irja Alho. 2004. Helsinki: Finnish Literature Society.

Itkonen, Terho. 1964. *Proto-Finnic Final Consonants I:1*. Helsinki: University of Helsinki.

Itkonen, Terho. 1989. *Nurmijärven murrekirja* [Book of the Nurmijärvi dialect]. Helsinki: Finnish Literature Society.

Jarva, Vesa. 2008. "Old Helsinki Slang and Language Mixing." *Journal of Language Contact – VARIA* 1:52–80.

Jussila, Raimo, Erja Nikunen, and Sirkka Rautoja, eds. 1992. *Suomen murteiden taajuussanasto. A Frequency Dictionary of Finnish Dialects*. Helsinki: Institute for the Languages of Finland.

Kallio, Petri. 2007. "How Uralic is Stadin Slangi?" In *Language and Identity in the Finno-Ugric World*, edited by Rogier Blokland and Cornelius Hasselblatt, 176–191. Maastricht: Shaker.

Liuttu, Pentti. 1951. "Helsingin slangin keskeistä sanastoa" [Essential vocabulary of Helsinki Slang]. MA thesis. University of Helsinki.

Meakins, Felicity. 2013. "Mixed Languages." In *Contact Languages: A Comprehensive Guide*, edited by Peter Bakker and Yaron Matras, 159–228. Berlin: Mouton de Gruyter.

Mikkonen, Jenni. 2014. "Vanhan Helsingin slangin ruotsalaisperäiset sanat nauhoitetussa keskustelussa" [Swedish loan words in the recorded conversation of Old Helsinki Slang]. MA thesis. University of Jyväskylä.

Nahkola, Kari. 1999. "Nykyslangin sananmuodostusoppia" [Aspects of word formation in Finnish slang]. *Virittäjä* 103:195–221.

NS = *Nykysuomen sanakirja* [Dictionary of Modern Finnish]. Porvoo: WSOY.

Paunonen, Heikki. 1993. "From a Small Swedish Town to a Finnish City." In *Language Variation and Change* 5:51–59.

Paunonen, Heikki. 1995. *Suomen kieli Helsingissä. Huomioita Helsingin puhekielen historiallisesta taustasta ja nykyvariaatiosta.* [The Finnish language in Helsinki. Observations on the historical background and modern variation in spoken Finnish in Helsinki.] Helsinki: University of Helsinki.

Paunonen, Heikki. 2000. *Tsennaaks Stadii, bonjaaks slangii. Stadin slangin suursanakirja.* [Dictionary of Helsinki Slang.] Porvoo: WSOY.

Paunonen, Heikki. 2006. "Vähemmistökielestä varioivaksi valtakieleksi" [From minority language to varying main language]. In *Helsinki kieliyhteisönä*, edited by Kaisu Juusela and Katariina Nisula, 13–99. Helsinki: University of Helsinki.

Saukkonen, Pauli, Marjatta Haipus, Antero Niemikorpi, and Helena Sulkala, eds. 1979. *Suomen kielen taajuussanasto. A Frequency Dictionary of Finnish.* Porvoo: WSOY.

Sivula, Jaakko. 1995. "Korpus ja kirosana" [Corpus and swear words]. In *Murteiden matkassa. Juhlakirja Alpo Räisäsen 60-vuotispäiväksi* [Dialects. Commemorative volume for the honour of Alpo Räisänen at his 60th birthday], 239–248. Studia Carelica Humanistica 6. Joensuu: University of Joensuu.

SMS = *Suomen murteiden sanakirja 1–8* [Dictionary of Finnish dialects 1–8]. Helsinki: Kotimaisten kielten tutkimuskeskus. 1985–2008.

Tadmor, Uri. 2009. "Loanwords in the World's Languages: Findings and Results". In *Loanwords in the World's Languages. A Comparative Handbook*, edited by Martin Haspelmath and Uti Tadmor, 55–75. Berlin: Mouton de Gruyter.

Waris, Heikki. 1973. *Työläisyhteiskunnan syntyminen Helsingin Pitkänsillan pohjoispuolelle* [The rise of the working class community on the north side of Helsinki's "Long Bridge"]. Helsinki: Weilin+Göös.

White, Leila. 2001. *Suomen kielioppia ulkomaalaisille* [A Grammar book of Finnish]. Helsinki: Finn Lectura.

WOLD = World Loanword Database. 2015. Accessed March 30, 2015. http://wold.clld.org/.

Wälchli, Bernhard. 2005. "Relexicalization vs. Relexification: the Case of Stadin Slangi Finnish." Unpublished manuscript.

Contributors

Vesa Jarva http://orcid.org/0000-0001-7965-9083

Vesa Jarva is University Lecturer in Finnish language at the University of Jyväskylä, Finland. He has also taught Finnish as a foreign language in the Netherlands, Lithuania, Hungary, and Estonia. Jarva has researched spoken Finnish, especially loanwords and ideophones. His PhD thesis concerned Russian loanwords and expressivity in Finnish dialects. He has also co-edited (with Timo Nurmi) a dictionary of modern colloquial Finnish *Oikeeta suomee*.

Vesa Koivisto http://orcid.org/0000-0003-1256-6477

Vesa Koivisto is Professor in Karelian language and culture at the University of Eastern Finland, Joensuu. He has studied derivation and verbal morphology in Finnish and other Finnic languages and has published monographies on these fields. He has also co-authored *Iso suomen kielioppi* (Descriptive Grammar of Finnish, 2004). He leads the project "Dialect Corpora of Border Karelia and Ingrian Finnish" (The Foundation for Advancement of Karelian Culture, 2016–2017).

Niina Kunnas http://orcid.org/0000-0002-2703-0600

Niina Kunnas is University Lecturer at the University of Oulu, Finland. The goal of her research is to generate new knowledge about northern language varieties as well as minority languages. She works within the context of sociolinguistics, minority language studies, as well as folk linguistics. Kunnas also teaches courses related to her research themes and supervises theses concerning language variation and change, language ideologies, and language policy.

Johanna Laakso ⓘ http://orcid.org/0000-0002-4892-9885

Johanna Laakso, PhD from the University of Helsinki, 1990, has been the chair of Finno-Ugric studies at the University of Vienna, Austria since 2000. Her research interests include historical and contact linguistics, morphology (in particular, word formation), multilingualism and minority issues, and gender linguistics. She has collaborated in various research projects, such as the EU-FP7 research project ELDIA ("European Language Diversity for All", 2010–2013); together with Annekatrin Kaivapalu and Helka Riionheimo, she coordinates the research network VIRSU (Finno-Ugric languages as target languages).

Anna-Riitta Lindgren ⓘ http://orcid.org/0000-0001-8315-8206

Anna-Riitta Lindgren *was the* Professor of Finnish linguistics 1994–2015 at The Arctic University of Norway, Tromsø, and has been professor emerita since 2015. She has published books and articles on the Kven dialects and on the sociology of multilingualism in North Calotte and in Helsinki.

Jenni Mikkonen ⓘ http://orcid.org/0000-0002-9737-1136

Jenni Mikkonen has a Master's Degree in Finnish language from the University of Jyväskylä. She has studied Finnish, foreign languages, arts, and literature. Her MA thesis focused on Swedish loanwords in Old Helsinki Slang. Mikkonen currently teaches Finnish language to immigrants in Rovaniemi.

Leena Niiranen ⓘ http://orcid.org/0000-0001-9488-0130

Leena Niiranen has been Professor in Finnish linguistics at The Arctic University of Norway, Tromsø since 2013. Her research interests are the learning of Finnish in a bilingual and formal learning environment, the education policy of Finnish and Kven in Norway, language revitalization, and language contact.

Marjatta Palander ⓘ http://orcid.org/0000-0002-4370-8493

Marjatta Palander is Professor in Finnish language at the University of Eastern Finland, Joensuu. Her research interests are in dialectology, sociolinguistics, and folk linguistics. She has published monographs on sound change in progress, variation in transitional dialects, a life-span study of an idiolect, and perceptual dialectology. She lead the FINKA research project "On the Borderline of Finnish and Karelian: Perspectives on Cognate Languages and Dialects" (The Academy of Finland, 2011–2014) and the project "Language Corpora of the Border Areas of Finland and Russia" (Kone Foundation, 2013–2015).

Dennis R. Preston is Regents Professor of Linguistics, Director of RODEO (Research on the Dialects of English in Oklahoma), and Co-Director of the Center for Oklahoma Studies, all at the Oklahoma State University, USA. He is also University Distinguished Professor Emeritus at Michigan State University. He has been a visiting professor at numerous US and overseas institutions and was Director of the Linguistic Society of America Institute in 2003. He was President of the American Dialect Society and has served on the Executive Board of that society and others. His work focuses on sociolinguistics and dialectology. Recently, he has published several book-length compilations together with James Stanford (2009), Nancy Niedzielski (2010), and Alexei Prikhodkine (2015). He is a fellow of the Linguistic Society of America and the Japan Society for the Promotion of Science and holds the Officer's Cross of the Order of Merit of the Polish Republic.

Helka Riionheimo ⓘ http://orcid.org/0000-0002-9294-6201

Helka Riionheimo is Professor in Finnish at the University of Eastern Finland, Joensuu. Her main academic interests are contact linguistics, dialectology, sociolinguistics, Finnic languages, and language endangerment and attrition. Her publications include a monograph on the contact of Ingrian Finnish and Estonian (2007) and journal articles in, e.g., *Studies in Language* and *Multilingua*. She currently leads the project "Translation, Revitalization and the Endangered Karelian Language" (Kone Foundation, 2015–2018) and has previously led the project "CROSSLING: Language Contacts at the Crossroads of Disciplines" (Kone Foundation, 2011–2014).

Tamás Péter Szabó ⓘ http://orcid.org/0000-0001-5105-5202

Tamás Péter Szabó is a University Teacher at the Department of Teacher Education, University of Jyväskylä. He holds the title of Docent in Applied Linguistics with a specialisation in Linguistic Landscape Studies. He has investigated various forms of discourse, ideology, and interaction in Hungarian and Finnish education. His earlier works focus on repair in classroom interaction with a special regard to the co-construction of institutional roles in education. His recent publications address the management of diversity in institutional settings, schoolscapes, and agency in interaction. The publications include a Special Issue "Studying the visual and material dimensions of education and learning" for *Linguistics and Education* (edited with Petteri Laihonen), and papers on videographic methods in schoolscape studies in *Linguistic Landscape* (with Robert A. Troyer).

Abstract

On the Border of Language and Dialect

Edited by Marjatta Palander, Helka Riionheimo and Vesa Koivisto

This volume considers the linguistic borders between languages and dialects, as well as the administrative, cultural and mental borders that reflect or affect linguistic ones; it comprises eight articles examining the mental borders between dialects, dialect continua and areas of mixed dialect, language ideologies, language mixing and contact-induced language change. The book opens with Dennis R. Preston's review article on perceptual dialectology, showing how this field of study provides insights on laymen's perceptions about dialect boundaries, and how such perceptions explain regional and social variation. Johanna Laakso problematizes the common notion of languages as having clear-cut boundaries and stresses the artificialness and conventionality of linguistic borders. Vesa Koivisto introduces the Border Karelian dialects as an example of language and dialect mixing. Marjatta Palander and Helka Riionheimo's article examines the mental boundaries between Finnish and Karelian, demonstrated by the informants when recalling their fading memories of a lost mother tongue. Niina Kunnas focuses on how speakers of White Sea Karelian perceive the boundaries between their language and other varieties. Within the framework of language ideology, Tamás Péter Szabó highlights the ways in which linguistic borders are interactionally (co)constructed in the school environment in Hungary and Finland. Anna-Riitta Lindgren and Leena Niiranen present a contact-linguistic study investigating the vocabulary of Kven, a variety lying on the fuzzy boundary of a language and a dialect. Finally, Vesa Jarva and Jenni Mikkonen approach demographically manifested linguistic boundaries by examining the Old Helsinki slang, a mixture of lexical features derived from Finnish and Swedish. Together, the articles paint a picture of a multidimensional, multilingual, variable and ever-changing linguistic reality where diverse borders, boundaries and barriers meet, intertwine and cross each other. As a whole, the articles also seek to cross disciplinary and methodological boundaries and present new perspectives on earlier studies.

Index

acoustic analysis 30
adaptation 67, 78, 196, 198, 224, 239, 240, 250
adessive-allative 73, 111
adessive-ablative-allative 111
affricate 101, 103, 106, 115, 116, 232, 242, 243
apocope 108, 109, 115, 223

Baltic Finnic, see Finnic languages
bilingual 48, 51, 52, 57, 65, 103, 194, 195, 196, 198, 212, 215, 228, 232, 248
bilingualism 64, 98, 227, 249
Border Karelian, see Karelian
borrowing 9, 13, 191–197, 199, 200, 202, 206, 207, 215–217, 222, 224–226, 233–235, 237, 248–250

code-switching 98, 99, 102, 226, 245
conjugation (see also verb type) 212–215, 235, 240, 245–247, 250
consonant gradation 71, 72, 100, 105, 108
contact-induced change 10, 42, 45, 63, 191, 192, 235, 247, 250
contact-linguistic(s) 63, 86, 117, 226
content word 222, 234–236, 238, 248, 249
convergence 7, 8, 230
cross-linguistic influence 9

derivatives 192, 198, 202, 204, 205, 207–214, 216, 240, 242
    causative 197, 198, 297, 208, 216
    diminutive 208, 211, 212, 216
    essentiative 204
dialect atlas 75, 76

dialect continuum 7, 8, 56, 59, 65, 124, 192
dialect mixing 11
diglossic 125, 196
diphthongisation 85, 101, 108, 109, 115
discourse analysis 11, 29, 127
divergence 7, 8, 47, 191, 193, 194, 217
diversity 12, 13, 33, 48–50, 70, 79, 156–159, 163, 174, 183, 184, 186
dominant language 8, 9, 59, 67, 97, 104, 114, 116, 194, 199

Eastern Finnish, see Finnish
English 10, 13, 28, 30, 31, 43–45, 47, 49, 115, 147, 162, 163, 165–183, 185, 186, 235, 236
enregisterment 147
erasure 147, 148, 186
etymology 17, 241
eye-tracking measure 32

factor analysis 24
Far North Finnish, see Finnish
finnicization 63, 64, 67–69, 78
Finnic languages 10, 13, 41, 57, 63, 64, 74, 77–79, 87, 100, 107, 192, 226
Finnish
    Eastern Finnish 7, 8, 11, 47, 61, 63, 67, 70, 71, 76, 85, 87, 90, 95, 96, 100, 101, 103, 106, 107, 109, 110, 113, 116
    Far North Finnish 191–194, 197, 200, 203, 207, 208, 210
    Ingrian Finnish 57, 146, 147
    Savo dialect 61, 87, 96, 108–110, 115
    Standard Finnish 67, 71, 73, 96, 101, 109, 114, 193, 197, 200, 203, 222, 223, 225, 229, 231–233, 235, 237–239, 241–250

257

folk etymology 17
folk linguistic(s) 10, 17, 33, 85, 86, 91, 92, 94, 95, 114, 116, 117, 126, 146, 147, 215
foreign language 13, 46, 157, 159, 163–165, 167, 171, 172, 175, 183, 186
forensic linguistics 91
fractal recursivity 147
frequency
    lexical 214, 215, 238
    textual 214, 215, 235
frequentative 205, 209–211, 216, 240
function word 222, 223

gemination 105, 106, 115–117

hand-drawn map 21, 22
heritage language 12, 90, 91, 102, 104, 124
heritage speaker 91, 102, 117
Hungarian 40, 43, 44, 49, 156–158, 162–164
hypercorrect 72, 85, 106, 115, 242, 243, 249
hyperdialectal 107

iconization 147, 148
ideology 7, 10, 12, 13, 17, 38, 39, 126, 127, 147, 149, 156–160, 162–165, 172, 178, 183–186
imitation 12, 85, 86, 91–97, 99, 103–117, 143
imperative 96, 110, 113, 203, 246
Ingrian Finnish, see Finnish
innovation 22, 52, 62, 69, 73, 193, 195, 213, 214, 215, 222, 224, 239, 245, 250
integration strategies 201, 216
interaction 7, 12, 13, 29, 47, 50, 98, 157, 160–163, 167, 168, 174, 177, 183–186
intonation 95, 115

Karelian
    Border Karelian 9, 11, 12, 56–79, 85–117
    Karelian Proper 11, 12, 57, 59, 71, 73, 74, 76, 87, 92, 100, 110, 111, 124, 131, 134, 146
    Olonets Karelian, Olonetsian 11, 12, 47, 56, 57, 59, 64, 65, 69–74, 76, 87, 89, 92, 100–102, 107–111, 124, 126, 129, 130–135, 137, 142–146, 148, 155
    South Karelian 57, 59, 62, 65, 70–73, 76, 87, 89, 124, 129, 131–137, 139, 143, 145, 146, 148

Tver Karelian 56, 62, 70, 132, 133, 135–137, 148
White Sea Karelian 47, 73, 78, 87, 107, 123–125, 127–129, 131–135, 137, 140–149
Kven 8, 13, 191–217

language attitude 10, 17, 27, 32, 126
language contact 7, 9, 12, 13, 42, 52, 56, 57, 63, 77, 79, 86, 98, 192, 195, 214, 226, 230, 242, 250
language exam 172
language ideology 10, 12, 13, 17, 126, 127, 156, 159, 160, 162, 164, 185
language memory 12
language mixing 10, 75
language nest 87
language regard 17, 33, 127
language shift 8, 12, 42, 67, 68, 90, 194, 215
language variety 7, 9, 13, 29, 30, 33, 48, 49, 77, 79, 93, 167, 192, 193, 195, 226
latent speaker 85, 90, 117
lay term 95
lexical map 76
lexical strength 198
Likert scale 28
linguistic attitude 10, 11, 86
linguistic diversity 13, 33, 156, 184, 186
listening task 12, 91, 123–125, 127, 132, 133, 135, 146, 148, 155
little arrow method 17–19
loan verb marker 201, 203, 204
loan word 14, 95, 107, 108, 197, 200, 205, 223, 235
Ludian 57, 107, 124, 131–133, 137–140, 145, 148, 155

matched-guise technique 28, 32
matrix language 226, 229, 232, 244
Meänkieli 8, 193, 194, 201, 203, 205, 208, 215
metalanguage 29, 94, 95, 99, 127
metadiscourse 12, 158, 162
minority language 8, 9, 13, 57, 59, 79, 87, 149, 192, 193, 196
mixed dialect 10, 11, 69, 77, 78
mixed language 64, 139, 193, 223, 226
momentane 211, 212
monolingualism 11, 38, 44, 156
mother tongue 13, 38, 44, 46, 48, 49, 91, 124, 129, 144, 157, 158, 163, 164, 175, 183, 186, 199, 231
multidimensional scaling 24

multilingualism 10, 11, 13, 38, 42, 45, 47, 48–51, 156, 157–159, 163, 180, 183, 184, 194, 215

Norwegian 8, 13, 48, 191, 193–195, 199–206, 215, 217

Old Helsinki Slang 14, 222, 224, 225, 228, 229

palatalization 70, 71, 101, 105, 107, 115, 116
paralexification 226, 249, 250
passive 71, 103, 107, 110, 112, 209, 211, 213, 245
perceptual (dialectology) 16–19, 21–24, 34, 79, 123, 147, 148
performance speech 91
person(al) ending 73, 108, 110, 247, 248
prosodic (feature) 103, 115
Proto-Karelian 63, 87

reaction time 32, 33
relexification 249
rememberer 90, 96, 98
replication 13, 47,191, 192, 195,196, 198, 200–202, 206, 208–211, 216, 217
resynthesis 16, 30, 31
revitalization, revitalize 79, 86, 87, 193, 194, 199
Romani 102
Russian 56, 57, 59, 65–67, 71, 76–79, 87, 95, 96, 98, 102, 104, 107, 112, 113, 116, 124, 125, 130, 131, 139–142, 145, 146, 148, 176, 178, 183, 223, 224, 230, 233, 235, 237, 239–241, 243

Saami 41, 48, 69, 117, 191, 192, 194, 196–201, 206–217
Savo dialect, see Finnish
Scandinavian 191, 192, 197–202, 213, 216, 217

schoolscape 156, 157, 160–163, 178, 182, 183, 185, 186
schwa vowel 116
second language acquisition/learning 45, 91, 116
semantic differential scale 27, 28
semi-speaker 91, 98
slang 222–226, 228–233, 235, 238–241, 243, 244, 248–250
slang suffix 232, 233, 235, 240–244, 249, 250
South Karelian, see Karelian
speech pathology 91
speech rhythm 114
speech tempo 115
standard language 21, 67, 157–159, 185, 193, 217, 223, 224, 239
Standard Finnish, see Finnish
Swedish 47, 159, 176, 178, 183, 191, 193, 196, 197, 200–206, 208, 217, 222–233, 235–245, 247–250

theme interview 92, 125, 127
transfer 116
transitional dialects 59
Tver Karelian, see Karelian

Veps 57, 107, 132, 137–140, 145
verb type (see also conjugation) 196, 201–209, 211, 213, 214, 216, 217
verbalizer 201, 203–208, 210, 216, 217
White Sea Karelian, see Karelian
vocabulary 49, 64, 77, 95, 96, 103, 123, 140, 148, 191, 193, 196, 207, 217, 222–226, 230, 232, 233, 235, 237–239, 242, 248–250
word-boundary gemination 105, 106, 115, 116

zero-person construction 113

Studia Fennica Ethnologica

Memories of My Town
The Identities of Town Dwellers and Their Places in Three Finnish Towns
Edited by Anna-Maria Åström, Pirjo Korkiakangas &
Pia Olsson
Studia Fennica Ethnologica 8
2004

Passages Westward
Edited by Maria Lähteenmäki & Hanna Snellman
Studia Fennica Ethnologica 9
2006

Defining Self
Essays on emergent identities in Russia Seventeenth to Nineteenth Centuries
Edited by Michael Branch
Studia Fennica Ethnologica 10
2009

Touching Things
Ethnological Aspects of Modern Material Culture
Edited by Pirjo Korkiakangas, Tiina-Riitta Lappi &
Heli Niskanen
Studia Fennica Ethnologica 11
2008

Gendered Rural Spaces
Edited by Pia Olsson &
Helena Ruotsala
Studia Fennica Ethnologica 12
2009

Laura Stark
The Limits of Patriarchy
How Female Networks of Pilfering and Gossip Sparked the First Debates on Rural Gender Rights in the 19th-century Finnish-Language Press
Studia Fennica Ethnologica 13
2011

Where is the Field?
The Experience of Migration Viewed through the Prism of Ethnographic Fieldwork
Edited by Laura Hirvi &
Hanna Snellman
Studia Fennica Ethnologica 14
2012

Laura Hirvi
Identities in Practice
A Trans-Atlantic Ethnography of Sikh Immigrants in Finland and in California
Studia Fennica Ethnologica 15
2013

Eerika Koskinen-Koivisto
Her Own Worth
Negotiations of Subjectivity in the Life Narrative of a Female Labourer
Studia Fennica Ethnologica 16
2014

Studia Fennica Folkloristica

Venla Sykäri
Words as Events
Cretan Mantinádes in Performance and Composition
Studia Fennica Folkloristica 18
2011

Hidden Rituals and Public Performances
Traditions and Belonging among the Post-Soviet Khanty, Komi and Udmurts
Edited by Anna-Leena Siikala & Oleg Ulyashev
Studia Fennica Folkloristica 19
2011

Mythic Discourses
Studies in Uralic Traditions
Edited by Frog, Anna-Leena Siikala & Eila Stepanova
Studia Fennica Folkloristica 20
2012

Cornelius Hasselblatt
Kalevipoeg Studies
The Creation and Reception of an Epic
Studia Fennica Folkloristica 21
2016

Genre – Text – Interpretation
Multidisciplinary Perspectives on Folklore and Beyond
Edited by Kaarina Koski, Frog & Ulla Savolainen
Studia Fennica Folkloristica 22
2016

Storied and Supernatural Places
Studies in Spatial and Social Dimensions of Folklore and Sagas
Edited by Ülo Valk & Daniel Sävborg
Studia Fennica Folkloristica 23
2018

Studia Fennica Historica

Modernisation in Russia since 1900
Edited by Markku Kangaspuro & Jeremy Smith
Studia Fennica Historica 12
2006

Seija-Riitta Laakso
Across the Oceans
Development of Overseas Business Information Transmission 1815–1875
Studia Fennica Historica 13
2007

Industry and Modernism
Companies, Architecture and Identity in the Nordic and Baltic Countries during the High-Industrial Period
Edited by Anja Kervanto Nevanlinna
Studia Fennica Historica 14
2007

Charlotta Wolff
Noble conceptions of politics in eighteenth-century Sweden (ca 1740–1790)
Studia Fennica Historica 15
2008

Sport, Recreation and Green Space in the European City
Edited by Peter Clark, Marjaana Niemi & Jari Niemelä
Studia Fennica Historica 16
2009

Rhetorics of Nordic Democracy
Edited by Jussi Kurunmäki & Johan Strang
Studia Fennica Historica 17
2010

Fibula, Fabula, Fact
The Viking Age in Finland
Edited by Joonas Ahola & Frog with Clive Tolley
Studia Fennica Historica 18
2014

Novels, Histories, Novel Nations
Historical Fiction and Cultural Memory in Finland and Estonia
Edited by Linda Kaljundi, Eneken Laanes & Ilona Pikkanen
Studia Fennica Historica 19
2015

Jukka Gronow & Sergey Zhuravlev
Fashion Meets Socialism
Fashion industry in the Soviet Union after the Second World War
Studia Fennica Historica 20
2015

Sofia Kotilainen
Literacy Skills as Local Intangible Capital
The History of a Rural Lending Library c. 1860–1920
Studia Fennica Historica 21
2016

Continued Violence and Troublesome Pasts
Post-war Europe between the Victors after the Second World War
Edited by Ville Kivimäki and Petri Karonen
Studia Fennica Historica 22
2017

Personal Agency at the Swedish Age of Greatness 1560-1720
Edited by Petri Karonen & Marko Hakanen
Studia Fennica Historica 23
2017

Pasi Ihalainen
The Springs of Democracy
National and Transnational Debates on Constitutional Reform in the British, German, Swedish and Finnish Parliaments, 1917–19
Studia Fennica Historica 24
2017

Studia Fennica Anthropologica

On Foreign Ground
Moving between Countries and Categories
Edited by Marie-Louise Karttunen & Minna Ruckenstein
Studia Fennica Anthropologica 1
2007

Beyond the Horizon
Essays on Myth, History, Travel and Society
Edited by Clifford Sather & Timo Kaartinen
Studia Fennica Anthropologica 2
2008

Timo Kallinen
Divine Rulers in a Secular State
Studia Fennica Anthropologica 3
2016

Studia Fennica Linguistica

Minimal reference
The use of pronouns in Finnish and Estonian discourse
Edited by Ritva Laury
Studia Fennica Linguistica 12
2005

Antti Leino
On Toponymic Constructions as an Alternative to Naming Patterns in Describing Finnish Lake Names
Studia Fennica Linguistica 13
2007

Talk in interaction
Comparative dimensions
Edited by Markku Haakana, Minna Laakso & Jan Lindström
Studia Fennica Linguistica 14
2009

Planning a new standard language
Finnic minority languages meet the new millennium
Edited by Helena Sulkala & Harri Mantila
Studia Fennica Linguistica 15
2010

Lotta Weckström
Representations of Finnishness in Sweden
Studia Fennica Linguistica 16
2011

Terhi Ainiala, Minna Saarelma & Paula Sjöblom
Names in Focus
An Introduction to Finnish Onomastics
Studia Fennica Linguistica 17
2012

Registers of Communication
Edited by Asif Agha & Frog
Studia Fennica Linguistica 18
2015

Kaisa Häkkinen
Spreading the Written Word
Mikael Agricola and the Birth of Literary Finnish
Studia Fennica Linguistica 19
2015

Linking Clauses and Actions in Social Interaction
Edited by Ritva Laury, Marja Etelämäki, Elizabeth Couper-Kuhlen
Studia Fennica Linquistica 20
2017

On the Border of Language and Dialect
Edited by Marjatta Palander, Helka Riionheimo & Vesa Koivisto
Studia Fennica Linquistica 21
2018

Studia Fennica Litteraria

Aino Kallas
Negotiations with Modernity
Edited by Leena Kurvet-Käosaar & Lea Rojola
Studia Fennica Litteraria 4
2011

The Emergence of Finnish Book and Reading Culture in the 1700s
Edited by Cecilia af Forselles & Tuija Laine
Studia Fennica Litteraria 5
2011

Nodes of Contemporary Finnish Literature
Edited by Leena Kirstinä
Studia Fennica Litteraria 6
2012

White Field, Black Seeds
Nordic Literacy Practices in the Long Nineteenth Century
Edited by Anna Kuismin & M. J. Driscoll
Studia Fennica Litteraria 7
2013

Lieven Ameel
Helsinki in Early Twentieth-Century Literature
Urban Experiences in Finnish Prose Fiction 1890–1940
Studia Fennica Litteraria 8
2014

Novel Districts
Critical Readings of Monika Fagerholm
Edited by Kristina Malmio & Mia Österlund
Studia Fennica Litteraria 9
2016

Elise Nykänen
Mysterious Minds
The Making of Private and Collective Consciousness in Marja-Liisa Vartio's Novels
Studia Fennica Litteraria 10
2017